The Thames & Hudson
Dictionary of Ancient Egypt

Toby Wilkinson

The Thames & Hudson
Dictionary of Ancient Egypt

With 316 illustrations, 163 in colour

Thames & Hudson

For Dad

Frontispiece: The Ramesseum, the mortuary temple of Ramesses II in western Thebes.

Title-page: Scarab-shaped pendant of gold inlaid with lapis lazuli, carnelian and other semiprecious stones, from the tomb of Tutankhamun.

First published in the United Kingdom in 2005 by Thames & Hudson Ltd, 181A High Holborn, London WC1V 7QX

www.thamesandhudson.com

British Library Cataloguing-in-Publication Data
A catalogue record for this book is available from the British Library

ISBN-13: 978-0-500-05137-5
ISBN-10: 0-500-05137-2

Picture research by Sally Nicholls

Printed and bound in China by Everbest Printing Co Ltd

Contents

Preface

This book is intended as a handy reference guide to the ancient civilization of the Nile Valley. It is aimed at a general readership, as well as at those with a special or academic interest in the subject. The book's objective is to be the most comprehensive, single-volume dictionary of ancient Egypt currently available in the English language. Entries cover the rulers, officials, deities and archaeological sites of Egypt (and, to a lesser extent, Sudan); major topics such as art and religion; and terms peculiar to Egyptology or used with a special meaning. A particular feature is a separate entry for every significant king of Egypt from the unification of the country in c. 3000 BC to the conquest of Alexander the Great in 332 BC.

Inevitably, decisions about what to include and what to leave out had to be made. The guiding principle was that the book should be a dictionary, not an encyclopedia; hence, extended essays on broad themes have generally been omitted, in favour of more, shorter, entries on specific subjects. Likewise, bibliographical information has not been given for each individual entry; but readers are referred to the suggestions for further reading at the end of the book.

There are many variant spellings in use for ancient Egyptian personal names. As a general rule, this book uses those that conform most closely to a translitera-tion of the original Egyptian, rather than, for example, the alternative Greek forms. However, for ease of use, alternate spellings are given as cross-references and in the entries themselves. For archaeological sites, main entries use the names (ancient or modern) most commonly used in other Egyptological works; again, alternate names have been included to aid the reader. The abbreviations KV and QV refer to tombs in the Valley of the Kings and Valley of the Queens respectively, numbered, according to custom, by their order of discovery. There is, as yet, no general agreement among scholars about ancient Egyptian dates, although a consensus may be emerging. The dates for individual rulers and dynasties follow Bill Manley (ed.), *The Seventy Great Mysteries of Ancient Egypt* (Thames & Hudson, 2003).

How to use this book

Intended as much for the beginner as the specialist, and thus assuming no previous knowledge of ancient Egypt or Egyptology, the entries in this dictionary are as self-sufficient as possible. However, to avoid cumbersome repetition, it has occasionally been necessary to use specialist terms defined elsewhere in the dictionary. Such terms have been given as cross-references, indicated by the use of SMALL CAPITALS.

Extensive use of cross-references has also been made to encourage the reader to follow a subject from

one entry to another, and hence to explore more widely the fascinating culture of ancient Egypt.

Entries are arranged in strict alphabetical order; the only exceptions are place-names beginning with the prefix el- which appear under the main element of the name, for example el-Omari as Omari, el-. Works of literature are arranged by the first word of the title by which they are most commonly known. Thus, the *Dispute of a Man with his Ba* appears under D, and the *Tale of Sinuhe* under T.

The text is richly illustrated, to give an impression of the brilliance and sophistication of ancient Egyptian civilization. Several of the pictures are published here for the first time; others are only rarely reproduced outside the specialist literature. Two important entries of widespread relevance, temple and tomb, are illustrated with cutaway diagrams showing, in each case, a typical layout. Illustrations are usually on the same page or double-page spread as the entries they accompany.

The chronology and king-list at the beginning of the book are intended for reference purposes, although dates (BC or AD) are also given in the individual dictionary entries for kings and periods. A special map section at the back of the book contains plans of the three archaeological sites – Saqqara, Giza and the Valley of the Kings – and the two monuments – Karnak and Luxor temples – most often visited by tourists to Egypt; these are followed by a general map of Egypt with inset maps of the Delta and Thebes. In place of an extensive bibliography, more suited to a specialist publication, the book concludes with suggestions for further reading. All the titles listed are in the English language and are written in an accessible style. They are arranged in broad categories to assist the reader who wishes to follow up in more detail a particular aspect of ancient Egypt.

Acknowledgments

Several colleagues very kindly read earlier drafts of the book, and made a number of helpful corrections, comments and suggestions. In particular, thanks are due to Aidan Dodson, Peter Grose-Hodge, Geoffrey Martin and Sarah Cullis. The author is also indebted to the editorial and production staff at Thames and Hudson for their continued enthusiasm and support, and to Michael Bailey for his unfailing patience.

The pyramids of Dahshur seen across Lake Dahshur. From left to right: the 'Bent Pyramid' and 'Red Pyramid' of Sneferu (4th Dynasty), and the 'Black Pyramid' of Amenemhat III (12th Dynasty).

King-list and chronology

The dates of ancient Egypt are generally assumed to be among the most secure in the ancient world – accurate to within two centuries c. 3000 BC; accurate to within two decades c. 1300 BC; and precise from 664 BC. But this still means that there are no precise dates for most of the period covered by this book. Different books give different dates for the same event, with the result that, for example, Narmer might have become king in 3100, 3050 or 2950 BC and the Battle of Kadesh might have taken place in 1297, 1286 or 1275 BC. Nevertheless, although there is not complete agreement among experts, there are options which are widely favoured. The dates used in this book are listed below, alongside the names of the kings of ancient Egypt.

Egyptologists normally employ a method of dividing the kings of ancient Egypt into 31 *dynasties*, following the practice of the Egyptian priest, Manetho, who wrote a history of his nation shortly after 300 BC. In general these dynasties correspond to particular ruling families, although in the more obscure eras of history some dynasties appear to be little more than convenient groupings of kings, some of whom were contemporary rulers in different parts of Egypt. In fact, Manetho is quite clear about this last point – that often there was more than one line of kings in Egypt.

Modern Egyptologists have grouped the dynasties into broader periods known as 'Kingdoms', when, normally, there was only one king throughout Egypt. The *Old Kingdom* (c. 2575–2125 BC) is the age of the Great Pyramid and the Great Sphinx. The *Middle Kingdom* (c. 2000–1630 BC) was an age of renewed national unity, and of a great flowering of art and literature. The *New Kingdom* (c. 1539–1069 BC) is often described as the imperial, or golden, age of ancient Egypt – the time of Amenhotep III, Akhenaten and Ramesses II, when Egypt was the richest and most powerful nation in the world. The *Late Period* (664–332 BC) became the final assertion of ancient Egyptian independence in the wider world, after which the country was conquered by Alexander the Great and later was absorbed by the Roman Empire.

EARLY DYNASTIC PERIOD
'Dynasty O' c. 3100 BC
Existence uncertain
Ka (?)
Scorpion (?)

1st Dynasty
c. 2950–c. 2775
Narmer
Aha
Djer
Djet
Den
Anedjib
Semerkhet
Qaa

2nd Dynasty
c. 2750–c. 2650
Hetepsekhemwy
Nebra
Ninetjer
Weneg (?)
Sened (?)
Peribsen
Khasekhem(wy)

3rd Dynasty
c. 2650–c. 2575
Netjerikhet (Djoser)
Sekhemkhet
Khaba
Sanakht
Huni

OLD KINGDOM
4th Dynasty
c. 2575–c. 2450
Sneferu
Khufu (Cheops)
Djedefra
Khafra (Chephren)
Menkaura (Mycerinus)
Shepseskaf

5th Dynasty
c. 2450–c. 2325
Userkaf
Sahura
Neferirkara Kakai
Shepseskara Izi
Neferefra
Niuserra Ini
Menkauhor
Djedkara Isesi
Unas

6th Dynasty
c. 2325–c. 2175
Teti
Userkara (?)
Pepi I
Merenra Nemtyemsaf
Pepi II

7th/8th Dynasty
c. 2175–c. 2125
Numerous ephemeral kings

FIRST INTERMEDIATE PERIOD
9th/10th Dynasty
c. 2125–c. 1975
Several kings, including:
Khety I
Khety II
Merikara

11th Dynasty
c. 2080–c. 1940
Intef I
Intef II
Intef III

MIDDLE KINGDOM
Mentuhotep II
c. 2010–c. 1960
Mentuhotep III
c. 1960–c. 1948
Mentuhotep IV
c. 1948–c. 1938

12th Dynasty
c. 1938–c. 1755
Amenemhat I
c. 1938–c. 1908
Senusret I c. 1918–c. 1875
Amenemhat II
c. 1876–c. 1842
Senusret II
c. 1842–c. 1837
Senusret III
c. 1836–c. 1818
Amenemhat III
c. 1818–c. 1770
Amenemhat IV
c. 1770–c. 1760
Sobekneferu
c. 1760–c. 1755

13th Dynasty
c. 1755–c. 1630
Seventy kings, including
(order uncertain):
Sobekhotep I
Amenemhat V

Ameny Qemau
Sobekhotep II
Hor
Amenemhat VII
Ugaf
Khendjer
Sobekhotep III
Neferhotep I
Sahathor
Sobekhotep IV
Sobekhotep V
Ay (I)

SECOND INTERMEDIATE PERIOD
Mentuemsaf
Dedumose
Neferhotep II

14th Dynasty
Numerous ephemeral
 kings

15th Dynasty
 c. 1630–c. 1520
Six kings, including:
Salitis
Sheshi
Khyan
Apepi *c. 1570–c. 1530*
Khamudi *c. 1530–c. 1520*

16th Dynasty
Numerous ephemeral kings

17th Dynasty
 c. 1630–c. 1539
Numerous kings, probably
 ending:
Intef V
Intef VI
Intef VII
Sobekemsaf II
Senakhtenra (Taa?)
Seqenenra Taa (II)
Kamose
 c. 1541–c. 1539

NEW KINGDOM
18th Dynasty
 c. 1539–c. 1292
Ahmose *c. 1539–c. 1514*
Amenhotep I
 c. 1514–c. 1493
Thutmose I *c. 1493–c. 1481*
Thutmose II *c. 1481–c. 1479*
Thutmose III
 c. 1479–c. 1425
 and Hatshepsut
 c. 1473–c. 1458

Amenhotep II
 c. 1426–c. 1400
Thutmose IV *c. 1400–c. 1390*
Amenhotep III
 c. 1390–c. 1353
Amenhotep IV (Akhenaten)
 c. 1353–c. 1336
Smenkhkara
 c. 1336–c. 1332
Tutankhamun
 c. 1332–c. 1322
Ay (II) *c. 1322–c. 1319*
Horemheb *c. 1319–c. 1292*

19th Dynasty
 c. 1292–c. 1190
Ramesses I *c. 1292–c. 1290*
Seti I *c. 1290–c. 1279*
Ramesses II *c. 1279–c. 1213*
Merenptah *c. 1213–c. 1204*
Seti II *c. 1204–c. 1198*
Amenmesse *c. 1202–c. 1200*
Siptah *c. 1198–c. 1193*
Tawosret *c. 1198–c. 1190*

20th Dynasty
 c. 1190–c. 1069
Sethnakht *c. 1190–c. 1187*
Ramesses III *c. 1187–c. 1156*
Ramesses IV *c. 1156–c. 1150*
Ramesses V *c. 1150–c. 1145*
Ramesses VI *c. 1145–c. 1137*
Ramesses VII
 c. 1137–c. 1129
Ramesses VIII
 c. 1129–c. 1126
Ramesses IX *c. 1126–c. 1108*
Ramesses X *c. 1108–c. 1099*
Ramesses XI
 c. 1099–c. 1069

THIRD INTERMEDIATE PERIOD
21st Dynasty
 c. 1069–c. 945
Smendes *c. 1069–c. 1045*
Amenemnisu
 c. 1045–c. 1040
Psusennes I *c. 1040–c. 985*
Amenemope *c. 985–c. 975*
Osochor (Osorkon 'the
 elder') *c. 975–c. 970*
Siamun *c. 970–c. 950*
Psusennes II *c. 950–c. 945*

22nd Dynasty *c. 945–c. 715*
Shoshenq I *c. 945–c. 925*
Osorkon I *c. 925–c. 890* and
 Shoshenq II *c. 890*
Takelot I *c. 890–c. 875*

Osorkon II *c. 875–c. 835*
Shoshenq III *c. 835–c. 795*
Shoshenq IV *c. 795–c. 785*
Pimay *c. 785–c. 775*
Shoshenq V *c. 775–c. 735*
Osorkon IV *c. 735–c. 715*

23rd Dynasty *c. 830–c. 715*
Takelot II *c. 840–c. 815*
Pedubast I *c. 825–c. 800*
 and Iuput I *c. 800*
Shoshenq VI *c. 800–c. 780*
Osorkon III *c. 780–c. 750*
Takelot III *c. 750–c. 735*
Rudamun *c. 755–c. 735*
Peftjauawybast
 c. 735–c. 725
Shoshenq VII *c. 725–c. 715*

24th Dynasty
 c. 730–c. 715
Tefnakht *c. 730–c. 720*
Bakenrenef *c. 720–c. 715*

25th Dynasty
 c. 800–657
Alara *c. 800–c. 770*
Kashta *c. 770–c. 747*
Piye *c. 747–c. 715*
Shabaqo *c. 715–c. 702*
Shabitqo *c. 702–690*
Taharqo 690–664
Tanutamani 664–657

LATE PERIOD
26th Dynasty 664–525
Nekau I 672–664
Psamtik I 664–610
Nekau II 610–595
Psamtik II 595–589
Apries 589–570
Amasis 570–526
Psamtik III 526–525

27th Dynasty (Persian)
 525–404
Cambyses 525–522
Darius I 521–486
Xerxes 486–466
Artaxerxes I 465–424
Darius II 424–404

28th Dynasty 404–399
Amyrtaeos 404–399

29th Dynasty 399–380
Nepherites I 399–393
Psammuthis 393
Hakor 393–380
Nepherites II 380

30th Dynasty 380–343
Nectanebo I 380–362
Teos 365–360
Nectanebo II 360–343

31st Dynasty (Persian)
 343–332
Artaxerxes III 343–338
Arses 338–336
Darius III 335–332

MACEDONIAN PERIOD
 332–309
Alexander III (the Great)
 332–323
Philip Arrhidaeus 323–317
Alexander IV 317–309

PTOLEMAIC PERIOD
 309–30
Ptolemy I 305–282
Ptolemy II 285–246
Ptolemy III 246–221
Ptolemy IV 221–205
Ptolemy V 205–180
Ptolemy VI 180–145
Ptolemy VIII and Cleopatra
 II 170–116
Ptolemy IX 116–107
 and Cleopatra III 116–101
Ptolemy X 107–88
Ptolemy IX (restored)
 88–80
Ptolemy XI
 and Berenice III 80
Ptolemy XII 80–58
Cleopatra VI 58–57
 and Berenice IV 58–55
Ptolemy XII (restored)
 55–51
Cleopatra VII and Ptolemy
 XIII 51–47
Cleopatra VII and Ptolemy
 XIV 47–44
Cleopatra VII and Ptolemy
 XV 44–30

ROMAN PERIOD
 30 BC–AD 395

Aba *see* Ibi

Abgig Site in the FAYUM where an immense STELA of King SENUSRET I once stood. Carved from a single block of granite and formerly described as an obelisk, the monument is the only surviving example from ancient Egypt of a stela combining great height with a rounded top; its original purpose is unclear. A column of inscribed HIEROGLYPHS on one side, near the top, gives the NAMES and ROYAL TITLES of Senusret I. The monument was relocated in modern times to the provincial capital of MEDINET EL-FAYUM. No archaeological work has been carried out at Abgig and the site's ancient significance remains unknown. It is highly likely that further traces of MIDDLE KINGDOM activity remain to be discovered in the area.

Abu Ghurab (Abu Ghurob) Area of the MEMPHITE NECROPOLIS on the west bank of the NILE, north of ABUSIR. A cemetery of 1st Dynasty mud-brick tombs lies at the edge of the cultivation, but the site is most famous for its 5th Dynasty monument, the SUN TEMPLE of NIUSERRA, which is the best-preserved example of its kind. Its relief decoration includes countryside and wildlife scenes depicting the seasons of the year. The monument originally comprised a colossal truncated obelisk (a representation of the BENBEN STONE); a large open courtyard with an altar for offerings; and a range of subsidiary buildings, including an area for slaughtering and butchering cattle.

Abu Rawash (Abu Roash) The northernmost site in the Memphite NECROPOLIS, on the west bank of the NILE, north of GIZA. Cemeteries of late Predynastic and Early Dynastic date are located around the foot of a small hill; on the hilltop, high officials of the 1st Dynasty built their MASTABA tombs, in one case accompanied by two BOAT BURIALS. Further north, to the west of the modern village of Abu Rawash, a large descending corridor cut into the bedrock, boat pits and stone fragments are all that remain of the unfinished 4th Dynasty pyramid complex of DJEDEFRA. The particular choice of location remains a mystery, although the imposing natural setting and a connection with HELIOPOLIS (which lies directly opposite, on the other side of the Nile) may have been factors. Also at Abu Rawash is a large brick monument of the OLD KINGDOM, built around a knoll of rock. Its precise date and function are unclear. There are further tombs of the 4th and 5th Dynasties in the vicinity.

Abu Simbel Site in NUBIA, originally on the east bank of the NILE, now on the eastern shore of Lake Nasser,

*The façade of the main temple at **Abu Simbel**, dominated by four seated colossi of Ramesses II. This rock-cut temple was moved from its original position when the Aswan High Dam was built in the 1960s.*

just north of the present-day border between Egypt and Sudan. Although there are 18th Dynasty monuments in the vicinity, Abu Simbel is most famous for the two 19th Dynasty rock-cut temples of RAMESSES II. In 1968, to save them from the rising waters of Lake Nasser as a result of the building of the ASWAN High Dam, the temples were cut into blocks and re-erected inside an artificial mountain on the desert plateau, 64 m (210 ft) above their original location. The international operation, conducted under the auspices of UNESCO, caught the public imagination and Abu Simbel today is a popular tourist attraction.

The larger temple is dedicated to a quartet of gods: AMUN-RA, Ra-Horakhty, PTAH and the deified Ramesses II. Its façade is dominated by four colossal seated statues of Ramesses, each 22 m (71 ft) high, arranged in two pairs flanking the entrance. The main axis of the temple is orientated so that on two days of the year (21 February and 21 October) the rising sun penetrates to the sanctuary, where it illuminates the statue of the king. Reliefs inside the temple include a famous depiction of the BATTLE OF KADESH and, outside, the text of the 'marriage stela' which sealed the peace between the two warring parties through a diplomatic union between Ramesses II and a Hittite princess. The smaller temple at Abu Simbel is officially dedicated to HATHOR, although the decoration gives prominence to Queen NEFERTARI, Ramesses II's chief wife, as a manifestation of the goddess. The façade is dominated by six standing statues, four of the king and two of his queen.

Abusir Area of the MEMPHITE NECROPOLIS between SAQQARA and ABU GHURAB. The site is dominated by four pyramid complexes of the 5th Dynasty, built for SAHURA, NIUSERRA, NEFERIRKARA, and the ephemeral king NEFEREFRA. All four pyramids are in various states of ruin; the last was never finished but was adapted to form a MASTABA. The monument of Sahura departed from earlier tradition by placing greater emphasis on the mortuary temple and VALLEY TEMPLE, less on the pyramid itself. Imaginative architectural use of differently coloured stones and an elaborate decorative scheme focusing on the king characterize the buildings. In the complex of Neferirkara, archaeologists discovered a collection of PAPYRUS documents detailing the operation of the king's mortuary cult; they provide valuable evidence for religious practice and organization in the pyramid age.

Among the other principal monuments at Abusir are the pyramids of 5th Dynasty QUEENS; the mastaba of Ptahshepses (VIZIER and Niuserra's son-in-law), one of the largest private tombs of the Old Kingdom; the CENOTAPH of KHENTKAWES; the intact LATE PERIOD tomb of Iufaa; and the shaft tomb of Wadjhorresnet (chancellor under CAMBYSES and DARIUS I). The name Abusir is also applied to a 1st Dynasty cemetery at the southern end of the site, which is more properly considered a continuation of north Saqqara.

Abydos (el-Arabah el-Madfuna) Site of religious significance on the west bank of the NILE in northern UPPER EGYPT, with important archaeological remains of all periods.

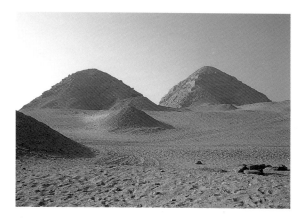

The 5th Dynasty pyramids at **Abusir** *comprise the funerary monuments of Sahura, Neferirkara, Niuserra and Neferefra.*

Relief from the temple of Seti I at **Abydos**, *showing the young king sitting on the lap of the goddess Isis.*

A large burial-ground (Cemetery U) was established on the low desert in the PREDYNASTIC PERIOD; eventually this became reserved for high-status individuals. When excavated in the late 1980s, the largest of these tombs, U-j, was found to contain a royal sceptre in ivory, hundreds of imported wine jars, and large numbers of inscribed bone labels comprising the earliest corpus of hieroglyphic WRITING yet discovered. From the beginning of the 1st Dynasty, the area known as the UMM EL-QAAB (contiguous with Cemetery U) became an exclusively royal cemetery. At least nine rulers of the 1st Dynasty, and the last two kings of the 2nd Dynasty, built imposing mud-brick tombs, surrounded by smaller subsidiary tombs for their retainers. In addition, most kings also built a separate funerary enclosure – often delineated by lines of further subsidiary tombs – closer to the NILE, near the cultivation, and facing the town of Abydos. Decorated in the PALACE-FAÇADE style, the enclosures were originally plastered and whitewashed to resemble the royal compound at MEMPHIS. The remains of one enclosure can be seen incorporated in the walls of a Coptic town, Deir Sitt Damiana. Another, the 2nd Dynasty SHUNET EL-ZEBIB, remains an imposing monument and has been the focus of recent excavations. A fleet of twelve wooden boats, discovered nearby in 1991, has been dated to the 1st Dynasty reign of DJER.

The town of Abydos (Kom es-Sultan) contained further 1st Dynasty burials, and remains from later periods, including KA CHAPELS, a MIDDLE KINGDOM mayor's house, and an area for FAIENCE production. The temple, originally dedicated to KHENTIAMENTIU, became the principal cult centre of OSIRIS in the late OLD KINGDOM, transforming Abydos into one of Egypt's most important religious sites. During the Middle Kingdom, the tomb of Djer was identified as the tomb of Osiris and an elaborate procession, re-enacting the myths surrounding the god, took place annually from temple to tomb. Many private individuals erected CENOTAPHS and STELAE on either side of the ceremonial route (known as the 'Terrace of the Great God'), in order to share in the offerings which accompanied the festival. At this period, the area surrounding the Early Dynastic funerary enclosures was opened up for private burials, and became one of the largest cemeteries in Egypt.

Meanwhile, royal activity was concentrated at South Abydos where SENUSRET III built a mortuary temple and a subterranean tomb. Hewn into the cliff, the burial chamber may have been the king's final resting place. A large planned settlement nearby probably accommodated those who served the royal mortuary cult. This area witnessed further royal building projects at the beginning of the NEW KINGDOM, notably cult monuments for TETISHERI, AHMOSE NEFERTARI and AHMOSE, some of which were in the form of pyramids.

Recent work has uncovered reliefs depicting Ahmose's battles against the HYKSOS. Cult activity continued at the site well into the RAMESSIDE period.

The main standing monuments at Abydos, and the focus of modern tourist activity, are the New Kingdom temples of SETI I and RAMESSES II. The earlier structure is famous for its beautiful painted reliefs and an extensive KING-LIST. Its unique plan comprises seven sanctuaries, dedicated to the main state gods of the 19th Dynasty, the principal deities of the Osiris myth, and the deified Ramesses himself. Behind the temples is the OSIREION. Abydos also has major cemeteries of the THIRD INTERMEDIATE PERIOD and LATE PERIOD, including the tomb of Iuput, High Priest of AMUN in the 22nd Dynasty.

Adaima Site on the west bank of the NILE in UPPER EGYPT, a short distance to the south of Esna, comprising cemetery and settlement remains dating from the PREDYNASTIC PERIOD to the 1st Dynasty. Detailed study of the human remains from graves has shed new light on prehistoric BURIAL CUSTOMS.

Admonitions of Ipuwer Literary work of the late MIDDLE KINGDOM in which the theme of 'national distress' is treated at greater length and intensity than in other examples of the genre (*see* LITERATURE). The work is presented as an extended lament by a wise man called Ipuwer, who admonishes an unnamed almighty power for letting chaos overturn the established order. The description of chaos is vivid, if contradictory, and used to be regarded as an account of the FIRST INTERMEDIATE PERIOD. The text is now recognized as a purely fictional work. It is preserved in a single copy on a 19th Dynasty PAPYRUS; many gaps make translation particularly difficult.

aegis In Egyptian RELIGION, a shield-shaped device (from the Greek for 'shield') comprising a representation of a broad collar of beads surmounted by the head of a deity. The aegis was a potent symbol of protection, and was customarily shown at the prow and stern of a god's sacred barque, with the particular head being that of the deity in question. AMULETS in aegis form

Late Period bronze **aegis** *from Saqqara, depicting the head of the goddess Isis wearing a crown of uraeus serpents; she is flanked by two falcon-heads representing the god Horus.*

first appear in the NEW KINGDOM, usually depicting AMUN-RA, BASTET, BES, HATHOR or MUT. In the following THIRD INTERMEDIATE PERIOD, FAIENCE finger-rings with aegis bezels became popular.

Ægyptiaca Ancient Egyptian objects found outside Egypt, for example in other regions bordering the Mediterranean.

afterlife beliefs A belief in life after death was one of the defining facets of ancient Egyptian culture. Much of our evidence for pharaonic civilization and its prehistoric antecedents is of a funerary nature: grave goods, PYRAMIDS, mummies, TOMBS. The Egyptians' apparent obsession, at all periods, with BURIAL CUSTOMS reflects a deep conviction that eternal life was possible providing that the proper preparations were made. Provision of sustenance for the spirit and preservation of the body (from the OLD KINGDOM onwards by MUMMIFICATION) were two prerequisites for achieving immortality. A 'goodly burial' could help to ensure that the eternal aspects of humanity – the BA, the KA, the AKH, the NAME and the shadow – were all properly nurtured.

The antiquity of afterlife beliefs is demonstrated by the inclusion of FUNERARY OBJECTS in burial chambers from earliest Predynastic times. As for the details of ancient Egyptian concepts of the afterlife, the sources of evidence are many and varied; they include grave goods, FUNERARY TEXTS, tombs and TOMB DECORATION. In the late PREDYNASTIC and EARLY DYNASTIC PERIODS, eternity seems to have been conceived of,

essentially, as a continuation of earthly existence. In a royal context, the tomb was thus required to provide a palace in microcosm, in which the king might carry out the rituals of KINGSHIP for eternity, accompanied by his retainers. In the 3rd Dynasty, a cosmic element was introduced into royal afterlife beliefs, identifying the starry sky as the king's ultimate destination. This concept underlay the architecture and orientation of the Old Kingdom pyramids.

The rise of the OSIRIS myth at the end of the Old Kingdom changed the concept of the royal afterlife, giving the deceased king a key role in the solar cycle (the sun, as it passed through the underworld, being joined with Osiris). It also led to the wider dissemination of afterlife beliefs, beyond the king and his immediate circle, in what has been termed 'the democratization of the afterlife'. The once exclusively royal PYRAMID TEXTS were adopted for use in private burials as the COFFIN TEXTS. In the new theology, ordinary individuals, too, could look forward to a blessed existence in the company of Osiris; although, to achieve this end, a last judgment, the WEIGHING OF THE HEART, had to be successfully passed. Tomb scenes of the MIDDLE KINGDOM and NEW KINGDOM picture the afterlife for a private individual as an agricultural idyll in the 'Field of Reeds' where the deceased would be surrounded by abundance and be free of the more unpleasant aspects of daily life. By contrast with ordinary mortals, the king had to prepare for a more dangerous journey in the company of RA, helping to defeat the serpent APOPHIS each night, and again each morning, as the SOLAR BARQUE entered and left the underworld. The royal tombs in the VALLEY OF THE KINGS illustrate the anticipated journey, and the many hazards that had to be overcome.

In the LATE PERIOD, confidence in the promise of immortality, and the corresponding view of death as a mere interruption, seem to have been slowly undermined, even though extracts from the Pyramid Texts and other funerary texts continued to be used in tombs. Literature from this period suggests a growing horror of death, and a determination to enjoy earthly life.

agriculture Egypt's prosperity depended upon the fertility of its soil. The cultivation of crops in Egypt began in prehistoric times on the shores of Lake FAYUM, in natural basins in the NILE Valley, and at oases and wells in the drier regions on either side. The successful practice of agriculture was at all periods closely linked with the annual INUNDATION and the seasons. In pharaonic times, fields were generally situated on the floodplain of the Nile. In the autumn (September–November), as soon as the flood waters receded, leaving behind well-watered ground covered by a layer of fertile silt, new plants were sown. Seed was scattered by hand and trampled in by livestock. Winter and spring (December–May) were the main growing periods, and crops were harvested in the summer (June–July) before the inundation arrived again. Cereal crops were reaped with sickles, threshed by livestock on a threshing floor, winnowed by hand, then stored in granaries. With the aid of artificial IRRIGATION, it became possible to grow two crops a year; the introduction of the SHADUF (a device for raising water) in the NEW KINGDOM made this easier and more widely practised. The relative ease with which the country could produce agricultural surpluses underpinned pharaonic civilization; the royal court and state building projects were supported through taxation, which was levied as a proportion of all crops grown. Although in theory all land belonged to the king, in practice plots could be bought and sold, or rented, by private individuals, temples and other institutions. The principal crops were emmer (an early type of wheat), barley and flax; free-threshing wheat was only introduced in the PTOLEMAIC PERIOD. Pulses,

perhaps grown as a second crop to improve the soil, may have been an important source of food for the general population, although there is little evidence for their cultivation. Vegetables, including onions, beans, lettuce and garlic, were grown in small GARDENS situated on higher land, requiring manual watering throughout the growing season.

A-Group *see* Nubia

Aha (*c.* 2925 BC) King of the early 1st Dynasty, whose name is more accurately rendered as Hor-Aha ('HORUS the fighter'). He was the successor of NARMER and predecessor of DJER. Identified by some scholars as the legendary MENES, Aha is best known for the monuments which survive from his reign: the tomb of a high official at SAQQARA (number 3357); and the king's own mortuary complex at ABYDOS, comprising dozens of individual chambers cut into the desert gravel. One yielded objects bearing the name Benerib (literally 'sweet heart'), who may have been Aha's wife. A further large tomb was built during his reign at NAGADA, for Queen NEITHHOTEP, probably Aha's mother. Objects bearing Aha's name have been found throughout Egypt, though not yet from surrounding lands; but

Idealized scene of **agriculture** *painted on the wall of the 19th Dynasty tomb of Sennedjem at Deir el-Medina, showing the harvesting of corn and flax.*

inscribed labels suggest contemporary royal interest in the border regions (specifically the DELTA and NUBIA).

Ahhotep Name borne by at least one, and possibly two, QUEENS at the beginning of the NEW KINGDOM. The earlier and more famous one (sometimes referred to as Ahhotep I) was the daughter of King TAA I, the sister and wife of his successor TAA II, and the mother of AHMOSE I. Her life thus spanned the end of the SECOND INTERMEDIATE PERIOD and the rise of the New Kingdom (18th Dynasty), and she may have played an important role in the battles to expel the HYKSOS. A ceremonial STELA erected by her son at KARNAK praises her heroism in the struggle to liberate Egypt from foreign occupation. She probably acted as regent during Ahmose's minority, and perhaps continued to govern on his behalf when he was away on military campaigns. Her tomb has not been identified, but her coffin was found in the royal cache at DEIR EL-BAHRI.

The second queen named Ahhotep (who may have been the same person as Ahhotep I) also died in the reign of Ahmose, but she seems to have been the wife of his predecessor KAMOSE. Her intact tomb was discovered in 1859 at DRA ABU EL-NAGA. It contained her mummy inside a gilded coffin, ceremonial weapons inscribed for Ahmose, a necklace of gold flies (perhaps a reward for valour in wartime), model BARQUES in gold and silver, and items of JEWELRY.

Ahmose (I) (throne name: Nebpehtira) (c. 1539–c. 1514 BC) First king of the 18th Dynasty (NEW KINGDOM). He was the son of TAA II, but only acceded to the throne after the death of KAMOSE, possibly his elder brother. Ahmose was very likely a child at his accession, and effective power was exercised by his mother Queen AHHOTEP. The latter part of his reign was dominated by the final expulsion of the HYKSOS, and the re-emergence of Egypt as a sovereign power. Details of these military campaigns are shown in reliefs at ABYDOS, and are also included in AUTOBIOGRAPHIES from private tombs of the period, most famously that of AHMOSE SON OF ABANA at ELKAB. Engagement with the Hyksos drew Egypt into the power politics of the wider LEVANT; in a series of campaigns, Ahmose succeeded in extending the borders of Egyptian influence deep into PALESTINE and beyond. He thus laid the foundations for the Egyptian 'empire' of the NEW KINGDOM. He also reasserted Egyptian power over NUBIA, undertaking at least two military expeditions and establishing a new administrative centre at BUHEN.

Ivory label of **Aha**, *a king of the early 1st Dynasty, from Nagada, originally attached to a jar of precious oil; the king's name appears at top right.*

Within Egypt, Ahmose's reign witnessed a renaissance of royal power. He reorganized the system of internal government, reopened the limestone quarries at TURA, and embellished the temples of AMUN and MONTU at KARNAK. However, few major monuments survive from his reign, apart from two mud-brick buildings at Abydos, one of them a small pyramid for the king himself, the other a cult building dedicated to his grandmother TETISHERI. Ahmose's tomb has never been located; it is probably at DRA ABU EL-NAGA where his predecessors of the 17th Dynasty were buried. The king's mummy, found in the royal cache at DEIR EL-BAHRI, suggests that he died relatively young, in his mid-thirties.

Ahmose II *see* Amasis

Ahmose Nefertari Wife of AHMOSE, and mother of AMENHOTEP I. One of the most influential royal women in Egyptian history, her parentage is disputed: her father was either KAMOSE or, more likely, TAA II (thus making her Ahmose's sister). Like TETISHERI and AHHOTEP I, Ahmose Nefertari enjoyed high office and was the second female member of the royal family (after Ahhotep I) to bear the title GOD'S WIFE OF AMUN. This gave her an important role in the cult of Amun, the pre-eminent cult of the time, bringing with it control of extensive land-holdings, and thus considerable economic power.

She probably ruled as regent during the early years of Amenhotep I's reign. Certainly, mother and son were closely linked in later popular RELIGION. They were regarded as the joint founders of the workmen's village at DEIR el-MEDINA, and as such were worshipped by its inhabitants throughout the NEW KINGDOM. Ahmose Nefertari probably outlived her son and may have played a crucial role in the eventual succession of THUTMOSE I. Her tomb has not been located, but her coffin and mummy were discovered in the royal cache at DEIR el-BAHRI.

Ahmose son of Abana Official of the early 18th Dynasty, whose rock-cut tomb at ELKAB contains one of the most famous AUTOBIOGRAPHIES from ancient Egypt. The inscription recounts his career as an officer in the marine corps of the ARMY under three successive kings, AHMOSE, AMENHOTEP I and THUTMOSE I. As a

Relief from the temple of Amun-Ra at Karnak showing Ramesses II before the deified **Ahmose Nefertari**; she was revered as the ancestress of the 18th Dynasty.

Detail from the 19th Dynasty funerary papyrus of Ani showing the god **Aker** as twin lions seated back to back, framing the hieroglyph for 'horizon'.

young man, Ahmose son of Abana took part in the siege of AVARIS, which marked the final stage of the expulsion of the HYKSOS from Egypt. Campaigns later in Ahmose's career were directed against NUBIA and PALESTINE. Particularly fascinating are the references in his tomb inscription to uprisings against pharaonic rule within Egypt. Such incidents are rarely mentioned in texts, and give a valuable insight into Egypt's internal politics at the beginning of the NEW KINGDOM.

Aker An earth god. In the PYRAMID TEXTS, Aker is mentioned as the god who guards the entrance to the underworld. He was occasionally represented as a strip of land with human heads at either end, but was more usually shown as two LIONS seated back to back, or as the conjoined forequarters of two lions or SPHINXES. In these forms, Aker symbolized the western and eastern horizons, the entrance and exit to the underworld. He became particularly closely associated with the passage of the sun god RA through the underworld. The hollow-like shape of Aker's body gave rise to his particular association with the socket that held the mast on the SOLAR BARQUE. This, in turn, conferred on Aker APOTROPAIC qualities, and it is in this role that he often appears in the decoration of MIDDLE KINGDOM magic wands, used in childbirth rituals. Aker was also believed to cure snake bites and counteract the effects of harmful substances.

akh In Egyptian RELIGION, the eternal, transfigured spirit of a dead person that resulted from the reunion of their BA and KA in the afterlife. The *akh* was believed to be enduring and unchanging, and to live in the underworld forever. Together with the *ba*, *ka*, NAME and shadow, the *akh* was one of five elements that constituted a complete individual. In Egyptian ART, it was usually represented as a mummy-like figure.

Akhenaten (throne name: Neferkheperura-Waenra) (c. 1353–c. 1336 BC) Tenth king of the 18th Dynasty, the son of AMENHOTEP III and TIYE. A figure of enduring fascination, Akhenaten presided over a series of radical changes in ART and RELIGION. He succeeded to the throne as Amenhotep IV and, early in his reign, founded a new temple to the ATEN (sun disc) at KARNAK. The question of whether he initially ruled in a CO-REGENCY with his father is still unresolved. In his fifth regnal year, he changed his name to Akhenaten ('effective for the Aten') to indicate his devotion to the sun disc, and founded a new capital city, called

Akhetaten ('Horizon of the Aten'), at the site of AMARNA; hence his reign and its immediate aftermath are termed the 'Amarna period'. The king swiftly set about promoting the cult of the Aten as the only acceptable form of religion; other cults were persecuted, and the names of their deities, especially AMUN, were effaced from monuments throughout Egypt. Akhenaten's motives are much debated, but since all access to the Aten was through the intermediaries of the king and queen, the primary effect of his changes was to elevate the status of the ROYAL FAMILY. His chief wife, NEFERTITI (by whom he had six daughters – TUTANKHAMUN may have been his son by a secondary wife), certainly played an unusually prominent role in religion and politics; she may eventually have succeeded Akhenaten as the next ruler, SMENKHKARA, although this remains a matter of debate. The king's new art style similarly set the royal family apart from the rest of humanity, showing them with strangely elongated skulls, large thighs, distended bellies and long, narrow limbs. Akhenaten had himself shown with both male and female attributes, perhaps to emphasize his connection with the sole creator god. Although dominated by such radical departures, his eighteen-year reign also witnessed significant developments in foreign relations, as recorded in the AMARNA LETTERS. Akhenaten had a decorated tomb prepared for himself in the royal wadi at Amarna; but his body may have been removed shortly after his death. In later periods, his reign was seen as an offence against MAAT, the goddess of truth, justice and harmony; Akhenaten was expunged from the official record or, when mention was unavoidable, was referred to euphemistically as 'the enemy of Akhetaten'.

akhet see calendar

Akhetaten *see* Amarna

Akhmim Site on the east bank of the NILE in MIDDLE EGYPT, and capital of the ninth Upper Egyptian NOME. Akhmim was an important cult centre of MIN; blocks and statues from a temple built by RAMESSES II were found during salvage excavations. Little more is known about the town itself, which lies buried beneath the modern village. The nearby White Monastery, constructed in the 4th century AD, and one of the most important centres of early Christianity in Egypt, incorporates reused blocks from some of the pharaonic buildings. The two cemeteries which served Akhmim

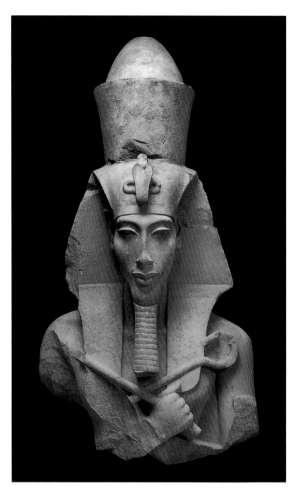

Upper part of a colossal statue of **Akhenaten**, from Karnak; the king is shown in the exaggerated style characteristic of the early part of his reign.

during the OLD KINGDOM have been excavated at Hawawish on the east bank and Hagarsa on the west bank. The tombs include those of the 6th Dynasty NOMARCHS. In the 18th Dynasty, Akhmim became important through its links with the royal family. YUYA and TUYU, parents of Queen TIYE, came from Akhmim, as did Tutankhamun's overseer of tutors, Sennedjem. King AY may also have been a native of Akhmim; he restored its temples and dedicated a new one to Min at nearby el-Salamuni. Numerous graves from the Ptolemaic, Roman and Christian periods have also been excavated in the vicinity.

Akhtoy *see* Khety

Akkadian Semitic language of northern MESOPOTAMIA (named after the site of Akkad). It is divided into three broad chronological/cultural phases, namely Old

Akkadian (3rd millennium BC), Assyrian and Babylonian (2nd and 1st millenniums BC). Akkadian was written in the CUNEIFORM script borrowed from the SUMERIANS of southern Mesopotamia. During the Egyptian NEW KINGDOM, Akkadian (in its Babylonian form) was the diplomatic language throughout the LEVANT. Hence, the AMARNA LETTERS are written in the Babylonian language.

alabaster *see* travertine

Alara (c. 800–c. 770 BC) King of KUSH during the THIRD INTERMEDIATE PERIOD, and founder of the royal line whose later members, from PIYE onwards, ruled Egypt as the 25th Dynasty.

Alashiya *see* Cyprus

alcoholic drinks *see* beer, wine

Alexander the Great (336–323 BC) Macedonian ruler who succeeded his father Philip II in 336 BC and conquered Egypt four years later at the age of 20. Welcomed by the Egyptian population as their liberator from the hated Persians, Alexander legitimized his position by visiting the ORACLE of AMUN in the SIWA OASIS, which declared him the son of AMUN-RA. He honoured the traditional gods and founded a new city, ALEXANDRIA, in 331 BC. After only a brief stay in Egypt, he departed to continue his conquests, leaving his trusted officials in charge. When he died in 323 BC, power passed first to his half-brother Philip Arrhidaeus (323–317 BC), then to his son Alexander IV (317–309 BC). Neither was able to keep all Alexander's

conquests united in a single empire, and the different areas became separate states, ruled by his generals. Egypt fell to the general Ptolemy, who became king (and founder of the Ptolemaic Dynasty – *see* PTOLEMAIC PERIOD) after Alexander IV's death in 305 BC. Alexander's body is said to have been brought back to Egypt for burial, but his tomb has never been identified.

Alexandria City founded by ALEXANDER THE GREAT in 331 BC on the site of an earlier settlement (Ra-Kedet, Rakhotis). Occupying a strategic location on a narrow peninsula on the Mediterranean coast, Alexandria replaced MEMPHIS as the capital of Egypt by 320 BC. It was a thriving city – essentially Greek, rather than Egyptian, in character – throughout the PTOLEMAIC PERIOD and ROMAN PERIOD. Its most famous buildings were the Library and Museum (said to have burned down in the 3rd century AD), and the Pharos Lighthouse (one of the Seven Wonders of the Ancient World), situated on a separate island linked by a bridge to the mainland. A series of earthquakes in the 4th to 6th centuries AD destroyed many monuments, but recent underwater excavations have found blocks from the lighthouse and statues from the palace quarters. Elsewhere in the city, the principal monuments include a Roman stadium, baths and gymnasium complex; a temple to SERAPIS; and, nearby, Pompey's Pillar, a granite column erected by the Roman Emperor Diocletian. Today Alexandria is Egypt's second city, with a new Library recently opened recalling past glories.

Amara Site on both banks of the NILE in Upper NUBIA. The settlement on the west bank (Amara West), founded in the RAMESSIDE period, may originally have

Aerial view of part of the central city at **Amarna***; the large rectangular building in the centre of the picture is the Small Aten Temple, fronting onto the Royal Road (left).*

been connected with gold mining or trade expeditions, but seems to have succeeded SOLEB as the residence of the Deputy of KUSH, one of the two Egyptian administrators reporting to the VICEROY OF KUSH. Other major archaeological remains include a temple, built during the reign of RAMESSES II, and a series of cemeteries. On the opposite bank of the Nile, the site of Amara East comprised a town and temple of the MEROÏTIC period.

Amarna (Tell el-Amarna) Site on the east bank of the NILE in MIDDLE EGYPT where AKHENATEN founded his new capital, named Akhetaten ('Horizon of the ATEN'). The ancient city originally included agricultural land on the west bank; today the name Amarna refers only to the remains on the east bank, situated in a prominent bay in the cliffs measuring some 10 km (6 miles) north to south by 5 km (3 miles) east to west. Founded in the fifth year of Akhenaten's reign, around 1350 BC, Akhetaten was occupied for about thirty years, until the reign of TUTANKHAMUN. It is therefore, in essence, a single-period site, and provides important insights into the life of a major settlement in the NEW KINGDOM. Its principal buildings were dismantled in the reign of RAMESSES II; the stone blocks were then reused in the construction of temples at HERMOPOLIS and at other sites. Limited reoccupation of Amarna took place during the THIRD INTERMEDIATE PERIOD, and in the ROMAN PERIOD. There is also a Christian church at the site from the Byzantine period.

The ancient city comprises a number of distinct quarters, strung out along the edge of the cultivation, from north to south. The North City included the main royal residence, the North Riverside Palace, which the king and queen would leave each day in an elaborate CHARIOT procession, travelling along the royal road to the government centre; this daily ceremonial is depicted on the walls of some of Amarna's ROCK-CUT TOMBS. The North Palace was a residence for female members of the ROYAL FAMILY, including KIYA and MERITATEN. The North Suburb was probably a late overspill from the main city.

The Central City housed the main government buildings, and was laid out on a grid system. To the west of the royal road was the Great Palace, used for ceremonial occasions; it was linked by a bridge with the King's House, on the east side of the road, which included a WINDOW OF APPEARANCE. The heart of the city was dominated by two temples to the Aten, surrounded by state bakeries, GLASS works and government offices, including the foreign ministry archives which yielded the AMARNA LETTERS. Among the numerous houses in the Central City and South Suburb was the workshop of the sculptor THUTMOSE, where the painted bust of NEFERTITI was discovered in 1912.

At the southernmost end of the city, the complexes of Kom el-Nana and Maru Aten probably served a ceremonial purpose connected with the Aten cult. To the east of the main ribbon of settlement, on the low desert plain, are a set of altars of unknown purpose and a workmen's village built to house those who were involved in the construction of the tombs for the royal family in the remote Royal Wadi, several kilometres to the east of the bay. Rock-cut tombs of high officials are concentrated in two groups, at the northern and southern ends of Amarna. The whole site is demarcated by a series of fifteen boundary STELAE cut into the cliffs. They record the circumstances surrounding the city's foundation. Excavations have taken place at Amarna since the 19th century AD. Today many of its buildings are threatened by expanding cultivation.

Amarna Letters Collection of clay tablets, inscribed in the CUNEIFORM script of MESOPOTAMIA, discovered at AMARNA in 1887 in the building which housed the foreign ministry archive. Around 360 tablets survive; many more were destroyed by illicit digging. Some of the letters date to the reign of AMENHOTEP III, but the

One of the **Amarna Letters***, an archive of diplomatic correspondence from the late 18th Dynasty; the clay tablet is written in cuneiform script.*

Sandstone head of **Amasis**, of unknown provenance; the distinctive features of 26th Dynasty Egyptian royal statuary may have influenced contemporary Greek sculpture.

majority were written during the reigns of AKHENATEN and TUTANKHAMUN. Most of the texts are in Babylonian – a dialect of AKKADIAN and the diplomatic language of the period – and a few in other languages of the LEVANT. They represent correspondence between the Egyptian court and other rulers in the region, including the 'great kings' of the HITTITES, MITANNI, ASSYRIANS, Babylonia and Alashiya (probably CYPRUS), and the minor rulers of dependent city states such as BYBLOS and Kadesh. All incoming letters were kept, but only a selection of the outgoing correspondence from the Egyptian court. Together, the archive

Painted relief of **Amenemhat I** from his funerary temple at Lisht; the king wears the false beard and uraeus, and holds the flail over his shoulder.

provides an unrivalled source for international relations during the late 18th Dynasty.

Amasis (Ahmose II) (throne name: Khnemibra) (570–526 BC) Fifth king of the 26th Dynasty. An ARMY general serving in NUBIA during the reign of PSAMTIK II, Amasis came to the throne following the defeat of his predecessor APRIES by Greek settlers in the DELTA. Amasis pursued an ambivalent policy towards Greece: in a gesture of goodwill, he financed the rebuilding of the temple of Apollo at Delphi, and continued to employ Greek mercenaries in the Egyptian army; but he restricted the activities of their merchant compatriots at NAUKRATIS. In a long and prosperous reign, Amasis conquered parts of CYPRUS and won control of its naval fleet; at home, he sponsored a large number of building projects, although his name was later effaced by CAMBYSES who conquered Egypt following the brief reign of Amasis's son and successor, PSAMTIK III. The tomb of Amasis was seen by HERODOTUS at SAIS, but the area where it probably lay has been totally destroyed.

Amduat Collective name for a set of funerary texts, composed in the 18th Dynasty (c. 1539–c. 1292 BC), describing the underworld. The Egyptian word *amduat* means 'that which is in the underworld', although the full name of the collection was 'Writings of the Hidden Chamber'. First attested in the tomb of THUTMOSE III, the texts took as their theme the sun god's night-time journey through the realm of OSIRIS. Lavishly illustrated copies of the Amduat feature prominently in the decoration of NEW KINGDOM royal tombs, especially those of the RAMESSIDE period. Selected scenes began to appear in private burials of the THIRD INTERMEDIATE PERIOD.

Amenemhat I (throne name: Sehetepibra) (c. 1938–c. 1908 BC) First king of the 12th Dynasty (MIDDLE KINGDOM). His family came from THEBES, and his name (meaning 'AMUN is at the fore') signalled his devotion to Amun, the local god. Of non-royal parentage (his father was a priest), Amenemhat is probably to be identified with the VIZIER of the same name who led a mining expedition to the WADI HAMMAMAT during the brief reign of MENTUHOTEP IV. Whether or not Amenemhat was the chosen heir, he seems to have taken steps to legitimize his accession and secure his family's position on the throne. Hence the PROPHECY OF NEFERTI, a literary work composed about this time, refers to a 'saviour' called Ameny (the shortened form of

Amenemhat) who rescues Egypt from a time of chaos. Amenemhat probably also began the practice of CO-REGENCY, to guarantee that his son would succeed him without a challenge. Nevertheless, according to two other contemporary works of literature, the INSTRUCTION OF AMENEMHAT I FOR HIS SON and the TALE OF SINUHE, Amenemhat was murdered in a palace conspiracy.

His HORUS NAME, Wehem-Mesut, 'repeater of births', signalled his reign as a time of renaissance. Although he may have begun a tomb at Thebes, close to those of his 11th Dynasty predecessors, he made a decisive return to OLD KINGDOM models by relocating the capital towards the apex of the DELTA (at ITJ-TAWY) and by beginning again the practice of pyramid building. The king's mortuary complex at LISHT is noteworthy for incorporating many reused blocks from Old Kingdom pyramids, especially the Great Pyramid of KHUFU at GIZA. There are different explanations for this: it may have been a time-saving device at a time when quarrying stone for large monuments was a largely forgotten practice; or a conscious attempt to harness the symbolic power and authority of powerful kings from the past.

Other reforms included reorganization of local government and the reintroduction of conscription to the army. Inscriptions at MEMPHIS record military activity in PALESTINE, while another at Korosko mentions a campaign to overthrow WAWAT (Lower NUBIA) in his final year on the throne. Together with the construction of the first fortress at SEMNA, this marked the beginning of a new policy of conquest and annexation in Nubia. Similar measures were taken to protect Egypt's northern frontier. A fortress at Qaret el-Dahr in the western Delta was designed to prevent incursions from Libya; while, to keep out raiders and migrants from Palestine, a series of fortifications called the 'Walls of the Ruler' was constructed in the northeastern Delta. An administrative building at Ezbet Rushdi near AVARIS confirms the level of royal interest in the region. Further building projects in the reign of Amenemhat I included additions to the temples at BUBASTIS and Memphis, as well as new work at KARNAK, TOD and ARMANT.

Amenemhat II (throne name: Nubkaura) (c. 1876–c. 1842 BC) Third king of the 12th Dynasty (MIDDLE KINGDOM). He succeeded his father, SENUSRET, after a two-year CO-REGENCY. His reign seems to have been characterized by active trade with the eastern Mediterranean region: the silver treasure found at TOD is dated to his reign, suggesting economic links with the

*Granite head from a colossal seated statue of **Amenemhat III**, erected in the temple of Bastet at Bubastis and later usurped by Osorkon III in the 22nd Dynasty.*

Aegean; while statues of his female royal relatives – perhaps diplomatic gifts – have been discovered as far afield as the Lebanon. The king is also attested in the temple of HATHOR at SERABIT EL-KHADIM, indicating that mining expeditions to the Sinai continued during his reign. A fragment of an ANNALS inscription from MEMPHIS provides a detailed account of events at the royal court, and is the best source for his reign.

His pyramid complex is one of the least-known royal monuments in Egypt. Built at DAHSHUR, it took the form of a long rectangular enclosure, aligned east–west, with a massive brick PYLON forming the entrance gateway to the mortuary temple. The pyramid's location close to the cultivation made it particularly vulnerable to quarrying; by the time archaeologists first investigated it at the end of the 19th century AD, all the casing stone had been stripped away, leaving mounds of limestone chippings which gave the monument its modern name, 'the white pyramid'. The removal of the original stone facing has exposed the rough construction of mud-brick compartments filled with sand. Excavations at the complex yielded exquisite examples of JEWELRY, made for the princesses Khnumet and Ita.

Amenemhat III (throne name: Nimaatra) (c. 1818–c. 1770 BC) Sixth king of the 12th Dynasty and son of

SENUSRET III. His long reign was the most prosperous of the MIDDLE KINGDOM, and is marked by inscriptions and buildings throughout Egypt and the surrounding areas. Trade with the LEVANT continued to flourish, attested by a royal SPHINX statue found in the region. Activity centred on the Egyptian port of BYBLOS, where objects bearing the king's name have been discovered. Frequent mining expeditions were sent to the Sinai (WADI MAGHARA, Wadi Nasb and Rud el-'Air) for TURQUOISE and perhaps also copper. The results can be seen in the fine JEWELRY of the period, and in a rare copper statue of the king.

Within Egypt proper, royal projects focused on the FAYUM region, where Amenemhat may have ordered large-scale IRRIGATION and land reclamation projects. Two colossal statues of him were erected at BIAHMU, and temples were built at MEDINET EL-FAYUM and MEDINET MAADI. So prominent were the king's monuments in the Fayum, that he was deified (as King Lamarres or Marres) by the local inhabitants in the PTOLEMAIC PERIOD.

A pyramid at DAHSHUR (today named 'the Black Pyramid') was intended as his final resting-place. However, due to the large number of underground chambers and passages, and the poor quality of the local bedrock, cracks began to develop and walls to buckle before the monument was finished. It was abandoned in the king's 20th year; the PYRAMIDION of black granite still survives. A new pyramid was begun at HAWARA in the Fayum; Classical authors nicknamed its multi-chambered mortuary temple the 'LABYRINTH'.

Amenemhat developed his father's distinctive style of royal SCULPTURE. The most typical statues are instantly recognizable with their narrow eyes and large protruding ears. Others deliberately hark back to ancient forms, suggesting an interest in antiquity and, more especially, in models from the EARLY DYNASTIC PERIOD and OLD KINGDOM.

Amenemhat IV (throne name: Maakherura) (c. 1770–c. 1760 BC) Seventh king of the 12th Dynasty. One of the least-known rulers of the MIDDLE KINGDOM, he succeeded AMENEMHAT III, who may not have been his father, and reigned for only a short time; he may have been the ancestor of the 13th Dynasty line. His major monument is the temple at MEDINET MAADI; he may also have built (or completed) the temple at QASR ES-SAGHA. He is attested in the temple at SERABIT EL-KHADIM, so Egypt's links with the TURQUOISE-mining area of the Sinai were evidently maintained during his

reign. A SPHINX statue of Amenemhat IV has been found in the Levant, suggesting that foreign contacts still flourished, although it may have reached there by trade at a later date. The king's pyramid complex has never been identified with certainty; one of the unnamed and unfinished pyramids at MAZGHUNA, to the south of DAHSHUR, has been mooted, probably wrongly, as a possible candidate.

Amenemhat V, VI, VII (throne names: Sekhemkara, Sankhibra, Sedjefakara, respectively) (mid-18th century BC) Ephemeral kings who reigned during the first half of the 13th Dynasty.

Amenemnisu (throne name: Neferkara) (c. 1045–c. 1040 BC) Second king of the 21st Dynasty who reigned for a brief period after the death of SMENDES.

Amenemope (throne name: Usermaatra-Setepenamun) (c. 985–c. 975 BC) Fourth king of the 21st Dynasty, buried at TANIS.

Amenhotep I ('AMUN is satisfied') (throne name: Djeserkara) (c. 1514–c. 1493 BC) Second king of the 18th Dynasty (early NEW KINGDOM); the son of AHMOSE I and AHMOSE-NEFERTARI. His mother may have acted as regent during the early part of his reign, which, as a whole, is poorly documented. He married his sister Meretamun. He was revered throughout the New Kingdom as the co-founder, with his mother, of the workmen's village at DEIR EL-MEDINA. He succeeded in bringing NUBIA under Egyptian control, and appointed a VICEROY OF KUSH to govern it. He also built a temple on the Nubian island of Sai. He commissioned small additions to the temple of KARNAK, and other work at ABYDOS, ELKAB, KOM OMBO and ELEPHANTINE. The location of his tomb remains in doubt. It is mentioned in an inspection list from the reign of RAMESSES IX, and is probably at DRA ABU EL-NAGA, although the undecorated monument (KV39) at the very edge of the VALLEY OF THE KINGS has also been suggested as a possible candidate. Amenhotep is known to have built a mortuary temple at DEIR EL-BAHRI.

Amenhotep II (throne name: Aakheperura) (c. 1426–c. 1400 BC) Seventh king of the 18th Dynasty, who assumed full power following a short CO-REGENCY with his father THUTMOSE III. Amenhotep evidently took pride in his physical strength and promoted a heroic image of KINGSHIP. On one relief, he is shown shooting an arrow through a solid bronze target. Trade with the eastern Mediterranean is suggested by FAIENCE apes bearing the king's CARTOUCHE found at Mycenae and Tiryns in Greece. He undertook temple building at Amada and Kalabsha in NUBIA, and in the THEBAN area. Little has survived of his mortuary temple, and the decoration of his burial chamber in the VALLEY OF THE KINGS remained unfinished at his death. However, the tomb (KV35) was reused in the 21st Dynasty for the interment of eight other royal mummies taken from their own tombs for safe keeping. The cache was discovered in 1898.

Amenhotep III (throne name: Nebmaatra) (c. 1390–c. 1353 BC) Ninth king of the 18th Dynasty, son of THUT-MOSE IV and MUTEMWIA. His reign of over thirty-five years is one of the best attested of the NEW KINGDOM, and was a golden age of art and architecture. Diplo-matic relations with the Levant are recorded in some of the AMARNA LETTERS; by contrast, there is little evidence for military activity, except for a campaign in his fifth year to quell an uprising in NUBIA. He presided over a set of lavish construction projects, supervised by his chief architect AMENHOTEP SON OF HAPU. New buildings included large parts of LUXOR TEMPLE; the third PYLON at KARNAK; a huge mortuary temple in western THEBES, the entrance to which was flanked by the COLOSSI OF MEMNON; and a palace at MALKATA with a huge artificial harbour, the BIRKET HABU, for the celebration of his SED FESTIVALS. His principal wife, TIYE, played an important role at court; the king also took at least three of his daughters as 'King's Wife'. His religious programme, designed to elevate the status of KINGSHIP, anticipated the more radical reforms of his son, AKHENATEN. Amenhotep built a tomb in the Western branch of the VALLEY OF THE KINGS (KV22), decorated with scenes from the AMDUAT.

Amenhotep IV *see* Akhenaten

Amenhotep son of Hapu High official of the 18th Dynasty who rose to prominence during the reign of AMENHOTEP III. Born in ATHRIBIS, Amenhotep son of Hapu moved to the royal court at THEBES and was pro-moted to the position of chief royal architect; he oversaw the construction of the king's mortuary temple and its colossal statues (the COLOSSI OF MEMNON), and the temple of SOLEB in NUBIA. As a mark of special royal favour, Amenhotep was allowed

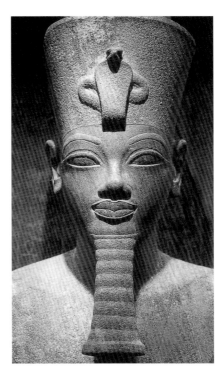

Detail of a red quartzite statue of **Amenhotep III**, *discovered in 1989 in a cache beneath the floor of Luxor Temple; the whole sculpture represents a portable figure of the rejuvenated king that would have been used during temple processions.*

Statue of **Amenhotep son of Hapu** *from the temple of Amun-Ra at Karnak; the classic pose of the Egyptian scribe emphasizes his membership of the literate ruling elite.*

Detail of the 19th Dynasty funerary papyrus of Hunefer, from Thebes; the monster **Ammut** awaits the result of the weighing of the heart, ready to consume the deceased if he fails the judgment.

Amulets were produced in many different shapes, from a variety of materials, and over a long period of time; those pictured here range in date from the First Intermediate Period to the Late Period.

to construct a cult temple among the royal mortuary temples in western Thebes, and to erect statues of himself – whose inscriptions chart his career – in the temple at KARNAK. Probably buried at QURNET MURAI on the west bank at Thebes, he became the focus of popular worship; he was posthumously deified, and venerated for three centuries after his death. In the LATE PERIOD, he was worshipped alongside the 3rd Dynasty official IMHOTEP for his supposed healing powers.

Amenirdis *see* God's Wife of Amun, Piye, Rudamun

Amenmesse (*c.* 1202–*c.* 1200 BC) King of the 19th Dynasty who usurped the throne for three years immediately before or during the reign of SETI II. He is perhaps the same individual as the VICEROY OF KUSH, Messuy, and began a tomb in the VALLEY OF THE KINGS (KV10).

Amenophis *see* Amenhotep I, II, III, IV

Ameny Qemau (*c.* 1750 BC) King (perhaps the third) of the 13th Dynasty who built a pyramid at DAHSHUR, now badly ruined. Its burial chamber was carved from a single block of granite, following the model of AMENEMHAT III's monument nearby.

Ammenemes *see* Amenemhat I, II, III, IV

Ammut In Egyptian RELIGION, a monster which was believed to dwell in the underworld. It waited beside the scales used in the WEIGHING OF THE HEART, ready to devour the hearts of those who did not secure entry to the afterlife. Ammut, which means 'devourer of the dead', was depicted with the head of a CROCODILE, the forequarters of a LION, and the hindquarters of a HIPPOPOTAMUS, thus combining three of the most fearsome beasts in one body.

Amratian *see* Predynastic period

amulet Small charm worn to afford its owner magical protection, or to convey certain qualities (for example, a LION amulet might convey strength, or a set-square amulet rectitude). Attested from the BADARIAN period onwards, amulets were produced both for the living and the dead. Particular amulets were placed at specific places in the mummy wrappings. The HEART SCARAB was a specialized form of amulet to protect the heart of the deceased in the afterlife. Amulets were made from a wide variety of materials, including FAIENCE, glass, and precious stones – with COLOUR often playing an important symbolic role – and in a wide variety of forms. They might depict sacred objects (such as the DJED PILLAR, TYET GIRDLE or WEDJAT EYE); animals (BULL's head amulets were particularly common in the late PREDYNASTIC PERIOD); or hieroglyphs (for example, ANKH or SA). From the NEW KINGDOM onwards, deities – especially household deities such as BES and TAWERET – were popular subjects for amulets.

Amun Originally a local god of the Theban region, Amun rose to prominence as THEBES itself became more important, eventually becoming the state god of NEW KINGDOM Egypt (with the exception of the AMARNA period, when the Amun cult suffered particular persecution). First mentioned in the PYRAMID TEXTS, Amun means 'the hidden one', and may have been associated with the power of the wind. Together with his original consort Amaunet, he was a member of the OGDOAD of HERMOPOLIS, and hence a god of creation. Through this association, he became closely linked with the sun god RA, and with the fertility god MIN. From the 12th Dynasty he was worshipped at KARNAK in his ITHYPHALLIC form, Amun KAMUTEF. At the beginning of the 18th Dynasty, Amun became the chief deity of Thebes, and was venerated in a TRIAD with MUT and KHONSU; their principal cult centre was the huge religious complex at Karnak, where Amun was worshipped in his combined form of Amun-Ra, King of the Gods, Lord of the Thrones of the TWO LANDS. LUXOR TEMPLE served as Amun's 'southern resting-place'; in the RAMESSIDE period and later, the god also had major temples at PER-RAMESSES and TANIS, and at various sites in Nubia. Befitting his exalted status, Amun was often depicted seated on a throne. In human form, he was shown wearing a short kilt and twin-plumed crown, his skin often coloured blue to emphasize his role in maintaining the fertility of Egypt. He could also be depicted as a ram (as in the avenue of CRIOSPHINXes at Karnak) to stress his procreative vigour; the GOOSE was another of his sacred animals. A number of popular shrines within the enclosure wall at Karnak allowed private individuals to petition Amun; he was believed to be able to cure eye problems.

Amyrtaeos (404–399 BC) Sole king of the 28th Dynasty, from SAIS. He liberated first the DELTA, then the whole of Egypt, from Persian rule. His reign was brief; he was deposed by a rival ruler from MENDES, NEPHERITES I.

Anat Warrior goddess, introduced to Egypt from the Levant where she was particularly associated with the seaport of Ugarit on the Syrian coast. First attested in Egypt towards the end of the MIDDLE KINGDOM and favoured during the HYKSOS period, Anat had become an important goddess in the DELTA by the 19th Dynasty, and was adopted by the RAMESSIDE kings as one of the patron deities of their military activities. RAMESSES II even named one of his daughters Bint-Anat ('daughter of Anat'). Sometimes identified with HATHOR, Anat was considered in Egyptian theology as a daughter of RA. She was usually depicted as a woman wearing a long dress and a tall plumed crown, holding weapons of war: a spear, battle axe and shield. In the THIRD INTERMEDIATE PERIOD, a precinct within the temple of MUT at KARNAK was dedicated to Anat.

ancestor busts Ancestor worship was an important feature of private RELIGION in ancient Egypt; small painted anthropomorphic busts could serve as the focus for such practices. Around 150 examples survive: one is from the MIDDLE KINGDOM town of KAHUN, most of the rest come from the NEW KINGDOM village

*Thutmose III kneels before **Amun**-Ra, who holds the sign of life to the king's nostrils, on an 18th Dynasty granite obelisk at Karnak; the god wears the characteristic twin plumes of a male deity.*

of DEIR EL-MEDINA. Made of stone, wood or clay, the busts seem mostly to have depicted male ancestors.

Anedjib (c. 2850 BC) Sixth king of the 1st Dynasty. Comparatively little is known about his reign. Inscriptions on two stone vessels from SAQQARA mention a SED FESTIVAL, suggesting that he may have reigned for a considerable period, perhaps in excess of thirty years. However, he is sparsely attested, being mentioned by name at only three sites in Egypt: Saqqara, HELWAN and ABYDOS. Two small marbles inscribed with Anedjib's SEREKH are now in a private collection. Otherwise, his major surviving monument is a tomb on the UMM EL-QAAB. Less elaborate than those of his immediate predecessors, the grave nevertheless yielded some important clues about the early development of the royal tomb. Inscribed stone vessels from the funerary equipment depict a stepped structure. If this is to be identified as the tomb superstructure, it would foreshadow the design of the STEP PYRAMID. Elsewhere, innovation in tomb architecture is demonstrated by another building of Anedjib's reign, the MASTABA of a high official at Saqqara (number 3508). Its burial chamber was covered by a stepped mound, entirely hidden within the superstructure.

Aniba Site on the west bank of the NILE in Lower NUBIA, north of the Second CATARACT. Founded in the 12th Dynasty, it comprised a large fortified settlement, a temple dedicated to HORUS Lord of Miam (the ancient name for Aniba), a series of cemeteries, and a separate settlement for the local Nubian (C-Group) population. In the NEW KINGDOM, Aniba was the administrative capital of WAWAT and the residence of one of the deputies to the VICEROY OF KUSH.

animal cults One of the most distinctive features of ancient Egyptian RELIGION was the reverence shown for certain animals that were regarded as the living manifestations of particular deities. The worship of the APIS bull is first attested in the EARLY DYNASTIC PERIOD, as is the cult of a sacred bull at BUTO. Cattle seem to have played a central role in religious beliefs from the PREDYNASTIC PERIOD; the animal cults of dynastic Egypt may be seen as a continuation of this tradition. Individual animals singled out for worship, such as the BUCHIS and MNEVIS bulls, had their own priesthoods and were buried with great ceremony. The popularity of animal cults reached a peak during the LATE PERIOD when whole species were revered; FALCONS, IBISES, monkeys and CATS were bred in huge numbers, to be donated as VOTIVE offerings by individual worshippers. They were mummified and buried in large underground galleries, especially at SAQQARA. Elsewhere, animal cults ranged from rams (at HERAKLEOPOLIS and ESNA) to CROCODILES (at MEDINET EL-FAYUM).

animal husbandry Livestock played a crucial part in the Egyptian economy from earliest times, with cattle, sheep, goats and PIGS the most important domesticated animals. Cattle may have been introduced to Egypt from the Levant, or may have been domesticated from native North African stock. Long-horned cattle were the dominant breed until the end of the OLD KINGDOM, when a shorter-horned variety was introduced, eventually becoming the more common. The humped zebu was introduced into Egypt from Asia in the 18th Dynasty. Cattle-herding is attested at NABTA PLAYA in the Western Desert as early as 8000 BC. Predynastic PETROGLYPHS in the Eastern Desert, together with contemporary settlement remains from the NILE

In ancient Egypt's farming economy **animal husbandry** *was crucially important and it acquired a corresponding significance in the wider culture; a wall painting from the 18th Dynasty tomb of Nebamun at Thebes shows cattle being brought for inspection.*

Valley, suggest a lifestyle in which herding played a central role. This may explain the dominance of cattle imagery in Egyptian culture, and the fact that implements used in animal husbandry, such as the crook, later became symbols of authority and items of ROYAL REGALIA. In early Predynastic times, cattle were probably kept for their renewable sources of food (milk and blood), being slaughtered for meat only on important occasions. In later periods, too, the availability of beef would have been confined to the wealthiest in society. In addition to their importance for food, cattle were also kept as draught animals. From at least the beginning of the 1st Dynasty, the fields of the DELTA provided important pasturage. Throughout pharaonic history, wealthy individuals and institutions owned large herds, which were branded to identify ownership. Cattle were so symbolic of wealth that the national census of resources was called the 'cattle count'.

Sheep and goats (originally from the Near East) were often grouped together under the name 'small cattle', indicating their inferior status. They were kept for milk, meat and wool. Goats were particularly well suited to the poorly vegetated scrub land at the desert margins, and may always have outnumbered sheep. Pigs played an important part in the Egyptian diet, despite their ambivalent position in the wider culture. Pens for pig-rearing were excavated at the AMARNA Workmen's Village, and pigs were included in NEW KINGDOM lists of temple assets, even if they were never presented as food offerings to deities. Ducks and geese were kept for eggs and meat from the PREDYNASTIC PERIOD; domestic fowl, first encountered on military campaigns in the Levant, were introduced in the 18th Dynasty. The HORSE was introduced in a military context during the SECOND INTERMEDIATE PERIOD; the DONKEY was the main pack animal until the introduction of the CAMEL in the THIRD INTERMEDIATE PERIOD.

Anket (Anuket, Anukis) Goddess of the First CATARACT region. Her main cult centre was on the island of SEHEL, but she was also worshipped further south, in NUBIA. First attested in the OLD KINGDOM, Anket was depicted as a woman wearing a tall plumed crown and holding a sceptre in the form of a papyrus reed. In the NEW KINGDOM, she formed a TRIAD with two other local deities, KHNUM and SATET.

ankh Egyptian word for 'life', written with the sign of a sandal-strap (a T-shape surmounted by a loop). This HIEROGLYPH was a powerful symbol and one of the most common in Egyptian religious iconography. Because of its cruciform shape, it was adopted by the COPTS as their distinctive form of cross.

Ankhesenamun ('She lives for AMUN') Third daughter of the late 18th Dynasty king AKHENATEN and his wife

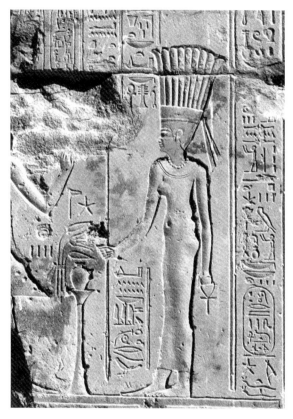

The goddess **Anket**, *wearing her distinctive feathered headdress, carved on a relief block from the Ptolemaic temple at Dakka in Nubia.*

Wall painting from the tomb of Amenhotep II in the Valley of the Kings showing the goddess Hathor holding the **ankh** *– the sign of life – to the king's nostrils.*

*Throne of Tutankhamun, showing the young king relaxing with his wife **Ankhesenamun** under the protective rays of the Aten; the figures of the king and queen are inlaid with silver sheet and semiprecious stones.*

*The Palermo Stone preserves a section of royal **annals** from the Early Dynastic period and Old Kingdom; the complete tablet was probably set up in a temple as part of a cult of the royal ancestors.*

NEFERTITI. She may have borne her father a daughter named Ankhesenpaaten-ta-sherit, before marrying her half-brother TUTANKHAMUN. Originally named ANKHESENPAATEN ('She lives for the ATEN'), she changed her name (as did her husband) to reflect the restoration of the cult of Amun and the demise of Aten worship following the death of Akhenaten. Her children by Tutankhamun were still-born or died in infancy; their mummies were found in his tomb (KV62). A ring bearing her name next to that of AY may suggest that Tutankhamun's successor married the dead king's young widow to legitimize his claim to the throne. Ankhesenamun is possibly to be identified as the queen who wrote to the HITTITES requesting a prince to marry after her own husband had died.

Ankhesenpaaten *see* Ankhesenamun

Ankhtifi NOMARCH of the third Upper Egyptian NOME during the 9th/10th Dynasty (*c.* 2125–2100 BC). His ROCK-CUT TOMB at el-MO'ALLA contains a biographical inscription which provides one of the most important accounts of political events in the FIRST INTERMEDIATE PERIOD. Although he nominally recognized the king in the north, Ankhtifi was an ambitious man who succeeded in extending his power, first over the neighbouring nome of EDFU and then over the southernmost nome of ELEPHANTINE. This gave him control over the whole of southern Upper Egypt and brought him into conflict with the equally ambitious rulers of THEBES. According to Ankhtifi's account, a disastrous famine afflicted Egypt during his time of office, and he was able to send supplies of grain to the nomes of DENDERA and THIS. Such an act would have been politically motivated, serving to isolate the Thebes-COPTOS alliance. A Theban attack on Ankhtifi's fortress at ARMANT effectively marked the beginning of hostilities in a protracted civil war. Ankhtifi seems to have retained regional dominance during his lifetime, but Theban expansion was ultimately unstoppable and his son exercised only local authority in the town of HIERAKONPOLIS.

annals Records of salient events arranged by reign, and in a year-by-year format. Those of the EARLY DYNASTIC PERIOD and OLD KINGDOM are preserved on the PALERMO STONE and several associated fragments. Such inscriptions, or the original records from which they were compiled, may have served as the basis for compiling KING-LISTS.

Antinoöpolis (el-Sheikh Ibada) Site on the east bank of the NILE in MIDDLE EGYPT, directly opposite HERMOPOLIS. The earliest remains belong to a temple of RAMESSES II, but the site is best known for the Roman city founded in AD 130 on the orders of the emperor Hadrian, to commemorate his favourite Antinous who drowned in the Nile nearby. Today virtually nothing remains of the city.

Anubis Funerary god concerned with burial and the afterlife. Frequently mentioned in the PYRAMID TEXTS which date back to the late OLD KINGDOM and the FIRST INTERMEDIATE PERIOD, Anubis may originally have been closely linked with the king, but as AFTERLIFE BELIEFS became more widespread his cult was extended to a broader section of the population. The god was depicted in canine form, or as a man with the head of a canine; usually identified as a JACKAL, the precise animal may be a composite creature combining attributes of the dog, jackal and fox. Dogs and jackals observed scavenging in cemeteries on the desert edge may have caused the ancient Egyptians to connect them with burial. Anubis was usually shown coloured black, symbolizing his funerary associations. A famous example is the statue found guarding the burial of

Scene from the 19th Dynasty tomb of Sennedjem at Deir el-Medina showing the god **Anubis** (or a priest wearing an Anubis mask) preparing the mummy of the tomb owner.

TUTANKHAMUN. The NEW KINGDOM NECROPOLIS seal used in the VALLEY OF THE KINGS bore the image of Anubis. The god performed several distinct roles, each indicated by a particular epithet. As 'Lord of the Sacred Land', he presided over the NECROPOLIS. 'He who is upon his mountain' referred to the common sight of a jackal standing on the edge of the desert escarpment, surveying the area below. 'The one who is in the place of embalming' denoted Anubis as the god of MUMMIFICATION; priests carrying out mummification may have worn Anubis masks for at least part of the process. As 'Lord of the NINE BOWS', Anubis was responsible for subjugating the hostile forces that might threaten the deceased in the tomb. The god also played a key part in the OPENING OF THE MOUTH ceremony, and escorted the newly deceased to the WEIGHING OF THE HEART. The cult of Anubis gradually absorbed those of other canine funerary deities, notably that of KHENTIAMENTIU, and was itself eventually assimilated into the cult of OSIRIS. Worshipped throughout Egypt, Anubis was also the principal deity of the 17th Upper Egyptian NOME.

Anuket, Anukis *see* Anket

Apedemak (Apedamak) War god of MEROË, who may also have been regarded as a patron deity of Upper NUBIA (he is referred to as 'splendid god at the head of Nubia, LION of the south'). During the MEROÏTIC period, Apedemak was the most important of the native Nubian deities. Besides a 'lion temple' at the site of Meroë itself, the god's main cult centre was at Musawwarat el-Safra, located in the desert to the east of the Sixth CATARACT; here, inscriptions in Egyptian HIEROGLYPHS give Apedemak the epithet 'strong of arm'. In another temple to the god at Naqa, in the same region, reliefs show him with the Egyptian deities HATHOR and AMUN, and in a TRIAD with ISIS and HORUS, emphasizing the high degree of Egyptian influence in Meroïtic religion. Apedemak was depicted as a lion or lion-headed man, occasionally as a three-headed lion or even a serpent-lion. He is usually shown wearing the triple crown; in anthropomorphic form he often carried a sceptre of special shape, surmounted by the figure of a crouching lion.

Apep *see* Apophis

Apepi (throne name: Aauserra) (*c*. 1570–*c*. 1530 BC) Penultimate king of the 15th Dynasty and the most important of the HYKSOS rulers who controlled northern Egypt during the SECOND INTERMEDIATE PERIOD. Apepi reigned for a long time, perhaps forty years, and he is attested as far south as GEBELEIN (although the stone block bearing his name may have been brought from elsewhere). The Rhind PAPYRUS is dated to his reign or that of his successor KHAMUDI. Towards the

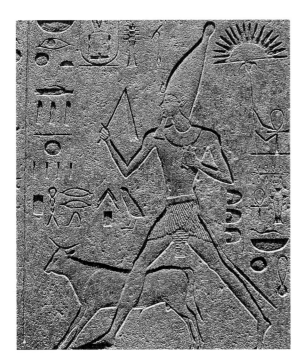

*A sandstone block from the 18th Dynasty Red Chapel of Hatshepsut at Karnak, showing the ruler running a ritual race with the **Apis** bull.*

end of Apepi's reign, the Theban ruler TAA II initiated military action against Hyksos rule; a RAMESSIDE papyrus gives an account of the ensuing battles. According to the stelae of Taa's successor KAMOSE, the Hyksos ruler entered into a strategic alliance with the ruler of KUSH, in an attempt to defeat the Thebans in a pincer movement. However, Kamose prevailed and besieged the Hyksos capital of AVARIS. Apepi's successor Khamudi was finally driven out of Egypt by AHMOSE's forces.

Aper-el Vizier during the reign of AKHENATEN, late 18th Dynasty (*c*. 1353–*c*. 1336 BC), whose Semitic name (compounded with the name of the god El) may suggest foreign ancestry. His rock-cut tomb has recently been excavated at SAQQARA.

Apis Sacred BULL of MEMPHIS and the focus of Egypt's most important bull cult, attested from the early 1st Dynasty. Apis was associated with PTAH, being regarded as his herald or his living image. Only one Apis bull existed at any one time. It was chosen following the death of its predecessor, and identified by means of particular markings, especially a white triangle on its forehead. It was kept in a special enclosure south of the temple of Ptah at Memphis, and provided with its own 'HAREM' of cows. It gave ORACLES and took part in processions. From the 18th Dynasty onwards, each successive Apis bull was mummified after its death, and buried in a series of underground galleries at SAQQARA, the SERAPEUM. The cow which had given birth to an Apis bull was associated with ISIS, treated with due reverence and, from the 26th Dynasty onwards, buried in a nearby set of catacombs, the Iseum. From early times, the Apis cult was closely connected with KINGSHIP; kings such as DEN and, later, HATSHEPSUT were shown running with the Apis bull. After death, the Apis was identified with OSIRIS. The resulting composite deity was worshipped in the PTOLEMAIC and ROMAN PERIODS as SERAPIS (hence the name Serapeum). After the NEW KINGDOM, the Apis was usually depicted in art as a bull with a sun disc between its horns, which had previously been the distinctive characteristic of the MNEVIS bull.

Apophis In Egyptian RELIGION, the huge SNAKE that embodied chaos and was the chief enemy of RA on his nightly journey through the underworld. Believed to have existed in the primeval waters from the beginning of time, Apophis attacked the SOLAR BARQUE every evening as it entered the underworld, and again every morning as it left. All those aboard were required to join together in defending Ra; SETH speared the serpent, and the stain of its blood was associated with the red sky at sunrise and sunset. First attested in the MIDDLE KINGDOM, the myth of Apophis plays a central role in NEW KINGDOM AFTERLIFE BELIEFS, and features frequently in FUNERARY TEXTS.

apotropaic Having the power to ward off evil. In ancient Egyptian RELIGION, earthly life and the afterlife were both characterized by a constant struggle between the forces of order and chaos. Evil threatened to disrupt individual lives and the whole of creation, but could be kept at bay – if not actually defeated – by magical means. Many everyday items, such as AMULETS, as well as FUNERARY OBJECTS and texts, were therefore designed to have an apotropaic function, to protect their owners against malign powers.

Apries (throne name: Wahibra) (589–570 BC) Fourth king of the 26th Dynasty. The son of PSAMTIK II, Apries undertook major building projects at MEMPHIS, in the DELTA, and in the BAHARIYA OASIS. He consolidated his power in UPPER EGYPT by having his relation Ankhneseneferibra adopted by NITIQRET as her successor to the office of GOD's WIFE OF AMUN. Further afield, he launched campaigns against Cyprus, Palestine and Phoenicia, and tried to stop a Babylonian advance at Jerusalem, but was defeated and driven south. A further Egyptian defeat by the forces of Cyrene led the army to mutiny, and the general AMASIS to depose Apries. He tried to regain the throne by invading Egypt with a Babylonian force, but was defeated and killed. Amasis nevertheless accorded him a full royal funeral.

Archaic Period *see* Early Dynastic period

Arensnuphis (Arsnuphis) MEROÏTIC god, probably of African origin, whose cult is first attested in the early Meroïtic period at Musawwarat el-Safra, in the desert to the east of the Sixth CATARACT. He was associated with the Egyptian gods ONURIS and SHU, and was combined with the latter through SYNCRETISM, as Shu-Arensnuphis, when his cult spread into Egyptian NUBIA during the PTOLEMAIC PERIOD. A KIOSK to Arensnuphis at PHILAE was jointly dedicated by Ptolemy IV and his Meroïtic contemporary King Arkamani (218–200 BC). In the temple of Dendur (originally 45 miles (75 km) south of Aswan, now in the Metro-

Painting in the 20th Dynasty tomb of Inherka at Deir el-Medina showing the serpent **Apophis** being decapitated by the great cat sacred to the sun god Ra.

politan Museum of Art, New York), Arensnuphis is shown being worshipped by the Roman emperor Augustus. The god was usually depicted as a man wearing a feathered crown, sometimes carrying a spear, but could also be shown as a LION, in common with other Meroïtic deities.

Armant Site on the west bank of the NILE in UPPER EGYPT, south of THEBES. Extensive prehistoric remains include areas of settlement, and a cemetery that has been used to chart the development of Predynastic Upper Egyptian culture. Until the early NEW KINGDOM, Armant was the capital of the fourth Upper Egyptian NOME. From the early MIDDLE KINGDOM onwards, its primary importance was as a cult centre of MONTU. The original temple, dating to the 11th Dynasty with later additions, was destroyed in the LATE PERIOD. A replacement was begun by NECTANEBO II, who also initiated the tradition of burying the sacred BUCHIS bulls in a special catacomb, the Bucheum. This practice was maintained for 650 years until the reign of the Roman emperor Diocletian. The cows worshipped as the mothers of the Buchis bulls were also interred in special tombs. A MAMMISI built by CLEOPATRA VII and Ptolemy XV Caesarion has been completely destroyed, but two gates of the ROMAN PERIOD survive.

army The ancient Egyptian word translated as 'army' could, in fact, refer to any organized expeditionary force of men, whether it was needed for mining, quarrying or fighting. Although military engagements are attested as early as the PREDYNASTIC PERIOD, there does not seem to have been a standing army in Egypt until the MIDDLE KINGDOM at the earliest, and no centrally organized national army until the NEW KINGDOM. Prior to the Middle Kingdom, soldiers were conscripted from each NOME whenever a military force was needed. Surprisingly large armies could be raised in this way. For example, the OLD KINGDOM official WENI boasts of having amassed a force of tens of thousands from the regions of Egypt for a campaign against the nomads of southern Palestine. Even at this early period, Egyptian soldiers were supplemented by large numbers of foreign mercenaries, many of them from NUBIA. Mercenaries remained an important feature of the Egyptian army throughout pharaonic history.

The fragmentation of political authority at the end of the OLD KINGDOM led to a situation where NOMARCHS raised and maintained their own local troops. This pattern persisted until the late Middle Kingdom, even though, following the reunification of Egypt, all armed forces were theoretically at the king's disposal. The full-scale military colonization of Nubia in the 12th Dynasty, which was based upon a network of permanently manned FORTRESSES, required a more developed military infrastructure. It is at this time that the armed forces acquired their own administrative apparatus (army SCRIBES). The Egyptian army in Nubia was well trained and supplied by the central government. In addition to its duties escorting trade shipments, the army carried out sophisticated surveillance operations throughout Lower Nubia, to protect Egyptian national interests.

The expulsion of the HYKSOS at the end of the SECOND INTERMEDIATE PERIOD drew Egypt into the politics of the eastern Mediterranean as never before. The defence of national borders and the creation of an empire required a permanent, national army for the first time. Even so, a scene in the Theban tomb of Userhat suggests that conscription remained a tool for raising extra manpower when the need arose.

The creation of a professional army in the 18th Dynasty is mirrored by a new militarism in royal ideology. Rulers such as THUTMOSE I and THUTMOSE III portrayed themselves as war leaders; the latter king included in his ANNALS a description of the Battle of MEGIDDO and used it as a potent piece of royal propaganda. As the army began to play an increasingly important role in national life, its power and influence also grew. Veterans were often granted parcels of land near the capital, apportioned by the king; this no doubt

*Wooden model of an **army** platoon, from the 11th Dynasty tomb of Mesehti at Asyut; the soldiers carry pikes and large shields, and were probably intended to guard the deceased in the afterlife.*

provided him with a convenient body of loyal reservists in case of a crisis. At the end of the 18th Dynasty, the commander-in-chief of the army, HOREMHEB, was able to gain the ultimate prize by claiming the throne, following the extinction of the royal line. He in turn chose a fellow army commander as his heir and successor (RAMESSES I).

With its military origins, the RAMESSIDE dynasty enhanced still further the standing of the army in national affairs. Through accounts like the Battle of KADESH, more is known about the internal organization of the army in the 19th Dynasty than at any other period of Egyptian history. The most basic unit was a platoon of 50 men; five of these units formed a 250-strong company, with its own scribe and commanding officer. Twenty companies formed a division of 5000 soldiers, usually commanded by a royal prince or other trusted confidant of the king. The army as a whole comprised four or five divisions, each named after a principal god. In the Battle of Kadesh, the divisions were called AMUN, RA, PTAH and SETH. Military texts suggest that the king himself led his troops into battle, although in reality this may not always have been the case. In peacetime, the army was divided for practical purposes into northern and southern sections, each commanded by a prince.

Throughout most of Egyptian history, there was no separate navy; but there were marines trained in naval warfare, and such troops were used to great effect by RAMESSES III in the battle against the SEA PEOPLES. In the LATE PERIOD, the Egyptian army came to rely increasingly on foreign mercenaries. Many of them were prisoners of war who could win freedom by serving the Egyptian king in battle. The large numbers of Greeks and Phoenicians who served in the SAITE army constituted important sections in an increasingly multi-ethnic population. (*See also* BOATS AND SHIPS, CHARIOT.)

Arsaphes *see* Herishef

Arses (338–336 BC) Ephemeral king of the 31st Dynasty (Second PERSIAN period).

Arsinoe Name of four QUEENS of the PTOLEMAIC PERIOD. Arsinoe I and II were wives of Ptolemy II, the second also being his sister who reigned at his side. Arsinoe III was the sister-wife of Ptolemy IV and was assassinated immediately after his death. Arsinoe IV was the daughter of Ptolemy XII, and the sister of

Ptolemy XIII, Ptolemy XIV and CLEOPATRA VII. She was proclaimed queen in opposition to Cleopatra, but subsequently captured, sent into exile, and finally assassinated on the orders of Mark Antony.

Arsnuphis *see* Arenshupis

art The ancient Egyptian LANGUAGE had no word for 'art', rather, art served an essentially functional purpose that was intimately bound up with RELIGION and ideology. To render a subject in art was to give it permanence. Hence, Egyptian art portrayed an idealized, not a realistic, view of the world. There was no tradition of individual artistic expression, since art served a wider, cosmic purpose of maintaining created order. It was bound by certain rules of representation (such as HIERARCHICAL SCALING), codified at the end of the PREDYNASTIC PERIOD. Art was diagrammatic rather than representational, each aspect of an object being depicted from its most characteristic angle. This gives Egyptian art its curious distorted perspective from a western, European viewpoint. Art and WRITING were considered parts of a unified system of representation; the modern distinction would not have been recognized by the ancient Egyptians. Our knowledge of Egyptian art is partial at best. Most examples that have

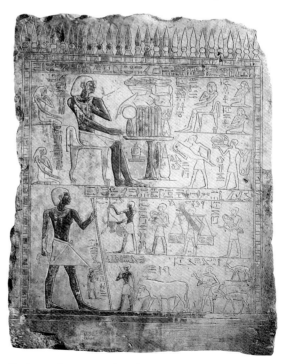

The late 12th Dynasty painted limestone stela of Amenemhat Nebuy from Abydos exemplifies the essential principles of ancient Egyptian **art***.*

survived were 'official art', produced for the ruling class; even within this category, reliefs and SCULPTURE in stone have survived much better than works in wood and other less durable media. There must also have been a flourishing tradition of 'popular' or 'folk' art, which was probably very different in character. Glimpses of other possible art styles may be seen during the FIRST INTERMEDIATE PERIOD, when regional and local traditions flourished; and during the AMARNA period when AKHENATEN instituted a deliberate break from pre-existing artistic traditions. A hybrid Greek-Egyptian style characterized works from the early PTOLEMAIC PERIOD.

Artaxerxes Name of three Persian kings, two of whom ruled Egypt (465–424 BC and 343–338 BC) during the 27th and 31st Dynasties respectively (the first and second periods of Persian domination).

Asasif Name given to two separate areas of the THEBAN NECROPOLIS. The southern area has six tombs of the LATE PERIOD but is otherwise little known. The northern area extends between DRA ABU EL-NAGA and KHOKHA, to the east of DEIR EL-BAHRI, and contains important ROCK-CUT TOMBS of the MIDDLE KINGDOM and NEW KINGDOM, some of the latter were reused in the THIRD INTERMEDIATE PERIOD. The earliest tombs, of the 11th Dynasty, are adjacent to the causeway of MENTUHOTEP II's mortuary temple. The 18th Dynasty tombs are oriented to the causeway of HATSHEPSUT's temple; they include the tomb of PUYEMRA. In the LATE PERIOD, several successive chief stewards of the GOD'S WIFE OF AMUN built large mortuary palaces in the vicinity.

Sketch on a New Kingdom ostracon from Deir el-Medina showing an unnamed goddess, probably **Astarte**, *in the form of a winged sphinx wearing an elaborate crown.*

Ashmunein, el- *see* Hermopolis

Asia, Western *see* Assyrians; Hittites; Israel; Kadesh, Battle of; Levant; Megiddo, Battle of; Mesopotamia; Mitanni; Sumerian

Assyrians People of north-eastern MESOPOTAMIA whose heartland was the city of Assur on the banks of the Tigris. During the reign of THUTMOSE III, the Assyrians and Egyptians maintained friendly relations, united in their common opposition to the MITANNI. There is little evidence for contacts in the following centuries; but when Assyria began its territorial expansion in the 1st millennium BC, it came into conflict with Egypt, as both powers tried to win and maintain the allegiance of the small city states in the LEVANT. The two states fought during the 23rd to 25th Dynasties, successive Assyrian invasions of Egypt paving the way for the rise of the 26th Dynasty (PSAMTIK I was originally installed as an Assyrian vassal king). Assyrian rule had little cultural impact on Egypt, and in the late 7th century BC the Assyrian empire was superseded by Babylonia as the dominant power in Mesopotamia.

Astarte Goddess of love and fertility, but also of war, whose cult was introduced from the LEVANT in the NEW KINGDOM. In Egypt, she was worshipped primarily as a warrior deity, in particular as the protectress of the king's battle CHARIOT (a role she shared with ANAT). She is mentioned on the Sphinx Stela of AMENHOTEP II, and a temple of Astarte was built at PER-RAMESSES. In Egyptian theology, she was regarded as the daughter of RA and wife of SETH. She was usually depicted as a naked woman on horseback, wearing the ATEF crown or a horned headdress, and brandishing weapons.

astronomy and astrology Close observation of the sky and stars is attested from an early period. The prehistoric stone circle at NABTA PLAYA was aligned with the midsummer sunrise and was designed to give advance warning of the summer solstice and the associated rainy season. A Predynastic PALETTE from Gerza shows a cow goddess with stars for ears and a star above her head; she may represent a particular constellation. Stars were to play a prominent role in Egyptian RELIGION, especially during the OLD KINGDOM. The title of the High Priest of HELIOPOLIS, 'Greatest of Seers', suggests an astronomical connection; it has also been suggested that the sacred BENBEN STONE of Heliopolis may have been a meteorite. Following the

*The painted ceiling in the royal tomb of Seti I is decorated with scenes related to **astronomy and astrology**, including depictions of the constellations in their ancient Egyptian forms.*

practice of 'stretching the cord', that is, laying out a temple or other sacred building (attested from the late 2nd Dynasty), which relied on astronomical observation, the 4th Dynasty PYRAMIDS were carefully aligned to the circumpolar stars. These were identified in the PYRAMID TEXTS as 'the Indestructibles', associated with the souls of dead kings. The four 'star shafts' in the Great Pyramid of KHUFU were aligned to Sirius and three other important constellations, Draco, Ursa Minor and Orion. The first and last of these were worshipped as deities in their own right, SOPDET and Sah respectively. The Pyramid Texts contain frequent references to stars as the king's companions in his celestial afterlife, while the ceilings of pyramid corridors and chambers were often decorated with stars. The HELIA-CAL rising of Sirius was the event which marked the beginning of the INUNDATION, and of the year in the Egyptian civil CALENDAR.

The Egyptians were well acquainted with the phenomenon by which the stars appear to move across the night sky. In the MIDDLE KINGDOM, COFFINS were often decorated with lists of the 36 groups of stars (decans) into which the night sky was divided. Tombs and temples of later periods often showed these decans on their ceilings; several RAMESSIDE royal tombs in the VALLEY OF THE KINGS are noted for their astronomical ceilings, most famously the tomb of SETI I. From the Middle Kingdom, Egyptian astronomy included knowledge of five planets: Mercury, Venus, Mars, Jupiter and Saturn. Although the Egyptians had the concept of auspicious and inauspicious days, true

astrology – the belief that the stars can affect human destiny – does not seem to have been a feature of religion until the PTOLEMAIC PERIOD. The Babylonian ZODIAC was only adopted in the 1st century AD.

Aswan Modern city, overlying an ancient site, on the east bank of the NILE in southernmost Upper Egypt. Situated at the northern end of the First CATARACT and marking Egypt's southern frontier, Aswan was of great strategic importance. The site has been continuously built over; the surviving remains date from the PTOLE-MAIC and ROMAN PERIODS. At that time, the settlement was a garrison for military campaigns against NUBIA. A fortified wall with watchtowers was built to the south of Aswan to guard against Bedouin raids. Two small temples of ISIS survive; blocks from a third were reused in the city wall. The local area was also the principal

*View of the Nile at **Aswan**, which marked the southern boundary of Egypt proper throughout the pharaonic period and was therefore always of strategic importance.*

source of granite throughout Egyptian history. PETRO-GLYPHS and inscriptions from all periods occur in the vicinity, while an unfinished obelisk and statues still lie in the main granite quarry to the south of the city. More extensive archaeological remains connected with Aswan and its ancient inhabitants are preserved on the nearby island of ELEPHANTINE and in the ROCK-CUT TOMBS at QUBBET EL-HAWA on the other side of the Nile. In the 1960s, the construction of the Aswan High Dam (the second of two dams across the Nile at Aswan) fundamentally changed the river's course. It also prompted a major international campaign of rescue archaeology to save the monuments of Lower Nubia from the rising waters of Lake Nasser.

Asyut Site on the west bank of the NILE in MIDDLE EGYPT. Strategically located at the start of the caravan route to the KHARGA OASIS and southwards to NUBIA, Asyut was capital of the thirteenth Upper Egyptian

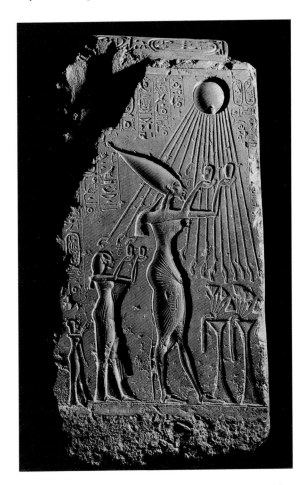

Fragment of a balustrade from the Great Palace at Amarna, with Akhenaten, Nefertiti and their eldest daughter Meritaten under the protective rays of the **Aten**, offering a libation to the sun disc.

NOME. It rose to prominence during the FIRST INTERMEDIATE PERIOD when its NOMARCHS were allies of the kings of HERAKLEOPOLIS against the Thebans. Inscriptions from the tombs of three successive nomarchs help to chart the progress of the civil war. Some of the earliest examples of COFFIN TEXTS have been found at Asyut in burials of this period. The site is also famous for the tomb of Hapdjefa I, nomarch during the reign of SENUSRET I, with its inscriptions detailing an elaborate series of contracts designed to ensure the perpetuation of the owner's mortuary cult. To date, only limited excavations have taken place at Asyut, and a single block is all that has been recovered from the local temple of WEPWAWET.

atef **crown** *see* crowns

Aten The sun disc, worshipped as a god during the 18th Dynasty and as the sole deity during the reign of AKHENATEN. The word *Aten* may have signified the radiant light of the sun rather than the physical disc. Its cult was promoted by AMENHOTEP III, before being given exclusive status by his son Amenhotep IV, who changed his name to proclaim that he was 'effective for Aten' (Akhenaten). The king built temples to the Aten at KARNAK, MEMPHIS and SESEBI; but the cult was most closely associated with his new capital city, AMARNA. The *Great Hymn to the Aten*, inscribed in the tomb of AY at Amarna, described the new official theology. The king and god ruled in a CO-REGENCY, demonstrated by the granting of a ROYAL TITULARY to the Aten. Moreover, Akhenaten alone was said to have true knowledge of the god, removing the need for any PRIESTS to interpret its will. The Aten cult remained an exclusive religion for the members of the ROYAL FAMILY and their closest circle of officials, winning little if any popular adherence. It faded soon after Akhenaten's death. The Aten was originally shown as a man with a FALCON's head, wearing the sun disc. In the art of the Amarna period it was depicted in more abstract form, as a disc wearing the URAEUS, and with rays extending from it, each of which terminated in a hand; some of the hands were empty, others offered the sign of life to Akhenaten and NEFERTITI.

Athribis Name of two sites in Egypt. The more important (Tell Atrib) is located in the central DELTA, on the Damietta branch of the NILE. It was the capital of the tenth Lower Egyptian NOME and the home town of AMENHOTEP SON OF HAPU. It is first mentioned in the

4th Dynasty, but there are no surviving monuments at the site earlier than the MIDDLE KINGDOM. The main features visible today are a temple of AMASIS, the tomb of a 26th Dynasty queen, and a settlement and cemetery of the PTOLEMAIC and ROMAN PERIODS. The site has suffered badly from the activities of SEBAKH (mud-brick) diggers.

Atum Primeval creator god and member of the ENNEAD of HELIOPOLIS. According to the Heliopolitan creation myth, Atum was self-engendered, the father of the gods, the creator from whom all else came, but also the god who would destroy everything at the end of the world. The god's hand, by which he brought forth SHU and TEFNUT through masturbation, stood for the female element contained within the sole creator. The cult of Atum became closely linked with that of the sun god. The composite RA-Atum represented a fusion of creative forces. In the context of the solar cycle, Atum was identified with the evening sun. He played a role in the mythology of KINGSHIP, sharing with the goddess SESHAT the task of recording the king's NAMES on the leaves of the ISHED TREE. Atum was usually depicted as a male figure wearing the double crown, but could also be shown with the head of a ram, or as a SCARAB. His principal cult centres were at Heliopolis and Per-Atem (biblical Pithom) in the DELTA.

autobiographies A popular genre of LITERATURE in ancient Egypt was the idealized description of an individual, extolling his accomplishments and ignoring any shortcomings, and hence far from a true autobiography. Such texts were most frequently inscribed in tombs; the earliest surviving examples (such as the autobiographies of WENI and HARKHUF) date to the late OLD KINGDOM. Although their primary purpose was to give permanence to the desired self-image of the tomb owner, autobiographical inscriptions giving details of specific events can be an important source for Egyptian HISTORY. Examples are the autobiographies of ANKHTIFI and AHMOSE SON OF ABANA, and the CHRONICLE OF PRINCE OSORKON at KARNAK.

Avaris (Tell el-Daba) Site in the north-eastern DELTA with remains spanning the FIRST INTERMEDIATE PERIOD to the beginning of the NEW KINGDOM. It has been the focus of excavations by an Austrian mission since 1966. Avaris was founded as a royal estate in the 9th/10th Dynasty. It was subsequently developed by the state during the 12th Dynasty, but rose to prominence as the capital of the HYKSOS during the 15th Dynasty; the town and surrounding region had already been settled by immigrants from the LEVANT during the late MIDDLE KINGDOM. DONKEY burials within the settlement illustrate the Middle Bronze Age culture of this immigrant population, who succeeded in establishing an Asiatic colony within Egypt. At the end of the SECOND INTERMEDIATE PERIOD, the Theban army laid siege to Avaris, prior to driving the Hyksos out of the Delta. A citadel with tombs of young men slain in battle has provided archaeological evidence to support the historical accounts. The early NEW KINGDOM rulers built a palace at the site, decorated with frescoes of bull-leaping influenced by similar paintings from Minoan CRETE. Avaris was subsequently abandoned in large part until the 19th Dynasty, when the RAMESSIDE kings founded their new capital, PER-RAMESSES, in the immediate vicinity.

Awibra Hor *see* Hor

Ay (I) (throne name: Merneferra) (early 17th century BC) King (perhaps the twenty-seventh) of the 13th Dynasty, and the last ruler of the dynasty to be attested in LOWER EGYPT. The end of his reign is generally taken to mark the end of centralized state control over the whole of Egypt, and hence the beginning of the SECOND INTERMEDIATE PERIOD. The PYRAMIDION from Ay's funerary monument was found at Faqus in

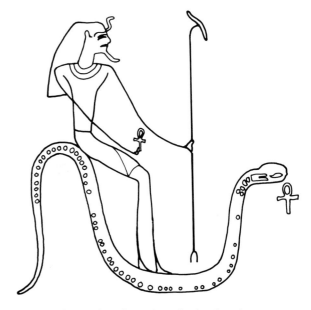

Drawing of a scene from the Amduat, showing the god **Atum** *– wearing royal regalia and holding a was sceptre – sitting on a serpent.*

the north-eastern DELTA; it had probably been transported there from a site in the NECROPOLIS of MEMPHIS or LISHT.

Ay (II) (throne name: Kheperkheperura) (*c.* 1322–*c.* 1319 BC) Fourteenth and penultimate king of the 18th Dynasty. An important official at the court of AKHENATEN, Ay may have been a royal relative, perhaps a brother of TIYE and/or the father of NEFERTITI. He rose from being superintendent of horses to the position of chancellor during TUTANKHAMUN's reign. At AMARNA, he began an impressive tomb, inscribed with the *Great Hymn to the Aten*. After the untimely death of Tutankhamun, Ay claimed the throne and had himself depicted in the young king's tomb (KV62) carrying out the funeral rites as legitimate heir. He may also have married Tutankhamun's widow, ANKHESENAMUN, to secure his position. Ay's own royal tomb (KV23), in the western VALLEY OF THE KINGS, had probably been intended for his predecessor; it includes scenes of hunting in the marshes, not usually found in royal tombs or in burial chambers. An elderly man at his accession, Ay reigned for only a few years; his death marks the end of the Amarna period.

Ayin Asil *see* Dakhla Oasis

Ay (II) performs the opening of the mouth ceremony on the mummy of Tutankhamun, in a scene from a wall painting in the boy king's tomb in the Valley of the Kings.

B

ba In Egyptian RELIGION, a concept with two distinct meanings. The *ba* was the aspect of an individual that made him/her unique, akin to the modern idea of personality. It played an important role in AFTERLIFE BELIEFS. The *ba* was thought to journey from the tomb to unite with the KA and become a transfigured spirit (AKH). It was represented as a human-headed bird; migrating birds were identified as *bas* flying between the tomb and the underworld. Egyptians believed that the physical body had to be reunited with the *ba* every night in order to survive for eternity. The term *ba* also signified the power or manifestation of a deity, as embodied in an animate or inanimate object. Hence the APIS bull was considered as the *ba* of OSIRIS, and the MNEVIS bull the *ba* of RA.

Baal Storm god and one of the most important deities of the Canaanites. By the 18th Dynasty, his cult had been introduced to Egypt. In the Egyptian pantheon, he was regarded as the brother and husband of ANAT, and was associated with SETH because of his disruptive nature. Hence, in texts describing the Battle of KADESH, the king is compared to Seth and Baal. Important cult centres of Baal existed at MEMPHIS and in the northern DELTA. The god was usually shown in human form with long hair and a Syrian-style pointed beard, wearing a conical helmet with horns at the base and carrying a sword or other weapons.

Badarian Term applied to the earliest Upper Egyptian culture of the PREDYNASTIC PERIOD (*c.* 5000–4000 BC). Named after the site of el-Badari in MIDDLE EGYPT, where material of the period was first excavated, the Badarian culture is characterized by fine handmade POTTERY, often burnished with a pebble to give a rippled finish. Other typical grave goods include small objects of IVORY, the earliest cosmetic PALETTES, and JEWELRY, some of it made from Red Sea shells. Badarian contacts with the area to the east of the NILE have been confirmed by the discovery of burials in the WADI HAMMAMAT and on the Red Sea coast. Badarian graves show variation in size and wealth, suggesting that the society was already unequal, with certain members enjoying greater prestige and access to resources. The Badarian culture thus marks the beginning of a process that was ultimately to lead to the creation of pharaonic civilization.

Bahariya Oasis Most northerly of the main Western Desert oases. Attested in Egyptian texts from the MIDDLE KINGDOM, it is mentioned on the stela of KAMOSE as the route used by the HYKSOS king to communicate with the ruler of KUSH. In the NEW KINGDOM, it was an important source of stone for royal building projects, and also the Egyptian front line against attacks by LIBYA. Apart from a NEW KINGDOM tomb, the region's standing monuments date to the 26th Dynasty and later periods. Notable are a series of chapels built by APRIES and AMASIS, a temple of ALEXANDER THE GREAT, and the recently discovered Valley of the Golden Mummies, a major NECROPOLIS of the ROMAN PERIOD.

Bakenrenef (Bocchoris) (throne name: Wahkara) (c. 720–c. 715 BC) Second and last king of the 24th Dynasty. His influence was probably restricted to his native city of SAIS, although later histories gave him undue prominence. His reign was brought to an end by the conquests of SHABAQO.

Balamun, Tell el- *see* Tell el-Balamun

Balat *see* Dakhla Oasis

Banebdjedet ('The ram, the lord of Djedet (Mendes)') Ram god of MENDES, where he was worshipped in a TRIAD with Hatmehit and HARPOCRATES. He was usually depicted as a ram or ram-headed man, but from the NEW KINGDOM he could be shown with four heads because of his associations with RA, OSIRIS, SHU and GEB. Like other ram gods, he was credited with strong sexual powers and was identified as the BA of Osiris.

barque (bark) *see* barque shrine, solar barque

barque shrine In Egyptian RELIGION a model boat in which the cabin was replaced by a shrine containing the cult image of a deity. It was kept in the sanctuary of a temple, and carried by PRIESTS in procession at important FESTIVALS. On long processional routes, such as that leading from KARNAK to LUXOR TEMPLE, small way-stations might be provided as resting places for the barque shrine.

Bashendi *see* Dakhla Oasis

Basta, Tell *see* Bubastis

Bastet Feline goddess whose main cult centre was at BUBASTIS (the name means 'House of Bastet'). In the PYRAMID TEXTS, she appears as the mother and nurse of the king, and in later periods she was regarded as a symbol of motherhood. She was also identified as the daughter of RA, and like other feline deities, combined

*The **ba** of the deceased, in the form of a human-headed bird, hovers over his mummified body, in a wall painting from the 19th Dynasty tomb of Amenemone at Thebes.*

*A Late Period bronze statuette of the cat goddess **Bastet** with a basket over one arm and holding a sistrum; she combined dangerous and protective attributes.*

dangerous and protective attributes. Perhaps originally a lioness deity, Bastet was more commonly depicted as a CAT or cat-headed woman. Her cult became very popular in the LATE PERIOD, giving rise to the manufacture and dedication of numerous bronze cat statues, and to the creation of special cemeteries for mummified cats at Bubastis and SAQQARA.

Bat Cow goddess, important in the PREDYNASTIC and EARLY DYNASTIC PERIODS. Depicted as a woman's head with the ears and horns of a cow, Bat had celestial connotations and is shown in a protective role on the NARMER PALETTE. She was the local goddess of the seventh Upper Egyptian NOME, and influenced the cult of HATHOR, eventually being assimilated into it during the MIDDLE KINGDOM.

battles *see* Kadesh, Megiddo

Bay Chancellor at the end of the 19th Dynasty in the reign of SIPTAH. Bay was instrumental in placing Siptah on the throne (according to Bay's own inscriptions), but he fell from grace and was executed late in the reign. Bay was granted the privilege – rare for a commoner – of a TOMB in the VALLEY OF THE KINGS (KV13).

beard Facial hair – in the form of beards and moustaches – went in and out of fashion in ancient Egypt. In general, careful grooming seems to have been a mark of social status: some NEW KINGDOM ostraca show workmen with unkempt hair and unshaven stubble. An elaborately plaited beard was an attribute of divinity, and most Egyptian gods were shown with beards. To demonstrate his quasi-divine status, the king wore a false beard, secured by a chin strap, as part of the ROYAL REGALIA. After death, when the king had become assimilated with OSIRIS, he was generally depicted with the god's long curly beard.

The head of the celestial cow goddess **Bat**, *a detail from the top of the early 1st Dynasty Narmer Palette, on which she watches over the figure of the king in a protective role.*

Beautiful Festival of the Valley A major festival of the THEBAN area which involved the statues of AMUN, MUT and KHONSU travelling from KARNAK across the NILE to DEIR EL-BAHRI. The festival's origins can be traced back to the MIDDLE KINGDOM, but it first became important in the NEW KINGDOM. For families, it was an occasion to visit the TOMBS of their relatives and offer prayers to their ancestors.

bee Bee-keeping is attested in Egypt from prehistoric times, and collectors are known to have gathered honey from wild bees along the desert edges. Bees were important as a source of honey – the main sweetener in Egyptian FOOD AND DRINK – and beeswax, used in MEDICINE and METALWORKING. Bee-keepers are depicted in the SUN TEMPLE of NIUSERRA at ABU GHURAB and in the 18th Dynasty tomb of REKHMIRA at THEBES. In a religious context, the bee was associated with LOWER EGYPT: one of the ROYAL TITLES introduced in the 1st Dynasty, *nesut-bity*, meant literally 'he of the sedge and bee' and related to the DUALITY of royal authority; the temple of NEITH at SAIS was known as 'the house of the bee'.

beer One of the staples of the Egyptian diet, beer was thick and nutritious but had a low alcohol content. The basic ingredients were water and partly baked BREAD. Sieved together, the resulting mixture was left to ferment; sugar from dates or honey could be added to accelerate the fermentation process. The finished product was enhanced with various flavourings, including dates, honey and herbs. The earliest evidence for beer production comes from the Predynastic town at HIERAKONPOLIS. Throughout Egyptian history, beer was produced by individual households, but also on an industrial scale for those employed on government building projects.

Behbeit el-Hagar Site in the northern central DELTA, about 10 km (6 miles) north of SEBENNYTOS. It is dominated by a ruined temple of ISIS, built in the 30th Dynasty and PTOLEMAIC PERIOD.

Beit el-Wali Rock-cut temple, originally located on the west bank of the NILE in Lower NUBIA, but moved in the 1960s to a new location near the ASWAN High Dam, to protect it from the rising waters of Lake Nasser. The temple was built by RAMESSES II and dedicated to AMUN-RA. Its reliefs include scenes of Egyptians attacking Syrian and Nubian settlements.

Beit Khallaf Site in Upper Egypt, dominated by a 3rd Dynasty cemetery with two huge and imposing tombs of mud-brick. The earlier tomb, Mastaba K1, contained seal impressions naming Netjerikhet (Djoser) and Nimaathap (the wife of Khasekhemwy). K1 is probably her tomb, and its vast size illustrates her importance as ancestress of the 3rd Dynasty, and perhaps Djoser's mother. The proximity of Beit Khallaf to the ancient town of This may indicate that Nimaathap was descended from the kings of the 1st Dynasty who came from the area. The later Mastaba, designated K2, is dated to the reign of Sanakht and contained a seal impression bearing the earliest known cartouche.

Belzoni, Giovanni *see* Egyptology

benben **stone** Sacred stone kept in the temple of Heliopolis. It played a prominent role in solar religion and hence in Egyptian sacred architecture. Pyramids, sun temples and obelisks were all designed to resemble the *benben*, which was depicted in art as pointed or conical in shape. It may have been a meteorite. Mythology interpreted the stone as a fallen star, or the petrified semen of Ra-Atum, and connected it to the benu bird.

Beni Hasan Site on the east bank of the Nile in Middle Egypt. The limestone cliffs contain a series of Middle Kingdom rock-cut tombs, made for the nomarchs of the sixteenth Upper Egyptian nome. Some of the tombs have colourful painted reliefs, including a famous scene in the tomb of Khnumhotep II showing a group of Asiatic traders arriving in Egypt. On the slope below the cliffs, numerous lower status burials provided archaeologists with a wealth of information about private burial customs in the 11th and 12th Dynasties.

Bent Pyramid *see* Dahshur

benu **bird** In Egyptian religion, the sacred bird of Heliopolis. First mentioned in the Pyramid Texts in connection with Atum, it came to be regarded as the manifestation of Ra and Osiris. In the New Kingdom it was frequently depicted in the Book of the Dead as a heron with a crest of two feathers. Closely linked with the benben stone, it was also the inspiration for the phoenix of Greek mythology.

Berenike (Medinet el-Haras) Port on the Red Sea coast, founded by Ptolemy II in the 3rd century BC to

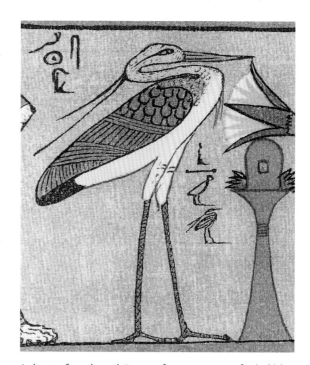

A vignette from the 19th Dynasty funerary papyrus of Ani which shows the **benu** *bird next to a ewer on a stand, topped by a water-lily.*

Detail of a painted relief from the 12th Dynasty tomb of Khnumhotep II at **Beni Hasan***, depicting the arrival in Egypt of a group of Asiatic traders.*

facilitate trade between Egypt, Arabia and more distant regions. It was connected by desert routes to EDFU and, later, to COPTOS. In the PTOLEMAIC PERIOD, it was the port to which cargoes of elephants were sent for military deployment; in the ROMAN PERIOD, trade shipments were mainly composed of consumer goods. Excavations have revealed warehouses, industrial areas, and a temple of SERAPIS.

Bersha, Deir el- *see* Deir el-Bersha

Bes Name given to a minor deity, or a number of similar deities and demons, which became popular in the NEW KINGDOM and later periods. Bes was venerated as a protective figure, guarding against snakes, but particularly associated with childbirth and children. Together with TAWERET, Bes played a prominent role in private (as opposed to state) RELIGION. He had no particular cult centre, but was a popular household deity. He was depicted as a DWARF-like figure with a mane, large staring eyes and a protruding tongue. The image was perhaps derived from a male lion rearing up on its hind legs.

Bes was often shown with a large belly and breasts, emphasizing his role in fertility; carrying knives or the HIEROGLYPH for protection (SA), signifying his protective role; or dancing with musical instruments, in his role as a god of popular celebration.

B-Group *see* Nubia

*Sandstone figure of **Bes** from the enclosure of the late Ptolemaic temple of Hathor at Dendera; Bes was a popular minor deity in the New Kingdom and later periods.*

Biahmu Site in the FAYUM where King AMENEMHAT III erected a cult building and a pair of colossal royal statues. Today, only their pedestals and a few scattered stone blocks survive.

biblical connections Although Egypt is mentioned in the Old and New Testaments, attempts to corroborate these accounts through the study of ancient Egyptian texts or through archaeology have proved extremely difficult, inconclusive and controversial. A fundamental point is the different aims of the two kinds of sources. While the Bible describes real and allegorical events that its writers considered particularly significant, the Egyptian written record portrays the world from a purely Egyptian viewpoint. Moreover, the events of the Old Testament are difficult to date with certainty, and their portrayal of events in Egypt does not tie in with the picture built up through excavation. Most attention has been paid to the accounts of Joseph and the Exodus, but there is still no agreement on the most likely historical setting for these events from an Egyptian perspective. Some writers have sought to make a connection between the monotheism of Moses and the religious reforms of AKHENATEN (*c.* 1353–*c.* 1336 BC); yet the word 'Israel' first occurs in a hieroglyphic inscription in the reign of MERENPTAH (*c.* 1213–*c.* 1204 BC), in a list of lands and peoples subjugated by the king. Stylistic connections between Egyptian and biblical texts indicate a common literary tradition across large parts of the ancient Near East, but little more.

Birket Habu *see* Amenhotep III, Malkata

birth house *see mammisi*

block statue *see* sculpture

blue crown *see* crowns

board games *see* games

boat burial The practice of burying a full-size boat (either an actual craft or a dummy) to accompany the deceased into the next world is attested from the 1st Dynasty. At this period, the tombs of certain high officials at SAQQARA, ABU RAWASH and HELWAN were provided with one or more boat burials, presumably to assist in an afterlife journey. A fleet of twelve cedar boats was interred next to the funerary enclosure of King DJER at ABYDOS. This early example of royal boat burials prefigures the famous cedar BARQUES buried in pits next to the Great Pyramid of KHUFU at GIZA. In later pyramid complexes of the OLD KINGDOM, a boat-shaped pit could take the place of an actual boat, but its magical purpose remained the same.

boats and ships Since the River NILE was the main artery for transport and communication in ancient Egypt, boats were vitally important. They are attested in ART from the early PREDYNASTIC PERIOD, and they played a crucial role in every sphere of Egyptian culture, including RELIGION. The sun god was believed to travel across the sky and through the underworld by boat; BARQUE SHRINES and processions by boat were important features of cultic activity.

For fishing trips and short journeys across the river, simple rafts and lightweight skiffs made from bundled PAPYRUS reeds were adequate. More robust vessels would have been required for longer journeys. Nevertheless, river transport was relatively straightforward, since the Nile current flowed from south to north while the prevailing wind blew from north to south. Travel upstream could therefore be accomplished with the help of a sail, while for downstream journeys the sail was furled – or a collapsible mast stowed – and the boat propelled with oars. A large oar at the stern was used for steering, and provided extra propulsion. The establishment of regular trade links with BYBLOS in the 2nd Dynasty gave Egypt access to supplies of high-quality coniferous woods, greatly facilitating the construction of sea-going ships. Remains of such vessels from the early NEW KINGDOM were discovered in 2005 in a cave on the Rea Sea coast at Wadi Gawasis.

The Egyptian LANGUAGE had more than a hundred different terms for boats, indicating a wide variety of forms for particular uses. Likewise, representations and TOMB MODELS of boats are relatively common. However, surviving examples of craft are rare. Prominent exceptions are the fleet of twelve cedar boats found next to the SHUNET EL-ZEBIB at ABYDOS, and the two SOLAR BARQUES of KHUFU at GIZA. The latter demonstrate sophisticated boat-building skills. The shell was built first from wooden planks, jointed, pinned or lashed together; the supporting frame was then inserted. The Egyptians built barges capable of moving stone blocks weighing over seven hundred tons and naval vessels for military engagements.

Bocchoris *see* Bakenrenef

Book of the Dead Name given by Egyptologists to the collection of funerary texts called by the ancient Egyptians the *Spells for Coming Forth by Day*. In use from the NEW KINGDOM until the early ROMAN PERIOD, the collection comprises around two hundred individual chapters, intended to provide the deceased with all the necessary information to achieve a successful afterlife. Many of the chapters are derived from the earlier PYRAMID TEXTS and COFFIN TEXTS. Selections were usually written on PAPYRUS and placed in the COFFIN, incorporated into the mummy wrappings, or rolled up and inserted into a statuette of PTAH-SOKAR-OSIRIS.

Vignette from the 18th Dynasty **Book of the Dead** *of Nakht, from Thebes; on this section of the funerary papyrus, the deceased is shown with his wife before the deities Osiris and Maat, with Nakht's house and garden in the background.*

Many copies have survived. The more elaborate versions included coloured illustrations (vignettes). Individual extracts might be inscribed on AMULETS or other ritual objects. Of particular importance were Chapter 6, the SHABTI text; Chapter 30A, commonly inscribed on HEART scarabs; and Chapter 125, concerning the WEIGHING OF THE HEART.

borders Geography provided ancient Egypt with natural borders: the Mediterranean Sea to the north, deserts to the west and east, and the First CATARACT of the NILE to the south. Although these barriers protected Egypt from foreign infiltration and attack for much of its history, they did not prevent the ancient Egyptians from exploring and exploiting the areas beyond the immediate confines of the Nile Valley. Egypt's natural borders were also reinforced at various periods by the construction of FORTRESSES, as much for economic as for military purposes. A fortress on ELEPHANTINE was built in the early 1st Dynasty, to mark Egypt's formal border with NUBIA and regulate trade. In the 12th Dynasty, AMENEMHAT I built the 'Walls of the Ruler' to protect the eastern DELTA from large-scale immigration of Palestinian peoples; while SENUSRET III erected a series of fortresses and a commemorative STELA at SEMNA to mark Egypt's new southern frontier with KUSH and ensure Egyptian control of trade convoys. In the NEW KINGDOM, RAMESSES II and other rulers reinforced Egypt's north-western and north-eastern borders with forts, designed to repel attack from LIBYA and the LEVANT respectively (for example, ZAWIYET UMM EL-RAKHAM). The area under Egyptian control was at its most extensive in the reign of THUTMOSE III, when the king erected border inscriptions on the bank of the River Euphrates in MESOPOTAMIA and at KURGUS in Upper Nubia.

bread The main staple of the ancient Egyptian diet, bread was symbolic of food in general. The HIEROGLYPH for 'offering' showed a loaf of bread on a mat, while the OFFERING FORMULA asked, above all, for the deceased to receive bread and BEER. Bread was made from emmer wheat – or occasionally barley – which had been threshed, winnowed and ground on a saddle quern (the rotary quern was introduced in the PTOLEMAIC PERIOD). Although yeast was known, bread was generally unleavened; it was baked in an oven or in the embers of a fire. Moulds were often used for baking as well as shaping bread, and are one of the most common types of POTTERY found in ancient Egyptian settlement sites. Different shapes of loaf were produced for different purposes; bread destined for offerings in temples or tombs was commonly formed into long narrow loaves. The Egyptian LANGUAGE had many different words for bread and cake.

breccia *see* stone

bronze *see* metalworking

Bubastis (Tell Basta) Site in the eastern DELTA, on the edge of the modern city of Zagazig. In ancient times it was located on the Pelusiac branch of the NILE, and benefited from its strategic importance for trade between Egypt and the LEVANT. First mentioned in the late PREDYNASTIC PERIOD, it flourished as the main cult centre of BASTET, with a cemetery of sacred CATS being developed in the 26th Dynasty. Monuments of all periods have been excavated at the site: KA CHAPELS of TETI and PEPI I; a large cemetery spanning the OLD KINGDOM and FIRST INTERMEDIATE PERIOD; a huge administrative complex of the MIDDLE KINGDOM, including the office and residence of the mayor, with an associated cemetery; chapels built for the SED FESTIVALS of AMENEMHAT III and AMENHOTEP III; and tombs of RAMESSIDE officials, including two VICEROYS OF KUSH. Bubastis rose to national prominence as the home town of the kings of the 22nd Dynasty. The principal temple to Bastet dates from this period; OSORKON II also built a temple to ATUM, and Osorkon III a temple to the lion god Mihos. Originally subordinate to HELIOPOLIS, Bubastis became the capital of the eighteenth Lower Egyptian NOME during the LATE PERIOD. The site continued to flourish in the PTOLEMAIC PERIOD, and in the ROMAN PERIOD when further temple building took place.

Buchis Sacred BULL worshipped in the THEBAN region from the 26th Dynasty onwards as the incarnation of MONTU. It was believed to cure diseases, especially those affecting the eyes. It took part in staged fights with other bulls in a special arena. From the SAITE period until the reign of the Roman emperor Diocletian, successive Buchis bulls were interred in their own cemetery on the desert edge at ARMANT (the Bucheion).

Buhen Site in Lower NUBIA, at the northern end of the Second CATARACT. A settlement was founded in the OLD KINGDOM to serve Egyptian mining expeditions. In the reign of SENUSRET I, a FORTRESS was built as part of the military annexation and occupation of Lower Nubia. Its defences included a massive curtain wall with spur walls to protect the flanks; a heavily fortified gateway; and semi-circular bastions with slits for archers. In the NEW KINGDOM, with the frontier further south, Buhen's strategic importance was reduced, and a new town was built outside the fortress walls. Following the construction of the ASWAN High Dam in the 1960s, the site – originally on the west bank of the NILE – was lost forever beneath the waters of Lake Nasser.

bull In common with many cultures in North Africa and the eastern Mediterranean, ancient Egyptians revered the bull as a symbol of strength, virility and fertility. The importance of bulls in early Egyptian RELIGION and ideology may be echoes of a prehistoric cattle-herding lifestyle from which pharaonic civilization eventually developed. From the beginning of Egyptian history, the bull was particularly closely associated with KINGSHIP. On the NARMER PALETTE, the ruler is shown as a bull, tearing down the walls of an enemy stronghold and trampling its inhabitants underfoot. A bull's tail remained an important part of the ROYAL REGALIA from the late PREDYNASTIC PERIOD to the very end of Egyptian civilization. Kings frequently bore the epithet 'strong bull', while a 1st Dynasty MASTABA at SAQQARA, built for a prominent member of the royal court, was decorated along its principal façade with a line of bulls' heads, modelled in clay. Sacred bull cults were popular and widespread in Egypt: at BUTO, MEMPHIS (the APIS bull), HELIOPOLIS (the MNEVIS bull) and ARMANT (the BUCHIS bull). The NILE INUNDATION was sometimes represented as a bull, probably because of its key role in renewing the fertility of Egypt.

burial customs AFTERLIFE BELIEFS, FUNERARY OBJECTS and TOMBS are all much better attested than the ceremonies and rituals which accompanied interments. From prehistoric times, the preferred location for cemeteries was on the west bank of the NILE, the place of sunset and the land of the dead. In the PREDYNASTIC PERIOD bodies were laid in the grave in a contracted position, recalling the baby in the womb; this custom was probably designed to assist in the individual's rebirth. An extended position became more usual from the OLD KINGDOM onwards, with the deceased laid on one side, looking towards the east in order to share in the daily rebirth promised by the rising sun. Grave goods were a feature of burials from

earliest times, indicating a belief in life after death. Greater numbers of funerary objects became customary as Egypt moved towards statehood at the beginning of the 1st Dynasty. From the EARLY DYNASTIC PERIOD onwards, differences in social status were expressed by the quantity and quality of grave goods, and by the

*Remains of the Middle Kingdom fortress at **Buhen** during excavation in the 1960s; it was designed to withstand attack by Nubians or desert tribespeople.*

*A wild **bull** is captured by Ramesses III to demonstrate his physical prowess; relief from his mortuary temple at Medinet Habu.*

*A Predynastic grave from Gebelein illustrates typical Egyptian **burial customs** – the provision of grave goods for the deceased and the preservation of the body (here by natural mummification).*

size and decoration of a tomb. One of the most important developments in burial customs was the widespread adoption of MUMMIFICATION in the Old Kingdom, designed to preserve the body of the deceased for eternity.

The funeral itself was accompanied by various rituals. An obscure ceremony called the Breaking of the Red Jars is attested in the Old Kingdom, while MIDDLE KINGDOM funerals sometimes involved a symbolic figure called a TEKENU. The funeral procession to the tomb was no doubt an occasion for mourning, with the MUU DANCERS playing an important role. The COFFIN might be borne aloft on carrying poles, transported on a cart, or dragged on a sledge drawn by people or oxen. Detailed depictions of funerals in NEW KINGDOM tombs show groups of mourners, offering bearers, libations and prayers. Once the mummy had been installed in the tomb, the OPENING OF THE MOUTH ceremony was performed to ensure that the deceased could derive sustenance from the offerings and hence survive in the afterlife. Wealthier individuals – who would usually prepare a tomb during their lifetime – attached great importance to making proper provision for their funerary cult, to guarantee a perpetual supply of offerings.

Busiris Classical name given to nine different towns in Egypt. The most famous (Abu Sir Bana) lies in the central DELTA on the Damietta branch of the NILE. Capital of the ninth Lower Egyptian NOME from the OLD KINGDOM to the LATE PERIOD, it was identified as the birthplace of OSIRIS and was one of the god's main cult centres. A few monuments have been found, but there have been no proper excavations.

The New Kingdom temple enclosure at **Buto**, located between the two main settlement mounds which may correspond to the twin cities Pe and Dep mentioned in Egyptian texts.

Butehamun THEBAN official at the end of the 20th/beginning of the 21st Dynasty, who was responsible for restoring the royal mummies of the NEW KINGDOM pharaohs after they had been violated by tomb robbers. Butehamun's name was thus inscribed on the wrappings of RAMESSES III's mummy, and has been discovered recently at burial sites in the desert to the west of THEBES.

Buto (Tell el-Fara'in) Site in the northwestern DELTA with remains from the PREDYNASTIC PERIOD to the ROMAN PERIOD. Two settlement mounds may correspond to the twin cities (Pe and Dep) mentioned in Egyptian texts from the beginning of the 1st Dynasty. A third mound, the site of the main temple, has yielded royal statues and STELAE of the NEW KINGDOM and LATE PERIOD. On the edge of the modern cultivation, modern excavations beneath the water-table, using pumping equipment, have revealed traces of Predynastic occupation, including evidence for a Palestinian element in the local population. In the early fourth millennium BC, Buto belonged to the Lower Egyptian cultural tradition; the spread of Upper Egyptian POTTERY types can be charted in successive archaeological layers, heralding the cultural unification of Egypt. In early times, Buto had a coastal location, ideal for trade between Egypt and the LEVANT. Today, it lies some distance inland, due to the advance of the Delta sediments. Ruined Roman pottery kilns dominate the site.

Byblos (Jebail) Port on the Lebanese coast, first settled in the Neolithic period and occupied more or less continuously until the 7th century AD. From at least the EARLY DYNASTIC PERIOD, it was Egypt's main source of high-quality timber for ship-building. A stone vessel fragment with the name of KHASEKHEMWY marks the earliest evidence for direct Egyptian involvement; contacts became more intensive from the OLD KINGDOM onwards, with commodities such as oil, resins and WINE being exported. The links between Byblos and Egypt were particularly strong in the 12th Dynasty, after which the native rulers of Byblos became heavily Egyptianized. The AMARNA LETTERS include several from the ruler of Byblos seeking military assistance. By the end of the NEW KINGDOM, however, Egyptian influence had declined and there is no evidence for close contacts after the 22nd Dynasty. Byblos gradually diminished in importance in the face of competition from other ports of the eastern Mediterranean, such as Sidon and Tyre.

C

Cairo Modern capital city of Egypt, strategically located at the apex of the DELTA where UPPER EGYPT and LOWER EGYPT meet.

calendar Based upon the monthly lunar cycle and the annual cycle of the INUNDATION, the ancient Egyptian civil calendar was divided into three seasons, *akhet* (inundation), *peret* (emergence) and *shemu* (summer). Each season comprised four equal months of thirty days. (Each day was divided into twenty-four units or 'hours', with the day-time and night-time each comprising twelve 'hours' of equal length. Hence the length of any particular 'hour' depended on the length of the day and hence on the particular time of year.) To make up the annual total of 365 days, five EPAGOMENAL days were added at the end of the year. The first day of the first month of *akhet*, New Year's Day, which coincided with the beginning of the inundation, was traditionally marked by the HELIACAL RISING of Sirius. However, because of the lack of a leap year, the civil calendar gradually fell out of step with the natural cycle of the seasons. Eventually, the calendar month of 'inundation' fell during the summer drought. This was rectified at the beginning of the ROMAN PERIOD by the introduction of the leap year. Dates in the civil calendar were expressed in terms of a king's regnal years, in the format: regnal year X of King N, month Y of *akhet/peret/shemu*, day Z. While the civil calendar, uniform throughout the country, was used for administrative purposes, a lunar calendar based upon strict observation of the moon was employed to determine the date of religious FESTIVALS. Observations were probably made locally, so that each town or city kept its own lunar calendar.

Cambyses (525–522 BC) Persian ruler who conquered Egypt in 525 BC, ushering in the first PERSIAN PERIOD (the 27th Dynasty). Cambyses was the son of Cyrus II, and a member of the powerful Achaemenid Dynasty that greatly extended Persian power throughout Asia and the Mediterranean. Having first threatened Egypt towards the end of the reign of AMASIS, Cambyses mounted a successful invasion against the next king, PSAMTIK III. Psamtik was defeated and captured at the Battle of Pelusium, then executed by the victorious Persians. Cambyses led his army on to MEMPHIS, capturing the city and formally annexing Egypt to the Persian empire.

Adopting the styles and titles of a PHARAOH, Cambyses mounted unsuccessful military campaigns against Carthage and NUBIA. A further defeat when trying to capture the SIWA OASIS gave rise to the legend of 'the lost army of Cambyses', said to have disappeared in the Western Desert. Although there is little contemporary evidence for large-scale oppression by the conquering Persians, the reign of Cambyses was vilified in later Egyptian tradition, probably because of the action he took to curb the economic power of the temples. In fact, according to inscriptions from his reign, he re-established the cult of NEITH at SAIS, and maintained the practice of burying the sacred APIS bull with all due rites. Cambyses died in Syria in 522 BC, on his way back to Persia, after just three years as ruler of Egypt.

camel The domesticated camel originated in Asia and is first attested in the NILE Valley in the 9th century BC; the earliest dated remains were found at QASR IBRIM. Today the camel is a common beast of burden throughout Egypt and North Africa.

*Set of limestone **canopic jars** made for the burial of the 21st Dynasty princess Neskhons at Deir el-Bahri; the stoppers represent the four sons of Horus (from left to right Qebehsenuef, Duamutef, Hapi and Imsety).*

Canaan *see* Palestine

canopic jars Vessels used for storing the internal organs removed during MUMMIFICATION, and named after the human-headed jars that were worshipped as personifications of Kanopos (the helmsman of Menelaeus in Greek mythology) by the inhabitants of ancient Canopus. The practice of evisceration is first attested in the burial of HETEPHERES in the early 4th Dynasty. Her organs were stored in a TRAVERTINE chest divided into four compartments. Later, each organ – the liver, lungs, stomach and intestines – was provided with a separate jar, of stone or pottery, and placed under the symbolic protection of one of the four SONS OF HORUS. During the FIRST INTERMEDIATE PERIOD, the stoppers of canopic jars began to be modelled in the form of human heads. From the late 18th Dynasty, they were more commonly modelled to resemble the heads of the protecting genii (baboon, JACKAL, FALCON and human). This became the standard for canopic equipment in the 19th Dynasty. In the THIRD INTERMEDIATE PERIOD, the mummified organs were generally returned to the body, but wealthy burials could still include a dummy set of jars. The last known royal set of canopic jars was made for APRIES. The manufacture of canopic equipment continued into the PTOLEMAIC PERIOD, but ceased by Roman times.

Carians People from the coast of Asia Minor (modern Turkey), opposite the island of Rhodes, who served as mercenaries in the Egyptian ARMY during the LATE PERIOD. A cemetery at SAQQARA, used by Carians based at MEMPHIS, has yielded a number of bilingual STELAE, allowing the decipherment of the Carian language.

Carnarvon, Lord *see* Egyptology

carnelian Orange-red gemstone (a variety of chalcedony) found in pebble form throughout the Eastern Desert. Its COLOUR gave it a symbolic association with the sun, and it was favoured for JEWELRY and inlays. In the MIDDLE KINGDOM, jewelry often used carnelian in combination with TURQUOISE and LAPIS LAZULI.

Carter, Howard *see* Egyptology

cartonnage Material made from layers of linen or PAPYRUS stiffened with plaster. Similar to *papier maché*, it was used above all for funerary items, such as mummy masks, mummy cases, and anthropoid COFFINS, and

was often painted or gilded with religious scenes or with an idealized representation of the deceased.

cartouche Oval frame in which certain ROYAL NAMES were written from the late 3rd Dynasty to the end of pharaonic culture. The cartouche (French for 'cartridge') was so named by Napoleon's expedition because its shape resembled a gun-cartridge. It represented a length of knotted rope, and symbolized everything encircled by the sun, hence emphasizing the king's cosmic role. The earliest attested cartouche occurs on a seal impression of the 3rd Dynasty king SANAKHT from BEIT KHALLAF. From the end of the 3rd Dynasty (the reign of HUNI), the king's birth name (and, from the 5th Dynasty, his throne name) was written inside a cartouche. This fact helped early scholars to recognize royal names in ancient Egyptian inscriptions, paving the way for the decipherment of hieroglyphic WRITING. Because of its protective connotations, a cartouche shape was adopted for some royal sarcophagi of the NEW KINGDOM, and for the burial chamber of THUTMOSE III.

cat Kept as domestic pets from the PREDYNASTIC PERIOD, cats are often depicted in private TOMBS of the MIDDLE KINGDOM and NEW KINGDOM sitting under their owners' chairs or taking part in HUNTING expeditions. The cat also had religious associations: as a manifestation of RA, battling with the serpent APOPHIS; or as the sacred animal of various deities. In the LATE PERIOD, large numbers of cats were mummified, and bronze cat statuettes manufactured, as offerings to BASTET. The ancient Egyptian word for cat, *miu* ('mew'), was onomatopoeic.

cataract Area of rapids in the course of the NILE, caused by changes in the underlying geology. There are six such stretches between ASWAN and Khartoum. The First cataract, which includes the islands of ELEPHANTINE and SEHEL, formed Egypt's southern border throughout pharaonic history. A series of FORTRESSES was built in the 12th Dynasty around the Second cataract to guard Egypt's border with KUSH.

cattle *see* animal husbandry

Cave of the Swimmers Name given to a site in the Wadi Sura, on the western side of the GILF KEBIR plateau. A shallow recess in the cliff is decorated with prehistoric paintings, including, most famously, a series of human

Pectoral of the 12th Dynasty princess Mereret from her tomb at Dahshur; a stunning example of Middle Kingdom craftsmanship, it is made from gold, inlaid with red **carnelian** and dark blue lapis lazuli.

Wooden box from the tomb of Tutankhamun, its top in the form of a **cartouche** containing the hieroglyphs for the king's name and title.

Gilded **cartonnage** mummy mask of Tuyu, mother-in-law of Amenhotep III, from her and her husband's tomb in the Valley of the Kings.

Ptolemaic bronze statuette of a **cat**, cast in two halves and used as a container for a mummified cat presented as a votive offering to the goddess Bastet.

figures in what appears to be swimming postures. The precise date and significance of these pictures remain unclear, but they may perhaps relate to trance-like religious experiences rather than swimming.

cavetto cornice Concave architectural moulding often used to decorate the tops of buildings (such as temple PYLONS) and objects (such as STELAE). Its distinctive shape may have been intended to imitate the appearance of primitive reed huts.

cenotaph Memorial or funerary structure set up at a location separate from the owner's actual tomb, especially at sites of religious significance. For example, at ABYDOS hundreds of cenotaph chapels were erected by private individuals along the processional way, while the OSIREION was a grand cenotaph for the god OSIRIS.

C-Group *see* Nubia

Champollion, Jean-François *see* Egyptology

chariot Assumed to have been introduced from the LEVANT during the HYKSOS period, the chariot is first attested in Egypt in the early 18th Dynasty, in an inscription from the tomb of AHMOSE SON OF ABANA, and on reliefs of AHMOSE from ABYDOS. The Egyptian chariot had two wheels of four or eight spokes each, and was drawn by a pair of HORSES. As well as being an important military innovation, allowing rapid attack and equally rapid withdrawal, chariots were used for HUNTING, sport and royal processions; they play a prominent role in royal iconography of the NEW KINGDOM. Tombs at AMARNA show the ROYAL FAMILY riding by chariot into the main city along the royal road. The best-known examples of actual chariots to have survived from antiquity were discovered in the tomb of TUTANKHAMUN. The Egyptian ARMY of the NEW KINGDOM had an elite corps of charioteers, called the *maryannu*.

Cheops *see* Khufu

Chephren *see* Khafra

children Childbirth and childhood were fraught with danger in ancient Egypt, and hence the focus of many private religious practices. Infant mortality was high, so a range of spells and magical devices was employed to protect newborn babies. Children were generally suckled for a long period – perhaps up to three years. In the case of royal children, wet-nurses would carry out this role. From at least the OLD KINGDOM, children wore a distinctive hairstyle, the SIDELOCK OF YOUTH; nakedness for children was probably common. TOYS and GAMES are well attested. Formal schooling was generally restricted to the male children of the literate elite; other boys would simply have learned a trade by watching their fathers. It is difficult to assess the status of children, since most of our evidence was produced by and for adults. However, the existence of wealthy child tombs in the PREDYNASTIC PERIOD suggests a degree of inherited status. Adolescence marked the end of childhood, but it is not known if a child's entry into the adult world was celebrated with any special rite of passage.

Gold centre of a fan from the tomb of Tutankhamun, with chased decoration showing the king in his **chariot** *hunting an ostrich; throughout the New Kingdom chariots were used as much for sport as for warfare.*

Chronicle of Prince Osorkon Autobiographical inscription carved on the 'Bubastite portal' at KARNAK which describes the political manoeuvrings and civil war between rival THEBAN claimants to the KINGSHIP during the reign of TAKELOT II (23rd Dynasty). Prince Osorkon, Takelot II's son, relates how he became High Priest of AMUN but was challenged by the rise to power of PEDUBAST I; he was twice expelled from THEBES, before finally defeating his rival and returning to office. The chronicle is one of the primary sources for the internal politics of Egypt in the late THIRD INTERMEDIATE PERIOD.

chronology For Egyptian prehistory (the PREDYNASTIC PERIOD), the most commonly used method of dating and ordering events or objects is by means of a relative chronology, based upon gradual stylistic changes in various classes of object, especially POTTERY. The SEQUENCE DATING system devised by Flinders Petrie at the beginning of the 20th century AD (*see* EGYPTOLOGY) has been revised from time to time, but still provides the basis for dividing the Predynastic period into broad cultural phases. Absolute chronology, or the determination of calendar dates BC, depends upon various scientific methods, notably radiocarbon dating and thermoluminescence.

For the historic period, beginning with the 1st Dynasty, scientific methods can still be used but, because of the large margin of error involved, are generally less accurate than historical chronology, based upon KING-LISTS, calendrical and astronomical records. The Egyptian dating system was based upon regnal years of kings, and did not use a fixed point such as the AD system. Hence, historical chronology depends to a great extent on establishing a reliable list of kings from the beginning of the 1st Dynasty, and an accurate length of reign for each ruler. Unfortunately, the sources of information are incomplete, and often difficult to interpret. Dates in the OLD KINGDOM were based either upon regnal years or the 'cattle count', but this latter event became annual rather than biennial in the 6th Dynasty. The picture is further confused by the fact that during the three intermediate periods distinct dynasties are known to have ruled simultaneously in different parts of the country.

Texts record five instances in the course of Egyptian history when the HELIACAL RISING of Sirius coincided with the first day of the civil CALENDAR. (The period of 1,460 (365 x 4) years that must have elapsed between each coincidence is called a 'Sothic cycle'.) Modern astronomical knowledge can now determine absolute dates for these occurrences, but the calculations depend upon where in Egypt (MEMPHIS, THEBES or ASWAN) the ancient observations were made. The end result is that the margin of error for establishing a precise chronology increases as one goes further back in time. Later dates are more secure than earlier ones, and the earliest fixed, certain date in Egyptian history is 664 BC, which marks the beginning of the 26th Dynasty.

Egyptologists have adopted MANETHO's system of dynasties to break the huge span of pharaonic history into more manageable periods of time, and have grouped dynasties into broader divisions: EARLY DYNASTIC PERIOD, Old Kingdom, FIRST INTERMEDIATE PERIOD, MIDDLE KINGDOM, SECOND INTERMEDIATE PERIOD, NEW KINGDOM, THIRD INTERMEDIATE PERIOD and LATE PERIOD, together with the PTOLEMAIC PERIOD and ROMAN PERIOD after the sequence of dynasties.

cippus (pl. cippi) Special form of STELA, attested from the NEW KINGDOM to the ROMAN PERIOD, which was designed to provide healing, and to protect against

*Slate **cippus** of the early Ptolemaic period, showing Horus as a child triumphing over a host of dangerous creatures (snakes, scorpions, crocodiles) under the protective gaze of Bes.*

bites and stings. A standard image showed the god HORUS as a naked child, standing on a CROCODILE and holding SNAKES, SCORPIONS and other dangerous animals in his outstretched arms. Water poured over a cippus was believed to have curative properties.

circumcision To judge from surviving mummies, most Egyptian males seem to have been circumcised, although the practice was by no means universal. It seems to have been carried out in early adolescence, and was probably done as much for hygienic reasons as for religious or aesthetic ones. The procedure is depicted in wall reliefs in the 6th Dynasty tomb of Ankhmahor at SAQQARA, and in the temple of MUT at KARNAK. It was carried out with a curved flint knife, but it is difficult to be certain if the foreskin was removed entirely. From the LATE PERIOD onwards, ritual purity demanded that all PRIESTS be circumcised. The practice was banned in the ROMAN PERIOD, although priests were exempted. There is no evidence for female circumcision in ancient Egypt.

Cleopatra Name of seven queens of Egypt during the PTOLEMAIC PERIOD. The last (51–30 BC) is the most famous, because of her involvement with Julius Caesar and Mark Antony, and the dramatic manner of her death. She was also the last ruler of Egypt until modern times to reside permanently in the country. She ruled first in a CO-REGENCY with her father Ptolemy XII, then with her brother Ptolemy XIII before he assumed sole authority. She was restored to power by Caesar in 48 BC, this time as co-regent with her younger brother and husband, Ptolemy XIV. Two years later, after visiting Rome, Cleopatra had her brother killed and in his place installed her son, whom she claimed had been fathered by Caesar. She subsequently had twins by, and married,

*Black basalt statue of **Cleopatra** VII wearing a triple uraeus serpent to distinguish her from other Ptolemaic queens; the statue would originally have been gilded to stress her divinity.*

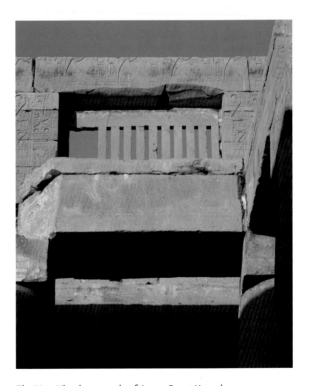

*The New Kingdom temple of Amun-Ra at Karnak uses **clerestory** windows high up in the walls to bring light into the hypostyle hall.*

Mark Antony. In 30 BC, after Rome had declared war on Egypt, Cleopatra committed suicide to avoid a humiliating defeat. Octavian (later the emperor Augustus) seized Egypt as his private estate, ushering in the ROMAN PERIOD.

clerestory Upper storey of a building with windows that allow light to filter down to the lower level. This architectural device is used most effectively in the HYPOSTYLE HALL of the temple of KARNAK.

clothing Artistic representations, supplemented by actual surviving garments, constitute our main sources of evidence for the clothes worn by ancient Egyptians. The two sources are not always in agreement, however, and it seems that representations were more concerned with highlighting certain attributes of the person depicted than with accurately recording their true appearance. For example, in ART created for men, WOMEN were often shown with restrictive, tight-fitting dresses, perhaps to emphasize their figures, or to denote their place in the home and their dependence on male relatives (neither of which was necessarily the case in real life).

As in most societies, fashions in Egypt changed over time; different clothes were worn at different seasons of the year, and by different sections of society. Particular office-holders, especially PRIESTS and the KING, had their own special garments.

For the general population, clothing was simple, predominantly of linen, and probably white or off-white in colour. It would have shown the dirt easily, and professional launderers are known to have been attached to the NEW KINGDOM workmen's village at DEIR EL-MEDINA. Men would have worn a simple loincloth or short kilt, supplemented in winter by a heavier tunic. High-status individuals could express their status through their clothing, and were more susceptible to changes in fashion.

Longer, more voluminous clothing made an appearance in the MIDDLE KINGDOM; flowing, elaborately pleated, diaphanous robes for men and women were particularly popular in the late 18th Dynasty and the RAMESSIDE period. Decorated textiles also became more common in the New Kingdom. In all periods, women's dresses may have been enhanced by colourful bead netting worn over the top. In the ROMAN PERIOD, Egypt became known for the manufacture of fine clothing. Sandals of leather or basketry are the most commonly attested types of footwear. Examples of these,

together with linen shirts and other clothing, were discovered in the tomb of TUTANKHAMUN.

cobra *see* snake, uraeus, Wadjet

coffin The earliest purpose-built funerary containers for bodies were simple rectangular wooden boxes, attested in the 1st Dynasty. A coffin swiftly became an essential part of the burial equipment. Known euphemistically as the 'lord of life', its primary function was to provide a home for the KA, and to protect

Painted inner **coffin** *of Montu Besenmut from his early 26th Dynasty burial at Thebes; the exterior is covered with texts to assist the deceased in the afterlife.*

the physical body from harm. In the 4th Dynasty, the development of longer coffins allowed the body to be buried fully extended (rather than curled up on its side in a foetal position). At the end of OLD KINGDOM, it became customary once more for the body to be laid on its side. The side of the coffin that faced east in the tomb was decorated with a pair of eyes so that the deceased could look out towards the rising sun with its promise of daily rebirth. Coffins also began to be decorated on the outside with bands of FUNERARY TEXTS, while pictures of food and drink offerings were painted on the inside to provide a magical substitute for the real provisions placed in the tomb. In the FIRST INTERMEDIATE PERIOD, decorated coffins became a substitute for TOMB DECORATION; in the MIDDLE KINGDOM, COFFIN TEXTS made their first appearance, sometimes accompanied by detailed maps of the underworld. Middle Kingdom coffins show a number of distinct regional styles, echoing the cultural fragmentation of the preceding period. In the 17th and early 18th Dynasties, the THEBAN area produced characteristic anthropoid *rishi* (feathered) coffins. These were replaced (except for kings) by other styles of anthropoid coffins which became the standard form throughout the country for the remainder of Egyptian history. The predominance of decorated tombs in the New Kingdom removed the need for object friezes, so coffins were generally undecorated on the inside. However, this situation was reversed again in the THIRD INTERMEDIATE PERIOD when new types of coffin decoration focused on the OSIRIS myth and extracts from the BOOK OF THE DEAD, to aid the resurrection of the deceased. In the PTOLEMAIC and ROMAN periods, a CARTONNAGE mask was often fixed directly onto the mummy wrappings as a substitute for a coffin.

Coffins were generally made of wood; those of high-status individuals used fine quality, imported cedar. From the Middle Kingdom onwards, wealthy

*Interior of the 12th Dynasty coffin of Sepi from el-Bersha, decorated with a frieze of funerary objects and extracts from the **Coffin Texts**, a collection of spells.*

individuals were often provided with a set of two or three nested coffins. The most sumptuous coffins might be inlaid with glass or precious stones, while royal coffins were often made from GOLD or silver.

Coffin Texts Collection of more than a thousand spells, from which selections were inscribed on coffins during the MIDDLE KINGDOM. Many different types of texts are represented, including HYMNS, prayers, offering lists, descriptions of the afterlife, and spells to assist the transformation and ascension of the deceased. Some were derived from the PYRAMID TEXTS, other were newly composed. The appearance and use of the Coffin Texts reflect the wider dissemination of AFTERLIFE BELIEFS after the end of the OLD KINGDOM (a process termed 'the democratization of the afterlife'). Two strands of belief are reflected in the texts: the journey with the sun god, and a blessed existence in the company of OSIRIS. Some texts were later absorbed into the BOOK OF THE DEAD.

Colossi of Memnon Pair of colossal statues of AMENHOTEP III, erected at the entrance to his mortuary temple (now largely destroyed) in western THEBES. Carved from quartzite sandstone, the statues show the seated king, flanked by figures of TIYE. The sides of the colossi carry reliefs of the god HAPY. In 27 BC, an earthquake damaged the northern statue, causing it to produce a whistling sound each morning. Greek visitors linked the statues with the Homeric character Memnon, singing to his mother, the goddess of the dawn. Repairs in the 3rd century AD silenced the colossus but the name has stuck. Today, the statues are one of the principal tourist attractions on the west bank at Thebes.

colour The ancient Egyptian LANGUAGE had four basic colour terms: *kem* (black), *hedj* (white/silver), *wadj* (green/blue) and *desher* (red/orange/yellow). Each carried symbolic associations. Black was the colour of the fertile alluvial soil, and carried connotations of fertility and regeneration. Hence statues of the king as OSIRIS often showed him with black skin. Black was also associated with the afterlife, and was the colour of funerary deities such as ANUBIS. White was associated with purity. Green/blue was the colour of vegetation, and hence of rejuvenation. Osiris could be shown with green skin; in the 26th Dynasty, the faces of COFFINS were often coloured green to assist in rebirth. This colour symbolism also explains the popularity of TURQUOISE and FAIENCE in FUNERARY EQUIPMENT. Red/orange/yellow was an ambivalent colour. It was, naturally, associated with the sun; red stones such as quartzite were favoured for royal statues which stressed the solar aspects of KINGSHIP. CARNELIAN had similar symbolic associations in JEWELRY. Red ink was used to write important names on PAPYRUS documents. However, red was also the colour of the deserts, and hence associated with SETH and the forces of destruction.

Egyptians had no basic word for blue, although a blue pigment based on LAPIS LAZULI was introduced in the OLD KINGDOM and was particularly associated with the night sky. GOLD, as a metal rather than as a colour, was associated with the flesh of the gods. Another important symbolic use of colour in Egyptian ART was to distinguish between male and female figures. Men were customarily depicted with tanned, red-brown skin; while women, ideally expected to remain at home, looking after the household, were shown with yellow, untanned skin.

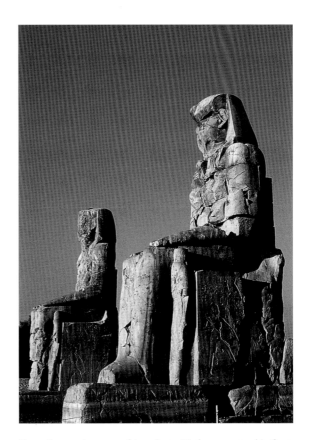

*The twin seated statues of Amenhotep III that once stood in front of his mortuary temple at western Thebes are today known as the **Colossi of Memnon**.*

*Stela of Amenemhat from his tomb at Asasif, western Thebes (early Middle Kingdom); the composition shows a particularly strong use of **colour**, notably to differentiate the skin of the men and women.*

Complaints of Khakheperra-seneb MIDDLE KING-DOM literary work, composed during or shortly after the reign of SENUSRET II, but preserved in a single 18th Dynasty copy. Like other texts of the 12th Dynasty, it deals with the themes of anarchy and national distress through an extended series of metaphors.

copper *see* metalworking

Coptic *see* Copts

Coptos (Guft, Qift) Site on the east bank on the NILE in UPPER EGYPT, 38 km (24 miles) north-east of Luxor. Strategically located at the mouth of the WADI HAMMA-MAT, gateway to the Eastern Desert and the Red Sea coast, Coptos was important from early times and was capital of the fifth Upper Egyptian NOME. In the PTOLE-MAIC and ROMAN PERIODS, it became a major trans-shipment point for trade with India. Throughout Egyptian history, Coptos was the major cult centre of MIN. Colossal statues of a fertility god dating to the late PREDYNASTIC period were unearthed in the temple enclosure. A series of decrees, exempting the temple personnel from CORVÉE LABOUR, provide a vivid picture of politics at the very end of the OLD KINGDOM; no fewer than eight decrees, each inscribed on stone and set up in the temple, were issued on a single day by one of the last kings of the 8th Dynasty, King Neteribau Neferkauhor. The earliest elements of the temple structure date to the 18th Dynasty; there are several other sacred buildings of the LATE PERIOD, Ptolemaic and Roman periods, and a number of Christian churches, in the vicinity. Since the end of the 19th

century AD, many of the most experienced workers ('Guftis') employed by archaeological expeditions have come from the area around Coptos.

Copts The Christian population of Egypt. The term is used both for the Egyptian people during the 4th to 8th centuries AD, when Egypt was a Christian country, and for the Christian population since the Arab conquest. The word 'Copt' is thought to derive from the ancient Egyptian Hut-ka-Ptah (Aigyptos in Greek), one of the names for MEMPHIS. The adjective 'Coptic' is used to describe the LANGUAGE, LITERATURE and culture of Christian Egypt; the historical period when Egypt was a Christian country; and the Egyptian Orthodox Church.

co-regency Period during which two kings reigned simultaneously. The practice, whereby the heir was crowned during his predecessor's lifetime, was initiated in the 12th Dynasty to ensure a smooth transition from one reign to the next. Many co-regencies have been suggested; some are hotly disputed by scholars.

corvée labour Work undertaken for the state by con-scripted members of the general population. Workers could be drafted for building projects, IRRIGATION works, mining expeditions or military campaigns. From time to time, royal decrees were issued to exempt the staff of particular institutions, especially TEMPLES. Although conscription was sanctioned by government departments, the actual draft was carried out by local officials, often backed up by the threat of physical force. So ubiquitous was the practice of corvée labour in ancient Egypt, that it was believed to extend even to the afterlife. Hence SHABTI figurines were designed to answer the summons and perform the required duties on behalf of the deceased.

cosmetics Use of makeup, especially around the eyes, was a characteristic feature of ancient Egyptian culture from Predynastic times. Kohl (eye-paint) was applied to protect the eyes, as well as for aesthetic reasons. It was usually made from GALENA, giving a silvery-black colour; during the OLD KINGDOM, green eye-paint was also used, made from MALACHITE. Egyptian WOMEN painted their lips and cheeks, using rouge made from red ochre. Henna was applied as a dye for hair, finger-nails and toenails, and perhaps also nipples. Creams and unguents to condition the skin were popular, and were made from various plant extracts.

creation myths The ancient Egyptians had three main myths to explain the creation of the universe. Each was rooted in a particular location; all played their part in the complex web of associations that characterized Egyptian RELIGION. Perhaps the most enduring and influential myth originated at HELIOPOLIS and centred on an ENNEAD of deities. ATUM, the self-generated creator god, brought forth a son and daughter (SHU and TEFNUT) from his own bodily fluids. Some versions of the myth indicate spitting, others masturbation, as the act of creation. The union between the first divine couple brought forth another brother–sister pair, GEB and NUT, who in turn created OSIRIS, ISIS, SETH and NEPHTHYS.

An extension to this basic framework was the Osiris myth, involving the god, his consort Isis, and their son HORUS. The murder of Osiris by Seth, and the resulting struggle for power, won by Horus, provided a powerful narrative linking the ideology of KINGSHIP with the creation of the cosmos. A second creation myth was developed at HERMOPOLIS, and is first mentioned in the MIDDLE KINGDOM. It envisaged an OGDOAD of

*The life-like 4th Dynasty painted limestone statue of the 'royal acquaintance' Nofret shows the importance of **cosmetics** in ancient Egypt, especially the use of eye-paint.*

deities coming into existence in the primeval waters of NUN and eventually giving rise to the PRIMEVAL MOUND and the sun god. The third creation myth originated at MEMPHIS and cast PTAH as the creator god, who brought forth order by means of the spoken word. This so-called 'Memphite Theology' represents a more academic view of creation and was probably developed in the NEW KINGDOM.

Crete Island in the Aegean which maintained sporadic links with Egypt from the OLD KINGDOM onwards. Regular contact is attested in the NEW KINGDOM in the form of Minoan pottery found at Egyptian sites, Egyptian objects found on Crete, and the remarkable frescoes of bull-leaping from an early 18th Dynasty palace at AVARIS. The last indicate a large degree of cultural exchange, echoed later in the dynasty in palace decoration at MALKATA and AMARNA. Several private tombs

*Dignitaries from **Crete** bringing offerings (including metal ingots and characteristic Minoan drinking vessels), in a scene from the tomb of the 18th Dynasty vizier Rekhmira at western Thebes.*

The **criosphinx** was a compound animal with the body of a lion and a ram's head; this avenue of criosphinxes leads to Karnak temple, the ram being an attribute of the temple's chief deity, Amun-Ra.

from the reigns of HATSHEPSUT and THUTMOSE III depict people bringing tribute from a land called Keftiu, usually identified as Minoan Crete. An inscription of AMENHOTEP III from THEBES lists Cretan place names, although after the 14th century BC, Mycenae replaced Crete as Egypt's main trading partner in the Aegean. Contacts with Crete resumed again in the 1st millennium BC (THIRD INTERMEDIATE PERIOD and LATE PERIOD).

crime and punishment The evidence for criminal activity and judicial sanctions in ancient Egypt is partial and patchy. The crimes attested in the written record range from petty theft to more serious offences such as tomb robbery and conspiracy against the king (the last known from the reigns of PEPI I and RAMESSES III). Punishments were similarly wide-ranging. The penalty for theft from an individual was to give back a multiple of the amount stolen. The theft of state property was more harshly punished, often involving beatings and mutilation; from the OLD KINGDOM onwards, beatings were carried out by a specialist group of officials. Other serious offenders could be exiled together with their families; this seems to have been the fate of political opponents. Capital punishment was apparently reserved for the severest crimes, such as high treason or the desecration of a temple. Those convicted in such cases might be given the option of taking their own lives; otherwise, death was by impalement or burning. Imprisonment is attested, including sentences with

hard labour, but it does not appear to have been particularly common. However, if an individual fled justice or deserted from CORVÉE LABOUR, his family could be imprisoned by the state. Failure to report a crime and conspiracy to conceal one were considered almost as serious as the offence itself, and were punished accordingly.

The existence of a LAW code in ancient Egypt is hotly debated. Punishments were probably based on precedent, and seem to have followed the rules of MAAT in making no distinction between people of different social status.

criosphinx In ancient Egyptian RELIGION, a compound animal with the body of a LION and the head of a ram. The god AMUN was occasionally depicted in this form, most famously in the avenue of criosphinxes flanking the processional way in front of the temple of KARNAK.

crocodile Feared and revered for its strength and ferocity, the crocodile was depicted in art from Predynastic times, and was worshipped as the god SOBEK. It would have been a common sight in ancient Egypt basking on sandbanks, and in IRRIGATION canals and in Lake FAYUM, as well as in the NILE.

Crocodilopolis see Medinet el-Fayum

crook see royal regalia

crowns In royal and religious symbolism, crowns played a central role, emphasizing different facets of KINGSHIP or identifying particular deities. The two most important royal crowns are both attested from the PREDYNASTIC PERIOD.

The white crown was tall and conical in shape, with a bulbous tip. From the 1st Dynasty onwards, it became associated with UPPER EGYPT, and was the more prestigious of the two royal crowns, perhaps signifying the divine office of kingship.

The red crown comprised a low squarish cap with a tall back-piece from which a coil projected. Although it may have originated at NAGADA, following the unification of the TWO LANDS the red crown became associated with LOWER EGYPT, and with the goddess NEITH. It seems to have been junior to the white crown, perhaps symbolizing the king's secular role. From the middle of the 1st Dynasty, the white and red crowns were combined to form the double crown, symbolic of the king's authority over both parts of his realm.

Another royal headdress, the blue crown, first appeared in royal iconography during the SECOND INTERMEDIATE PERIOD. It was shaped like a tall helmet and was covered with gold discs. It may have developed from an earlier cap crown, similar to the close-fitting cap worn by the god PTAH. The king was often shown wearing the blue crown in scenes of a military nature, although its symbolism seems to have been more universal.

Crowns worn by royal women included the vulture-cap (worn, for example, by NEFERTARI in scenes from her tomb) and the tall platform crown, the most famous example of which occurs on the painted bust of NEFERTITI. To identify themselves with important goddesses, such as HATHOR and ISIS, royal women might also be shown wearing cows' horns or a pair of ostrich feathers. The latter (the quintessential mark of

divinity) was typically worn by the gods AMUN and MIN. A more complex headpiece was the *atef* crown, combining the white crown with a plume on either side and a small disc at the top. Associated with the gods, it was also worn by the king at religious rituals. A triple *atef* crown first occurs in the reign of AKHENATEN. Further composite crowns became especially common in the PTOLEMAIC and ROMAN PERIODS. In Egyptian ART, the particular crown or headdress associated with a deity was often an important identifier, and could be transferred to a different deity in order to pass on certain attributes.

Not strictly crowns, but important items of ROYAL REGALIA nevertheless, were the various HEADDRESSES. It is assumed that crowns and other headpieces were made from various materials, including textiles and metals, but no actual examples have survived from ancient Egypt.

*Various **crowns** were used in ancient Egyptian art and sculpture to denote particular aspects of kingship; shown here (left to right, above and below) are the white crown, red crown, double crown, **atef** crown and blue crown.*

*Mummified **crocodile** from the early Roman period, 1st century AD. In ancient Egypt the crocodile was worshipped as the god Sobek, and the animals would have been found in the Nile and other waterways.*

cubit *see* weights and measures

cuneiform ('wedge-shaped') Script in which the Sumerian and Akkadian languages of MESOPOTAMIA were written. It was particularly suited to writing with a sharp stylus on clay tablets. When Babylonian (a form of Akkadian) became the diplomatic language of the Near East in the mid-second millennium BC, cuneiform was used widely throughout the LEVANT for correspondence between rulers; hence the AMARNA LETTERS are written in cuneiform.

cursive script Term used to describe the freehand style of WRITING in ink on PAPYRUS or OSTRACA. HIERATIC, DEMOTIC and cursive HIEROGLYPHS are all examples of cursive scripts. The last was a type of script similar to monumental hieroglyphs, but used in scribal training and for religious texts.

Cusae (el-Qusiya) Classical name for a site on the west bank of the NILE in MIDDLE EGYPT (ancient Egyptian Qis) which was the capital of the fourteenth Upper Egyptian NOME, and which formed the border between the HYKSOS and THEBAN areas of control during the SECOND INTERMEDIATE PERIOD. The tombs of the MIDDLE KINGDOM NOMARCHS of Cusae are at the nearby site of MEIR.

Cyprus Island in the eastern Mediterranean which maintained intensive trading links with Egypt from the SECOND INTERMEDIATE PERIOD to the 19th Dynasty. Egyptian stone vessels and SCARABS have been found on Cyprus, while sites in Egypt and NUBIA have yielded Cypriot pottery, including the distinctive base-ring juglets, thought to have been containers for opium. However, Cyprus's major export was copper; a shipwreck discovered off Uluburun in Turkey contained copper ingots and Egyptian GOLD objects.

The land of Alashiya, mentioned in the AMARNA LETTERS, is generally identified as Cyprus. Contacts with Egypt were disrupted in the late RAMESSIDE period, perhaps because of raids against Cyprus by the SEA PEOPLES. In the 26th Dynasty, APRIES launched a military campaign against Cyprus; the island eventually came under Ptolemaic control.

D

Daba, Tell el- *see* Avaris

Dahshur Area of the MEMPHITE NECROPOLIS to the south of SAQQARA, about 50 km (31 miles) from Cairo. The site is dominated by two well-preserved PYRAMIDS built by SNEFERU in the 4th Dynasty. The Bent Pyramid was the first to be designed as a true pyramid from the outset, and it retains more of its casing blocks than any other pyramid. The abrupt change of angle half-way up the monument was probably dictated by structural concerns. The Northern or Red Pyramid is second in size only to the Great Pyramid of KHUFU at GIZA. Dahshur also comprises an extensive cemetery of OLD KINGDOM MASTABAS, and four pyramid complexes of the MIDDLE KINGDOM, now badly ruined. The White Pyramid of AMENEMHAT II has been little studied. It was built with retaining walls radiating out from a central stone core. Nearby are tombs for the king's principal wife and four princesses. The pyramid of SENUSRET III – perhaps a CENOTAPH rather than his actual burial place – shows the strong influence of the STEP PYRAMID in its orientation, design and decoration. Adjacent mastabas contained JEWELRY and other FUNERARY OBJECTS for the daughters of Senusret III and AMENEMHAT III. The latter ruler also built a pyramid at Dahshur. Called the Black Pyramid, it was never used for the king's burial because of structural problems. However, it was later used for the burial of a 13th Dynasty king, Awibra HOR. The remains of another 13th Dynasty royal burial, the pyramid complex of Amenyqemau, have also been found at Dahshur.

Dakhla Oasis The most intensively studied of the Western Desert oases, and the administrative centre for the whole oasis region during much of pharaonic history. Long-term survey and excavation by British and French archaeologists have revealed remains from virtually every period of Egyptian civilization.

The modern settlement of Bashendi has given its name to the prehistoric culture discovered in the vicinity. Finds dating back to the sixth millennium BC include flint tools and weapons, grinding stones, JEWELRY and POTTERY. Later levels at the site also contained imported materials and large numbers of bones from domesticated animals, suggesting a mixed economy and contacts with the contemporary BADAR-

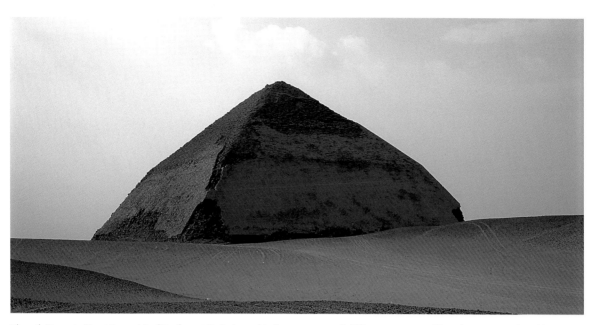

The 4th Dynasty 'Bent Pyramid' of Sneferu at **Dahshur**; this first attempt at building a true pyramid ran into structural problems during construction, requiring a reduction in slope half-way up the monument.

IAN culture to the east. Through such contacts, the Bashendi people may have contributed to the early stages of development of NILE Valley civilization. PETROGLYPHS elsewhere in the Dakhla Oasis indicate further activity in the PREDYNASTIC PERIOD.

In the OLD KINGDOM, a major town was founded at Ain Asil, together with an associated cemetery of large MASTABA tombs nearby at Qila el-Dabba. The two sites are known collectively as Balat and have provided valuable evidence for provincial urban life far away from the royal court. The regional governors, who ruled from Balat, presided over an important centre of pharaonic culture outside the boundaries of Egypt proper. Excavations have uncovered a PALACE which served as the governor's official residence for five generations in the late 6th Dynasty.

Scattered remains across the Dakhla Oasis suggest continued Egyptian involvement during the MIDDLE KINGDOM and NEW KINGDOM, but much archaeological work remains to be done to clarify the nature and extent of activity in these periods. By contrast, the extensive monuments of the ROMAN PERIOD have been studied in detail. They include the three large towns of Amheida, Mut and Ismant (known to the Romans as Trimithis, Mouthis and Kellis); aqueducts, and a temple to the Theban TRIAD of AMUN, MUT and KHONSU at Deir el-Haggar; and the tomb of Pet-Osiris at Muzzawaka, whose intricate decoration illustrates the agricultural products of the oasis.

dancing An important part of celebrations and religious rituals, dancing in ancient Egypt was usually carried out to musical accompaniment. It seems to have been performed by single-sex groups, since men and women are never shown dancing together. The specialist MUU DANCERS played a central role in funeral processions.

A group of women **dancing** and playing musical instruments carved on a limestone relief block from a 19th Dynasty tomb at Saqqara.

Darius Name of three Persian kings of Egypt.

Darius I (521–486 BC) was the second king of the 27th Dynasty, in succession to CAMBYSES. His reign is the best documented of the first PERSIAN PERIOD. Major developments during his reign included legal and administrative reforms, additions to the temple of HIBIS, and the completion of a canal linking the NILE to the Red Sea.

Darius II (424–404 BC) was the fifth and last king of the 27th Dynasty before AMYRTAEOS of SAIS reasserted Egyptian independence.

Darius III (335–332 BC) was the third and last king of the 31st Dynasty (second PERSIAN PERIOD). He ruled Egypt for only a year before ALEXANDER THE GREAT invaded the country and brought Persian domination to an end.

Daydamus (Didyme) One of a series of fortified outposts built in the Eastern Desert in the PTOLEMAIC PERIOD, near the northern end of the road from COPTOS to BERENIKE.

death *see* afterlife beliefs, burial customs

deben *see* weights and measures

decan *see* astronomy and astrology

Dedumose (throne names: Djedhetepra and Djedneferra) (c. 1600 BC) Name of two ephemeral kings of the late SECOND INTERMEDIATE PERIOD (16th or 17th Dynasty), whose authority was confined to UPPER EGYPT.

deification Although the ideology of KINGSHIP regarded the king in some ways as divine, it was unusual for individuals in ancient Egypt to be formally accorded divine status, either during their lifetime or posthumously. However, there are interesting exceptions to this rule. The founders of DEIR EL-MEDINA, AMENHOTEP I and AHMOSE NEFERTARI, were worshipped by the village's inhabitants throughout the NEW KINGDOM. From the late 18th Dynasty onwards, kings began to stress the divinity of their office as opposed to the mortality of the individual ruler. In NUBIA, which to some extent lay outside the realm of

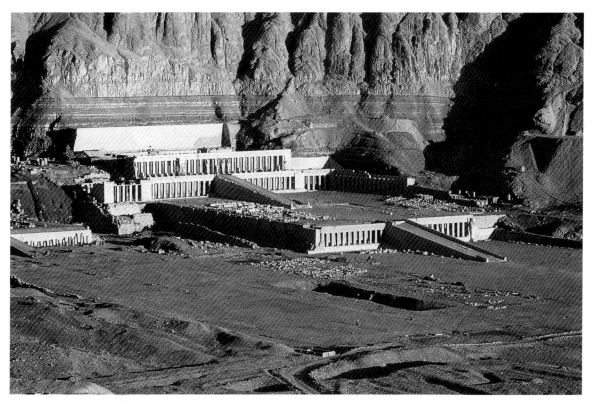

The 18th Dynasty mortuary temple of Hatshepsut at **Deir el-Bahri** *exploits the site to stunning effect, using the sheer cliff face as a backdrop for a highly original terraced design.*

the Egyptian pantheon, deification of the reigning king – or at least of KINGSHIP – became a feature of New Kingdom cult. AMENHOTEP III at SOLEB, AKHENATEN at Sedeinga, and RAMESSES II at ABU SIMBEL all stressed their quasi-divine status. Akhenaten took the process one step further, effectively elevating himself to full divinity by emphasizing his CO-REGENCY with the ATEN. In the LATE PERIOD, two high officials of the 3rd and 18th Dynasties respectively, IMHOTEP and AMENHOTEP SON OF HAPU, were deified and became the focus of popular cults; while in the ROMAN PERIOD, Hadrian deified his drowned lover Antinous, dedicating the city of ANTINOÖPOLIS to him.

Deir el-Bahri Site on the west bank of the NILE at THEBES, in a bay in the cliffs directly facing KARNAK. MENTUHOTEP II chose the site for his mortuary temple (now ruined), built to a radical design. The monument comprised a lower portico; a ramp leading to an upper level, with porticoes on four sides surrounding a central structure (variously reconstructed as a PYRAMID, a MASTABA or a replica of the PRIMEVAL MOUND), and tombs for the king's six wives; a PERI-STYLE court with a descending ramp to the burial chamber; and the earliest known HYPOSTYLE HALL leading to a rock-cut sanctuary. Mentuhotep's monument became one of the principal settings for the BEAUTIFUL FESTIVAL OF THE VALLEY. It was also the inspiration for the 18th Dynasty edifice which dominates Deir el-Bahri today, the mortuary temple of HATSHEPSUT. Comprising three colonnaded terraces, this monument is famous for its intricate reliefs, including scenes recording an expedition to PUNT. The main structure of the temple includes chapels of ANUBIS, HATHOR and AMUN. A smaller temple built by THUTMOSE III lies nearby. In the surrounding hillsides, high officials at the courts of Mentuhotep II, Hatshepsut and Thutmose III built their tombs. Famous examples include the burial of SENENMUT, and the tomb which was used in the THIRD INTERMEDIATE PERIOD to house a cache of royal mummies, removed from the VALLEY OF THE KINGS for protection.

Deir el-Ballas Site on the west bank of the NILE in UPPER EGYPT, 45 km (28 miles) north of THEBES. Dating to the SECOND INTERMEDIATE PERIOD and early 18th Dynasty, the site comprises a series of cemeteries, an extensive area of settlement, and two large buildings. The North Palace may have been a royal residence but the so-called South Palace was probably a fortress. Both seem likely to have been used by KAMOSE and AHMOSE during the wars against the HYKSOS.

Deir el-Bersha Site on the east bank of the NILE in MIDDLE EGYPT, best known for its ROCK-CUT TOMBS of the OLD KINGDOM and MIDDLE KINGDOM, especially those constructed for the NOMARCHS of the fifteenth Upper Egyptian NOME. The 12th Dynasty tomb of DJE-HUTYHOTEP is famous for its scene showing a stone colossus being dragged from the nearby quarries at HATNUB. The site also contains burials of the SECOND INTERMEDIATE PERIOD.

Deir el-Medina Site on the west bank of the NILE at THEBES, situated in a bay in the cliffs north of the VALLEY OF THE QUEENS. The principal feature is a walled village founded in the reign of AMENHOTEP I for the workmen who built the royal tombs in the VALLEY OF THE KINGS. Deliberately secluded, and guarded for extra security, the village was inhabited by successive generations of workmen and their families until the end of the 20th Dynasty, with only a brief period of closure during the reign of AKHENATEN. It was enlarged in the RAMESSIDE period. At the beginning of

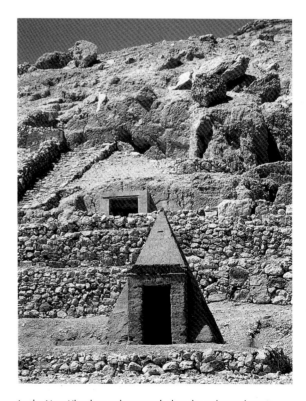

*In the New Kingdom, private tomb chapels at the workmen's village of **Deir el-Medina** were marked by small mud-brick pyramids.*

each week, the workmen would walk from the village, over the cliffs, to the Valley of the Kings; during the working week, they camped overnight a short distance from the Valley.

Large numbers of OSTRACA from Deir el-Medina provide a detailed picture of social and economic life during the NEW KINGDOM. Near the village (called by

*Painted relief from the 19th Dynasty tomb of Nefertari, Valley of the Queens, showing one of the underworld **demons** holding a pair of knives to defend the sun god during his nightly journey.*

*Ivory label from Abydos, depicting **Den** defeating a foreign enemy, with the caption 'first time of smiting the easterner'; the label was originally attached to a pair of sandals.*

the ancient Egyptians 'The Place of Truth') are several workmen's tombs of unusually rich decoration; a temple founded by AMENHOTEP III and largely rebuilt in the PTOLEMAIC PERIOD; tombs of the LATE PERIOD; and a Coptic monastery which gives the site its modern Arabic name ('monastery of the town').

Delta The northernmost part of Egypt (essentially synonymous with LOWER EGYPT) where the NILE divides into several distributaries as it flows into the Mediterranean Sea. The resulting triangular area of floodplain resembles the Greek letter delta (Δ). In antiquity there were at least five main branches of the Nile flowing through the Delta; today there are only two. The ancient Egyptians associated the Delta with the PAPYRUS plant, perhaps recognizing the region's resemblance to a flower-head perched on top of a stalk (the Nile Valley). Archaeology in the Delta, long neglected for practical reasons, has increased greatly in recent years.

democratization of the afterlife *see* afterlife beliefs, Coffin Texts, Pyramid Texts

demons Term used by Egyptologists to denote minor deities and other, lesser, supernatural beings. Those associated with the underworld included AMMUT and other malevolent demons which symbolized the forces of chaos and were believed to inhabit the edge of the world. Their benevolent counterparts, often shown in illustrations of the BOOK OF THE DEAD, were responsible for defending the sun god, using long knives. The messengers of the lion goddess SEKHMET formed the second main group of demons. They represented the goddess in her evil aspect, and were thought to be particularly active at the end of each year. Opposing them were the followers of OSIRIS.

demotic Cursive script, derived from HIERATIC, which it had largely replaced by the 26th Dynasty, except for funerary and religious texts. Used at first only for commercial and legal documents, it became widespread by the PTOLEMAIC PERIOD (its name is derived from the Greek for 'popular'). Until the advent of Roman rule, it was used alongside Greek, and is one of the three scripts carved on the ROSETTA STONE. The last surviving business documents written entirely in demotic date to AD 175–176. In the ROMAN PERIOD, Greek replaced demotic as the legal and administrative language; the last demotic inscription was written at

*The middle section of the Rosetta Stone is written in **demotic**, the vernacular and administrative script used for the Egyptian language during the Ptolemaic period.*

PHILAE in AD 452. Some signs from demotic were retained in the COPTIC script.

Den (Dewen, Udimu) (c. 2875 BC) Fifth king of the 1st Dynasty, and one of the best attested of the EARLY DYNASTIC PERIOD. He probably succeeded to the throne as a child, since his mother MERNEITH seems to have acted as regent for the early part of his reign. Den may have lived to celebrate a second SED FESTIVAL. During a long reign, part of which is recorded on the PALERMO STONE, he presided over important innovations in royal ideology and architecture. He was the first king to bear the *nesut-bity* title (*see* ROYAL TITLES), and the first to be shown wearing the double crown; both expressed the DUALITY of royal authority. His tomb at ABYDOS was the first to have a descending stairway; this gave access to the burial chamber, which was lined with granite slabs from ASWAN in an early example of the monumental use of STONE. A group of graves near the SERAPEUM at SAQQARA probably surrounded a cult enclosure for the king. High-status tombs for royal officials were built at ABU RAWASH, HELWAN and Saqqara. The tomb of the chancellor HEMAKA contained the earliest known roll of PAPYRUS (albeit a miniature one) and lavish FUNERARY OBJECTS. Remarkable craftsmanship is also demonstrated in a series of stone vessels carved in complex forms, ranging from flowers to imitations of reed baskets. Numerous imported vessels give the impression of sustained and intensive contact between Egypt and the LEVANT. In all areas, Den's reign witnessed an early flowering of pharaonic culture.

Dendera Site on the west bank of the NILE, in northern UPPER EGYPT, which became the capital of the sixth Upper Egyptian NOME in the OLD KINGDOM. Today Dendera is dominated by the well-preserved temple of HATHOR; the columns of its façade and HYPOSTYLE HALL are surmounted by Hathor-headed capitals. Texts in the temple crypt mention a building on the site from the reign of PEPI I, but the earliest kings attested are of the MIDDLE KINGDOM, named on reused blocks (a complete chapel of MENTUHOTEP III is now in the Egyptian Museum in Cairo).

The surviving monument dates from the 30th Dynasty to the ROMAN PERIOD. The exterior walls are decorated with reliefs showing CLEOPATRA and her son Caesarion. The roof has symbolic mortuary chapels for OSIRIS; one contains an early ZODIAC. The temple is similar in plan to its counterpart at EDFU, with which it maintained close cultic links. A mud-brick enclosure wall surrounds the principal buildings, which include two MAMMISIS, a small temple of ISIS, and an associated sanatorium for pilgrims.

The site retained its religious importance into the Christian period, when a basilica was built inside the sacred precinct. A nearby cemetery contains tombs dating from the EARLY DYNASTIC period to the FIRST

INTERMEDIATE PERIOD, including an important series of MASTABAS of the late Old Kingdom. There are also LATE PERIOD burials of sacred animals, especially cows.

deserts The ancient Egyptians distinguished the black land (*kemet*) of the NILE floodplain from the red land (*deshret*) of the deserts on either side. The hieroglyphic sign for 'desert' showed a range of three hills, reflecting the fact that the deserts are both raised above the floodplain and more mountainous. Egyptian attitudes to the deserts were ambivalent. RELIGION associated the Western Desert with the land of the dead, and the deserts in general with disorder and forces hostile to creation. Sacred places, like the temple at QASR ES-SAGHA, were built to defend Egypt from such threats. Yet the deserts were also important sources of materials, especially GOLD and various types of STONE. From the EARLY DYNASTIC PERIOD onwards, state-sponsored MINING AND QUARRYING expeditions were sent into the deserts to bring back high-value commodities. Routes through the deserts were also vitally important for communication and for trade between Egypt and neighbouring lands. When the Egyptians had to venture into the deserts, they placed their trust in the protective deities MIN and HATHOR.

Research has shown that for much of prehistory before 3500 BC the deserts were more humid than today. Archaeology, at sites like NABTA PLAYA, has revealed traces of advanced cattle-herding cultures that flourished in the wetter periods, and may have laid the foundations for Egyptian civilization. Yet, by historic times, the surviving inhabitants of the desert margins were belittled by official Egyptian ideology and cast as a threat to pharaonic rule.

Dewen *see* Den

didactic literature *see* wisdom literature

Didyme *see* Daydamus

diet *see* food and drink

diorite *see* stone

Diospolis Parva Collection of sites on the west bank of the NILE in northern UPPER EGYPT, between the modern villages of Hiw and Semaina. Flinders Petrie's excavations (*see* EGYPTOLOGY) in the area led him to compile the first CHRONOLOGY for the PREDYNASTIC PERIOD, based upon the SEQUENCE DATING of pottery styles.

diseases *see* medicine

Dispute of a Man with his Ba Famous text composed in the 12th Dynasty and surviving in a single, contemporary copy. Also known as *The Man Who Was Tired of Life*, or by its German name *Lebensmüde*, this difficult and intriguing work consists of a dialogue between a man who longs for death and his BA, which urges him to stop complaining and enjoy life. Four exquisite

The façade of the temple of Hathor at **Dendera**, *built in the reign of the Roman emperor Augustus in the 1st century AD; the column capitals are in the form of Hathor heads, each wearing a sistrum, symbolic of music and dance.*

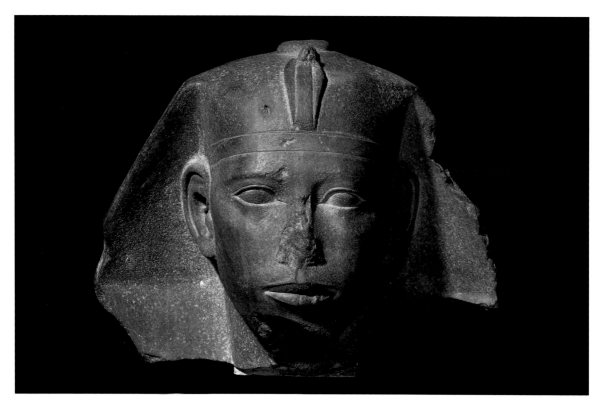

Red quartzite head of **Djedefra** from his pyramid temple at Abu Rawash; the head probably belonged to a sphinx statue.

poems at the end of the work deplore the misery of life and exalt death.

Divine Adoratrice Religious title held by WOMEN, often senior members of the ROYAL FAMILY, in the NEW KINGDOM and THIRD INTERMEDIATE PERIOD. Its precise significance is not fully understood, but it was connected with the cult of AMUN. First attested in the reign of HATSHEPSUT, the title was given by THUTMOSE III to the mother of his principal wife. In the Third Intermediate Period, it was usually held jointly with the office of GOD'S WIFE OF AMUN.

Djedefra (Radjedjef) (*c.* 2525 BC) Third king of the 4th Dynasty. The son and successor of KHUFU, he oversaw his father's burial; his name was found on the stone beams covering one of Khufu's boat pits at GIZA. Djedefra chose a new site, ABU RAWASH, for his PYRAMID complex, and was also the first king to bear the title Son of RA, associating himself with the solar cult of HELIOPOLIS. He reigned for less than a decade, leaving his pyramid unfinished. A stone head of the king from Abu Rawash may have belonged to the earliest SPHINX statue.

Painted relief from the temple of Seti I at Abydos, showing the king raising the ceremonial **djed** pillar, assisted by the goddess Isis.

Detail of the funerary stela of **Djet** from his tomb at Abydos; the king's name is written with a single serpent hieroglyph inside a serekh-frame, surmounted by the falcon god Horus.

Relief of **Djoser** from the chambers beneath his Step Pyramid at Saqqara; the king is shown performing the ritual run that formed part of the sed festival celebrations.

Djedkara *see* Isesi

djed **pillar** HIEROGLYPH for 'stability', consisting of a concave-sided upright with three or four cross-bars, perhaps representing a pole around which grain was tied. The symbol came to be identified as the backbone of OSIRIS, although it was originally associated with SOKAR. In the NEW KINGDOM, the ceremony of raising the *djed* pillar was a key element in royal ritual, symbolizing both the resurrection of Osiris and the enduring stability of KINGSHIP. The ceremony formed part of AMENHOTEP III's SED FESTIVAL at THEBES, and is also depicted in the temple of SETI I at ABYDOS.

Djehutyhotep NOMARCH of the fifteenth NOME of UPPER EGYPT during the reigns of AMENEMHAT II, SENUSRET II and SENUSRET III. His tomb at DEIR EL-BERSHA is famous for a scene showing the transport of a colossal statue.

Djeme *see* Medinet Habu

Djer (Zer) (c. 2900 BC) Third king of the 1st Dynasty. His tomb at ABYDOS on the UMM EL-QAAB was surrounded by 317 subsidiary graves for royal retainers, including women of the HAREM. The BOAT BURIALS found next to the SHUNET EL-ZEBIB may in fact have belonged to Djer's nearby funerary enclosure. Artifacts from his reign include a flint knife with a gold handle, a hoard of copper tools from a MASTABA at SAQQARA, and a headless FAIENCE statuette (depicting a seated king) from ELEPHANTINE. An ivory label suggests a royal visit to BUTO and SAIS, while trade with the LEVANT is indicated by imported pottery found in his tomb.

Djet (Uadji, Wadji, Zet) (c. 2875 BC) Fourth king of the 1st Dynasty. His reign seems to have been comparatively short, but produced two of the masterpieces of early Egyptian art, an IVORY comb engraved with religious iconography, and the king's funerary STELA from his tomb at ABYDOS. Foreign POTTERY from various sites indicates flourishing trade with the LEVANT. Other monuments built during Djet's reign include MASTABAS with PALACE-FAÇADE decoration at TARKHAN and GIZA.

Djoser (Zoser) (c. 2650 BC) First king of the 3rd Dynasty, known on contemporary monuments by his HORUS name Netjerikhet; NEW KINGDOM graffiti at

SAQQARA confirm this correspondence. The king is best known for his mortuary complex, the STEP PYRAMID at Saqqara, reputedly designed by IMHOTEP. Boundary STELAE from the complex name three royal women, probably Djoser's wife and two daughters; his mother, Nimaathap, is known to have been the consort of KHASEKHEMWY.

A life-size statue from Djoser's SERDAB in the Step Pyramid presents a striking image of royal power. However, comparatively little is known about his reign, and his other surviving monuments in Egypt are few. He is mentioned on inscriptions from BEIT KHALLAF and ELEPHANTINE, and at the TURQUOISE mines at WADI MAGHARA. Fragments from a shrine at HELIO-POLIS may indicate the growing importance of solar religion. The FAMINE STELA on the island of SEHEL purports to date to his reign, but is in fact Ptolemaic. Djoser was regarded by later generations as a pivotal figure in Egyptian history and in the Turin Canon (*see* KING-LISTS) his name is written in red ink, signalling the beginning of a new age. Certainly, he made the decisive switch from ABYDOS to Saqqara as the location of the royal tomb, and his own monument was Egypt's first PYRAMID.

dog An early Predynastic bowl shows a hunter holding four dogs on leashes (each animal with a small bell tied around its neck), attesting to the importance of domesticated dogs from an early period. In addition to their role in HUNTING, dogs were also valued as guard animals, and as faithful companions. Pet dogs were sometimes buried with their owner – one royal dog of the OLD KINGDOM had its own tomb at GIZA – and dogs were unique among animals in being given NAMES. These often reflect qualities of loyalty and bravery, but foreign names were also popular; indeed, dogs were imported from many neighbouring countries, especially LIBYA, NUBIA, the LEVANT and PUNT.

The dog was sacred to ANUBIS, and in the LATE PERIOD mummified dogs were buried in underground galleries at SAQQARA (the Anubieion). However, the subservience of dogs could be used as an insult when applied to humans. Hence, in the INSTRUCTION OF AMEN-EMHAT I FOR HIS SON, the king says 'I made the Asiatics do the dog walk'.

Various different types of dog, including breeds related to the saluki and the greyhound, are depicted in Egyptian art, although it is difficult to identify them with certainty.

dolomite *see* stone

donkey Probably indigenous to North Africa, wild asses have been found in Palaeolithic contexts. By the

*Relief of two **dog**s from the façade of the 12th Dynasty tomb of Sarenput I at Qubbet el-Hawa; the animals, of strikingly different breeds, were probably favourite pets of the tomb owner.*

Limestone relief with **donkeys** being driven across a threshing floor; the piece is unprovenanced, but probably came from a late 5th Dynasty tomb at Saqqara.

Neolithic period, they had been domesticated; the earliest donkey grave was excavated in the Predynastic village at MAADI. Throughout ancient Egyptian history, before the introduction of the CAMEL, donkeys were the main beasts of burden. HARKHUF recounts how he returned from an expedition to NUBIA with three hundred donkeys, laden with goods. MIDDLE KINGDOM inscriptions from the SINAI show a local Palestinian chief riding a donkey, evidently a source of amusement to the Egyptians of the time.

Dra Abu el-Naga Area of the THEBAN NECROPOLIS comprising the line of cliffs from the entrance to DEIR EL-BAHRI northwards as far as the wadi leading to the VALLEY OF THE KINGS. The area comprises tombs from the SECOND INTERMEDIATE PERIOD to the LATE PERIOD, most notably those of the 17th Dynasty kings. After the inauguration of the Valley of the Kings as the royal burial-ground, Dra Abu el-Naga remained in use for private burials throughout the NEW KINGDOM, including the tomb of a mayor of Thebes, KENAMUN, and many 19th Dynasty High Priests of AMUN.

dreams Believed to be a guide to future events, and a channel of communication for the gods, dreams and their interpretation were accorded great significance in ancient Egypt. THUTMOSE IV cited a dream to legitimize his accession to the throne. A RAMESSIDE papyrus describes different dreams and their meanings. In the LATE PERIOD, people would sometimes sleep within temple enclosures in the hope that an ORACLE would communicate with them in their dreams.

duality The concept that harmony was embodied in balanced opposites was fundamental in Egyptian thought. It found early artistic expression in the paired figures that feature prominently on many of the Predynastic ceremonial PALETTES. Egypt itself was conceived as a duality: the TWO LANDS of UPPER EGYPT and LOWER EGYPT, but also the black land of the floodplain and the red land of the DESERTS. It was the king's role to hold the two aspects in balance. Hence ROYAL TITLES and ROYAL REGALIA stressed the king's dual role. On a cosmic scale, the universe consisted of paired opposites: the land of the living and the land of the dead, heaven and earth, order (MAAT) and chaos. Here, too, the king was responsible for mediating between divine and human spheres, and for keeping the competing forces in balance.

Duamutef *see* Sons of Horus

dwarf People of restricted growth were not uncommon in ancient Egypt, and often seem to have been accorded positions of status and influence at court. They were thought to have a special talent for singing and dancing, and may have fulfilled a role not unlike court jesters in medieval Europe. In the 1st Dynasty, the

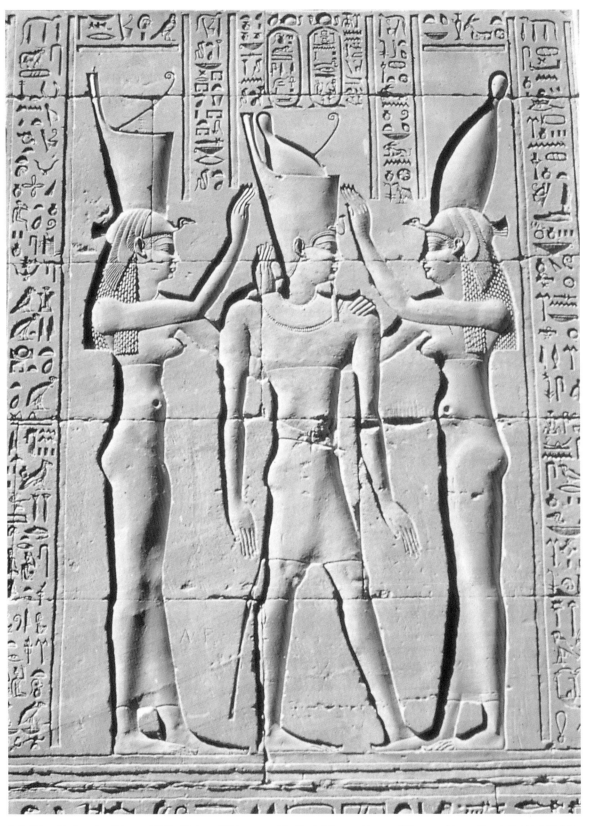

Relief from the temple of Horus at Edfu; Ptolemy VIII is crowned by the tutelary goddesses of Upper and Lower Egypt, Nekhbet (right) and Wadjet (left), symbolizing the **duality** *of the Egyptian realm.*

king's retainers buried in the royal cemetery at ABYDOS included several dwarfs. In the OLD KINGDOM, the dwarf Seneb attained high office and was able to commission a statue of himself with his family. The AUTO-BIOGRAPHY of HARKHUF, carved on the façade of his tomb at QUBBET EL-HAWA, recounts how the diplomatic mission to NUBIA under his command brought back a dwarf (or perhaps a pygmy from central Africa) for the amusement of the young King PEPI I.

dyad *see* sculpture

dynasty The system of ruling lineages or dynasties into which Egyptian history is traditionally divided was devised by the priest MANETHO in the 3rd century BC. To his original 30 dynasties, a 31st has been added, corresponding to the second period of Persian domination; some scholars also group the late Predynastic kings into a 'Dynasty 0'. Manetho's dynasties match quite closely the groupings of rulers suggested by ancient KING-LISTS, and are based mainly upon changes in the location of the royal tomb or capital city. They are not always true dynasties (i.e. family lineages), and some represent contemporary or overlapping sequences of rulers, especially during the Intermediate Periods.

Group statue of the Old Kingdom court **dwarf** *Seneb and his family; in an ingenious composition, the small figures of his son and daughter take the place of his legs.*

E

Early Dynastic period (c. 2950–c. 2575 BC) The first in the sequence of broad divisions of ancient Egyptian history devised by Egyptologists. It comprises the first three (or, for some scholars, the first two) dynasties of kings. Formerly termed the Archaic Period, the Early Dynastic period marks the formative phase of pharaonic civilization when administration, art and architecture all underwent rapid development. Since the 1970s, archaeological work at sites throughout Egypt has shed new light on this crucial period.

Because of the vagaries of preservation and excavation, the 1st Dynasty, although the most remote, is also the best understood phase of the Early Dynastic period. Large-scale monuments have not survived especially well, being mostly made of mud-brick. However, thousands of small objects from the royal tombs at ABYDOS and the contemporary elite burials at SAQQARA testify to the cultural sophistication of the early royal court and the outstanding skills of its craftsmen. WRITING on bone labels and seal impressions records mostly NAMES and titles, attesting to the development of an increasingly complex administrative system.

The 2nd Dynasty is marked by the relocation of the royal NECROPOLIS from Abydos to Saqqara, perhaps hinting at more profound political or religious changes. A hiatus in the royal succession in the middle of the dynasty may indicate a period of civil unrest, but order seems to have been restored after a relatively short time. The end of the dynasty, and especially the reign of KHASEKHEMWY, heralds the arrival of the pyramid age with its massive royal building projects.

The end of the Early Dynastic period in the 3rd Dynasty is dominated by the construction of the STEP PYRAMID, an enterprise that was made possible by the concentration of economic and political power at the royal court. This process reached its apogee in the OLD KINGDOM (c. 2575–c. 2125 BC).

Edfu Site on the west bank of the NILE in southern UPPER EGYPT with remains from virtually every period of Egyptian history. Tombs of the EARLY DYNASTIC PERIOD suggest the existence of an early town; this grew in importance in the OLD KINGDOM when Edfu replaced HIERAKONPOLIS as the most important regional centre. The Old Kingdom town walls still stand to a considerable height. Nearby, a major NECROPOLIS includes MASTABAS from the 6th Dynasty onwards.

Today, the most visible structure at Edfu is the Ptolemaic temple of HORUS, the largest intact temple in Egypt; it took 180 years to build (237 to 57 BC). Remnants of an earlier, RAMESSIDE temple show the usual orientation towards the Nile, whereas the Ptolemaic building is oriented towards the south. Clever use of light and darkness lends an air of mystery to the inner parts of the temple. In the sanctuary, a granite NAOS once held the cult image of Horus of Behdet, the local form of the FALCON god. Three colossal statues of Horus stand outside the gateway and by the door leading to the HYPOSTYLE HALL. The walls of a corridor separating the main temple from the outer enclosure wall are covered with extensive texts. As well as recording important religious myths, such as the conflict between Horus and SETH, the inscriptions also describe the numerous rituals and FESTIVALS that were celebrated in the temple each year; some of these linked Edfu with the temple of HATHOR at DENDERA.

Near the main building stands a ruined MAMMISI. Beyond, excavations have uncovered parts of the Roman and Byzantine town, including baths and houses.

education Formal schooling was a rarity in ancient Egypt. The majority of the population was illiterate, and would have learned practical skills from their parents; there may have been a system of apprenticeship before boys could practise a trade independently. For the small literate elite that formed the ruling class (estimated to have comprised between 1 percent and 5 percent of the population) education in reading and WRITING was carried out at scribal schools. Literary works such as KEMIT and the SATIRE OF THE TRADES, which were used (perhaps even composed) for educational purposes and which satirized other occupations, suggest that discipline at school was strict. WISDOM LITERATURE served to teach morality, as well as reading and writing. Repeated copying of set texts was one of the principal methods of scribal training; correct speaking was also highly valued.

A few members of the elite may have had a broader education, including some MATHEMATICS and astronomy. This was carried out in a school attached to a government institution (a HOUSE OF LIFE), or at the royal court itself. In the NEW KINGDOM, the sons of foreign rulers who owed allegiance to the PHARAOH were brought to Egypt to be educated at court together with the king's own children so that they might absorb Egyptian cultural values; this would, it was hoped, guarantee their continued loyalty.

Egyptian blue Material related to, but distinct from, FAIENCE and GLASS. Also called frit, Egyptian blue was made from quartz, alkali, lime and one or more colouring agents (especially copper compounds). These were heated together until they fused to become a crystalline mass, of a uniform colour throughout (unlike faience in which the core and the surface layer are of different colours). Egyptian blue could be worked by hand, or

Peristyle forecourt and pronaos of the temple of Horus at **Edfu**; this best-preserved of Egyptian temples was built during the reigns of Ptolemy VIII to Ptolemy XII.

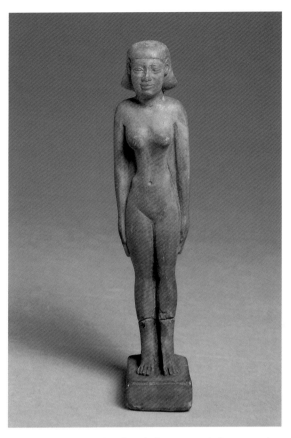

Early Ptolemaic statuette of a naked woman made from **Egyptian blue**, *a glass-like material also known as frit, using a combination of moulding and hand-carving.*

pressed into moulds, to make statuettes and other small objects. It could also be ground to produce a pigment. It is first attested in the 4th Dynasty, but became particularly popular in the PTOLEMAIC PERIOD and in the ROMAN PERIOD, when it was known as *caeruleum*.

Egyptology The study of ancient Egypt, its LANGUAGE, LITERATURE and culture. The ancient Egyptians were aware of their own history, and took an interest in monuments from earlier periods. THUTMOSE IV recounts on the Dream STELA at GIZA how he cleared the sand from around the Great SPHINX, while in the 19th Dynasty KHAEMWASET undertook a series of restoration and excavation projects among the OLD KINGDOM monuments of the MEMPHITE NECROPOLIS. The first extensive account of Egyptian culture was written by HERODOTUS, reflecting the Classical world's fascination with pharaonic civilization.

A number of European travellers of the 16th to 18th centuries AD brought back reports about Egypt and its monuments, but the history of Egyptology as a modern discipline began in 1798 with Napoleon's expedition to Egypt. His scientists and architects made detailed studies of the standing monuments. The results – the first comprehensive set of accurate maps and drawings – were published between 1809 and 1822 in a massive, 24-volume work, the *Description de l'Egypte*.

This impressive project opened up the mysteries of ancient Egypt to an audience of scholars and enthusiasts, and paved the way for the most significant single breakthrough in the history of Egyptology, the decipherment of hieroglyphic WRITING. The discovery and subsequent analysis of the ROSETTA STONE – for example by Thomas Young (1773–1829) – provided the key which, in 1822, enabled Jean-François Champollion (1790–1832) to announce that he had cracked the code.

Following the Napoleonic expedition, the first quarter of the 19th century AD was a period dominated by treasure hunting rather than archaeology. Consular agents and adventurers were hired by European governments to bring back objects and monuments for the great museum collections in London, Paris, Berlin and Turin. Foremost among such collectors was Giovanni Belzoni (1778–1823) who worked for the British Consul-General Henry Salt and brought back many of the largest monuments in the British Museum. The beginnings of a more scientific approach were apparent, however, in the work of independent scholars like John Gardner Wilkinson (1797–1875), who spent twelve years in Egypt, from 1821 to 1833, studying monuments and faithfully copying inscriptions. Another major contribution was made by Karl Richard Lepsius (1810–1884) who, from 1842 to 1845, led an ambitious and well-equipped Prussian expedition to Egypt and Sudan. The resulting twelve-volume publication, *Denkmäler aus Aegypten und Aethiopien* (1849–59), remains perhaps the most massive work in the history of Egyptology.

With excavations increasing rapidly, there was an urgent need for oversight and regulation, to prevent sites being plundered or destroyed. So, in 1858, the Khedive of Egypt appointed Auguste Mariette (1821–1881) as the first Conservator of Egyptian Monuments. Mariette created an Egyptian Antiquities Service, established the framework for the more orderly study and conservation of monuments, and also founded the Egyptian Museum in Cairo. His work was continued by his successor, Gaston Maspero (1846–1916), who insisted that archaeologists should produce proper publications of their work. With the

*The early history of **Egyptology** is captured in this painting by Paul Philippoteaux, showing the unwrapping of a mummy in the presence of various dignitaries; the man leaning over the mummy's head is the eminent 19th-century French Egyptologist Georges Daressy.*

establishment of the first academic posts in Egyptology at European universities, the subject achieved respectability.

The late 19th century AD witnessed the birth of archaeology as a scientific discipline, and the beginning of the great age of excavation in Egypt. The founding father of Egyptian archaeology was Flinders Petrie (1853–1942). He was the first archaeologist to realize the value and potential importance of even the smallest details, and his excavation reports set a new standard for archaeological publications. He also worked at most of the major sites in Egypt, paving the way for subsequent generations of scholars. The growth of archaeology resulted in the founding of national institutes, based in Egypt, to coordinate excavations. By the early 20th century, German, Dutch, French and American institutes had been established; their work continues today.

The discovery of TUTANKHAMUN's tomb in 1922 by Howard Carter (1874–1939) and Lord Carnarvon (1866–1923) was an international media event. It generated a wave of popular interest in Egyptology that has not abated since. The construction of the ASWAN High Dam in the 1960s, and the resulting threat to sites in NUBIA, sparked a massive international campaign of rescue archaeology. New scientific specialisms were brought to Egyptology for the first time, setting the scene for modern excavations which now routinely employ a huge range of specialist techniques and disciplines. At the beginning of the 21st century AD, Egyptology is perhaps more popular than at any time in its history.

electrum Natural alloy of GOLD and silver, obtained from the mountains of the Eastern Desert and NUBIA. The ancient Egyptian word for electrum, *djam*, was previously translated as 'fine gold'. Electrum seems to have been even more highly valued in pharaonic times than gold, probably because of its extra radiance.

Elephantine Island in the NILE, close to the modern city of ASWAN, at the head of the First CATARACT. The site's name, in both ancient Egyptian (Abu) and Greek, reflected its role in the IVORY trade. German excavations since the 1970s have revealed the history of Elephantine, which seems to have begun as two separate islands that became joined by the end of the EARLY DYNASTIC PERIOD.

From Predynastic times, the local population worshipped at a small shrine, nestling between natural granite boulders. Numerous VOTIVE objects discovered here include strange HEDGEHOG plaques, which may indicate a distinctive religious tradition. By the OLD KINGDOM, the shrine was explicitly dedicated to the goddess SATET who, together with KHNUM and ANKET, formed the local TRIAD. The shrine underwent successive phases of rebuilding and expansion, the first stone temple being erected in the 11th Dynasty. Elsewhere on the island a large temple to Khnum became the principal focus of state religion, while a sanctuary to the deified local hero HEQAIB attracted popular worship throughout the FIRST INTERMEDIATE PERIOD and MIDDLE KINGDOM. A NILOMETER was constructed to measure and record the height of the annual INUNDATION which, according to Egyptian mythology, originated from a cavern under Elephantine.

The earliest settlement, on the eastern side of the island, dates from the PREDYNASTIC PERIOD, and expanded steadily over time. Remains have been uncovered from virtually every period of Egyptian history. At the beginning of the 1st Dynasty, one of the first acts of the new Egyptian state was to construct a fortress on Elephantine, overlooking the main shipping channel. This reflected the site's importance as an administrative and customs point guarding Egypt's southern frontier, a role it was to retain throughout the pharaonic period. At the end of the 3rd Dynasty, a small granite PYRAMID, together with associated government buildings, was probably constructed for HUNI.

Elephantine served as the capital of the first Upper Egyptian NOME, and it was the natural starting point for trade and military expeditions to NUBIA. In the LATE PERIOD, it was home to a prominent community of Jewish mercenaries.

Elkab Site on the east bank of the NILE in southern UPPER EGYPT, most famous for its decorated ROCK-CUT TOMBS of the SECOND INTERMEDIATE PERIOD and NEW KINGDOM, and its imposing LATE PERIOD town wall. Excavations by British and Belgium archaeologists have revealed human activity from early prehistoric to Christian times, including remains of settlements, cemeteries and temples. The site has also given its name to the flint tool industry of the late Palaeolithic period ('Elkabian'), first identified at campsites in the vicinity.

Known to the ancient Egyptians as Nekheb, Elkab benefited from its location at the mouth of the Wadi Hellal, an important route from the Nile Valley to the Eastern Desert. Rocky outcrops in the Wadi are covered with prehistoric PETROGLYPHS, and with inscriptions of later periods, the latter mostly carved by priests serving in the local temple. Also in the Wadi are a small temple of AMENHOTEP III, dedicated to the local VULTURE goddess NEKHBET and HATHOR, 'lady of the entrance to the valley'; a stone chapel, built in the reign of RAMESSES II by the VICEROY OF KUSH Setau; and the Ptolemaic temple of a lioness deity.

From the 1st Dynasty, Nekhbet was revered as the representative (or 'tutelary') goddess for the whole of

*Painted relief from the 18th Dynasty tomb of Ahmose at **Elkab** showing the deceased and his wife seated before an offering table.*

*Drawing of a detail from the second golden shrine of Tutankhamun, showing the **ennead** of Heliopolis with the king himself in the place of Horus; from left to right the deities are Ra, Atum, Shu, Tefnut, Geb, Nut, Osiris, Isis and Tutankhamun (Horus).*

Upper Egypt. This perhaps reflected Elkab's geographical setting – with its narrow strip of cultivated land, it epitomizes the Upper Egyptian landscape – rather than its political importance. Nevertheless, the presence of a large Predynastic cemetery and the discovery of a granite block inscribed with the name of KHASEKHEMWY suggest that Elkab was a flourishing centre from an early period. The first town was surrounded by a circular wall, stretches of which still survive. However, partial erosion by the river and an expanding population led in time to the settlement of a much larger area which, in the 30th Dynasty, was enclosed by massive, rectangular, mud-brick walls. OSTRACA and other objects from the PTOLEMAIC and ROMAN PERIODS provide valuable insights into the economy and way of life at the time – the town was then called Eileithyiaspolis, Nekhbet having been equated with the Greek birth goddess Eileithyia.

Elkab enjoyed particular prominence during the 18th Dynasty. The main temple of Nekhbet, in the centre of the town, was rebuilt in sandstone. A smaller adjoining temple dedicated to THOTH and SOBEK, and a further temple outside the town wall were also constructed. In the cliffs behind the town, rock-cut tombs were built for local officials of the 17th and 18th Dynasties, including AHMOSE SON OF ABANA and PAHERI. Further tombs were built in the RAMESSIDE period. The latest remains at Elkab are the walls of a Coptic monastery.

encaustic Heated mixture of wax and pigment, used as a painting medium (from the Greek for 'burned in'). The encaustic technique was popular during the ROMAN PERIOD; the best examples are the so-called 'mummy portraits', funerary portraits on wooden boards which were discovered near the site of HAWARA in the FAYUM.

ennead Group of nine deities (from the Greek for 'nine'). In ancient Egyptian thought, the number nine signified the concept of 'many' (three times three, or a plurality of pluralities). Egyptian RELIGION featured several groupings of nine deities; the most important, known as the 'great ennead', comprised the nine gods who played a central role in the creation myth of HELIOPOLIS: ATUM (known as the 'bull of the ennead'), SHU, TEFNUT, GEB, NUT, OSIRIS, ISIS, SETH and NEPHTHYS.

epagomenal Term applied to the five days at the end of each year in the Egyptian civil CALENDAR, inserted after the twelve thirty-day months to bring the total number of days in the year to 365.

Esna Site on the west bank of the NILE in southern UPPER EGYPT, most famous for its temple dedicated to the TRIAD of KHNUM, NEITH and Heka (the god of MAGIC). A temple at Esna is mentioned in a text from the reign of THUTMOSE III. However, the earliest part of the visible structure, the west wall of the HYPOSTYLE

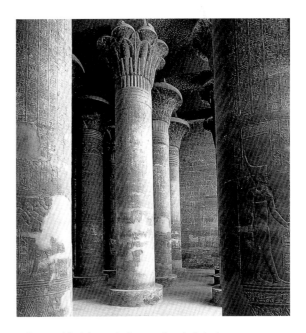

*Columns with elaborately decorated capitals in the pronaos at **Esna**; the temple, dedicated to Khnum, was built during the Roman period in the 1st and 2nd centuries AD.*

HALL, dates to the PTOLEMAIC PERIOD, while the rest of the building is Roman. Texts on the columns describe the various FESTIVALS celebrated in the temple, and also record HYMNS to Khnum.

Much of the temple still lies under the modern town. Small-scale excavations have revealed parts of a processional way that once connected the temple to a quay on the river bank; the associated inscriptions name the Roman emperor Marcus Aurelius. Known to the ancient Egyptians as Iunyt or Ta-senet, Esna was renamed Latopolis by the Greeks in honour of the Nile perch (*Lates niloticus*), which had its own sacred NECROPOLIS at the site. Palaeolithic remains have also been found at Esna. The stone tools, which are the principal evidence for the Esnan lithic industry, suggest a mixed pattern of subsistence based on the cultivation of plants as well as on HUNTING and gathering.

execration texts Documents, known from the late OLD KINGDOM onwards, which list people or places regarded by the Egyptians as hostile. According to Egyptian belief, knowing someone's name conferred power over them; further magical techniques could also be employed to defeat malign forces, such as writing the texts on statuettes of bound captives, or on POTTERY jars which were then smashed. This achieved the ritual destruction of the enemies named. Sometimes execration texts mention merely the NINE BOWS; on other occasions they give detailed names and places. However, standard lists of enemies were often repeated in later periods, so execration texts have proved of limited use in identifying particular foes of the Egyptians.

Most of the surviving texts come from the cemeteries of MEMPHIS and THEBES. A collection from the MIDDLE KINGDOM fortress of MIRGISSA may have been intended to provide an extra, magical, line of defence, to assist the garrison; they include texts written on a human skull.

Eye of Ra In Egyptian RELIGION, a separate deity which combined peaceful and vengeful aspects through its association with HATHOR and SEKHMET respectively. In one myth, the eye of the sun god travelled to NUBIA; in another, it took part in the mass slaughter of humans and had to be appeased by trickery. The Eye of Ra was also closely identified with the cobra goddess WADJET and hence with the URAEUS which spat fire at the king's enemies.

F

faience Ceramic material, made from quartz sand (or crushed quartz), small amounts of lime, and plant ash or NATRON. The ingredients were mixed together, glazed and fired to a hard shiny finish. Faience was widely used from the PREDYNASTIC PERIOD until Islamic times for inlays and small objects, especially SHABTI figures. More accurately termed 'glazed composition', Egyptian faience was so named by early Egyptologists after its superficial resemblance to the tin-glazed earthenwares of medieval Italy (originally produced at Faenze). The Egyptian word for it was *tjehenet*, which means 'dazzling', and it was probably used, above all, as a cheap substitute for more precious materials like TURQUOISE and LAPIS LAZULI. Indeed, faience was most commonly produced in shades of blue-green, although a large range of colours was possible.

The method of manufacture comprised two stages. First, the body material was mixed with water, and moulded into shape (either by hand, or by pressing it

The 'Carnarvon Chalice', a fine example of craftsmanship in **faience** dating to the 22nd Dynasty. The Egyptians used this ceramic material to produce a vast range of objects.

into a clay mould). Moulds for rings and other small items have been excavated in large numbers at AMARNA and QANTIR. Second, the glaze was applied in one of three ways. In the efflorescence process, the glazing material of soda, lime and silica was mixed with the body material and effloresced on the surface as the piece dried; after firing it melted to form a glaze. In the cementation process, the object was surrounded by powdered glazing material which bonded to the surface during firing; any excess was removed by careful sanding. In application glazing, the object was coated with glazing material in dry or paste form, and then fired.

falcon Often observed soaring high over the NILE Valley, the falcon was a perfect metaphor for distant majesty, and was associated from prehistoric times with the supreme celestial deity, HORUS. The early identification of the king with Horus led to the widespread use of the falcon in pharaonic ART, especially in royal contexts. The BA was most commonly depicted as a human-headed falcon, while a falcon on a plumed staff was the symbol of the west and its associated NECRO-POLIS. In the LATE PERIOD, huge numbers of mummified falcons and other birds of prey were buried in underground galleries at SAQQARA, attesting to the popularlity of ANIMAL CULTS at this time. Although the falcon was always most closely connected with Horus, it was also the sacred bird of the gods MONTU and SOKAR, and was occasionally associated with HATHOR.

false door Representation of a symbolic doorway, oriented to the west and built into the fabric of a tomb or mortuary temple. It was designed to serve as the point of contact between the realms of the living and the dead. Usually modelled in stone or wood, the false door was probably derived from the PALACE-FAÇADE decoration of 1st Dynasty elite tombs. It first appeared as a regular feature of tombs in the early OLD KINGDOM, and remained a key element of ancient Egyptian mortuary architecture throughout the pharaonic period. The 'door' itself was a narrow niche, in front of which visitors would place offerings for the deceased. In some examples, such as the tomb of MERERUKA, a life-size statue of the deceased (representing his KA) is shown emerging from the doorway to receive the offerings. The lintel over the door was inscribed with the standard OFFERING FORMULA, accompanied by the name and titles of the deceased. Often, there would also be a representation of the deceased, sitting in front of an OFFERING TABLE.

famine Although Egypt was famous in the ancient world for its agricultural productivity, there can be little doubt that, from time to time, prolonged periods of low, or excessively high, INUNDATIONS led to crop failure and famine. Unambiguous references to such events, however, are extremely rare: WRITING was a sacred medium, designed as much to perpetuate an ideal order as to record reality. Moreover, the ruling elite that produced the written record was also responsible for the well-being of Egypt and would not have wished to admit its failure in so public and permanent

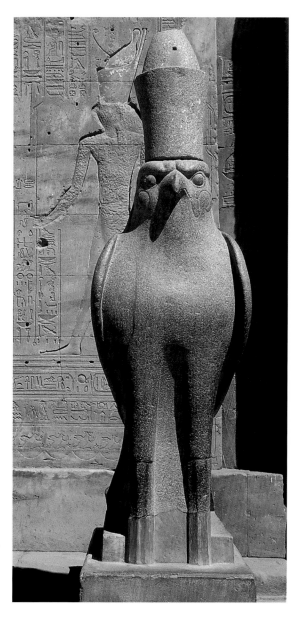

A monumental granite statue of a **falcon** wearing the double crown, representing the god Horus, in the Ptolemaic temple at Edfu.

a fashion. Nevertheless, there are occasional glimpses of hunger and its effects. Most famous are the reliefs of emaciated people from the causeway leading to the PYRAMID of UNAS. It has been suggested that famine may have been a contributory factor in the collapse of the OLD KINGDOM state. From the succeeding FIRST INTERMEDIATE PERIOD, there are references to famine in the tomb AUTOBIOGRAPHIES of ANKHTIFI at MOALLA and Hetepi at ELKAB. A 20th Dynasty papyrus refers to 'the year of the hyenas', which may be a euphemism for a period of famine. More problematic is the 'Famine Stela' on the island of SEHEL. Although its text, which refers to a seven-year famine, purports to be a decree of the 3rd Dynasty ruler DJOSER, the inscription in fact dates to the PTOLEMAIC PERIOD and the famine mentioned may never have taken place.

Limestone relief fragment showing emaciated bedouin suffering the effects of **famine**, from the causeway of the 5th Dynasty pyramid complex of Unas at Saqqara.

Farafra Oasis Today the least populated of the Western Desert oases, although occupying the largest depression. It was known to the ancient Egyptians as Ta-ihu ('land of cows'), perhaps harking back to its importance as a gathering place for semi-nomadic cattle-herders. Traces of Neolithic occupation dating back to 7000 BC have been excavated in the centre of the oasis, providing evidence for the early cultivation of cereal crops. More extensive settlement remains and PETROGLYPHS have also been discovered in the nearby Wadi el-Obeyid.

The Farafra Oasis is first mentioned in Egyptian texts of the 5th Dynasty, when it may have been jointly administered with the tenth Upper Egyptian NOME. In later periods, it was chiefly renowned as a source of raw materials: in the MIDDLE KINGDOM TALE OF THE ELOQUENT PEASANT, the central character brings wooden staves from the Farafra Oasis; in the 19th Dynasty, the area supplied stones for the building projects of RAMESSES II. At the same period, the oasis served as a first line of defence against infiltrations from LIBYA.

Little archaeological work has taken place in the oasis and few ancient remains have been uncovered, none of pharaonic date. Best known are the ROMAN PERIOD ROCK-CUT TOMBS at Ain Jallow and Ain Bishoi.

Fara'in, Tell-el *see* Buto

Faras Site in NUBIA near ABU SIMBEL; it was an important Christian centre in the Coptic period, its cathedral containing many painted murals.

farming *see* agriculture, animal husbandry

Fayum Low-lying fertile region in the Western Desert, centred on Lake Fayum (Lake Moeris, Birket el-Qarun). This large body of fresh water, fed from the NILE by the Bahr Yusuf channel, attracted settlement from prehistoric times. Excavations have uncovered evidence of hunter-gatherer (Fayum B) and early farming (Fayum A) communities on the lake shore. Occupation was particularly dense between 5500 BC and 4500 BC. Few remains of the late Predynastic, EARLY DYNASTIC PERIOD or OLD KINGDOM have been found in the Fayum, but the region saw an upsurge of activity in the 12th Dynasty, whose kings improved IRRIGATION, brought a greater area of land under cultivation, and founded royal estates and new cult temples.

Middle Kingdom monuments are scattered throughout the region, at sites such as ABGIG,

A **Fayum** portrait, probably from el-Rubayat, painted in encaustic on a wooden panel and dating to the mid-2nd century AD. The portrait would originally have been attached to the woman's mummy.

BIAHMU, HAWARA, MEDINET MAADI and MEDINET EL-FAYUM. The last was the principal cult centre of the crocodile god SOBEK. Few remains have been discovered from the NEW KINGDOM and THIRD INTERMEDIATE PERIOD, but increasing interest was shown in the Fayum from the LATE PERIOD onwards.

A particularly intense phase of activity took place in the PTOLEMAIC and ROMAN PERIODS, from which time come the famous and often very lifelike 'Fayum portraits' painted in ENCAUSTIC on cloths and boards attached to mummies. Several new towns were founded by Ptolemy II as part of a land reclamation project. Some, such as Karanis (Kom Aushim) became large cities by the 1st and 2nd centuries AD, although they later fell into decline and were abandoned by the 4th century AD.

festivals Festivals were a common feature of Egyptian religious practice. The Festival Hall of THUTMOSE III at KARNAK lists 54 different feast days, while a similar text at MEDINET HABU lists 60. Most festivals, whether of national or purely local importance, were annual events, celebrated on fixed days in the CALENDAR. Liturgical texts allow the details of certain festivals to be reconstructed. The central element was invariably a procession in which the cult image of a deity would be transported from one place to another. This provided a rare opportunity for the general population to come into contact with the deity and thereby to participate in state RELIGION; it might also be an occasion for ORACLES. Festivals also provided people with welcome additions to their regular diet, since the large amounts of food presented at such occasions would be redistributed to the population afterwards, in a 'reversion of offerings'. The most important national festivals included the New Year Festival and the Festival of SOKAR. At THEBES in the NEW KINGDOM, the OPET FESTIVAL and the BEAUTIFUL FESTIVAL OF THE VALLEY were among the most significant. Celebrated much less regularly, the SED FESTIVAL was of a different nature entirely, focusing on the ideology of KINGSHIP.

Field of Reeds *see* afterlife beliefs

First Intermediate Period (c. 2125–c. 1975 BC) Phase of ancient Egyptian history immediately following the collapse of the OLD KINGDOM centralized state. For much of the First Intermediate Period, the kings of the 9th/10th Dynasty (actually a single ruling family) from HERAKLEOPOLIS were widely recognized as the sole legitimate authority, even in UPPER EGYPT. However, the ambitions of a rival family from THEBES eventually led to the outbreak of civil war and a protracted series of battles between the two sides. Eventually, the Theban forces were victorious and the country was reunified under King MENTUHOTEP II, ushering in a new era of centralized control, the MIDDLE KINGDOM.

The reasons for the disintegration of central control at the end of the Old Kingdom are still not entirely clear, but may have included climatic factors, as well as the dynastic turmoil surrounding the royal succession after the extremely long reign of King PEPI II. Nonetheless, the authority of the court was maintained for a time by the numerous and ephemeral kings of the 8th

Fish and fishing *from a reed boat with a net and line, shown in intricate detail in a relief from the 5th Dynasty tomb of princess Idut at Saqqara.*

*The 'Botanical Garden' reliefs in the festival hall of Thutmose III at Karnak depict the exotic **flora and fauna** encountered by the king during his military campaigns in Palestine and Syria.*

Dynasty, who are thus sometimes assigned to the Old Kingdom. The ensuing political fragmentation of the country had long-lasting effects. The NOMES, especially in Upper Egypt, gained a new autonomy; this was reflected in the lavish burials of their governors, and in the development of distinctive regional artistic traditions. Both phenomena survived into the Middle Kingdom. Another result of the diminution of royal authority was that religious ideas and BURIAL CUSTOMS previously restricted to the king and his immediate circle spread to a much wider section of the population. The rise of the OSIRIS cult and the development of the COFFIN TEXTS were important aspects of this process, dubbed 'the democratization of the afterlife'. It was once believed that works of LITERATURE focusing on the themes of disorder and social dislocation, such as the PROPHECY OF NEFERTI and the ADMONITIONS OF IPUWER, represented eye-witness accounts of the First Intermediate Period. However, they are now recognized as fictional compositions of the succeeding Middle Kingdom.

fish and fishing Fishing has been an important subsistence activity in Egypt since prehistoric times. The earliest art from the NILE Valley – PETROGLYPHS on the cliffs at el-Hosh near ELKAB, dating to before 5000 BC – show strange curvilinear designs that have been interpreted as fish-traps. Besides the River Nile, the Mediterreanean and Red Seas, and Lake FAYUM, are also rich in fish. Pictorial evidence from TOMBS illustrates the detailed knowledge Egyptians had of differ-

ent fish species, and the various methods employed to catch them: traps, nets, lines and harpoons. Wealthy individuals kept fish in ponds; at DEIR EL-MEDINA, fishermen were employed to supplement the rations given to its inhabitants. Yet, despite the importance of fish in the diet, they were viewed ambiguously. The *Tilapia* fish was venerated because of its habit of brooding its young in its mouth, which suggested a connection with ATUM. Local fish deities are also attested, including the OXYRHYNCHUS fish and the goddess of MENDES, Hat-Mehit. By contrast, catching and eating fish became TABOO in the LATE PERIOD, because, according to Egyptian RELIGION, a fish had eaten the severed penis of OSIRIS.

flail *see* royal regalia

flora and fauna Evidence for the plant and animal life of ancient Egypt comes from archaeological, textual and artistic sources. In the NILE Valley and well-watered desert valleys, scrub-like vegetation predominated, characterized by grasses and shrubby plants interspersed with small trees such as acacia, tamarisk and dom-palm. The river banks provided a habitat for moisture-loving plants, including sycamore fig, willow, and dense thickets of reeds. LOTUS and PAPYRUS grew on the water's edge and in IRRIGATION canals. With the beginning of AGRICULTURE, an estimated 170 new species of plants were introduced and naturalized; further crop plants were introduced during the course of ancient Egyptian history.

Egypt was rich in wildlife, reflecting its varied ecosystems. The seasonal grasslands of the low desert supported large numbers of ostrich and game animals (elephant, giraffe, hartebeest, oryx, addax, wild cattle, ibex, gazelle, wild ass and Barbary sheep), as well as their predators (leopard, lion and hyena). The Nile floodplain attracted abundant bird life, especially waders and raptors; 75 different bird species have been identified in Egyptian ART. Aquatic wildlife such as CROCODILE and HIPPOPOTAMUS, and numerous types of fish thrived in the Nile. Common types of monkey included baboons, Barbary apes and African green monkeys. Domesticated animals included, from early times, CATTLE, sheep, goat, DONKEY, PIG, GOOSE, DOG and CAT. To these were added the HORSE in the SECOND INTERMEDIATE PERIOD; the mule and hinny, and domestic fowl in the NEW KINGDOM; and the CAMEL in the LATE PERIOD.

fly A common and persistent pest in Egypt, the fly had a symbolic importance throughout pharaonic history. In Egyptian art it was always depicted as if seen from above, with its wings folded back. Stone AMULETS in this distinctive form were made as early as the PRE-DYNASTIC PERIOD; they were probably intended to afford the wearer some protection against the insects. In the OLD KINGDOM and MIDDLE KINGDOM, the fly was sometimes shown on MAGIC objects, including wands used in childbirth rituals. In this context, the fly's productive breeding habits were probably being invoked. In the NEW KINGDOM, valour in military service was recognized with the award of a golden fly,

reflecting the insect's reputation for persistence in the face of opposition. The jewelry of Queen AHHOTEP included a gold chain with three fly pendants.

Followers of Horus Collective name given in the TURIN CANON to the kings – some real, some mythical – who ruled Egypt between the time of the gods and the accession of MENES.

food and drink Diet in ancient Egypt depended largely upon social status, but was varied, balanced and nutritious. The staples for all sections of society were BREAD and BEER. These were supplemented by a wide range of vegetables (including onions, garlic, cucumber, radishes, lettuce, celery, aquatic plants and their tubers); pulses (peas, beans and lentils); and fruit (figs, dates, grapes, persea and dom-palm nuts). Protein was provided by dairy products (milk, butter and perhaps cheese), fish and poultry (ducks and geese and their eggs). Meat (pork, mutton and beef) was a luxury mainly reserved for the elite, except at FESTIVALS; chicken bones have not been found at Egyptian sites before the PTOLEMAIC PERIOD. In the OLD KINGDOM, attempts were made to breed various wild animals for food, including cranes, hyenas and oryxes. HEDGE-HOGS and mice may also have been eaten on rare occasions. The main sweeteners, for drinks and cakes, were honey and carob gum. New foods were introduced through trade at various periods, including olives in the NEW KINGDOM. Methods of food preparation ranged from drying and salting to roasting, grilling, frying, stewing and boiling. WINE, made from grapes,

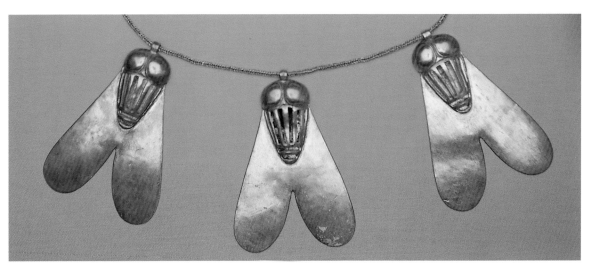

The **fly** was a symbol of perseverance, hence the award of golden flies for bravery on the field of battle; these three belonged to queen Ahhotep and were found in her early 18th Dynasty tomb at western Thebes.

dates or figs, was a popular drink among wealthier Egyptians, who probably ate three meals a day, whereas poorer people generally only had two.

fortresses Military architecture was highly developed in ancient Egypt from an early period. Fortresses and fortified walls were built at frontier points, to defend the country from hostile invasion and to regulate the movement of goods and people. The 1st Dynasty fortress on ELEPHANTINE and the OLD KINGDOM fortress at Ayin Asil in the DAKHLA OASIS are good examples, as are the 'Walls of the Ruler' built by AMEN-EMHAT I along the eastern edge of the DELTA, and the chain of fortresses built in the NEW KINGDOM along the northern coast of the SINAI. There were probably also garrisons and fortified towns within Egypt, especially during periods of political instability, but these are not well attested. When Egypt expanded its frontiers during the MIDDLE KINGDOM and New Kingdom, fortresses were built in newly conquered territory to assert and maintain control. The most striking example is the chain of fortresses built during the 12th Dynasty in Lower NUBIA, between the First and Second CATARACTS. They were sophisticated buildings, designed to repel attack and withstand periods of siege. Reliefs of SETI I show the fortress of Sile, on Egypt's north-eastern border, surrounded by a moat filled with CROCODILES, as an extra line of defence. The militaristic character of the RAMESSIDE period is emphasized by the design of the gatehouse of MEDINET HABU, which is modelled on a Syrian fortress. A major fortress of RAMESSES II has recently been excavated at ZAWIYET UMM EL-RAKHAM close to Egypt's border with LIBYA. Few examples of military architecture have survived from the THIRD INTERMEDIATE PERIOD or LATE PERIOD. In the PTOLEMAIC and ROMAN PERIODS, many new fortresses were built, especially in the Eastern Desert to guard mines and trade routes between the NILE and the Red Sea. Examples include MONS CLAUDIANUS and DAYDAMUS.

foundation deposits These refer to collections of VOTIVE offerings, buried at important locations in, or beneath, the foundations of a building, prior to its construction, in order to give it magical protection. The practice was generally confined to state projects such as temples, palaces and fortresses. It formed an integral part of the foundation ceremony, and is attested from the EARLY DYNASTIC PERIOD to the PTOLEMAIC PERIOD. For example, the temple of HATSHEPSUT at

DEIR EL-BAHRI was provided with fourteen brick-lined pits containing ritual objects. Foundation deposits provide excellent evidence for dating buildings.

frog A common sight and sound in the waterways and marshes of Egypt, the frog often occurs in huge numbers after the mating season. Hence the ancient Egyptians used a tadpole as the HIEROGLYPH for the number 100,000, and they regarded the frog as a powerful symbol of fertility and creation. Small FAIENCE figurines of frogs were deposited as VOTIVE objects in early shrines, emphasizing the central importance of fertility in popular RELIGION. A larger frog statue of Egyptian ALABASTER, dated to the 1st Dynasty, probably served as the cult image of a deity. In later eras, the frog was most commonly identified with HEQAT, the goddess of childbirth who presided over the final stages of labour. Frogs were often depicted on the 'magic wands' used in MIDDLE KINGDOM childbirth rituals. Ring-bezels and AMULETS in the shape of frogs were worn by women to ensure fertility. This practice even survived the religion reforms of AKHENATEN, frog amulets being manufactured at AMARNA during his reign.

According to the Roman historian Pliny, the ancient Egyptians believed that the frog reproduced spontaneously, giving it further regenerative associations. In one of the most important CREATION MYTHS, four of the eight deities comprising the OGDOAD of HERMOPOLIS were shown as frog-headed. Stone vessels in the shape of frogs are known from the PREDYNASTIC PERIOD; as grave goods they would have served to

Predynastic ivory statuette of a **frog**, *probably a votive offering. The ancient Egyptians regarded the frog as a symbol of fertility and creation.*

assist in the rebirth of the deceased. A later version of the same belief is reflected in the frog amulets included among mummy wrappings. Frogs also appear in the marsh scenes found in tombs of the OLD KINGDOM and Middle Kingdom, once again for their resurrective symbolism. In the NEW KINGDOM, the frog hieroglyph could be written after the name of a dead person to express the wish that they might 'live again'. After the conversion of Egypt to Christianity, the frog was retained by the COPTS as a symbol of rebirth; this may explain its occurrence as a decorative motif on POTTERY lamps from the Roman city of Karanis in the FAYUM.

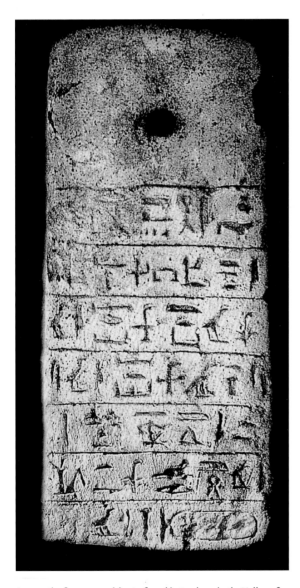

*Among the **funerary objects** found in tomb 55 in the Valley of the Kings was a magic brick inscribed with the name of Akhenaten. Magic bricks were intended to protect the tomb from malign forces.*

frontiers *see* borders

funerary cone *see* funerary objects

funerary objects The importance of AFTERLIFE BELIEFS in ancient Egyptian culture ensured that great attention was paid to providing the dead with the necessary offerings and equipment to assist their successful rebirth and eternal existence. The quantity and quality of grave goods depended upon a person's wealth and status. Some objects were made specially for the burial; others were deposited in the tomb because they had belonged to the deceased or been used in his lifetime. The most basic necessities were food and drink, to nourish and sustain the KA. They were often placed on an OFFERING TABLE. The funerary equipment often included other personal items, such as COSMETICS and JEWELRY (and, in the troubled times of the FIRST INTERMEDIATE PERIOD, weapons).

Besides these everyday items, special objects with a particular ritual function were generally included in a burial. Intended to protect and assist the deceased by magical means, the nature and range of these artifacts changed over time, according to religious beliefs. In the PREDYNASTIC PERIOD, figurines may have been intended to assist rebirth, while MACEHEADS both reflected and guaranteed the dead person's status. The beginning of MUMMIFICATION in the OLD KINGDOM brought with it a whole host of new funerary objects, including CANOPIC JARS and AMULETS which were placed among the mummy wrappings. Servant statues and other TOMB MODELS acted as emergency substitutes for the scenes of food and drink preparation painted on tomb walls. RESERVE HEADS were a particular feature of burials at GIZA in the 4th and 5th Dynasties. For wealthy burials of the OLD KINGDOM onwards, a statue to act as a substitute body was particularly desirable.

From the beginning of the MIDDLE KINGDOM, the extension of afterlife beliefs to a wider section of society gave rise to a new array of funerary objects. Foremost among these was the SHABTI. Elaborate tomb models, statuettes of hippos, HEDGEHOGS and jerboas also featured in some burials, as did ritual objects, such as magic wands, associated with childbirth and therefore rebirth. Tombs in the THEBAN NECROPOLIS were sometimes provided with baked clay cones, inserted above the doorway. These funerary cones remained popular in the NEW KINGDOM, when they were usually inscribed with the name and titles of the tomb owner.

From the 18th Dynasty, wealthy interments were usually provided with a papyrus copy of the BOOK OF THE DEAD, to guarantee success in the judgment before OSIRIS. Other specialist equipment included magic bricks to protect the tomb from malign forces, and germinating OSIRIS BEDS to assist with resurrection.

From the beginning of Egyptian history to the end of the ROMAN PERIOD, the first line of protection for the body of the deceased was the COFFIN. Royal burials were usually provided with several nested coffins inside a stone SARCOPHAGUS.

funerary texts *see Book of the Dead, Coffin Texts, Pyramid Texts*

furniture Although, by modern standards, ancient Egyptian houses would have been very sparsely furnished, WOODWORKING and cabinet-making were highly developed crafts. All the main types of furniture are attested, either as surviving examples or in TOMB DECORATION. Chairs were only for the wealthy; most people would have used low stools. Beds consisted of a wooden frame, with matting or leather webbing to provide support; the most elaborate beds also had a canopy, hung with netting, to provide extra privacy and protection from insects. The feet of chairs, stools and beds were often modelled to resemble bulls' hooves or, in later periods, lions' feet or ducks' heads. Wooden

furniture was often coated with a layer of plaster and painted. Royal furniture was more elaborate, making use of inlays, veneers and marquetry. FUNERARY OBJECTS from the tomb of TUTANKHAMUN include tables, boxes and chests, a gilded throne, and ritual beds shaped like elongated hippos and cattle. The burial equipment of HETEPHERES included a set of travelling furniture, light and easy to dismantle. Such furniture must have been used on military campaigns and other royal journeys.

Simple wooden lattice-work stool from Amarna, an example of the **furniture** *found in the houses of ordinary people during the New Kingdom; the top is pierced with holes to take a woven seat.*

A folding camp-bed from the tomb of Tutankhamun illustrates the kind of portable **furniture** *often favoured by royalty in the 18th Dynasty.*

G

galena Lead sulphide, used by the ancient Egyptians to make black pigment for eye paint. It was mined at sites in the Eastern Desert, principally GEBEL ZEIT.

games The ancient Egyptians enjoyed a wide variety of board games and athletic pursuits. Prominent in the first category was *senet* ('passing'). This was for two players, using a board of 30 squares, arranged in three rows of ten. Players had equal numbers of pieces, usually seven, which they moved according to the throw of a stick or knuckle-bone. The game became a standard part of funerary equipment, as it was regarded as

*Wooden model of Meketra's house and **garden** from his 11th Dynasty tomb at Thebes; the ideal Egyptian garden, shown here, consisted of a shady grove of trees surrounding a central pool.*

a metaphor for the struggle to achieve a blessed afterlife. A second popular board game was *men* ('endurance') which is attested from the 1st Dynasty. It was probably a race game, and was played on a long narrow board which was employed as the HIEROGLYPH for the word 'endure'. Another early game, which disappeared after the FIRST INTERMEDIATE PERIOD, was *mehen* ('serpent'), played on a round board in the shape of a coiled SNAKE. Like *senet*, it seems to have had significance in a funerary context. A board game for two players, with twenty squares, was introduced from the LEVANT but its rules are not known.

Sporting activities mentioned in texts or depicted in art include acrobatics, archery, stick fighting, boxing, swimming and running. The MIDDLE KINGDOM tombs at BENI HASAN contain many detailed illustrations of sports such as mock combat, juggling, jousting from rafts, and dozens of different wrestling positions. In the reign of TAHARQO, units of the ARMY took part in a race from MEMPHIS to the FAYUM.

gardens Three types of garden are attested from ancient Egypt: temple gardens, private gardens and vegetable gardens. Some temples, such as those at DEIR EL-BAHRI, were provided with groves of trees, especially the sacred ISHED TREE (persea). Private pleasure gardens are known from an 11th Dynasty tomb model of MEKETRA, and from TOMB DECORATION of the NEW KINGDOM. They were typically surrounded by a high wall, planted with trees and flowers, and provided with shady areas. Plants were cultivated for fruit and fragrance. Flowers included cornflowers, poppies and daisies, while the pomegranate, introduced in the New Kingdom, became a popular shrub. The gardens of wealthier individuals were arranged around an ornamental pool for fish, waterfowl and water-lilies. Vegetable plots, whether privately owned or belonging to

*Board **games** were popular in ancient Egypt; this example, with an ivory-veneered box, was found in the tomb of Tutankhamun and may have been used by the king during his lifetime.*

temples, were laid out in squares divided by water channels, and located close to the NILE. They were irrigated by hand, or (from the late 18th Dynasty) by means of the SHADUF.

Geb God who personified the earth. He had a pivotal position in the Heliopolitan ENNEAD, being the son of SHU and TEFNUT, the brother-husband of the sky goddess NUT, and the father of OSIRIS, ISIS, SETH and NEPHTHYS. As earth god, Geb was associated with vegetation and fertility, but also with the grave. He was also an important deity for the ideology of KINGSHIP and is frequently mentioned in the PYRAMID TEXTS. Geb was usually represented as a male human figure, often reclining on one side with his arm bent, but could also be portrayed as a white-fronted GOOSE or with a white-fronted goose on his head. He often has green skin and sometimes plants decorated his body. A universal deity, he had no specific cult centre.

Gebel Barkal Site on the east (locally north) bank of the NILE in Upper NUBIA, opposite NAPATA. Its principal topographical feature is an isolated sandstone hill with a free-standing pinnacle which was believed to resemble either a URAEUS wearing the white crown, or an erect penis. The mountain was regarded as sacred from at least the 18th Dynasty, and was revered as 'the pure mountain'. It was identified as the original home of the sun god's uraeus, the EYE OF RA. The site was also sanctified as the main cult centre of AMUN in Nubia,

because the pinnacle recalled his procreative form. The first temple to Amun was built by THUTMOSE III; SETI I and RAMESSES II undertook further construction projects. After a period of neglect, the Amun cult and temple were revived by the native Nubian kings of the

Fragment of a limestone relief from a 3rd Dynasty shrine at Heliopolis, showing the earth god **Geb** *seated wearing a tight-fitting robe.*

The holy mountain of **Gebel Barkal** *rises over the site of Napata in Upper Nubia; the Egyptians believed it to be the southern abode of the god Amun-Ra.*

25th Dynasty. ALARA and KASHTA built a PALACE of mud-brick, PIYE restored the temple, and TAHARQO added new buildings.

The site suffered after the invasion of PSAMTIK II's army, but remained an important religious centre, closely associated with Nubian KINGSHIP.

Gebelein Site on the west bank of the NILE in UPPER EGYPT, 30 km (19 miles) south of THEBES. It comprises two low hills, lying parallel to the river. The main early settlement was located next to the northern/western hill; well-preserved pottery kilns of the EARLY DYNASTIC PERIOD lie nearby. On the slopes of the hill, successive archaeological missions have excavated major cemeteries of the PREDYNASTIC PERIOD. Artifacts discovered there include two important early statuettes and a unique painted linen cloth. Numerous FIRST INTERMEDIATE PERIOD graves include some of Nubian mercenaries who served in the 11th Dynasty Theban army during the civil war against the 9th/10th Dynasty. The southern/eastern hill was dominated by a temple to HATHOR, founded as early as the 2nd Dynasty, embellished in the reign of MENTUHOTEP II, and still in use in the ROMAN PERIOD. At the foot of the hill lies an unexcavated settlement.

Finds from Gebelein, many of which are now in Turin's Museo Egizio, include a cache of 4th Dynasty administrative papyri; and OSTRACA in DEMOTIC and Greek, reflecting the life of mercenaries stationed at the site in the PTOLEMAIC PERIOD.

Gebel el-Arak knife handle Carved handle of HIPPOPOTAMUS IVORY belonging to a flint knife, dated to the late PREDYNASTIC PERIOD, which was bought by a French archaeologist at Gebel el-Arak near ABYDOS and is now in the Louvre, Paris. The scenes on the handle show the influence of the iconography of MESOPOTAMIA. One side depicts wild animals, presided over by a male figure in SUMERIAN costume holding apart two lions (the Mesopotamian motif known as 'Master of the Beasts'). The other side shows a battle, on land and on water; two of the ships involved in the naval engagement are of Mesopotamian design.

Gebel el-Silsila Site of sandstone quarries and monuments on both sides of the NILE in UPPER EGYPT, 65 km (41 miles) north of ASWAN. A Predynastic cemetery on the east bank and PETROGLYPHS on both banks indicate early activity at the site. The quarries, which are primarily on the east bank, were used from the 18th Dynasty until the ROMAN PERIOD. They swiftly became the principal source of sandstone in Egypt. On the west bank, inscriptions of all periods are accompanied by a series of shrines and other monuments, including a SPEOS of HOREMHEB with 19th and 20th Dynasty additions, and a large STELA of SHOSHENQ I.

Gebel Sheikh Suleiman *see* Nubia

Gebel Tjauti Site in the Western Desert commanding an ancient track between Luxor and Farshut. It has recently been discovered and recorded by a team of

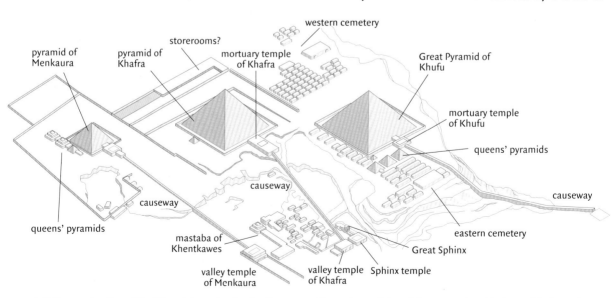

Artist's reconstruction of the **Giza** plateau showing the three pyramid complexes of the 4th Dynasty rulers, Menkaura, Khafra and Khufu, each with a long causeway reaching down to a valley temple next to the ancient course of the Nile.

American archaeologists. Inscriptions on the rock face include a large tableau of the PREDYNASTIC PERIOD, perhaps recording a decisive military encounter in the unification of Egypt; an important series of inscriptions from the FIRST INTERMEDIATE PERIOD, one by Tjauti, the NOMARCH of COPTOS, who still owed allegiance to the 9th/10th Dynasty; and graffiti left by desert scouts in the MIDDLE KINGDOM.

Gebel Uweinat *see* Uweinat

Gebel Zeit Mountain range on the Red Sea coast, with extensive remains of mine workings from the MIDDLE KINGDOM to the NEW KINGDOM. From the 12th Dynasty onwards, GALENA (lead sulphide) was the main objective of Egyptian expeditions, which generally set out from the THEBAN region. The oldest mining inscription dates to the reign of AMENEMHAT III, while the main workings date to the SECOND INTERMEDIATE PERIOD. They include a miners' settlement; and

chapels dedicated to HATHOR 'mistress of galena', to HORUS 'lord of the deserts', and to MIN and PTAH.

Gerzean *see* Predynastic period

gesso Thin layer of fine plaster which was often gilded; the technique was frequently used in the manufacture of CARTONNAGE objects.

Gilf el-Kebir High plateau in the extreme south-west of Egypt, close to the border with Libya. It is renowned for its prehistoric rock-art, notably the CAVE OF THE SWIMMERS.

Giza Area of the MEMPHITE NECROPOLIS, now on the edge of the modern city of Cairo; it is most famous for the three PYRAMID complexes of KHUFU, KHAFRA and MENKAURA, and the Great SPHINX. Pre-OLD KINGDOM activity at the site is attested by the discovery of Predynastic pots, and by two large tombs of the EARLY

The pyramids of Menkaura, Khafra and Khufu at **Giza** *are the quintessential monuments of ancient Egypt. In the foreground are the smaller pyramids of queens.*

DYNASTIC PERIOD. The plateau was chosen by Khufu as the location for his pyramid, the largest ever built and the only surviving Wonder of the Ancient World. It shows remarkable precision in its alignment and construction, and was accompanied by three subsidiary pyramids (probably for the king's wives) and five boat pits, two of which contained dismantled SOLAR BARQUES made from cedar. Modern construction work at Giza has uncovered parts of Khufu's causeway, but his VALLEY TEMPLE remains to be found. To the west and east of his Great Pyramid are cemeteries for members of the ROYAL FAMILY and high officials. Also dating to the reign of Khufu is the tomb of his mother, HETEPHERES. The Khafra complex comprises a large pyramid with some of its casing stones still in place, a single subsidiary pyramid, five boat pits, a pyramid temple, the remains of a causeway, and a well-preserved valley temple. Adjacent to the last is the Great Sphinx, which is generally dated to the reign of Khafra, at least in its finished form, although there remains some dispute about its precise age. It is the first monumental royal statue, and was venerated in the NEW KINGDOM and later periods as an image of HOREM-AKHET. THUTMOSE IV erected a giant STELA between its paws, while TUTANKHAMUN built a hunting lodge nearby. The pyramid of Menkaura is much smaller than its two predecessors, and was partially cased in red granite from ASWAN. Its well-preserved pyramid temple contained many fine dyad and TRIAD statues. The huge workforce employed in constructing the Giza pyramids was housed in a large town, a short distance away, at the foot of the plateau. This was surrounded by a stone enclosure wall ('The Wall of the Crow') and served by an industrial area including bakeries and breweries. A nearby cemetery for workers contains over 300 tombs. Some skeletons show signs of lower back stress, probably a result of the hard physical labour needed to build the pyramids. The quarries at Giza, from which much of the building stone was extracted, are also important archaeological sites.

During the 26th Dynasty, Giza once again became an important cemetery, with a number of large tombs concentrated around the causeway of Khafra.

glass Although the glassy materials FAIENCE and EGYPTIAN BLUE were manufactured in Egypt from an early period, the technology for making glass itself was only perfected in the early 18th Dynasty. It was probably imported from the LEVANT, since the Egyptian words for glass are of foreign origin. The FUNERARY OBJECTS of AMENHOTEP II included many glass artifacts, demonstrating a range of different techniques. At this period, the material was costly and rare, and may have been a royal monopoly. However, by the end of the 18th Dynasty, Egypt probably made sufficient quantities to export glass to other parts of the Eastern Mediterranean. Glass workshops have been excavated at AMARNA and PER-RAMESSES. The raw materials – silica, alkali and lime – were readily available in Egypt, although ready-made ingots of blue glass were also imported from the Levant and have been found in the cargo of the Uluburun shipwreck off the southern coast of Turkey. An ingot of rare red glass has been found at Per-Ramesses. The first stage of the glass-making process involved heating the ingredients together at between 700°C and 850°C. The resulting crystalline material was then crushed into a fine powder and reheated at 1000°C to produce molten glass which could be coloured and shaped. After the end of the NEW KINGDOM, glass-making declined in

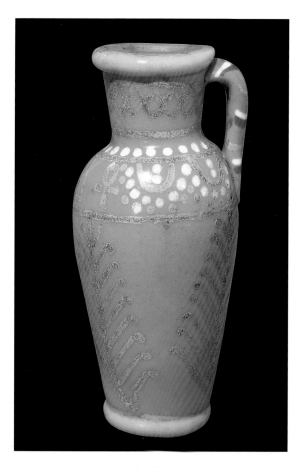

Blue **glass** jug from Thebes, inscribed with the name of Thutmose III of the 18th Dynasty; it is one of the earliest known glass vessels from Egypt.

Egypt, but was resurrected in the PTOLEMAIC and ROMAN PERIODS when ALEXANDRIA was a renowned centre of glass production.

God's Wife of Amun Office held by prominent royal women during the NEW KINGDOM, THIRD INTERMEDIATE PERIOD and LATE PERIOD. The title referred to the myth of the king's divine birth, according to which his mother was impregnated by the god AMUN. The God's Wife of Amun was required to play the part of Amun's consort in religious rituals. Ostensibly sacred, the office was used as a political tool for ensuring royal authority over the THEBAN region and the powerful priesthood of Amun. It is first attested at the beginning of the 18th Dynasty, when it was given by AHMOSE I to his mother AHHOTEP. In the early New Kingdom, the title was usually held by the king's principal wife. RAMESSES VI conferred the offices of God's Wife of Amun and DIVINE ADORATRICE on his daughter, setting the precedent for future appointments. Each subsequent holder was a king's daughter, and was expected to remain an unmarried virgin. In order to assist the royal succession, she would adopt the daughter of the next king as her heiress. In this way, the office helped ensure a smooth transfer of power between the 25th and 26th Dynasties. In the SAITE period, the God's Wives of Amun were wealthy and powerful individuals, becoming effectively rulers of THEBES after the office of High Priest of Amun lapsed. Their status is illustrated by the tomb of Amenirdis at MEDINET HABU. During the 25th Dynasty, the title God's Wife of Amun became linked to that of 'God's Hand', referring to the female principle inherent in the creator god ATUM which allowed him to bring forth SHU and TEFNUT by masturbation.

gold The golden treasure of TUTANKHAMUN has come to symbolize the wealth of ancient Egypt, and illustrates the importance of gold in pharaonic culture. Indeed, the burial chamber in a royal tomb was called 'the house of gold'. According to Egyptian RELIGION, the flesh of the gods was made of gold. A shining metal that never tarnished, it was the ideal material for cult images of deities, for royal funerary equipment, and to add brilliance to the tops of OBELISKS. It was used extensively for JEWELRY, and was distributed to officials as a reward for loyal service ('the gold of honour'). The oldest map in the world is a geological map of the gold mines in the WADI HAMMAMAT, from the reign of RAMESSES IV. However, the presence of gold-bearing

Gold *falcon head with twin-plumed headdress from the temple at Hierakonpolis; dating to the 6th Dynasty, this magnificent example of the goldsmith's art was originally mounted on a wooden statue base, forming a cult image of the god Horus.*

rocks in the Eastern Desert was known about, and exploited, from a much earlier period. Control of gold supplies may account for the growth and importance of HIERAKONPOLIS and NAGADA in the PREDYNASTIC PERIOD; the ancient name of Nagada was Nubt ('the golden'). Even more extensive reserves were to be found in NUBIA, in the Wadi el-Allaqi and the Wadi Gabgaba; a desire to gain access to new sources of gold may have been one of the principal motives for Egyptian control of Nubia in the MIDDLE KINGDOM, and again in the NEW KINGDOM. Several tombs of the 18th Dynasty show Nubians presenting gold as tribute. The hard and dangerous work of mining was often carried out by convicts. Egypt was famous throughout the Near East for its abundant gold reserves, which must have given it considerable economic and political leverage. In one of the AMARNA LETTERS, the king of the MITANNI writes to his Egyptian counterpart that 'in my brother's country gold is as plentiful as dirt'.

goose Kept for food (eggs and meat) from prehistoric times, geese would have been a common sight in the villages and on the waterways of ancient Egypt. Geese were frequently depicted in ancient Egyptian ART, one of the most famous examples being a painted relief of different species of geese from the 4th Dynasty tomb of Nefermaat and Atet at MEIDUM. The white-fronted goose was also used as a HIEROGLYPH, and was closely associated with the god GEB. The god sometimes bore the epithet 'the great cackler', while ISIS, as the daughter of Geb, could be referred to as 'the egg of the goose'. In the NEW KINGDOM, the goose was regarded as sacred to AMUN; a flock of geese was kept on the sacred lake in the temple of KARNAK.

government The administration of ancient Egypt was dominated symbolically and structurally by the office of KINGSHIP. The king combined the roles of head of state, head of government, head of the armed forces and theoretical high priest of every cult, even if, in practice, the exercise of some of these duties on a day-to-day basis was delegated to others. The royal court was synonymous with the state apparatus, government offices being based in the complex of buildings surrounding the royal residence. The royal household itself was an important department of government throughout pharaonic history, involving the management of royal estates as well as various functions concerned with the palace and royal ceremonial. During the EARLY DYNASTIC PERIOD, most, if not all, of the highest positions at court seem to have been held by members of the ROYAL FAMILY (as is the case in some Middle Eastern monarchies today). Only in the OLD KINGDOM were the highest echelons of government, including the position of VIZIER, opened up to people of non-royal birth. As Egypt's internal and external administration grew more complex, particularly in the New Kingdom, new offices were created; hand in hand with the expansion of the bureaucracy went an increasing professionalization.

From the foundation of the Egyptian state, management of the economy was the primary focus of government. WRITING seems to have been developed principally as a tool of economic administration, and the machinery of government was concerned, above all, with the assessment and collection of taxes to sustain the royal court and fund royal building projects. The treasury was therefore the most important department of state, presided over by the 'royal chancellor' who, together with the vizier and the overseer of works, was one of the highest officials in the land during the Old Kingdom. A regular census of the country's economic wealth gave the government the information it needed to levy and collect taxes, agricultural and mineral. Some of this revenue was used for the manufacture of secondary products, and the remainder was stored in state warehouses. The redistribution of produce to state employees was a major governmental activity, and it underpinned the ancient Egyptian economic system.

Local government was organized in tiers. Individual communities were governed by mayors, with some judicial decisions being exercised by town councils. Larger districts or NOMES were controlled on behalf of the king by administrators, later NOMARCHS. The peripheral regions (deserts and oases) had their own governors. In the late Old Kingdom, the office of 'overseer of Upper Egypt' was created to enhance royal authority over the part of the country most distant from the capital at Memphis; the New Kingdom division of the vizierate into northern and southern offices achieved much the same purpose. However, the centralizing tendency of Egyptian government was in permanent tension with a strong sense of local and regional identity which reasserted itself at times of weakened central control.

Conquered territories were administered separately. Before the 18th Dynasty an 'overseer of foreign lands' sufficed, but the creation of an Egyptian empire in the New Kingdom necessitated a more complex administrative structure. Each of Egypt's three northern provinces in the LEVANT had its own governor who presided over a series of garrison commanders and local princes. In NUBIA, the VICEROY OF KUSH governed on the king's behalf, delegating some responsibilities to his two deputies; at a community level, decisions were taken by the mayors of Egyptian colonies or by local Nubian chiefs.

Hand in hand with the creation of an empire went the formation of a standing army. This required appropriate political oversight, provided by the commander-in-chief of the armed forces (often the king's eldest son) who was assisted by northern and southern chief deputies. The New Kingdom likewise witnessed the creation of a formal administrative structure to provide central control of the increasingly powerful priest-hoods. In practice, however, the major temples may have retained a high degree of autonomy over their own affairs.

At all periods of pharaonic history, the key to Egypt-ian government was writing. The literate elite formed the governing class; 'SCRIBE' was synonymous with 'administrator'. The political structures put in place by the royal court were remarkably successful in main-taining effective control over a large geographical area, while employing only a relatively small number of people. The efficiency of this system contributed greatly to the longevity of ancient Egyptian civilization.

grave goods *see* funerary objects

Greatest of Seers Title held by the High Priest of HELIOPOLIS. It suggests the early importance of ASTRONOMY AND ASTROLOGY in ancient Egyptian RELI-GION.

Great Green *see* Wadj-Wer

Great Hymn to the Aten *see* hymns

Greeks *see* Amasis, Mycenaean, Naukratis, Ptolemaic period

Gurob *see* harem

The 18th Dynasty granodiorite pair statue of Sennefer and his wife Senai from Karnak shows the ancient Egyptians' love of elaborate **hair and wigs**.

H

hair and wigs The ancient Egyptians paid close atten-tion to their personal appearance, and hair was an important component of this. Hair-dressing imple-ments feature prominently among FUNERARY OBJECTS, while hairdressers were employed by wealthier individ-uals, as depicted on the coffin of Kawit, wife of MEN-TUHOTEP II. Artificial hair-extensions and the use of henna as a hair-dye are attested at HIERAKONPOLIS as early as the PREDYNASTIC PERIOD. Wigs, often highly elaborate, were favoured by the elite throughout Egypt-ian history. Heavy, shoulder-length wigs for women were considered to increase their sexual attractiveness. For men, shorter wigs were generally favoured. Wigs were usually made from human hair, padded with veg-etable fibres. Both wigs and natural hair were probably scented with INCENSE. A wig-maker's workshop has been excavated at DEIR EL-BAHRI. Hairstyles and wig styles changed over time, reflecting age and status as well as fashion. Children wore their hair in a distinctive SIDELOCK OF YOUTH until adolescence. Moustaches and short beards were popular in the OLD KINGDOM for high officials. From the NEW KINGDOM onwards, PRIESTS had their heads shaved, for reasons of ritual purity. The king wore a false beard as part of his ROYAL REGALIA, while male deities were often depicted with a curly beard. Spreading ashes over the hair, and tearing the hair, were common gestures of mourning.

Hakor (Hakoris) (throne name: Khnemmaatra) (393–380 BC) Third king of the 29th Dynasty; his reign lasted for little more than a decade and may have been interrupted by one or more usurpers. He made an alliance with the ruler of Salamis in CYPRUS and com-missioned a pair of SPHINXES for the temple at BUTO.

Hapi *see* Sons of Horus

Hapy God of the INUNDATION and bringer of fertility. He was associated with the River NILE in general, but more specifically with the Nile flood. He was depicted in ART as a man with blue skin, a swollen belly, and large pendulous breasts; he wore a loincloth, and carried PAPYRUS and LOTUS plants; he was often shown with a clump of papyrus on his head. Although vener-ated throughout Egypt, he was particularly popular in areas of Nile rapids, notably GEBEL EL-SILSILA and the First CATARACT region. An annual festival of Hapy celebrated the beginning of the inundation. From the 19th Dynasty onwards, temple reliefs and statue bases often showed two figures of Hapy binding the papyrus and lotus plants around the hieroglyphic sign for 'unite', perhaps emphasizing the Nile as the unifying thread in Egyptian geography.

harem Institution for the female members of the ROYAL FAMILY and their servants, without any erotic connotations. Mentioned in the 1st Dynasty in connection with weaving, the harem was probably always a centre of textile production; texts suggest it was an economic institution of national importance, supported by taxation, with its own estates and administration. Children, including in the NEW KINGDOM those of foreign vassals, were probably brought up in the harem. The women who lived there occasionally became involved in conspiracies against the reigning king, to judge from the autobiography of WENI and a judicial PAPYRUS from the reign of RAMESSES III. Harems were often attached to royal PALACES and villas. Texts mention a harem at MEMPHIS, while excavations at Gurob on the southeastern edge of the FAYUM have revealed an establishment founded by THUTMOSE III that remained in use throughout the 18th Dynasty.

Harkhuf High official of the 6th Dynasty from ELEPHANTINE, who was Overseer of Foreign Lands and responsible for expeditions to NUBIA in the reigns of MERENRA and PEPI II. The façade of Harkhuf's rock-cut tomb at QUBBET EL-HAWA is carved with a famous autobiographical inscription giving details of four

such expeditions; it provides important details about Egypt's early relations with Nubia. On the first expedition, Harkhuf accompanied his father as far as YAM, to open up trade routes to sub-Saharan Africa. His second trip took eight months, and on his third he followed the ruler of Yam who had gone to fight Libyan tribes in the Western Desert. Harkhuf's description of the political situation beyond Egypt's borders can be linked to the resurgence of Nubian autonomy under the C-Group. From his fourth and final expedition he brought back a DWARF (or pygmy) for the young Pepi II. A copy of the king's excited letter to Harkhuf is included in the tomb inscription.

Harper's Songs *see Songs of the Harper*

Harpocrates (Hor-pa-khered, 'Horus the child') The god HORUS as a child, referred to in the PYRAMID TEXTS as 'the child with his finger in his mouth'. According to ancient Egyptian RELIGION, the child Horus was raised in secret – to protect him from his uncle SETH – by his mother ISIS at Chemmis in the marshes of the DELTA. Although usually linked with Isis and OSIRIS, Harpocrates could also form a TRIAD with other pairs of adult deities, such as MONTU and Raettawy at MEDAMUD. The child god was often shown seated on his mother's lap, and was the main element of decoration on CIPPUS plaques. Closely linked with Harpocrates were HARSIESE and Hor-nedj-it-ef ('Horus who champions his father'), stressing his role as son and heir of Osiris.

Harsaphes *see* Herakleopolis

Harsiese (deity) ('Horus son of Isis') Child form of the god HORUS which stressed his ancestry and thus his legitimacy. According to Egyptian RELIGION, Harsiese performed the OPENING OF THE MOUTH ceremony for his dead father, thus securing his legitimate succession to the throne.

Harsiese (official) Probably the son of SHOSHENQ II (22nd Dynasty), he was appointed High Priest of AMUN at THEBES early in the reign of OSORKON II (c. 875 BC). Harsiese may subsequently have claimed ROYAL TITLES, following the model of PINEDJEM I earlier in the THIRD INTERMEDIATE PERIOD, from whom he seems to have been directly descended. Harsiese was buried at MEDINET HABU in a FALCON-headed SARCOPHAGUS, hence imitating royal BURIAL CUSTOMS.

*Relief of the Nile god **Hapy** on the side of one of the Colossi of Memnon, at the site of the 18th Dynasty mortuary temple of Amenhotep III in western Thebes.*

Hathor Cow goddess with a variety of roles in Egyptian RELIGION. She may originally have been a celestial deity. Early representations of a cow goddess show stars in place of the ears, but it is difficult to be certain if such images depict Hathor or BAT, whose cult and iconography were absorbed by Hathor in the OLD KINGDOM. Hathor was depicted in various guises: as a cow, a woman with cow's ears, or a woman with a headdress comprising cows' horns and sun disc. Her name, attested from the early 1st Dynasty and meaning 'mansion (i.e. residence) of HORUS', had heavenly connotations, since Horus was himself a celestial god. Hathor was closely associated with KINGSHIP: because the king was regarded as the incarnation of Horus, Hathor became his divine mother (although this role was usurped in later periods by ISIS). In this, and in her solar connection, Hathor features prominently in the PYRAMID TEXTS. At EDFU in the PTOLEMAIC and ROMAN PERIODS, she was worshipped as 'lady of the sky', the daughter of RA and wife of Horus.

Hathor was also the goddess of music, joyfulness and sexuality (and was hence identified by the Greeks with Aphrodite). The SISTRUM used in musical celebrations was often decorated with a Hathor head, as was the MENAT counterpoise. She was one of the deities invoked to protect new-born children, and her cult at MEMPHIS – where she was worshipped as 'lady of the sycamore' – had connections with fertility. By contrast, and in common with many Egyptian goddesses, she also had a vengeful aspect, and in one myth was sent by RA to destroy humanity.

Hathor also had an important role as protector of Egyptians outside the NILE Valley. In the SINAI, especially at SERABIT EL-KHADIM, she was worshipped as 'lady of TURQUOISE'; her cult was also celebrated at BYBLOS. Within Egypt, her principal cult centre from the Old Kingdom onwards was at DENDERA. A CALENDAR in the Ptolemaic temple lists more than twenty-five FESTIVALS celebrating the goddess. Hathor was also important in western THEBES, where as 'lady of the west' she had a funerary role, receiving and nurturing the setting sun each evening. From an early period, DEIR EL-BAHRI was associated with Hathor – a PETROGLYPH of a cow is carved high up on the cliff face. HATSHEPSUT incorporated a shrine to Hathor in her mortuary temple.

Hat-Mehit *see* fish and fishing

Hatnub Site of TRAVERTINE (calcite) quarries in the Eastern Desert of MIDDLE EGYPT, 18 km (11 miles)

Painted limestone pillar topped with an image of the goddess **Hathor,** *from the Hathor chapel in the 18th Dynasty temple of Hatshepsut at Deir el-Bahri; the deity is shown in her typical form blending human and bovine characteristics.*

south-east of AMARNA and the main source of this material from the OLD KINGDOM to the ROMAN PERIOD. Hatnub (ancient Egyptian for 'mansion of gold') was connected to the NILE Valley by means of a long dry-stone road, with markers at intervals. The tomb of DJEHUTYHOTEP at DEIR EL-BERSHA includes a scene of a colossal statue being transported from Hatnub. The quarry itself comprises three main zones. Ancient remains include incised CARTOUCHES of KHUFU, inscriptions giving details of mining expeditions, and a series of dry-stone huts for the quarry workers.

Hatshepsut ('Foremost of noblewomen') (throne name: Maatkara) (c. 1473–c. 1458 BC) Fifth ruler of the 18th Dynasty. The daughter of THUTMOSE I, she married her half-brother (the future THUTMOSE II) by whom she had a daughter, Nefrura. After her husband's death, his son by another wife was crowned king as THUTMOSE III and married his half-sister Nefrura. Since the young king and his wife were both children, Hatshepsut acted as regent. She subsequently assumed full power and had herself crowned king, adopting ROYAL TITLES. She promoted the story of her divine birth in order to legitimize her accession, and was often portrayed (in text and image) as male, to accord with the traditions of KINGSHIP.

Her reign – strictly a CO-REGENCY with Thutmose III – was marked by the prominence of the high official SENENMUT, and by innovation and excellence in ART and architecture. She built the first rock-cut temple in

*Painted limestone head of **Hatshepsut** from her mortuary temple at Deir el-Bahri; despite her gender, she wears the traditional false beard of kingship.*

Egypt at SPEOS ARTEMIDOS, its façade bearing an inscription crediting her with the defeat of the HYKSOS. At KARNAK, she commissioned a pair of OBELISKS, built the eighth PYLON and the beautifully decorated Red Chapel, and erected a series of way-stations on the processional route to LUXOR TEMPLE. In western THEBES, she built a small temple to AMUN at MEDINET HABU (with Thutmose III); and two tombs, one of them (KV20 in the VALLEY OF THE KINGS) usurped from Thutmose I but probably never used for Hatshepsut's burial. However, her most famous monument is her mortuary temple at DEIR EL-BAHRI. Modelled on the neighbouring temple of MENTUHOTEP II, its lavish decoration includes the famous scenes of an Egyptian expedition to PUNT.

Activity beyond the borders of Egypt is further attested by the dedication of shrines at WADI MAGHARA and BUHEN, and the organization of military campaigns against NUBIA and the LEVANT. After the 20th year of Thutmose III, Hatshepsut disappears from the official record. Later in Thutmose's sole reign, her name and image were systematically effaced from monuments, and screen walls were built to hide her obelisks at Karnak. These actions have been inter-

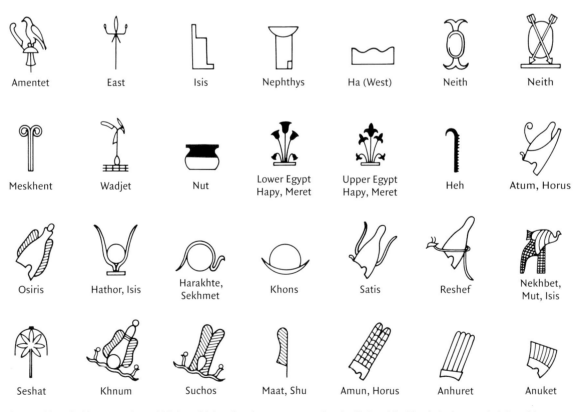

Amentet	East	Isis	Nephthys	Ha (West)	Neith	Neith
Meskhent	Wadjet	Nut	Lower Egypt Hapy, Meret	Upper Egypt Hapy, Meret	Heh	Atum, Horus
Osiris	Hathor, Isis	Harakhte, Sekhmet	Khons	Satis	Reshef	Nekhbet, Mut, Isis
Seshat	Khnum	Suchos	Maat, Shu	Amun, Horus	Anhuret	Anuket

*When not identified by name, the multifarious deities of ancient Egypt can often be distinguished by their characteristic **headdresses***

preted as the king taking revenge against his mother-in-law, but may simply have been motivated by a desire to erase what was seen as an anomaly in the line of succession.

Hawara Site at the entrance to the FAYUM where AMEN-EMHAT III built his second PYRAMID complex, after his monument at DAHSHUR developed structural problems. The architects of the Hawara pyramid learned from this experience, incorporating several stress-relieving devices in its construction; the burial chamber was carved from a single, gigantic block of quartzite. The pyramid's original casing of TURA limestone was robbed in antiquity, exposing the mud-brick core. The complex is the largest and most elaborate of its type from the MIDDLE KINGDOM. It is orientated north–south and was surrounded by a panelled enclosure wall, both features demonstrating the influence of DJOSER'S STEP PYRAMID. The pyramid temple had numerous chapels and was known to Classical authors as 'the Labyrinth'. An adjacent cemetery contains burials from the late Middle Kingdom to the ROMAN period.

hawk *see* falcon

headdresses Besides the various CROWNS worn by kings, queens and deities, three basic types of royal head-covering are known from ancient Egypt. The bag-shaped headdress, known as the *afnet*, is attested from the middle of the 1st Dynasty, as is the slightly more elaborate *khat* headdress which has lappets hanging down to the shoulders. The pleated head-cloth with turned-out facings, called the *nemes*, first appears on the statue of DJOSER from his STEP PYRAMID complex. It became the most common form of head-covering for the king, and could be worn in combination with a crown.

heart The most important organ of the human body in Egyptian culture, believed to be the centre of emotions and memory, and the seat of wisdom and personality. Because it was thought it could reveal a person's true character, it was left inside the body after MUMMIFICA-TION. A 'heart SCARAB' was often placed inside the mummy wrappings, above the organ itself, and was inscribed with a spell to prevent the heart from testifying against its owner at the final judgment. The WEIGHING OF THE HEART determined whether the deceased had led a life in accordance with MAAT. In the NEW KINGDOM, heart AMULETS were sometimes

included among the FUNERARY OBJECTS. The ancient Egyptians seem not to have understood the heart's role in the circulation of the blood.

hebsed *see sed* festival

hedgehog The hedgehog was a popular motif in ancient Egyptian ART from the PREDYNASTIC PERIOD onwards. The animal was believed to have guiding powers and, for this reason, was sometimes depicted attached to the prow of a ship, looking backwards. Because of its ability to roll into a ball to defend itself, it may also have had solar connotations. An association with rebirth or magical protection seems to be indicated by the frequent inclusion of FAIENCE hedgehogs among MIDDLE KINGDOM FUNERARY OBJECTS.

Underside of a **heart** *scarab of the 18th Dynasty general Djehuty; the text is from the* Book of the Dead, *and was designed to prevent the heart of the deceased from testifying against him.*

Faience **hedgehog** *from a 12th Dynasty tomb; such models were popular grave goods during the Middle Kingdom, but their precise symbolism remains obscure.*

Hedgehog plaques were common VOTIVE offerings in the early temple at ELEPHANTINE, while hedgehog AMULETS were popular in the NEW KINGDOM. In the LATE PERIOD, containers for eye-paint were often modelled in the shape of hedgehogs. In TOMB DECORATION, the animals may be shown in desert HUNTING scenes, or being carried in cages as offerings, perhaps to be eaten.

Heh God who personified the concept of infinity. In the Hermopolitan CREATION MYTH, he was a member of the original OGDOAD together with his consort Hauhet. He also had a cosmic role, supporting the legs of the celestial cow, and lifting the SOLAR BARQUE back into the sky at sunrise. Frequently depicted in AMULET form, and in royal iconography, Heh was shown as a male figure with a divine beard, kneeling and holding in each hand a notched palm branch (the HIEROGLYPH for 'year'); he was sometimes shown with a palm branch on his head and/or with ANKH signs suspended from his arms. The image of the god was used as the hieroglyph for 'million' and associated with the king's wish for 'millions of years' of rule.

Heket *see* Heqat

heliacal rising Term applied to the rising of Sirius, the dog star, when it is visible above the horizon just before sunrise. This event traditionally marked New Year's Day in the Egyptian civil CALENDAR.

Heliopolis (Tell Hisn) Site on the north-eastern edge of modern Cairo, near the apex of the DELTA. A Predynastic cemetery with burials of goats and DOGS was excavated in the southern part of the site. Fragments of a shrine built by DJOSER attest to its early importance as a religious centre. Heliopolis rose to prominence in the OLD KINGDOM as the principal cult centre of RA (hence its Greek name 'city of the sun'). Its ancient Egyptian name was Iunu (biblical On). Throughout pharaonic history, it was one of the most important religious sites in Egypt, renowned for its learning and theological expertise; its ENNEAD formed the basis of the most popular CREATION MYTH.

Heliopolis was connected to the river by a canal, and comprised a vast complex of religious buildings. At the centre of the main temple – dedicated to ATUM and Ra-Horakhty – was the BENBEN STONE. Neither stone nor temple has survived. Today the site is largely covered by modern buildings, and few ancient remains have been unearthed besides buildings of the RAMESSIDE period and the burials of MNEVIS bulls. The only major standing monument is an obelisk of SENUSRET I. Heliopolis was destroyed in the Persian invasions of 525 and 343 BC, and had been partly abandoned by the 1st century AD. In the ROMAN PERIOD, most of its remaining statues and obelisks were taken away to ALEXANDRIA and Rome; in the medieval period, its buildings were used as convenient sources of stone for the construction of Cairo.

Helwan Site opposite SAQQARA on the east bank of the NILE, more correctly known as el-Maasara or Ezbet el-Walda. It served as the main NECROPOLIS for MEMPHIS in the EARLY DYNASTIC PERIOD and comprises tens of thousands of graves from the 1st and 2nd Dynasties, ranging from simple pits to imposing MASTABA tombs, together with burials from later periods. Monasteries were built at the site in the Christian period, while prehistoric settlement and cemetery remains have been excavated at nearby el-Omari.

Hemiunu High official of the 4th Dynasty who served KHUFU as VIZIER, royal chancellor, overseer of royal scribes, and overseer of all construction projects of the king. In the last capacity, he would have directed the construction of the Great PYRAMID. His own tomb at GIZA (G 4000) was provided with a SERDAB containing a seated statue showing Hemiunu as corpulent and satisfied.

Heqaib (Pepinakht Heqaib) High official of the late 6th Dynasty, who was Overseer of Foreigners during the reign of PEPI II (perhaps in succession to HARKHUF) and hence responsible for relations with NUBIA and the Eastern Desert. He took part in two military campaigns to reimpose Egyptian authority in Lower Nubia. He built a tomb at QUBBET EL-HAWA, but is better known as the focus of a local cult on ELEPHANTINE, where he was venerated as an intermediary between humans and gods. His sanctuary was patronized by members of the elite and royalty during the MIDDLE KINGDOM; excavations have revealed more than fifty statues and 26 STELAE. During the annual Festival of SOKAR, a statue of Heqaib was carried through the streets of Elephantine.

Heqat FROG goddess associated with childbirth, especially the final stages of labour. 'Servant of Heqat' may have been a designation for midwife. First attested in the PYRAMID TEXTS, the goddess was frequently depicted on MIDDLE KINGDOM magical objects connected with childbirth, such as wands and clappers. AMULETS of Heqat were also popular. A relief in the temple of SETI I at ABYDOS shows the king presenting offerings to Heqat; VOTIVE offerings from the early temple at Abydos may indicate that a frog cult was particularly popular in this area from Predynastic times. A temple to Heqat was built in the PTOLEMAIC PERIOD at Qus, near COPTOS, while a procession in her honour is mentioned in the tomb of PETOSIRIS at TUNA EL-GEBEL. She was often associated with the ram god KHNUM in his creator aspect.

Herakleopolis (Ihnasya el-Medina) Site on the east bank of the Bahr Yusuf channel in MIDDLE EGYPT, near the entrance to the FAYUM. It was important from an early period as the main cult centre of the ram god HER-ISHEF (Harsaphes, identified by the Greeks with their god Herakles, hence the name Herakleopolis). It was also the capital of the twentieth Upper Egyptian NOME.

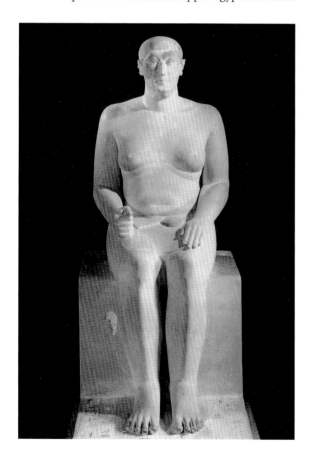

Seated limestone statue of the 4th Dynasty vizier and overseer of works, **Hemiunu,** *from his tomb at Giza; his corpulence emphasizes worldly success and affluence.*

Its ancient Egyptian name Nen-nesu may indicate a connection with the ideology of KINGSHIP. The town achieved particular prominence in the FIRST INTERMEDIATE PERIOD as the home of the 9th/10th Dynasty, and in the THIRD INTERMEDIATE PERIOD as the original power base of SHOSHENQ I before he became king. Cemeteries of both periods have recently been excavated by Spanish archaeologists. Building work in the temple of Herishef was carried out by SOBEKNEFERU and in the RAMESSIDE period, and repairs were made in the 26th Dynasty.

Herihor High official in the reign of RAMESSES XI who played a central role in internal politics at the end of the 20th Dynasty. Combining the offices of army general and High Priest of AMUN, Herihor was appointed by the king to bring the southern half of Egypt, especially the THEBAN region, back under central control; this followed an uprising which the VICEROY OF KUSH, Panehsy, had failed fully to quell.

Herihor duly succeeded Panehsy and eventually became VIZIER as well, thus holding the four most important offices of state. In the temple of KHONSU at KARNAK he went one step further, writing his last name in a CARTOUCHE and adopting ROYAL TITLES. His burial equipment also shows the same assumption of royal trappings. His appointment by Ramesses XI formalized the administrative division of Egypt (with SMENDES carrying out a similar range of functions in LOWER EGYPT) and paved the way for the political fragmentation of Egypt in the THIRD INTERMEDIATE PERIOD.

Herishef (Arsaphes, Harsaphes, Heryshef) Ram god of HERAKLEOPOLIS, attested from the 1st Dynasty. His name, meaning 'he who is upon his lake' probably referred to a topographical feature (perhaps a SACRED LAKE) in the locality.

Hermopolis (el-Ashmunein) Site on the west bank of the NILE in MIDDLE EGYPT, opposite DEIR EL-BERSHA. The ancient name for the city, Khemenu ('eight town'), referred to the local grouping of eight deities, the OGDOAD which lay at the heart of one of the Egyptian CREATION MYTHS. The town controlled a large area of fertile floodplain, and was capital of the fifteenth Upper Egyptian NOME, whose NOMARCHS were buried at Deir el-Bersha, Sheikh Said and TUNA EL-GEBEL.

From the NEW KINGDOM, Hermopolis was connected to the Nile by a canal. It was also important as a

Colossal quartzite sculpture of a baboon at **Hermopolis**; the piece was carved in the 18th Dynasty for the temple to the local god Thoth built by Amenhotep III.

Detail of a carved wooden panel of **Hesira** from his early 3rd Dynasty tomb at Saqqara; six such panels were originally installed in niches along the corridor of the tomb chapel.

starting point for a route to the BAHARIYA OASIS. Hermopolis was one of the principal cult centres of THOTH, identified by the Greeks with their god Hermes (hence the Classical name for the site). It was also the home town of Nimlot, a minor dynast of the THIRD INTERMEDIATE PERIOD.

AMENEMHAT II founded a temple to AMUN at the site, of which a monumental gateway remains. RAMESSIDE buildings extensively reused TALATAAT blocks from nearby AMARNA. The entire temple enclosure was rebuilt in the 30th Dynasty. Modern remains include colossal quartzite statues of baboons (sacred to Thoth), temple buildings of various dates, and a MIDDLE KINGDOM cemetery. A 5th century AD Christian cathedral lies over a temple in Greek style that was built for, and dedicated to, Ptolemy III and Queen Berenike.

Herneith Royal woman of the 1st Dynasty, perhaps the wife of DJER or DJET. Her MASTABA at North SAQQARA, was completed in the reign of DEN and was decorated in the PALACE-FAÇADE style. A stone lintel over the entrance, decorated with a frieze of LIONS, ranks as one of the earliest examples of TOMB DECORATION; a DOG buried near the threshold may have been a much-loved pet. Herneith's FUNERARY OBJECTS included fine jewelry.

Herodotus Greek historian born at Halicarnassus in the 480s BC. His nine-volume *History*, focusing on the Persian invasions of Greece, includes a long account of Egypt, its history, geography and culture (comprising the whole of Book II and the beginning of Book III). Much of his information seems to have been drawn from a visit he made to Egypt around 450 BC. Nevertheless, the accuracy of his account is decidedly mixed, although it remains an important source for events in LATE PERIOD Egypt.

Heryshef *see* Herishef

Hesira High official of the early 3rd Dynasty during the reign of DJOSER. His diverse offices included overseer of royal scribes and chief dentist. His MASTABA at SAQQARA, north of the STEP PYRAMID, was one of the earliest to incorporate a SERDAB; the tomb chapel contained paintings of FUNERARY OBJECTS, and a series of remarkable wooden panels, each carved with the figure of Hesira, his name and titles.

Hetepheres Early 4th Dynasty queen and chief wife of Sneferu, mother of Khufu, and probably also the daughter of Huni. Her sumptuously furnished tomb at Giza included a suite of portable furniture (now reconstructed from the surviving gilded elements) and one of the earliest sets of canopic equipment.

Hetepsekhemwy (c. 2750 BC) First king of the 2nd Dynasty; his reign is rather poorly attested. Seal impressions from the tomb of Qaa at Abydos indicate that Hetepsekhemwy oversaw the burial of his predecessor in the traditional royal necropolis; but Hetepsekhemwy chose a new site, Saqqara, for his own tomb. Comprising sets of rock-cut underground galleries, aligned north–south, the monument was robbed of its superstructure and most of its contents in antiquity. Objects bearing Hetepsekhemwy's name have been found at Helwan and Badari; others have been discovered reused in the later royal tombs of Peribsen, Khasekhemwy and Menkaura.

Hiba, el- Site on the east bank of the Nile in Middle Egypt, 30 km (19 miles) south of Herakleopolis. Founded in the New Kingdom, it was an important border town in the Third Intermediate Period, and the site of a fortified residence of the Theban rulers during the 23rd Dynasty. In the eleventh year of the reign of Takelot II, Prince Osorkon, High Priest of Amun and the king's son, sailed south from el-Hiba to crush a rebellion at Thebes. Today, the site of el-Hiba is dominated by the remains of a temple built by Shoshenq I.

Hibis Site of a temple in the Kharga Oasis. Begun by Psamtik II, with additions by Darius I, Hakor and later rulers, the monument is the only relatively intact structure in Egypt from the 26th Dynasty and Persian period. It was dedicated to Amun of Hibis and 'Amun-Ra of Karnak who dwells in Hibis'. An ancient town surrounding the temple lies under the modern cultivation and has never been excavated.

Hierakonpolis (Kom el-Ahmar) Site on the west bank of the Nile in southern Upper Egypt. Known to the ancient Egyptians as Nekhen, it was one of the largest and most important centres of political and cultural development in the Predynastic period. The archaeological remains cover a large area of floodplain and low desert, stretching westwards along a major wadi.

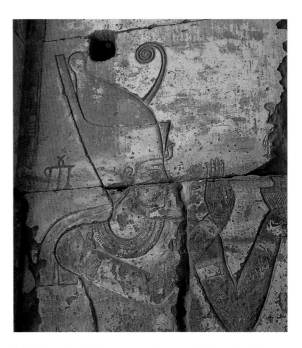

*Relief of Darius I in the temple of Amun at **Hibis** in the Kharga Oasis; it is the best-preserved building of the Persian period in Egypt.*

*Wall painting from a Predynastic tomb (T100) at **Hierakonpolis**; the scene comprises a flotilla of boats, perhaps connected with funeral rites, surrounded by motifs associated with royal authority.*

Reliefs in the 5th Dynasty tomb of Kagemni at Saqqara illustrate the principle of **hierarchical scaling**, whereby the most important figure in a scene (here Kagemni) was shown at a larger scale than subordinate figures.

Limestone ostracon from Deir el-Medina inscribed in **hieratic** with an extract from the Instruction of Amenemhat I for his Son.

The most prominent standing monument is a mudbrick cult enclosure of KHASEKHEMWY, 'the Fort'. Excavations at Hierakonpolis since the end of the 19th century AD have uncovered a wealth of remains from the early periods of Egyptian civilization. Early discoveries included a Predynastic painted tomb (T100), and a walled town with a temple of HORUS. Among the VOTIVE offerings found in the temple were a gold FALCON's head from a cult image of Horus; a life-size copper statue of PEPI I; and the collection of early objects known as the MAIN DEPOSIT.

More recent expeditions have revealed a Predynastic elite cemetery with ELEPHANT and cattle burials; PETROGLYPHS and guard posts; a ceremonial centre, probably the earliest surviving temple in Egypt; residential and industrial zones, including a potter's workshop; and a gateway from an early royal palace, decorated in the distinctive PALACE-FAÇADE style. Rock-cut tombs from the OLD KINGDOM, MIDDLE KINGDOM, NEW KINGDOM and ROMAN PERIOD, and additions to the temple by HATSHEPSUT, THUTMOSE III and RAMESSES XI, illustrate the continuing importance of the site throughout Egyptian history. This was largely due to its role as a major cult centre of Horus (hence its name in Greek, 'city of the hawk'). However, Hierakonpolis was gradually eclipsed as a regional administrative centre by nearby EDFU.

hierarchical scaling A system used in ancient Egyptian ART to indicate the relative status of human and divine figures, whereby the larger the figure in a particular composition, the greater its symbolic importance.

hieratic A CURSIVE SCRIPT, based on hieroglyphic signs, used from the end of the EARLY DYNASTIC PERIOD onwards. Perfectly suited to writing with a pen on PAPYRUS and OSTRACA, it was the script that SCRIBES were taught. It was always written from right to left, generally in columns until the 11th Dynasty, then in horizontal lines. Different styles of hieratic developed in the MIDDLE KINGDOM, 'business hieratic' eventually developing into DEMOTIC.

hieroglyph A sign in the ancient Egyptian 'hieroglyphic' WRITING system. The earliest recorded hieroglyphs have been found on bone labels from a Predynastic tomb at ABYDOS, dating to c. 3150 BC. The last hieroglyphic inscription was carved at PHILAE on 24 August AD 394. For the intervening 3,500 years, Egyptian writing remained a remarkably conservative system, and the preserve of a tiny literate minority, while the spoken LANGUAGE underwent considerable change. Fully formed hieroglyphs were used primarily on the walls of temples and funerary monuments (hence their name, from the Greek for 'sacred carvings'), while a more CURSIVE SCRIPT, better suited to writing with ink on PAPYRUS or OSTRACA, was generally employed for administrative, legal and literary purposes.

Hieroglyphic writing records only the consonants. The three basic types of signs are phonetic, conveying sound (a single consonant, or combinations of two or three); logographic, conveying meaning; and determinatives, denoting the general concept or category to which the preceding word belongs. Hieroglyphs were written without punctuation or spaces between words. They could be arranged in horizontal lines from left to right, or from right to left, or in vertical columns, depending on requirements. Writing and ART effectively belonged to a unified system of representation. Hence, individual signs which showed dangerous animals (such as SNAKES) were often deliberately mutilated to prevent them causing harm.

In the pharaonic period, fewer than 1,000 signs were used. This number was greatly expanded (to more than 6,000) in the PTOLEMAIC and ROMAN PERIODS, when hieroglyphic writing had become the preserve of priests, and different temples developed their own systems. The decipherment of hieroglyphs, made possible by the ROSETTA STONE, which was inscribed with the same decree in thre scripts, including hieroglyphs, was successfully accomplished by Jean-François Champollion in 1822; it stands as a major milestone in the history of EGYPTOLOGY.

hippopotamus The NILE supported herds of hippos until the NEW KINGDOM, and these large beasts would have been a common sight in earlier periods. They were a popular subject in Egyptian ART from the BADARIAN period onwards, and are a common decorative theme on early painted bowls. Hippos would have posed a real danger to fishermen and others crossing the river, so they were viewed with fear and awe. HUNTING a hippopotamus was a symbolically important ritual in the PREDYNASTIC PERIOD, becoming associated with KINGSHIP and, in later periods, with the triumph of HORUS over SETH (since the latter god could be represented as a hippopotamus). This accounts for the scenes of hippos being speared which feature in many private tombs of the OLD KINGDOM. Despite such connotations, hippos were also wor-

shipped for their positive attributes. A large limestone statue of a hippopotamus dating to the EARLY DYNASTIC PERIOD was probably the cult image of a deity. The female hippo became associated with TAWERET, while FAIENCE hippos were popular FUNERARY OBJECTS in the MIDDLE KINGDOM, probably because of their association with the fertility of the Nile, and hence regeneration.

history The modern concept of objective, factually based history seems to have had little place in ancient Egyptian culture. Texts, including ostensibly historical works such as AUTOBIOGRAPHIES and KING-LISTS, were composed primarily for religious reasons, to reflect an ideal view of the world. Hence it is often difficult to discern historical fact in such accounts. The 12th Dynasty ANNALS of AMENEMHAT II from MEMPHIS, and the TURIN CANON compiled in the RAMESSIDE period, may have aspired to a true record of facts, but the modern historical tradition only began with the writings of HERODOTUS.

Carved **hieroglyph**s on one of the 3rd Dynasty wooden panels of Hesira from Saqqara.

River scene from the 5th Dynasty tomb of princess Idut at Saqqara, showing a female **hippopotamus** giving birth to its calf.

A wooden statue of **Hor** found in his tomb at Dahshur; the upraised arms on the figure's head identify it as the king's ka or spirit.

Hittites An Indo-European speaking people of obscure origin who settled in central Anatolia (modern Turkey) in the 3rd millennium BC. Contact with Egypt seems to have begun in the SECOND INTERMEDIATE PERIOD, a vase fragment inscribed with the name of the HYKSOS king KHYAN having been found at the Hittite capital Hattusas (Boghazköy). The Hittites discovered the technique for smelting iron, and this highly prestigious material was imported into Egypt in small amounts during the NEW KINGDOM.

Hittites are first mentioned (as 'Hatti') in Egyptian texts during the reign of THUTMOSE III; imperial expansion brought the two powers increasingly into competition, particularly after the Hittites conquered and absorbed the kingdom of the MITANNI. At first, relations were friendly. AKHENATEN signed a treaty with the Hittite ruler Shuppiluliuma, and at the end of the AMARNA period, a widowed Egyptian queen (ANKHESENAMUN or NEFERTITI) sent a letter to the Hittite ruler requesting one of his sons as her husband; the prince was murdered on his way to Egypt, preventing the marriage from taking place. Thereafter relations between Egypt and the Hittites worsened, culminating in the Battle of KADESH during the reign of RAMESSES II. The resulting stalemate led to the signing of a formal peace treaty. The new alliance was cemented by a diplomatic marriage between Ramesses and a Hittite princess.

Hittite troops subsequently served in the Egyptian army and were garrisoned at PER-RAMESSES. MERENPTAH sent supplies of grain to the Hittites during a time of famine. The Hittite empire crumbled during the 13th century BC, perhaps under pressure from the SEA PEOPLES. Hittite mercenaries are shown fighting on the side of the Sea Peoples on reliefs at MEDINET HABU.

Hor (throne name: Awibra) (late 18th century BC) King of the 13th Dynasty, buried at DAHSHUR, close to the PYRAMID of AMENEMHAT III. His tomb contained a beautiful wooden statue of the royal KA, depicted as a naked man with the ka HIEROGLYPH on his head.

Horemakhet *see* Horus

Horemheb ('Horus in festival') (throne name: Djeserkheperura) (c. 1319–c. 1292 BC) Fourteenth and last king of the 18th Dynasty. Originally from HERAKLEOPOLIS, he first rose to prominence in the reign of AKHENATEN (if he is to be equated with a Paatenemheb mentioned at AMARNA), and became head of the army under TUTANKHAMUN. Although appointed crown prince, he failed to become king after Tutankhamun's death, possibly because of a coup mounted by AY. Only after Ay's demise did Horemheb eventually succeed to the throne, no doubt assisted by his power-base in the armed forces and perhaps bolstered by a connection with the 18th Dynasty ROYAL FAMILY (his wife Mutnodjmet may have been NEFERTITI's sister).

His reign marked a new beginning after the Amarna period, and his military connections brought a new dimension to the ideology of KINGSHIP. To legitimize his accession, he timed his coronation to coincide with the OPET FESTIVAL. He then embarked on a programme of major administrative reforms, and undertook building projects at LUXOR, KARNAK and GEBEL EL-SILSILA. He usurped Ay's mortuary temple in western THEBES and may have instituted a formal policy to destroy or appropriate his predecessor's monuments. As army general, he had commissioned an elaborate tomb at SAQQARA with detailed reliefs showing prisoners of war from campaigns in the LEVANT and NUBIA. As king, he built a new tomb in the VALLEY OF THE KINGS (KV57), the first to be laid out on a straight axis from entrance to burial chamber.

Having no surviving children, Horemheb adopted a fellow army officer as his heir (later RAMESSES I), and was hence revered after his death as the founder of the 19th Dynasty. His cult was celebrated until the 30th Dynasty.

Hornedjitef *see* Harpocrates, Horus

horse It is generally accepted that the horse was introduced to Egypt from the LEVANT during the SECOND INTERMEDIATE PERIOD, in conjunction with the use of the CHARIOT in warfare. First mentioned on the STELA of KAMOSE, the horse appears in Egyptian art from the beginning of the 18th Dynasty. Horses were used to pull chariots in battle, hunting expeditions and ceremonial processions, but were not generally ridden until the LATE PERIOD. From their first appearance in Egypt, they were status symbols for royalty, and the AMARNA LETTERS refer to horses being exchanged as gifts between rulers. The tombs of the 25th Dynasty kings at EL-KURRU and NURI included elaborate horse burials.

Horus FALCON god, closely connected with KINGSHIP. Originally a celestial deity, whose name means 'the distant one', Horus became associated with the king

from the late PREDYNASTIC PERIOD. The image of the soaring falcon was evidently considered a fitting metaphor for Egypt's ruler, and the king came to be regarded as the earthly incarnation of Horus. This was expressed most succinctly in the SEREKH, the frame surrounding the king's primary name which was

Limestone relief block from the 18th Dynasty tomb of **Horemheb** at Saqqara, showing him as commander-in-chief of the army under Tutankhamun, receiving the 'gold of honour' (necklaces of gold discs) from the king.

An 18th Dynasty limestone sculptor's model with the head of a **horse**, originally from Amarna but found at Hermopolis; such pieces would have been used as master copies and kept in a sculptor's workshop for reference purposes.

Limestone pair statue of the pharaoh Horemheb and **Horus** *the falcon-headed god of kingship.*

surmounted by the Horus falcon. The falcon perched behind the king's head in the seated statue of KHAFRA from his VALLEY TEMPLE conveys the same idea. In the TURIN CANON, the Predynastic rulers of Egypt are called the FOLLOWERS OF HORUS, emphasizing the link between the god and the monarchy.

The rise of the OSIRIS myth during the OLD KINGDOM reinforced the legitimacy of succession by identifying each ruler (equated with Horus) as the son and heir of his deceased predecessor (equated with Osiris). Particular forms of Horus, such as HARSIESE, HARPOCRATES and Hor-nedj-itef, were developed to emphasize his relationship with Osiris and Isis. Horus could also be paired with SETH to express the reconciliation and balance of opposing forces embodied in the institution of kingship. According to Egyptian myth,

Horus struggled with his uncle SETH to avenge the murder of Osiris. During the encounter, Horus lost an eye, which was restored as the WEDJAT EYE by HATHOR. His healing power was emphasized in the LATE PERIOD, CIPPUS plaques becoming popular in private religion.

Horus was worshipped in local forms at sites throughout Egypt, including HIERAKONPOLIS ('Horus of Nekhen'), EDFU ('Horus of Edfu'), LETOPOLIS ('Horus Khenty-irty'), and Behdet in the DELTA, where he was portrayed as a winged sun disc. More usually, the god was shown as a falcon or falcon-headed man. Because of his celestial nature – the sun and moon were interpreted as his eyes – Horus became closely linked through SYNCRETISM with RA, as Ra-Horakhty ('Ra-Horus of the horizon'). Horus was particularly associated with the sunrise, and in this form could also take the name Horemakhet ('Horus in the Horizon'); in the NEW KINGDOM, the Great Sphinx at GIZA was worshipped as an image of Horemakhet.

Horus name *see* royal titles

Horus Son of Isis *see* Harsiese

Horwerra Official of the 12th Dynasty who led an expedition to the TURQUOISE mines of the south-western SINAI early in the reign of AMENEMHAT III. Details of the expedition, including the personnel involved and the trials and tribulations of their mining work, are given in the text of a commemorative STELA erected by Horwerra at SERABIT EL-KHADIM.

House of Life Institution of learning attached to a TEMPLE where PRIESTS were taught to read, copy and compose sacred texts, as well as being instructed in ASTRONOMY AND ASTROLOGY, geography, MEDICINE, MATHEMATICS, LAW, theology, and the interpretation of DREAMS. A House of Life would also have included a scribal school for the children of the elite, and it may have played a role in supervising temple workshops. A closely linked institution was the House of Books (the temple library).

Houses of Life are known to have existed at MEMPHIS, AKHMIM, COPTOS, ABYDOS, ESNA and EDFU; one has been excavated at AMARNA.

human sacrifice A practice best attested in the EARLY DYNASTIC PERIOD, but rare thereafter. The 1st Dynasty royal tombs at ABYDOS indicate that the killing of retainers to accompany a newly deceased king into the afterlife took place on a significant scale at this period. Contemporary labels also indicate that human sacrifice could occur in a cultic context. An inscription from the reign of AMENHOTEP II refers to the ritual execution of seven Syrian princes in the temple of KARNAK. However, in general, the Egyptians seem to have abhorred the indiscriminate killing of humans, as indicated by the TALES OF WONDER in which KHUFU is portrayed as a tyrant for suggesting that a prisoner be executed.

In NUBIA, human sacrifice was practised in connection with the royal burials at KERMA during the SECOND INTERMEDIATE PERIOD.

humour and satire The ancient Egyptians undoubtedly had a well-developed sense of humour, but unequivocal examples are difficult to identify with certainty in the surviving record, because humour depends to such a large degree on context. Official art and texts served an essentially religious purpose, so afforded few opportunities for humour. One exception may be the reliefs at DEIR EL-BAHRI showing the large and grotesque wife of the ruler of PUNT. More certain, and more frequent, are examples of humour in non-official contexts, notably disrespectful cartoons of HATSHEPSUT near Deir el-Bahri, a late NEW KINGDOM satirical PAPYRUS, and comic scenes on OSTRACA from DEIR EL-MEDINA. The SATIRE OF THE TRADES uses comic exaggeration to belittle every profession save that of SCRIBE.

Huni (c. 2600 BC) Fifth and last king of the 3rd Dynasty, attested on contemporary monuments by his CARTOUCHE, but probably identical to the king whose STELA (now in the Louvre) gives the HORUS name Qahedjet. A series of small step PYRAMIDS, perhaps originally markers of the royal cult or of royal estates, may have been built for Huni. Surviving examples are located at ELEPHANTINE (named 'Diadem of Huni'), south EDFU, el-Kula near HIERAKONPOLIS, Tukh near NAGADA, Sinki near ABYDOS, and ZAWIYET EL-AMWAT. Remains which may belong to a further monument in the series have recently been excavated at ATHRIBIS. A further monument in the same series, at SEILA, is dated to the reign of Sneferu. Their construction may have been connected with a reorganization of provincial government.

Huni's funerary monument has not been securely identified. The pyramid at MEIDUM has been attributed to him, despite graffiti at the site which credit his successor SNEFERU with its construction. It is possible that Sneferu only finished the monument. The ANNALS of the 5th Dynasty on the PALERMO STONE mention an estate of Huni, indicating that his memory was still revered long after his death.

hunting Although of marginal importance as a means of obtaining food – compared to ANIMAL HUSBANDRY, AGRICULTURE and fishing – hunting was a highly symbolic activity with a prominent role in KINGSHIP and RELIGION. Above all, hunting wild animals, whether birds, desert animals or the hippopotamus, demonstrated the power of the hunter, whether king or commoner, over the unruly forces of nature, epitomizing the triumph of order over chaos. Hence hunting became a metaphor for royal authority and the universal aspiration to defeat the ultimate chaos of death. From the PREDYNASTIC period onwards, rulers had themselves depicted in the act of hunting. In early scenes, the hunters often wear special costumes, incorporating attributes of the animals they wished to defeat (horns, ostrich feathers) or to emulate (dogs' tails). In the NEW KINGDOM, AMENHOTEP III issued commemorative SCARABS to record his lion hunts; TUTANKHAMUN's tomb equipment included a painted box with scenes of hunting and warfare (equating wild animals with the human enemies of Egypt); and RAMESSES III

*The ancient Egyptians had a keen sense of **humour and satire**, though it rarely finds expression in official works of art; an exception is this 20th Dynasty papyrus which depicts animals engaged in human activities such as playing a board game and herding goats.*

commissioned a scene at MEDINET HABU showing him hunting a wild bull. From the OLD KINGDOM, private TOMB DECORATION frequently included scenes of hunting in the desert or in the marshes. Hunting would have involved a combination of chase, ambush and traps. An 18th Dynasty royal hunting park was excavated at SOLEB, and Tutankhamun built a hunting lodge near the sphinx at GIZA. It is possible that the hunting of certain animals, such as lions, was a privilege reserved for the king.

Hyksos Term used to denote the 15th Dynasty kings of foreign origin who ruled Egypt from AVARIS during the SECOND INTERMEDIATE PERIOD (c. 1630–c. 1520 BC). Derived via Greek from the Egyptian phrase *hekau khasut* ('rulers of foreign lands'), the term is sometimes used, incorrectly, to refer to the people of similar ethnic background who settled in the DELTA during the late MIDDLE KINGDOM. The Hyksos rulers probably originated from near BYBLOS in the LEVANT; their sphere of influence in Egypt is marked by the distribution of the distinctive TELL EL-YAHUDIYA POTTERY. The 15th Dynasty is generally thought to have comprised six kings, reigning for just over a century. According to MANETHO, the first Hyksos ruler was Salitis, who probably succeeded in unifying several small Delta states and/or conquering MEMPHIS. The most prominent of his successors are KHYAN and APEPI. KHAMUDI, the last king, was defeated by the army of AHMOSE. Other Hyksos rulers mentioned in inscriptions include SHESHI, Yannaasi (or Yansas-Aden), a son of Khyan, and SEKERHER.

Despite their non-Egyptian names and culture, the 15th Dynasty kings adopted ROYAL TITLES, maintained Egyptian forms of government and scholarship – the Rhind PAPYRUS dates to this period – and patronized various traditional cults. The major deities worshipped by the Hyksos kings were SETH (equivalent to their own BAAL), ANAT and ASTARTE. The Hyksos may have exercised a degree of sovereignty over vassal rulers in southern Palestine, although this has been disputed on the basis of archaeological evidence.

The 15th Dynasty certainly maintained active trade links with the Levant. Objects bearing the names of Hyksos rulers have been found as far afield as Knossos on CRETE and Baghdad in modern Iraq. Although they

A painting in the 18th Dynasty tomb of Nakht at western Thebes showing the tomb owner **hunting** in the marshes; he stands on a papyrus skiff, accompanied by his wife and children, and uses a throwstick to bring down water fowl.

were vilified in later Egyptian tradition, the Hyksos succeeded in strengthening Egypt's links with the rest of the Near East, paving the way for imperial expansion in the NEW KINGDOM. While their immediate cultural impact was confined to the Delta, they transformed Egyptian military technology in the long term, through the introduction of the HORSE, CHARIOT and curved sword.

hymns Texts eulogizing a particular deity were common in ancient Egypt. They survive on STELAE, on PAPYRUS documents, and on the walls of TEMPLES and TOMBS. They constitute an important source for understanding Egyptian RELIGION. It is likely that they were originally composed in order to be recited orally, as part of an act of worship. Besides literary works such as the *Cycle of Hymns to Senusret III*, hymns may be divided into three main categories. Hymns to OSIRIS were popular during the MIDDLE KINGDOM and NEW KINGDOM; frequently inscribed on funerary stelae, they praise the god as king of the dead and ruler of the underworld.

Hymns to HAPY were popular in the New Kingdom, surviving in numerous copies; they extol the god as bringer of fertility and may have been recited at the time of the INUNDATION. Hymns to the sun are the best represented of all hymns, occurring in royal and private contexts. They generally celebrate the god's triumphant passage through the underworld. A particular type of hymn to the sun is the *Litany of Ra*, inscribed in many RAMESSIDE royal tombs.

Most famous, with a special place in Egyptian religious literature, is the *Hymn to the Aten*, composed during the AMARNA period. It is preserved in two versions, the longer one known as the *Great Hymn to the Aten*, the shorter one as the *Lesser Hymn to the Aten*. The hymn reflects AKHENATEN's particular theology, praising the ATEN as the source of all life, and sustainer of the world.

hypaethral Architectural term meaning 'open to the sky', used to describe a building with no roof (such as the KIOSK of Trajan at PHILAE).

hypostyle hall Temple courtyard filled with rows of columns (hypostyle is Greek for 'resting on pillars'). An important element in Egyptian temple architecture, it symbolized the reed swamp which grew at the edge of the PRIMEVAL MOUND. Columns could be of different sizes, the largest flanking the temple's main processional axis and smaller ones forming the side aisles. The earliest surviving example of a hypostyle hall is in the mortuary temple of MENTUHOTEP II at DEIR EL-BAHRI. The most impressive, with 134 columns, is at KARNAK, and is lit by CLERESTORY windows.

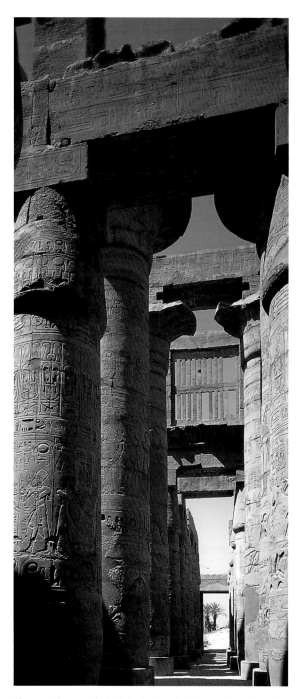

The great **hypostyle hall** *in the temple of Amun-Ra at Karnak, built and decorated in the reigns of Seti I and Ramesses II.*

Bronze statuette of an **ibis**, dating to the Late Period or Ptolemaic period; the bird was sacred to the god Thoth, and bronze statuettes were donated by worshippers as votive offerings.

Late Period statuette of an **ichneumon** from Thebes. This animal, also known as 'pharaoh's rat', was valued for its ability to kill vermin and snakes.

Late Period bronze statuette of the deified **Imhotep**, given as a votive offering; the base is inscribed with the name and titles of the donor.

I

Ibi (Aba) (throne name: Hakara) (c. 2150 BC) King of the 8th Dynasty who began a PYRAMID complex at south SAQQARA, close to the funerary monument of PEPI II. Its burial chamber was originally inscribed with selections from the PYRAMID TEXTS. According to the TURIN CANON, Ibi only reigned for two years; this would explain why his pyramid was never finished.

Ibia (throne name: Wahibra) (early 17th century BC) Ephemeral king of the late 13th Dynasty.

ibis Wading bird with a long curved beak. Three different species are attested in ancient Egyptian ART. The most important was the sacred ibis, which was regarded as an incarnation of THOTH; in the LATE PERIOD and PTOLEMAIC PERIOD, the birds were bred in captivity, mummified in their thousands, and placed in underground galleries at TUNA EL-GEBEL and SAQQARA as VOTIVE offerings. The hermit ibis was used as the hieroglyph for the AKH, and for the verb 'to shine'. The third species attested in reliefs is the glossy ibis. The word ibis is derived via Greek from the ancient Egyptian *hib*.

ichneumon Type of mongoose, also known as the 'pharaoh's rat', valued by the ancient Egyptians for its skill in killing vermin and SNAKES. It lived in reed swamps, and was often depicted in tomb scenes stealing birds' eggs. The ichneumon became a sacred animal in the MIDDLE KINGDOM. By the RAMESSIDE period it was associated with the spirits of the underworld because its ability to kill snakes was associated symbolically with RA's struggle against APOPHIS. Many bronze figurines of ichneumons have survived from the LATE PERIOD and PTOLEMAIC PERIOD; some are shown wearing the sun disc.

Ikhernofret High official during the reigns of SENUSRET III and AMENEMHAT III in the late 12th Dynasty. According to Ikhernofret's commemorative STELA, set up next to the processional way at ABYDOS, he grew up and studied in the royal PALACE, and was ultimately appointed royal chancellor. He was sent by Senusret III to refurbish the cult statue of OSIRIS at Abydos, together with its shrine and barque. While carrying out this duty, he took part in the Festival of Osiris; his stela provides one of the most important sources for the accompanying ceremonies, and one of the few surviving narrative accounts of an Egyptian festival. Ikhernofret's CENOTAPH chapel at Abydos was used by many of his contemporaries as the location for their own commemorative stelae.

Illahun *see* Lahun

Imhotep High official of the 3rd Dynasty, closely associated with the STEP PYRAMID of DJOSER. A statue base of the king from the complex is inscribed with Imhotep's name and titles, emphasizing his unique status at court. He is described as 'royal chancellor, first under the king, ruler of the great mansion, member of the PAT, GREATEST OF SEERS, and overseer of masons and painters'. Later tradition regarded him as the architect of the Step Pyramid complex, while MANETHO (incorrectly) ascribed to him the invention of building with blocks of dressed stone. Imhotep was also credited with several works of WISDOM LITERATURE, although none has survived.

In the LATE PERIOD, he was deified as a god of wisdom, WRITING and MEDICINE, and linked with PTAH and THOTH; bronze statuettes show him as a seated SCRIBE. His cult centre at SAQQARA (the Asklepion) became a place of pilgrimage. Those seeking to be healed left VOTIVE offerings, including clay models of diseased limbs and organs. He was also worshipped at DEIR EL-MEDINA alongside AMENHOTEP SON OF HAPU; and at KARNAK, DEIR EL-BAHRI and PHILAE. The Greeks identified him with their own god of healing, Asklepius. His tomb has not yet been discovered.

imiut Sacred symbol (or 'fetish') comprising the stuffed, headless skin of an animal tied to a pole standing in a pot. First attested in the 1st Dynasty, it became closely associated with the cult of ANUBIS. Models of an *imiut* were found in the tomb of TUTANKHAMUN.

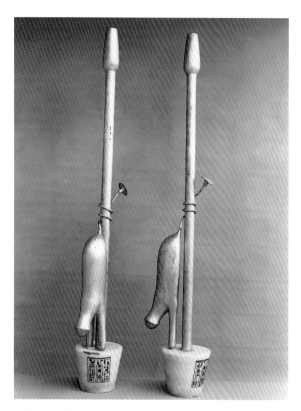

*Gilded wooden models of the **imiut**, a sacred symbol of the god Anubis, from the burial equipment of Tutankhamun. The fetish represented the stuffed, headless skin of an animal.*

*Female guests at a banquet wear cones of fat impregnated with **incense** on top of their wigs, in a wall painting from the 18th Dynasty tomb of Nakht at Thebes.*

Imsety *see* Sons of Horus

incense General term applied to a range of aromatic substances used in religious rituals and by individuals for cosmetic purposes. Incense trees were a major objective of the expedition sent by HATSHEPSUT to PUNT in the 18th Dynasty. In tomb scenes of the NEW KINGDOM, female guests at feasts are often shown wearing cones of fat, scented with incense, on top of their wigs. Several bronze censers (in which incense was burned) have survived from the LATE PERIOD.

incest Brother–sister marriages feature prominently in ancient Egyptian MYTHOLOGY, most notably among the nine principal deities of the Heliopolitan CREATION MYTH. The pairings of brother-husbands with their sister-wives (SHU and TEFNUT, GEB and NUT, OSIRIS and ISIS, SETH and NEPHTHYS) set a mythological precedent for incestuous relationships that helps to explain the occurrence of consanguineous marriages in the ROYAL FAMILY, especially during the NEW KINGDOM and PTOLEMAIC PERIOD. The practice seems to have been largely restricted to the king, and may have served to stress his divine status and his separateness from the rest of humanity. At the end of the 17th/beginning of the 18th Dynasty, three consecutive generations of the royal family witnessed the marriage of a brother and sister: TAA II and AHHOTEP I, AHMOSE I and AHMOSE-NEFERTARI, and AMENHOTEP I and Meritamun.

Sibling marriages were also common in the Ptolemaic royal family (for example, CLEOPATRA VI married two of her brothers, Ptolemy XIII and XIV). AKHENATEN may have gone one step further and fathered children by one or more of his daughters. At the end of the AMARNA period, TUTANKHAMUN married his half-sister, a practice that seems to have been more common in society at large. The marriage of full-blood siblings seems to have spread to the wider population only in the ROMAN PERIOD, when it was perhaps seen as a way of emphasizing their Egyptian cultural identity. In earlier periods, the use of the terms 'brother' and 'sister' to refer to a husband or a wife reflects Egyptian notions of endearment and respect rather than indicating incestuous relationships.

Instruction for Merikara Work of WISDOM LITERATURE which survives in three 18th Dynasty copies but is assumed to have been composed much earlier, in the FIRST INTERMEDIATE PERIOD. It is presented as a royal instruction from a king (KHETY) to his son, MERIKARA. Contemporary details include a reference to the destruction of THIS and the sacred sites of ABYDOS. More generally, the work sets out the rules by which a person should live, stressing moderate behaviour. The text also reflects on the institution and perils of KINGSHIP, and on divine retribution. It thus sets the tone for the 'pessimistic' genre so well represented in the literature of the MIDDLE KINGDOM.

Instruction of Amenemhat I for his Son One of the masterpieces of ancient Egyptian LITERATURE, dating from the early 12th Dynasty. Probably composed in the reign of SENUSRET I, the work is presented as an address by the deceased AMENEMHAT I to his son and successor. Unique in Egyptian literature is the theme of regicide, the old king recounting his murder in a palace coup. Written for dramatic impact, this powerful and imaginative work remained popular, especially for scribal training. The many surviving copies date from the NEW KINGDOM.

Instruction of Amenemope Work of WISDOM LITERATURE dating to the 20th Dynasty. Presented as a set of instructions from an official to his son, it comprises 30 chapters. Familiar themes include the importance of moderation in behaviour and honesty in setting field boundaries. More characteristic of the late RAMESSIDE period is the tone of personal piety. The work is rich in metaphors; elements of it were incorporated into the biblical Book of Proverbs.

Instruction of Any Work of WISDOM LITERATURE dating to the NEW KINGDOM. It reflects a 'middle-class' viewpoint, laying particular emphasis on moderate behaviour, skill in public speaking, showing respect to family and ancestors, making appropriate preparation for the afterlife, and honouring the gods. Unique in wisdom literature is the informal dialogue between Any and his son that comes at the end of the work.

Instruction of Hordedef The earliest known example of WISDOM LITERATURE, probably composed in the 5th Dynasty, but known only from much later copies. Ascribed to a son of KHUFU, the work stresses the importance of getting married, setting up a household, and preparing a proper burial in good time.

Instruction of a Man for his Son Work of WISDOM LITERATURE composed in the early 12th Dynasty, but surviving only in numerous fragments from the NEW KINGDOM. The complete text is difficult to recover; it may originally have formed part of a three-part work together with the *Instructions of Khety* and the *Loyalist Teaching*. In common with the latter, it stresses loyalty to the king. Particular importance is also attached to speaking correctly in different situations.

Instruction of Ptahhotep Work of WISDOM LITERATURE probably composed in the 6th Dynasty, although the surviving copies date from the MIDDLE KINGDOM and NEW KINGDOM. Presented as the sayings of a VIZIER during the reign of ISESI, it comprises 37 maxims on how to live life according to MAAT. Emphasis on knowing one's place in society, and on the dominance of men over women, would seem to support an OLD KINGDOM date of composition.

Intef I (Horus name: Sehertawy) (c. 2080 BC) THEBAN leader of the FIRST INTERMEDIATE PERIOD who challenged the authority of the ruling 9th/10th Dynasty by assuming ROYAL TITLES, thus proclaiming himself both king and head of a rival royal house (the 11th Dynasty). This act sparked civil war in the country. Intef I consolidated the Theban position in UPPER EGYPT by forming an alliance with COPTOS and attacking the fortresses of his rival, ANKHTIFI, at ARMANT. Intef's SAFF TOMB in western THEBES established the architectural pattern for royal tombs of the 11th Dynasty.

Intef II (Horus name: Wahankh) (c. 2062–c. 2012 BC) Second king of the 11th Dynasty. His fifty-year reign was the longest of any Egyptian king since PEPI II. Intef II vigorously pursued the civil war against the 9th/10th Dynasty of HERAKLEOPOLIS. Winning control over the seven southernmost NOMES of UPPER EGYPT, he next proceeded to attack the key site of ABYDOS, an episode referred to in the INSTRUCTION FOR MERIKARA and on Intef II's funerary STELA from THEBES. Also on the latter, the king boasts of launching attacks as far north as Aphroditopolis, at the apex of the DELTA; while HYMNS to RA and HATHOR hint at a more human frailty, emphasized by the prominent depiction of the king's pet DOGS. Besides his impressive SAFF TOMB in western Thebes, his major surviving monument is an octagonal pillar from KARNAK temple, part of the earliest known building at the site.

Intef III (Horus name: Nakhtnebtepnefer) (c. 2012–c. 2010 BC) Third king of the 11th Dynasty. Probably an

Intef II *making an offering of milk and beer, on his funerary stela from Thebes; the accompanying text is an extended hymn to Ra-Atum and Hathor.*

old man when his father, INTEF II, died, the new king reigned for just two years. His accession is recorded in a unique inscription on the STELA of a high official named Tjetji.

Intef IV (throne name: Sehetepkara) (c. 1700 BC) Ephemeral king of the mid-13th Dynasty.

Intef V (throne name: Sekhemra-wepmaat) (c. 1600 BC) King of the 17th Dynasty, whose authority was confined to UPPER EGYPT, perhaps more specifically the area around THEBES. His COFFIN (now in the Louvre, Paris) states that his burial was made by his brother INTEF VI. A fragment of Intef V's PYRAMIDION has recently been discovered at DRA ABU EL-NAGA, pointing to the likely location of the king's tomb.

Intef VI (throne name: Nubkheperra) (c. 1600 BC) King of the 17th Dynasty in succession to his brother INTEF V. The mud-brick PYRAMID marking his tomb has recently been excavated at DRA ABU EL-NAGA in western THEBES, as have fragments of his PYRAMIDION. An inscribed door-jamb from Gebel Intef in the Western Desert behind Thebes names Intef VI and his father SOBEKEMSAF.

Intef VII (throne name: Sekhemra-heruhermaat) (c. 1600 BC) Ephemeral king of the 17th Dynasty, known only from his COFFIN, now in the Louvre Museum, Paris, which was hastily converted into a royal coffin from a pre-existing private one. His reign must have been very brief, since he does not appear in any KING-LIST.

inundation Annual flooding of the NILE, when the river burst its banks, due to the high volume of water resulting from summer rains over the Ethiopian High-

*Wall relief from the Ramesseum depicting the goddess of writing, Seshat, inscribing the names of Ramesses II on the leaves of the sacred **ished** tree (persea).*

lands. This event marked the beginning of the year in the ancient Egyptian CALENDAR. The rise in the level of the river would have been noticed first at ASWAN in late June, and the Egyptians believed that the inundation originated in caverns below ELEPHANTINE. Further north, at MEMPHIS, the flood would have reached its height in September. Worshipped as the god HAPY, the inundation determined the agricultural cycle of seasons, and underpinned the land's productivity. As the waters spread out over the floodplain, a fresh layer of silt was deposited, renewing the fertility of the soil. The temporary flooding of the land also provided the state with an opportunity to mobilize large numbers of people for CORVÉE LABOUR. When the flood began to recede, water could be retained and channelled using simple IRRIGATION techniques.

The height of the annual inundation was measured by means of a NILOMETER, and would have provided a useful guide to the likely crop yield the following year. Hence it was regarded by the government as important information, and is given particular prominence in the ANNALS of the PALERMO STONE. The completion of the ASWAN High Dam in 1971 put an end to the annual inundation.

Inyotef *see* Intef I, II, III, IV, V, VI, VII

Irem *see* Yam

iron *see* Hittites, metalworking

irrigation The success of AGRICULTURE in the NILE Valley depended upon harnessing the floodwaters of the INUNDATION by means of dykes, ditches and canals. The valley naturally divided into a number of flood basins – upon which the NOMES were based – and irrigation could therefore be managed at a local level, without the need for massive state projects. However, according to the ideology of KINGSHIP, the ruler was ultimately responsible for the fertility of Egypt; hence on the SCORPION MACEHEAD, a late Predynastic king is shown carrying out an irrigation ritual, while a 1st Dynasty inscription mentions a (state-sponsored) canal near MEMPHIS.

Egyptian inscriptions of all periods make frequent reference to the dredging of canals, the repair of dykes, the re-establishment of field boundaries following the inundation, and other irrigation-related activities. Irrigation was revolutionized at periodic intervals by the introduction of new technology, notably the SHADUF in the NEW KINGDOM, and the animal-powered water wheel (*sakiya*) in the PTOLEMAIC PERIOD. In modern times, the construction of two dams at ASWAN changed forever the annual regime of the NILE, making possible perennial irrigation.

Isesi (Izezi) (throne name: Djedkara) (c. 2360 BC) Eighth king of the 5th Dynasty. His long reign, of more than thirty years, is relatively poorly attested. According to the biographical inscription from the tomb of HARKHUF, Isesi sent an expedition to PUNT which returned with a dancing DWARF. In order to make government more efficient, Isesi created the office of Overseer of UPPER EGYPT, based at ABYDOS. Another innovation was the abandonment of the 5th Dynasty tradition of building a SUN TEMPLE. Instead, he concentrated on his pyramid complex; this was the first to be built at south SAQQARA, and included a richly decorated mortuary temple, which was badly damaged in antiquity.

***ished* tree** In Egyptian RELIGION, the sacred persea tree, on the leaves of which THOTH or SESHAT wrote the king's names and titles, and the number of years of his reign.

Isis Goddess of uncertain origins who became one of the most important deities in the Egyptian pantheon. She was a member of the ENNEAD of HELIOPOLIS, the sister and wife of OSIRIS, and the mother of HORUS. The last aspect gave her a role in the ideology of KINGSHIP (because of the king's close identification with Horus), and this was emphasized by the writing of her name with the hieroglyph of a throne. According to the Osiris myth, she fulfilled the role of the ideal wife, seeking and reconstituting the dismembered body of her husband, following his murder by SETH. She made the first mummy from Osiris's dismembered corpse and aroused him in order to conceive Horus, whom she subsequently bore in the marshes of the DELTA. Then, by her cunning, she allowed her son to defeat Seth and assume the throne of Egypt.

Isis was depicted in human form, and was often shown cradling and suckling the infant Horus. As 'Isis great in magic', she was believed to have medicinal skills and to afford protection to the young. Her strong maternal associations gave rise to a connection with HATHOR; hence, from the NEW KINGDOM, Isis was often depicted wearing a headdress of a solar disc between a pair of cattle horns. The cow that gave birth

Ptolemaic bronze statuette of **Isis** *nursing her infant son Horus; this was one of the most popular images in religious art during the later periods of Egyptian history.*

to the APIS bull was regarded as a manifestation of Isis. Her other principal role was in funerary religion: together with her sister NEPHTHYS, she was believed to protect the deceased. Isis was worshipped throughout Egypt; from the LATE PERIOD onwards, her principal cult centre was on the island of PHILAE. Her cult spread throughout the Roman Empire and survived into the Christian period.

Ismant *see* Dakhla Oasis

Israel The term Israel is first attested in the ancient Egyptian sources on a victory STELA (the so-called 'Israel Stela') of MERENPTAH. The inscription lists a

number of defeated cities and peoples in the LEVANT, and includes the sentence 'Israel is laid waste; its seed is no more'. The HIEROGLYPHS make it clear that, to the Egyptians of the 19th Dynasty, 'Israel' signified a people rather than a territory. The biblical Israelites may, in origin, have been a semi-nomadic group from the highlands of central PALESTINE, who were more of an irritation than a threat to Egyptian authority in the region. By the THIRD INTERMEDIATE PERIOD, Egyptian texts indicate that 'Israel' had become a political and territorial entity with which Egypt was forced to engage as part of its wider foreign policy. However, relations between Egypt and Israel, despite their prominence in the Bible, are only sparsely documented in Egyptian inscriptions.

ithyphallic Term used to describe a male figure depicted with a prominent erect penis. Most represen-

The 'Israel Stela' of Merenptah from his mortuary temple at western Thebes; the inscription ends with a list of defeated peoples, including the only known occurrence in ancient Egyptian of the name **Israel**.

The **ithyphallic** fertility god Min, carved on a 12th Dynasty relief block from the temple of Min at Coptos dedicated in the reign of Senusret I.

tations of the god MIN, and many of AMUN-Min, show him in this form.

Itj-tawy Royal residence and capital city founded by AMENEMHAT I at the beginning of the 12th Dynasty (c. 1938 BC), and given the name Amenemhat-itj-tawy ('Amenemhat seizes the TWO LANDS'). Attested only in inscriptions, its precise location remains unclear. It most probably lay near LISHT where Amenemhat built his pyramid. An alternative possibility is that it was a southern suburb of MEMPHIS.

Iuput Name of two ephemeral kings of the late THIRD INTERMEDIATE PERIOD. Iuput I (c. 800 BC) was a ruler of the THEBAN region, probably a co-regent of PEDUBAST I. Iuput II (c. 720 BC) was a local ruler of LEONTOPOLIS who claimed ROYAL TITLES and, with his fellow DELTA potentates, submitted to PIYE when the latter invaded Egypt.

ivory From the BADARIAN period onwards, ancient Egyptian craftsmen used both elephant ivory (from tusks) and hippopotamus ivory (from teeth) to fashion small objects such as statuettes, gaming pieces, labels and cosmetic implements. A high-status material, ivory was always an important trade commodity. Elephant tusks were imported from NUBIA via ELEPHANTINE, while ivory is mentioned frequently in the AMARNA LETTERS.

Izezi *see* Isesi

J

jackal Often shown in desert hunting scenes in tombs of the OLD KINGDOM, MIDDLE KINGDOM and NEW KINGDOM, jackals would have been a familiar sight in ancient Egypt, prowling the cemeteries of the low desert or peering down from the adjacent cliffs. The earliest known representation of a jackal is a Predynastic schist statuette from el-Ahaiwa in UPPER EGYPT. In religious iconography, several gods could be shown in jackal (or less specific, canine) form, including WEPWAWET and KHENTIAMENTIU. The animal associated with ANUBIS may have been a jackal, or a composite creature with elements of the DOG, fox and jackal.

jewelry The ancient Egyptians exhibited a love of ornament and personal decoration from earliest Predynastic times. BADARIAN burials often contained strings of beads made from glazed steatite, shell and IVORY. Jewelry in GOLD, silver, copper and FAIENCE is also attested in the early PREDYNASTIC PERIOD; more varied materials were introduced in the centuries preceding the 1st Dynasty. By the OLD KINGDOM, the combination of CARNELIAN, TURQUOISE and LAPIS LAZULI had been established for royal jewelry, and this was to become standard in the MIDDLE KINGDOM. Less sophisticated pieces might use bone, mother-of-pearl or cowrie shells. The particular choice of materials depended upon practical, aesthetic and symbolic considerations. Some types of jewelry remained perennially popular, while others went in and out of fashion. In

Ivory *gaming pieces, in the form of lions and lionesses, from the tomb of a 1st Dynasty official at Abu Rawash.*

the first category were bead necklaces, bracelets, armlets and girdles. Bead aprons are first attested in the 1st Dynasty, while broad collars became a standard type from the early Old Kingdom. In the Middle Kingdom, anklets became fashionable for men as well as for women, but by the NEW KINGDOM they had fallen from favour, to be replaced by finger-rings and ear ornaments (rings and plugs). New Kingdom jewelry is generally more elaborate and garish than that

of earlier periods, and was influenced by styles from the Aegean and the LEVANT. Many fine examples were found in the tomb of TUTANKHAMUN. Jewelry, both royal and private, was replete with religious symbolism. It was also used to display the wealth and rank of the wearer. Royal jewels were always the most elaborate, as exemplified by the pieces found at DAHSHUR and LAHUN, made for princesses of the 12th Dynasty. In the 18th Dynasty, favoured courtiers were rewarded with the 'gold of honour' as a sign of royal favour.

The techniques of jewelry-making can be reconstructed from surviving artifacts and from TOMB DECORATION. A jewelers' workshop is shown in the tomb of MERERUKA; several New Kingdom tombs at THEBES contain similar scenes. Excavations in the industrial quarter at AMARNA have produced clay moulds for making faience rings, AMULETS and beads. Some jewelry was made specifically for burial, and most surviving pieces come from tombs. The very finest work would have been undertaken in TEMPLE workshops.

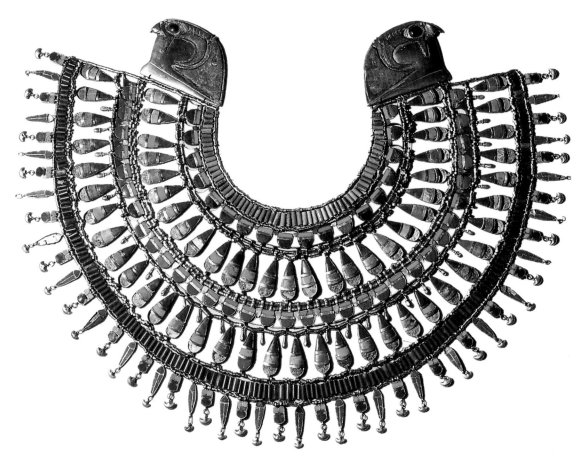

Two examples of ancient Egyptian **jewelry**: (top) pectoral of princess Sithathoriunet, from her tomb at Lahun; the combination of gold, carnelian, lapis lazuli and turquoise in a symbolic composition is typical of the 12th Dynasty; (bottom) 18th Dynasty beaded collar with falcon-head shoulder-pieces belonging to a wife of Thutmose III.

K

ka In Egyptian RELIGION, the life-force which gave each individual, whether human or divine, his or her particular character, nature and temperament. It was represented by the HIEROGLYPH of a pair of upraised arms. ⊔ The ka was believed to come into existence at birth, modelled by KHNUM on his potter's wheel at the same time as the physical body. Even after an individual's death, the ka continued to live as long as it was provided with the necessary protection and sustenance. Hence, a tomb was regarded as the 'house of a ka', the OFFERING FORMULA was designed to provide for the ka in perpetuity, and statues of the deceased were regarded as images of the ka. According to AFTER-LIFE BELIEFS, the successful union of the ka and BA would bring about the transformation of the dead into an AKH. The royal ka was of special importance and was celebrated during the OPET FESTIVAL. It was believed to pass unchanged from each king to his successor, transforming the mortal holder of the office into a semi-divine monarch.

ka chapel Building in the precincts of a provincial temple, established to provide its owner, after death, with the opportunity to participate in the rituals, and share in the offerings redistributed from the main cult. Like a temple in miniature, a ka chapel was endowed with its own estates to provide for the mortuary cult in perpetuity. Kings of the 6th Dynasty built several ka chapels, at BUBASTIS (TETI and PEPI II) and HIERAKON-POLIS (PEPI I); MENTUHOTEP II endowed one at DENDERA. The temple of OSIRIS-KHENTIAMENTIU at ABYDOS was the location for royal ka chapels from the OLD KINGDOM to the RAMESSIDE period. Private ka chapels are also attested, at ELEPHANTINE and in the DAKHLA OASIS. The term ka chapel may also be used to refer to the chamber in the superstructure of a tomb with the FALSE DOOR and OFFERING TABLE, providing the KA of the deceased with access to offerings.

Kadesh, Battle of Military encounter between the Egyptian army, under RAMESSES II, and the HITTITES, under their king Muwatallis. It took place in the 5th year of Ramesses II's reign (c. 1275 BC), near the city of Kadesh (Tell Neby Mend) on the River Orontes in central Syria. Thirteen copies of the Egyptian account

*Relief from the temple of Ramesses II at Abydos showing the aftermath of the Battle of **Kadesh**: slaughtered Hittite and Syrian soldiers, and horses, lie fallen on the banks of the River Orontes.*

survive on PAPYRUS and on the walls of Ramesses II's temples (including LUXOR TEMPLE, ABU SIMBEL and the RAMESSEUM). Kadesh was a strategically important town, commanding the route to inland Syria, and hence eagerly contested by the major powers in the region. Ramesses sent his main army northwards by an inland route, through territory under Egyptian control. An extra division of elite troops was dispatched along the coast. Misled by false information from two captured tribesmen, the main Egyptian force was subject to a surprise attack by the Hittites before it could con-

solidate its position. Only the arrival of the elite troops saved the Egyptians from immediate defeat. The battle continued the following day, but ended inconclusively. The Hittites then drove the Egyptians back south, successfully capturing their two northernmost provinces in the LEVANT. Eventually, Ramesses II signed a peace treaty with the new Hittite king Hattusilis III. Despite an ambiguous result, the Battle of Kadesh was presented in the Egyptian record as a great victory for the king.

Kagemni High official of the early 6th Dynasty. His MASTABA tomb, near the PYRAMID of TETI at SAQQARA, is famous for its beautifully decorated chambers.

Kahun Walled town near LAHUN at the eastern edge of the FAYUM. Although founded to house the personnel serving SENUSRET II's mortuary cult, it grew into a flourishing community with its own mayor. It is one of few surviving examples of a complete Egyptian settlement, and bears all the hallmarks of a state foundation, being laid out on a strict grid system. A wall divides the town into western and eastern sectors, the former comprising barrack-like dwellings for the general population, the latter administrative buildings and the larger villas of officials. Remarkable preservation of architecture and artifacts has provided a rich source of evidence for life in the MIDDLE KINGDOM. Most of the houses were single storey, with stairs to the roof. Walls were plastered and painted. Objects found inside the houses include items associated with private RELIGION, tools, agricultural and weaving equipment, GAMES and JEWELRY. Among the POTTERY were imports from CRETE and locally made imitations. Large numbers of HIERATIC papyri include the earliest known gynaecological text, religious documents, and private LETTERS. The site had a substantial foreign component to its population, illustrating the cosmopolitan nature of Middle Kingdom society.

Kalabsha Site on the west bank of the NILE in Lower NUBIA, 50 km (31 miles) south of ASWAN. First settled in the reign of AMENHOTEP II, the site is best known for its temple to the local Nubian god MANDULIS, built in the ROMAN PERIOD. To save the temple from the rising waters of Lake Nasser, it was dismantled in the 1960s and re-erected at a new site (New Kalabsha) just south of the Aswan High Dam.

Victory stela set up by **Kamose** in the temple of Amun-Ra at Karnak to commemorate his military successes against the Hyksos during the wars of reunification at the start of the 18th Dynasty.

Kamose (throne name: Wadjkheperra) (c. 1541–c. 1539 BC) Last king of the 17th Dynasty. The son or younger brother of TAA II, Kamose reigned for only three years, but made a decisive contribution to the THEBAN struggle against the HYKSOS. Details of his campaign, which extended Theban control as far north as CUSAE, are inscribed on two STELAE erected at KARNAK. They also record military activity against KUSH, an ally of the Hyksos. Kamose was buried at DRA ABU EL-NAGA, in a pyramid-style tomb.

Kamutef ('Bull of his mother') An epithet applied to AMUN-RA, MIN or the combined deity Amun-Min. It expressed the idea that the god was self-engendered, through impregnation of his own mother, and thus the concept of legitimate descent without ancestry. Amun-Min-Kamutef is depicted on the White Chapel of SENUSRET I at KARNAK.

Karanis *see* Fayum

Karnak Vast religious complex on the east bank of the NILE at THEBES (modern Luxor), and one of the greatest treasurehouses of ancient Egyptian ART, SCULPTURE and architecture. The monuments of Karnak were continuously added to and rebuilt, and they span a large part of pharaonic history, from the early MIDDLE KINGDOM to the ROMAN PERIOD.

The main temple, dedicated to AMUN-RA, was called in ancient Egyptian *ipet sut*, 'the most select of places'. It was founded in the 11th Dynasty, although most of the visible buildings date to the NEW KINGDOM. A survivor from the Middle Kingdom temple is the White Chapel of SENUSRET I, discovered as a series of reused blocks, and now re-erected in the Open Air Museum at the site. With the accession of the Theban 18th Dynasty, Amun-Ra was elevated to the position of state god; Karnak, his principal cult centre, became the focus of royal activity on an unprecedented scale. Endowed with huge estates, it was an economic institution of national importance, its priesthood the most powerful in the country. The temple of Amun-Ra is laid out along two ceremonial axes, with a large SACRED LAKE at their junction. The principal axis extends east to west, from the sanctuary to the front of the temple, where a stone quay originally connected with the Nile via a canal. The secondary axis runs north to south. A series of PYLONS and courts, embellished with obelisks (notably of HATSHEPSUT and THUTMOSE I), shrines and altars, were erected by successive kings, especially during the 18th and 19th Dynasties. Most impressive is the vast HYPOSTYLE HALL of SETI I and RAMESSES II. At the rear of the temple,

THUTMOSE III built a sumptuously decorated Festival Hall to celebrate his SED FESTIVAL. The present granite sanctuary was installed in the reign of Philip Arrhidaeus, ALEXANDER THE GREAT's successor.

A second major complex at Karnak is dedicated to the goddess MUT. Like the Amun precinct, it is surrounded by a high enclosure wall. At its centre is a horseshoe-shaped lake. Hundreds of statues of Mut in her leonine aspect, dedicated by AMENHOTEP III, were found in the temple. An avenue of sphinxes leads southwards from the Mut complex towards LUXOR TEMPLE. The third precinct, founded by Amenhotep III, is dedicated to MONTU and includes a small temple to MAAT. Besides these three principal enclosures, there are other, smaller buildings dedicated to PTAH, Opet and KHONSU. AKHENATEN built a series of temples to the ATEN outside Karnak's eastern enclosure wall; they were dismantled by HOREMHEB and their TALATAAT blocks reused in later constructions (at Karnak and Luxor). Reassembly of these reliefs is but one element of a huge international programme of recording, excavation and conservation being carried out at Karnak.

Kashta King of KUSH during the THIRD INTERMEDIATE PERIOD (c. 770–c. 747 BC), who expanded his contol into Lower NUBIA and assumed Egyptian ROYAL TITLES but cannot be said to have ruled Egypt. His predecessor was ALARA and his successor was PIYE.

Kawa Site on the east bank of the NILE in Upper NUBIA, 55 km (34 miles) south of KERMA. Remains include a shrine built by TAHARQO.

Kemet The ancient Egyptian name for Egypt. It means 'black land', and referred to the black fertile silt of the NILE Valley, by contrast with the 'red land' (*deshret*) of the deserts either side.

Kemit Text for scribal training, preserved in copies from the NEW KINGDOM, but composed in the early MIDDLE KINGDOM. It was evidently a well-known text, and is mentioned in the SATIRE OF THE TRADES. It comprises three sections: a selection of greetings used in letter writing; a narrative concluding with a model letter; and a selection of phrases used in idealizing AUTOBIOGRAPHIES.

Kenamun Name of two high officials of the 18th Dynasty. One was chief steward of AMENHOTEP II and superintendent of the royal dockyard near MEMPHIS; his tomb at western THEBES is famous for

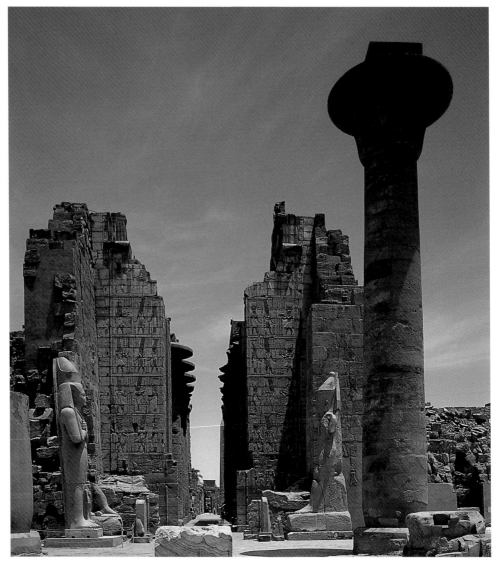

*View of the forecourt of the temple of Amun-Ra at **Karnak**, looking eastwards towards the second pylon and the Ramesside hypostyle hall; the large papyriform column in the foreground once formed part of a kiosk built by the 25th Dynasty king Taharqo.*

its decoration, and one of his SHABTIS is the earliest surviving piece of GLASS SCULPTURE. The other Kenamun was mayor of THEBES in the reign of AMENHOTEP III.

Kerma Site on the east bank of the NILE in Upper NUBIA, near the Third CATARACT. Occupying a strategic location astride trade routes between sub-Saharan Africa, the Red Sea and Egypt, Kerma may possibly be the land of YAM, mentioned in Egyptian inscriptions of the 6th Dynasty. The town was almost certainly the capital of the Kingdom of KUSH from the late OLD KINGDOM to the end of the SECOND INTERMEDIATE PERIOD. Today the site is dominated by two large mud-brick monuments dating from the 17th century BC,

known as the western and eastern *deffufa*. The former is probably the remains of a temple in the centre of the settlement, the latter a funerary chapel attached to the nearby cemetery for members of the ruling elite. The tumulus burials of the Kushite rulers yielded evidence of HUMAN SACRIFICE. A further cemetery on the desert edge, 3 km (2 miles) northeast of the town, is estimated to comprise over 30,000 graves. Kerma is the type-site for the Upper Nubian culture of the early 2nd millennium BC, characterized in the Second Intermediate Period by burnished tulip-shaped beakers and jugs of black-topped red pottery ('Kerma ware'). Kerma was destroyed in the early 18th Dynasty, probably during a campaign led by THUTMOSE II to annex Nubia.

Kha Architect and director of works at DEIR EL-MEDINA in the 18th Dynasty. The intact tomb of Kha and his wife Merit was discovered by an Italian expedition in the early 20th century AD. The contents, now in the Museo Egizio, Turin, show the range and quality of craftsmanship available to a member of the Deir el-Medina community.

Khaba (c. 2600 BC) King of the mid-3rd Dynasty. His position in the dynasty is not certain, but he was probably SEKHEMKHET's successor. He is very sparsely attested and probably reigned for only a few years. An unfinished pyramid (the 'Layer Pyramid') at ZAWIYET EL-ARYAN is attributed to him on the basis of inscribed stone vessels found in a nearby MASTABA. The name of Khaba has also been found on mud sealings at HIERAKONPOLIS and ELEPHANTINE.

Khababash (c. 335 BC) Ephemeral king who ruled briefly over LOWER EGYPT during the 31st Dynasty (the second PERSIAN PERIOD), probably in opposition to the Persians. The burial of an APIS bull at SAQQARA is dated to his reign; he is also known to have made a grant of land to the temple of WADJET at BUTO.

Khaemwaset ('Risen in THEBES') Fourth son of the 19th Dynasty king RAMESSES II, by his wife Isetnofret. Born during the reign of his grandfather SETI I, he accompanied his father on military campaigns while still a child. He became a priest of PTAH at MEMPHIS, rising to the rank of High Priest. His responsibilities included the cult of the APIS; to accommodate the burials of the sacred BULLS he founded the SERAPEUM, which was to remain in use for the next thousand years. He was also put in charge of his father's SED FESTIVALS. Dubbed 'the first Egyptologist', he had a strong personal interest in Egypt's past and especially the ancient monuments of the MEMPHITE NECROPOLIS. Inscriptions on many of the SUN TEMPLES and pyramids, notably the pyramid of UNAS, record restoration work carried out under his orders. He may even have conducted excavations at GIZA. A cult building of Khaemwaset has recently been discovered at SAQQARA, overlooking the pyramids of ABUSIR. He predeceased his father, and is assumed to have been buried in the Memphite area, although his tomb has not yet been located. In later tradition, he was revered as a magician.

Khafra (Khafre, Chephren) (c. 2500 BC) Fourth king of the 4th Dynasty. Probably a younger brother of

*Beaker of distinctive **Kerma** ware, found in the 17th Dynasty burial of a high-status woman at Qurna in western Thebes; remains of the string bag in which it was carried can still be seen.*

*Detail of a diorite statue of **Khafra** from his valley temple at Giza; the falcon perched behind the king's head symbolizes the god Horus protecting his earthly incarnation.*

his predecessor DJEDEFRA, he emulated his father KHUFU by building the second pyramid at GIZA. Its well-preserved VALLEY TEMPLE contained several seated statues of the king, carved in diorite from quarries at Gebel el-Asr in the Western Desert of Lower NUBIA. It is generally assumed that Khafra was responsible for carving the Great SPHINX from an existing knoll of rock.

Khamudi (c. 1530–c. 1520 BC) Last king of the HYKSOS 15th Dynasty, whose defeat by AHMOSE resulted in the

Statue of **Khasekhem** *from the temple at Hierakonpolis; the base is incised with figures of fallen combatants, labelled 'northern enemies', suggesting a period of civil war during the early part of the king's reign, before he changed his name to Khasekhemwy.*

reunification of Egypt and the beginning of the NEW KINGDOM.

Kharga Oasis Fertile region in the Western Desert, to the east of the DAKHLA OASIS and hence closer to the NILE Valley. It was important at all periods as a staging post on caravan routes between Egypt, the other oases, and NUBIA. On his expedition to YAM in the reign of MERENRA, HARKHUF took the 'oasis road' via Kharga. Administered by the governors of THIS from the 18th Dynasty, Kharga is listed in LUXOR TEMPLE as one of the regions which supplied stone for RAMESSES II's building projects. Few archaeological remains earlier than the 26th Dynasty have yet been unearthed, except for scattered prehistoric settlements and PETRO-GLYPHS, an isolated 4th Dynasty bowl, and MIDDLE KINGDOM pottery at sites in the north of the oasis. The principal standing monuments are the temple of AMUN at HIBIS, a series of settlements and fortresses dating to the ROMAN period, and an early Christian cemetery of decorated mud-brick tombs at Bagawat.

Khasekhem *see* Khasekhemwy

Khasekhemwy (c. 2675 BC) Last king of the 2nd Dynasty, and one of the best attested rulers of the EARLY DYNASTIC period. At the beginning of his reign, he adopted the HORUS NAME Khasekhem ('the power has appeared'). At this stage, his power may have been restricted to UPPER EGYPT. Later, for reasons which remain obscure but may have been connected with national reunification, he added the SETH animal to the top of his SEREKH and changed his name to the dual form Khasekhemwy ('the two powers have appeared'). His surviving monuments are numerous and impressive. Three from the first part of his reign were found in the temple of HORUS at HIERAKONPOLIS: a victory STELA recording action against NUBIA; and two life-size seated statues, inscribed on the base with images of slain enemies labelled as 'northern enemies 47,209', perhaps commemorating a successful campaign against LOWER EGYPT.

In the latter part of his reign Khasekhemwy built impressive mud-brick enclosures at Hierakonpolis ('the Fort') and ABYDOS (the SHUNET EL-ZEBIB), and undertook work in the temples at GEBELEIN and ELKAB. A stone vessel fragment with the name of Khasekhemwy has been found in the temple at BYBLOS, indicating the beginning of sustained trading contacts with the Lebanese coast. This would appear to be confirmed by a reference to shipbuilding on the PALERMO STONE, and the recent excavation of a fleet of cedar boats next to the Shunet el-Zebib.

Khasekhemwy's tomb at Abydos has a burial chamber lined with blocks of dressed limestone, fore-shadowing the construction of the STEP PYRAMID at SAQQARA. FUNERARY OBJECTS recovered from the tomb include a sceptre fashioned from the precious stone sard, with bands of gold; two limestone vases with sheet gold covers; and the earliest bronze vessels (a ewer and basin) yet found in Egypt. Khasekhemwy's wife, Nimaathap, was the mother of the next king, DJOSER.

kheker frieze Stylized representation of the knotted ends of matting, used as a decorative motif in ART and architecture from the 3rd Dynasty onwards. It alluded to the first shrine, which, according to Egyptian RELIGION, was built from reed mats and stood on the PRIMEVAL MOUND.

Khendjer (throne name: Userkara) (late 18th century BC) King (sixteenth or seventeenth) of the 13th Dynasty whose name may be of Asiatic origin. He reigned for only four years but left a number of monuments. His PYRAMID at south SAQQARA was the only such monument of the 13th Dynasty to be completed, and took inspiration from the earlier monument of AMEN-EMHAT III at HAWARA. Fragments of Khendjer's black granite PYRAMIDION were found near his pyramid. At ABYDOS, his name was inscribed on the stone bed installed in the tomb of DJER, which had come to be identified and venerated as the tomb of the god OSIRIS.

Khentiamentiu Funerary god of ABYDOS whose cult and attributes were absorbed by OSIRIS at the end of the OLD KINGDOM. Khentiamentiu, whose name 'foremost of the westerners' refers to the inhabitants of the land of the dead, was depicted as a JACKAL or DOG.

Khentkawes Mother of SAHURA and NEFERIRKARA, revered as the ancestress of the 5th Dynasty. She was buried at GIZA in a huge stone MASTABA, located close to the VALLEY TEMPLE of MENKAURA. Her funerary complex included a BOAT BURIAL and a pyramid town to accommodate the priests of her mortuary cult.

Khepri Creator god worshipped in the form of a SCARAB beetle. Because scarabs were seen to emerge from balls of dung, they were thought to be capable of spontaneous generation, and were thus linked with ATUM. Their habit of pushing a ball of dung along the ground also suggested a connection with the sun disc rising into the sky at dawn, and thus with the sunrise aspect of RA. Khepri is first mentioned in the PYRAMID TEXTS, and was depicted as a scarab or a man with a scarab's head.

Khety (Akhtoy) Popular name in the FIRST INTERMEDIATE PERIOD and early MIDDLE KINGDOM. It was borne by several kings of the 9th/10th Dynasty from HERAKLEOPOLIS (c. 2100 BC), one of whom is the unnamed author of the INSTRUCTION FOR MERIKARA. The SATIRE OF THE TRADES is attributed to a different author called Khety.

Khnum Ram god associated with the INUNDATION. First attested in the PYRAMID TEXTS, he later came to be regarded as the BA of the sun god. From the early 18th Dynasty, he was worshipped as a creator god who formed humans on a potter's wheel. His main cult centre was at ELEPHANTINE, where he was venerated in

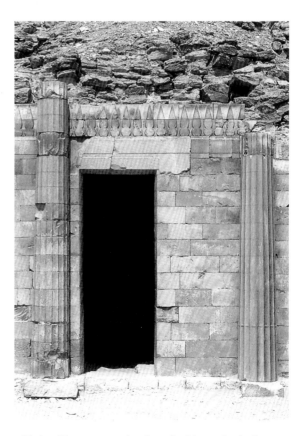

A **kheker frieze**, representing the stylized, knotted ends of a woven mat, decorates the upper façade of the 'House of the South' in the 3rd Dynasty Step Pyramid complex of Djoser at Saqqara.

The scarab-headed god **Khepri**, *in a painted relief from the 19th Dynasty tomb of Nefertari in the Valley of the Queens.*

a TRIAD with SATET and ANKET. The Famine STELA on SEHEL island records an appeal to Khnum made during a time of hunger caused by low NILE floods. It dates to the PTOLEMAIC PERIOD, as does the temple to Khnum at ESNA. Khnum was depicted as a long-horned ram, or as a man with a ram's head.

Khnumhotep (II) NOMARCH of the early 12th Dynasty whose rock-cut tomb at BENI HASAN has a famous scene showing the arrival in Egypt of a group of Asiatic traders. Khnumhotep's son, also called Khnumhotep (III), served in the Eastern Desert under SENUSRET II, and went on to achieve high office as royal chancellor and VIZIER. He died in the reign of AMENEMHAT III and was buried in a magnificent tomb at DAHSHUR; a narrative text inscribed on the monument's eastern façade records Egyptian involvement in a military dispute between BYBLOS and a neighbouring city-state on the north Syrian coast.

Khokhah Area of the Theban NECROPOLIS between ASASIF and SHEIKH ABD EL-QURNA. It contains the tombs of the OLD KINGDOM NOMARCHS of THEBES, together with private burials of the FIRST INTERMEDIATE PERIOD, 18th and 19th Dynasties. It was particularly popular for the tombs of high officials during the reigns of HATSHEPSUT, THUTMOSE III and AMENHOTEP III.

Khonsu Moon god with a complex set of associations. In the PYRAMID TEXTS and COFFIN TEXTS, he has a bloodthirsty nature, but in later periods he was worshipped as a healing deity. In the Theban region, he was regarded as the son of AMUN and MUT, and this association brought his cult to prominence in the NEW KINGDOM. In the 20th Dynasty, a temple to Khonsu was built within the precincts of the temple of Amun at KARNAK. Khonsu was linked with other child deities, especially SHU and HORUS, while at KOM OMBO he was worshipped as the son of SOBEK and HATHOR. He was usually depicted as a mummiform male, with the head of a FALCON, holding a sceptre and wearing the SIDE-LOCK OF YOUTH. His distinctive headddress comprised a crescent moon surmounted by a full moon. He could also be shown as a baboon.

Khufu (Cheops) (c. 2550 BC) Second king of the 4th Dynasty, and celebrated as the builder of the Great Pyramid at GIZA. Despite his fame, a tiny ivory statuette from ABYDOS is the only certain representation of him. He sent mining expeditions to HATNUB and the SINAI, and is also attested at BYBLOS. Later tradition viewed Khufu as a tyrant, as exemplified in the MIDDLE KINGDOM TALES OF WONDER.

Khyan (throne name: Suserenra) (c. 1610–c. 1570 BC) King of the HYKSOS 15th Dynasty, the predecessor of APEPI. He may have reigned for 40 years. He is attested in Egypt at GEBELEIN and BUBASTIS, where he seems to

*Painted relief from the temple of **Khnum** at Elephantine showing the ram-headed god, who was associated with the inundation, with the pharaoh Thutmose III, 18th Dynasty.*

*Granite statue of the god **Khonsu**, from his temple at Karnak; the child of Amun and Mut, Khonsu wears the sidelock of youth. His features are those of Tutankhamun, who commissioned the sculpture.*

*Ivory statuette of **Khufu** from Abydos; this tiny sculpture (about 7.6 cm/3 in high) is the only certain representation of the king who built the Great Pyramid.*

have carried out temple building, and further afield on objects found at Knossos (CRETE), Hattusas (capital of the HITTITES) and Baghdad. Khyan was the first Hyksos ruler to adopt full ROYAL TITLES, instead of the epithet *heka-khasut* ('ruler of foreign lands').

king-lists The ideology of KINGSHIP demanded that the institution be seen as an inheritance from the gods, passing in an unbroken line through a succession of legitimate rulers down to the current holder. In accordance with this myth of monarchy, lists of rulers were drawn up for display in sacred contexts, to reinforce the legitimacy of the king and celebrate his royal ancestors. The earliest such list is the PALERMO STONE, dating to the late OLD KINGDOM. Despite the likelihood that such king-lists were used by the priest MANETHO to compile his HISTORY of Egypt, they cannot be regarded as objective sources, but instead as tools by which the royal court promoted an idealized view of itself. The two most extensive king-lists from cult contexts are those from the temples of SETI I and RAMESSES II at ABYDOS. Both begin with MENES and end with the reigning king. They omit those rulers who were seen as having departed from the ideal, such as the HYKSOS, HATSHEPSUT, and the kings of the AMARNA period, notably AKHENATEN. THUTMOSE III had a shorter list of ancestors inscribed at KARNAK. A yet more abbreviated list was included in a private tomb at SAQQARA, indicating the popularity of the cult of royal ancestors in the late NEW KINGDOM. Other, shorter groups of kings were occasionally included in texts. A MIDDLE KINGDOM quarrying inscription in the WADI HAMMAMAT names five kings and princes of the 4th Dynasty. The exception among king-lists is the RAMESSIDE PAPYRUS known as the Turin Canon. Uniquely, it seems to have aspired to completeness, and included even the Hyksos rulers, though much has now been lost.

kingship The ideology surrounding the king was perhaps the single most important and pervasive influence on ancient Egyptian civilization. The institution of monarchy lay at the centre of state RELIGION, the multifarious roles of the king featured prominently in ART, while the celebration of the king's unique status produced a dazzling array of monuments, including the pyramids and the tombs in the VALLEY OF THE KINGS. The concept of the ruler can be traced back to the PREDYNASTIC PERIOD, and is most fully expressed in the ROYAL TITLES. These emphasized the king's symbolic

The Abydos **king-list**, *carved on the wall of a corridor in the temple of Seti I; the list was the focus of the cult of the royal ancestors, allowing Seti and his son, the future Ramesses II, to associate themselves with their long line of forebears.*

role in balancing and reconciling opposing forces, be they HORUS and SETH, the geographical halves of the Egyptian realm, or the many other manifestations of DUALITY inherent in the ancient Egyptian world-view. The primary duty of the king was to safeguard the continuity of the country and of created order, by upholding the values of MAAT, maintaining the cults of the gods and goddesses, and defeating Egypt's enemies.

At the heart of kingship ideology lay a conundrum, the need to reconcile the obvious mortality of the king with his quasi divine status. From a very early stage, the king was explicitly associated with the gods. His Horus name, the earliest royal title, proclaimed him as the earthly incarnation of the celestial deity. Yet the title 'son of RA', which was introduced in the 4th Dynasty, clearly identified the king as junior partner in his relationship with the supreme god. The king effectively occupied an intermediary position between human and divine states, making him the natural channel of communication. In a further development of this ideology, a distinction was drawn between the divinity of the office of kingship (which, by means of the royal KA, passed unchanged down the generations), and the mortality of the individual holder. This difference may be reflected in the two words for 'king', *nesut* and *bity*.

The Egyptian king was an absolute ruler: head of state and of government, ultimate judicial authority, commander of the armed forces, and high priest of every cult. In practice, the last responsibility was delegated to royal appointees, although temple decoration upheld the theory by showing the king himself carrying out the necessary rites before the deity. The office of kingship usually passed from father to son. However, according to ideology, succession depended, above all, on carrying out the duties of an heir, especially supervising the burial of the preceding king with all the necessary rites. This conformed to the notion that each new ruler acted as Horus for his predecessor, identified with OSIRIS. Hence, in the tomb of TUTANKHAMUN, his successor AY – who was not the nominated heir – is shown performing the OPENING OF THE MOUTH ceremony. The myth of divine birth could also be deployed to bolster a ruler's legitimacy, as was done by HATSHEPSUT. Despite palace coups, assassinations, periods of political fragmentation and other challenges to the monarchy, the official record promoted the notion that kingship had passed in an unbroken succession since the time of the gods. Remarkably, the institution remained the only acceptable form of government, and the defining facet of Egyptian civilization, for more than three thousand years.

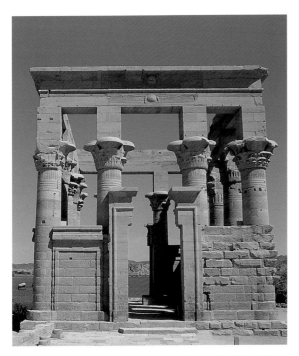

The **kiosk** built by the Roman emperor Trajan on the island of Philae, now relocated along with its adjacent monuments to the nearby island of Agilqiyya.

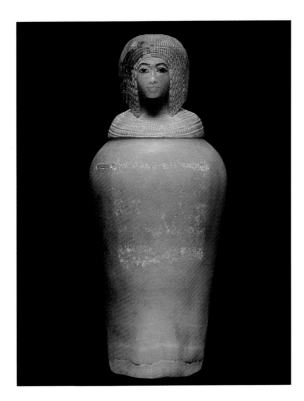

One of four canopic jars found in tomb 55 in the Valley of the Kings; it was probably made for Akhenaten's secondary wife **Kiya**, before being adapted for use by a different individual at the end of the Amarna period.

kiosk Small temple with an openwork perimeter of pillars. The best examples are the White Chapel of SENUSRET I at KARNAK and Trajan's kiosk at PHILAE.

Kiya Secondary wife of AKHENATEN, thought by some to have been the mother of TUTANKHAMUN. She is prominent at AMARNA in the early part of Akhenaten's reign, and bore the unique title 'Greatly Beloved Wife'; on WINE dockets she is referred to as 'The Noble Lady'. She has been identified by some scholars as princess Tadukhepa, daughter of the king of the MITANNI, who was sent to cement relations with Egypt, but there is no independent evidence for this theory. She disappears from the record at AMARNA after Akhenaten's 11th regnal year, coinciding with NEFERTITI's rise to prominence. Kiya's monuments were taken over by MERITATEN; her COFFIN and CANOPIC JARS were reused for a royal burial (KV55) in the VALLEY OF THE KINGS.

kohl *see* cosmetics

Kom Abu Billo Site in the western DELTA; as the town of Terenuthis, it flourished in the PTOLEMAIC and ROMAN PERIODS as a trading centre for salt and NATRON.

Kom el-Ahmar *see* Hierakonpolis

Kom el-Hisn Site in the western DELTA, about 12 km (7.5 miles) south of NAUKRATIS. The town mound has been greatly eroded by SEBAKH diggers, but still preserves remains of OLD KINGDOM houses. The town may have been a state-sponsored cattle-breeding centre or a trading post on the route to LIBYA. In the MIDDLE KINGDOM, a temple was built to the goddess SEKHMET-HATHOR; a decorated tomb of the period has recently been excavated. In the NEW KINGDOM, the town became capital of the third Lower Egyptian NOME. The cemetery contains graves dating from the FIRST INTERMEDIATE PERIOD to the New Kingdom.

Kom Ombo Site on the east bank of the NILE in southern UPPER EGYPT, best known for its temple to SOBEK and Haroeris ('HORUS the elder'). Reused blocks suggest a temple was first founded in the MIDDLE KINGDOM, but the surviving remains at the site date from the 18th Dynasty onwards. The current temple, with well-preserved decoration, is situated in an elevated position overlooking the Nile; it was built mainly in the PTOLEMAIC and ROMAN PERIODS. It is unique in Egypt for its dual dedication, reflected in its plan, with

*The temple of **Kom Ombo**, built during the reign of Ptolemy XII, is unique in its twin dedication to the gods Sobek and Haroeris.*

twin ceremonial axes and twin sanctuaries; it is also unusual in having a corridor surrounding the main building on three sides. Mummified CROCODILES have been found in the vicinity, even though the temple gives primacy to Haroeris over the crocodile god Sobek. A Ptolemaic MAMMISI stands to the west of the temple. In the Ptolemaic period, Kom Ombo was an administrative centre for the first Upper Egyptian NOME, and a market for the ELEPHANTS brought from Ethiopia via the Red Sea to serve in the Egyptian ARMY. Further archaeological sites in the surrounding region include prehistoric settlements and a Coptic church.

Koptos *see* Coptos

Kurgus Site on the west bank of the NILE in the Fourth CATARACT region of Upper NUBIA, where THUTMOSE I and THUTMOSE III each carved an inscription to define the southernmost extent of Egyptian control.

Kurru, el- Site on the west bank of the NILE in Upper NUBIA, downstream of the Fourth CATARACT. The town may have been the residence of the ancestors of the 25th Dynasty, before the rise of GEBEL BARKAL. A major royal necropolis comprises the tumulus burials of the KUSHITE kings, and the PYRAMID tombs of the 25th Dynasty rulers PIYE, SHABAQO, SHABITQO and TANU-TAMANI, together with burials of their queens and 24

horse burials. Each pyramid had an underground burial chamber, reached by a long descending staircase, and an undecorated funerary chapel. In the mid-7th century BC, el-Kurru was replaced as the main royal cemetery by NURI, and was subsequently abandoned.

Kush Kingdom in the Third CATARACT region of Upper NUBIA, and Egypt's main enemy during the MIDDLE KINGDOM and SECOND INTERMEDIATE PERIOD. From their capital at KERMA, the kings of Kush controlled a large fertile area and valuable trade routes between the NILE Valley and sub-Saharan Africa. No written records exist from the Kushite side, so the history and development of Kush must be traced in the Egyptian sources. The name Kush is first mentioned on a STELA of SENUS-RET I, erected at BUHEN to celebrate his conquest of Lower Nubia. The wish to defend this newly annexed territory from attack, and to restrain the Kushite threat, seems to have been the primary motive for the construction, in the 12th Dynasty, of a line of fortresses stretching from ASWAN to the Second cataract. Peaceful coexistence between the two powers came to an end with the onset of the Second Intermediate Period. Kush expanded into Lower Nubia following the Egyptian withdrawal, then formed an alliance with the HYKSOS kings against the THEBAN rulers of the 17th Dynasty, as recorded on the stela of KAMOSE. Evidence has recently come to light at ELKAB for a major Kushite invasion of

UPPER EGYPT, perhaps as far north as CUSAE, at this period. Kush was finally defeated by THUTMOSE I who conquered Kerma and imposed Egyptian colonial rule over Nubia. The VICEROY OF KUSH governed the entire territory on behalf of the king, but periodic military campaigns were still required to put down rebellions. The retreat of Egyptian forces at the end of the NEW KINGDOM paved the way for a resurgence of Kushite power. In a reversal of fortune, a line of Kushite kings from NAPATA succeeded in conquering Egypt, where they ruled as the 25th Dynasty. After the ASSYRIAN invasion, the last Kushite king, TANUTAMANI, was forced to retreat back to his Nubian heartland. The kingdom of Kush, eventually based at MEROË, remained a regional power until the 4th century   . In Egyptian texts of the New Kingdom, the term Kush is sometimes used to refer to the southern half of Egyptian-controlled Nubia (the northern half being known as WAWAT).

Kushite Belonging to, or characteristic of, the territory of KUSH.

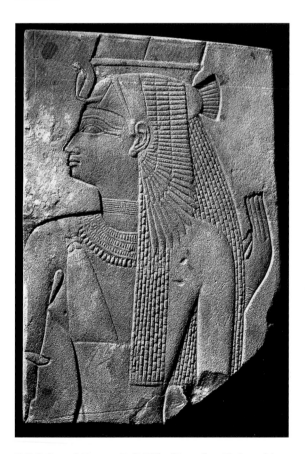

Relief of a 25th Dynasty God's Wife of Amun from Thebes, with some of the distinctive features of **Kushite** *art, such as the prominent wing of the nose and the shortened lower half of the face.*

L

labyrinth Name given by Classical authors to the mortuary temple of AMENEMHAT III at HAWARA, because of its numerous chapels and corridors, though very little survives today.

Lahun (el-Lahun, Illahun) Site at the eastern edge of the FAYUM, 70 km (44 miles) south of DAHSHUR, where SENUSRET II built his funerary complex. The PYRAMID itself was originally faced with limestone, and was constructed in mud-brick around a natural knoll of rock, with stone retaining walls to give greater stability. A hoard of JEWELRY belonging to princess Sithathoriunet was found in a nearby shaft tomb. Originally, a row of trees stood alongside the outer enclosure to recall the sacred grove of the OSIRIS myth. Eight MASTABA superstructures of uncertain purpose lie to the west of the pyramid. The remains of the VALLEY TEMPLE have been located a little to the east of the pyramid, at the edge of the town of KAHUN.

language The ancient Egyptian language belongs to the Afro-Asiatic family, and is related to the Berber and Tuareg languages of North Africa. Foreign words, especially from neighbouring Semitic languages, entered Egyptian at all periods, and there was a major influx of Greek vocabulary in the ROMAN PERIOD. Since most of our evidence for ancient Egyptian occurs in the more conservative, written form of the language, it is difficult accurately to assess the development of spoken Egyptian. Nevertheless, it is clear that the two forms had diverged considerably by the MIDDLE KINGDOM, with separate grammatical elements replacing inflected verb endings in the spoken language. Knowledge of how Egyptian was pronounced is also scanty, since the WRITING system did not record vowels until the introduction of the Coptic script in the 3rd century AD.

lapis lazuli Dark blue semi-precious stone highly valued by the ancient Egyptians because of its symbolic association with the heavens. It was imported via long-distance trade routes from the mountains of northeastern Afghanistan, and was considered superior to all other materials except GOLD and silver. Coloured GLASS or FAIENCE provided a cheap imitation. Lapis lazuli is first attested in the PREDYNASTIC PERIOD. A temporary interruption in supply during the 2nd and

3rd Dynasties probably reflects political changes in the Near East. Thereafter, it was used extensively for JEWELRY, small figurines and AMULETS.

Late Period (664–332 BC) The last of the broad phases into which Egyptologists divide pharaonic history. It comprises the centuries between the end of the THIRD INTERMEDIATE PERIOD and the conquest of Egypt by ALEXANDER THE GREAT. Some scholars place the 25th Dynasty in the Late Period, even though Egypt was not truly unified until the beginning of the 26th Dynasty. Others regard the SAITE period as distinct, and begin the Late Period with the 27th Dynasty.

The Late Period as a whole is well documented, with many surviving monuments, but is not as intensively studied as the NEW KINGDOM. In common with the preceding Third Intermediate Period, the Late Period was characterized by the prominence of different ethnic groups within the Egyptian population. It was also an era of personal piety, when ANIMAL CULTS flourished. Court culture looked back to the OLD KINGDOM for inspiration, producing an archaizing style.

law The evidence for the ancient Egyptian legal system comprises records of trials and judgments, preserved on PAPYRUS, OSTRACA, and in tomb inscriptions. At its most fundamental, ancient Egyptian law was based upon the concept of MAAT. Hence, in contrast to other ancient societies, Egypt stressed equality before the law for men and women, for people of high and low status. This changed only in the PTOLEMAIC PERIOD when the Greek legal system ran in parallel to Egyptian law, favouring Greeks. During the pharaonic period, the king was the ultimate judicial authority, and could enact laws by decree. In practice, he delegated authority to the VIZIER, whom anyone with a grievance had the right to petition, even if gaining access must have been difficult in practice.

There may have been a legal code, although none has survived. At the very least, records would have been kept of previous cases and judgments so that subsequent decisions could be based upon legal precedent. Courts (*djadjat*, *qenbet*) are attested from the OLD KINGDOM, each town having its own court consisting of local councillors, so that there was little difference between administrative and judicial authority. There

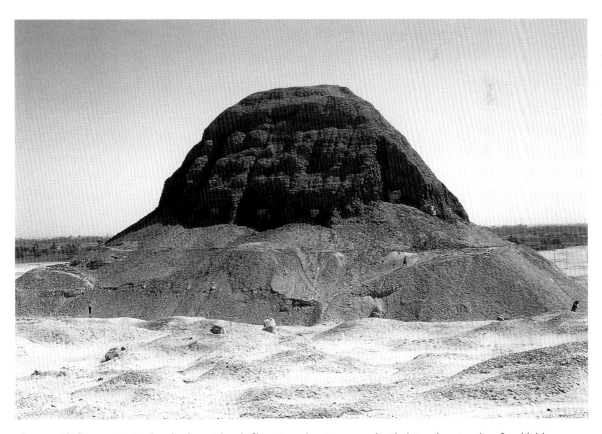

The pyramid of Senusret II at **Lahun** has been stripped of its outer casing stones, exposing the internal construction of mud-bricks.

Early 18th Dynasty bracelet of queen Ahhotep, made of gold inlaid with **lapis lazuli**; *the dark blue stone was highly prized for Egyptian jewelry at all periods.*

was a tiered structure of courts: the local court in MEMPHIS was subordinate to a higher court in HELIOPOLIS, the local court at DEIR EL-MEDINA to a great court in THEBES. A higher level of appeal could be made to the vizier, and ultimately to the king. Difficult cases were sometimes referred to ORACLES for a solution; this became increasingly popular from the NEW KINGDOM onwards.

Evidence has survived for different levels of CRIME AND PUNISHMENT, and for laws of inheritance and divorce, but boundary disputes and matters of land tenure probably constituted the majority of cases brought before the courts. Important sales and other transactions might also be subject to legal registration. In criminal cases, each side put their case before a panel of judges; witness statements were heard; and a judgment was given in the form 'A is right, B is wrong'. In all cases, court proceedings were recorded by SCRIBES.

Leontopolis (Tell el-Muqdam) Site in the central DELTA which became capital of the eleventh Lower Egyptian NOME in the PTOLEMAIC PERIOD. Three statue bases from the site date to the 12th Dynasty, but they may have been brought from elsewhere. The town was probably founded in the NEW KINGDOM or THIRD INTERMEDIATE PERIOD, and may have been a power base of the 23rd Dynasty.

It is assumed that the royal tombs of this period were located in the local temple, which was dedicated to the LION god Mihos (hence the Greek name Leontopolis, 'lion city'). Only the tomb of Queen Kamama,

of unknown antecedents, has been located. Recent excavations have indicated that the town flourished during the first PERSIAN PERIOD.

Lepsius, Karl Richard *see* Egyptology

Letopolis (Ausim) Site on the west bank of the Rosetta branch of the NILE, in the south-western DELTA, 13 km (8 miles) northwest of Cairo. It was the capital of the second Lower Egyptian NOME; its local FALCON god, Khenty-irty (later absorbed by the cult of HORUS), is attested as early as the 3rd Dynasty. To date, only a few monuments have been uncovered, dating to the LATE PERIOD.

letters Many examples of ancient Egyptian correspondence, private, royal and diplomatic, have survived on PAPYRUS, clay tablets, or transcribed on monuments. Particularly important collections include an archive of letters between the 11th Dynasty Theban farmer Hekanakhte and members of his family; private correspondence from KAHUN; the MIDDLE KINGDOM SEMNA despatches (a series of military communications between Egyptian troops in NUBIA and their commanders in THEBES); the AMARNA LETTERS; and a large number of private letters and simple notes from DEIR EL-MEDINA.

Since most of the population was illiterate, scribes would have been employed when writing or reading letters was required. Letter-writing was a skill learned by studying model examples and texts such as the KEMIT. While there must have been a messenger service for official documents, private letters were probably delivered informally.

letters to the dead The ancient Egyptians believed in the power of the dead to affect the lives of the living, for better or worse. Individuals thus sought to communicate with their deceased relatives, to request help or ask for forgiveness. Fewer than twenty such letters have survived, dating from the OLD KINGDOM to the NEW KINGDOM. They were usually written on PAPYRUS or inscribed on POTTERY, and placed in the funerary chapel of the intended recipient. In the LATE PERIOD, letters to dead individuals were probably replaced by direct appeals to deities.

Levant The region bordering the eastern Mediterranean, comprising coastal Syria, Lebanon, and Israel. The term is used interchangeably with Syria-Palestine and the Near East.

Libya Egyptians came into contact, and conflict, with the semi-nomadic peoples living to the west of the NILE Valley from an early period. A ceremonial PALETTE from the end of the PREDYNASTIC period depicts a hoard of booty labelled as the produce of Tjehenu, which was the usual name for northern Libya, as far south as the FAYUM, until the NEW KINGDOM. By contrast, Tjemehu designated southern Libya, to the west of UPPER EGYPT and NUBIA. A cylinder of NARMER shows the king smiting a group of Libyan captives. In this case, the symbolism may be purely ritual, since Libyans, together with Nubians and the 'Asiatic' inhabitants of the LEVANT, were portrayed as archetypal enemies of Egypt from the very beginning of the Egyptian state. Hence, a scene of the king smiting a Libyan chief is included in the mortuary temple of SAHURA, and reappears fifteen hundred years later in the temple of TAHARQO at KAWA. By the New Kingdom, Libyan peoples called the Meshwesh (or Ma) and Libu, probably from the coastal region of Cyrenaica, were attempting to settle in the western DELTA, and were proving a persistent irritant to the Egyptian authorities. RAMESSES II built a fortress at ZAWIYET UMM EL-RAKHAM to defend Egypt against Libyan attack. MERENPTAH launched a campaign to push them back, but they returned at periodic intervals, most notably as allies of the SEA PEOPLES in the reign of RAMESSES III. Prisoners of war were settled in the Delta and gradually became a powerful group in Egyptian society; their descendants achieved power as the 22nd and 23rd Dynasties.

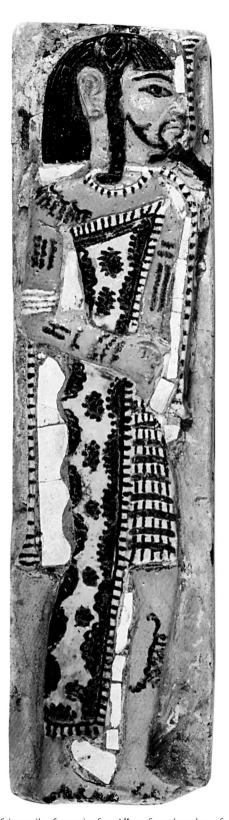

Glazed faience tile of a captive from **Libya**, *from the palace of Ramesses III in his mortuary temple at Medinet Habu, Thebes; he is shown in characteristic dress with tattoos on his arms and legs.*

lion Admired and revered for its strength, ferocity and appearance, the lion was closely associated with the ruler from Predynastic times. Kings kept tame lions as pets; one animal was buried with its master in a 1st Dynasty royal tomb at ABYDOS. Another lion burial has been discovered at SAQQARA. The SPHINX, a human-headed lion, became a powerful symbol of kingship from the early 4th Dynasty. HUNTING lions was considered the ultimate test of royal power; AMENHOTEP III issued commemorative SCARABS to celebrate a particularly successful hunting expedition, and a lion hunt is depicted on the painted box from the tomb of TUTANKHAMUN.

Already rare by the pharaonic period, lions seem nevertheless to have survived in small numbers on Egypt's desert margins. Because of this habitat, they were identified as the guardians of the eastern and western horizons. In Egyptian RELIGION, the sun could be represented as a lion, and a lion deity, AKER, was believed to guard the entrance to the underworld. Another lion deity, Mihos, was the local god of LEONTOPOLIS. However, most lion deities, such as SEKHMET, were female. Lions' paws were popular decorative motifs for the feet of beds and chairs, and temple gargoyles were often shaped like lions' heads.

Ptolemaic statue of a **lion** *in the temple enclosure at Medinet Maadi, on the edge of the Fayum.*

Lisht Site on the west bank of the NILE in northern MIDDLE EGYPT, 50 km (31 miles) south of CAIRO. Lisht was chosen by AMENEMHAT I as a new royal NECROPOLIS, probably because of its proximity to the 12th Dynasty capital of ITJ-TAWY. Amenemhat and his son SENUSRET I built their PYRAMID complexes on either side of a broad valley. The earlier pyramid, in the northern part of the site, reused blocks from OLD KINGDOM monuments at SAQQARA and GIZA. It was the first major royal pyramid to be constructed since that of PEPI II, and combined Old Kingdom MEMPHITE and 11th Dynasty THEBAN architectural traditions. Remains of ramps, slipways and stone-dressing stations provide important evidence about pyramid construction techniques.

The pyramid of Senusret I, located in southern Lisht, marked a return to Old Kingdom proportions, but used a new construction technique based on a grid of retaining walls filled with rubble. The main pyramid was surrounded by ten subsidiary pyramids, one of them for the royal KA; all lay within an enclosure wall, decorated with large SEREKH panels. Ten life-size seated statues of the king were found near the mortuary temple, and two painted wooden statues in a private tomb at Lisht. A court cemetery at the site comprises burials of high officials, and thousands of lesser graves, from the MIDDLE KINGDOM and ROMAN PERIOD.

Litany of Ra *see* hymns

The construction of the pyramid of Amenemhat I at **Lisht** *(seen here beyond a modern Islamic cemetery) marked a deliberate return to Old Kingdom architectural forms at the beginning of the 12th Dynasty.*

literature Many different types of text have survived from ancient Egypt, even though the total corpus must represent only a fraction of what was written. The term 'literature' is sometimes applied to the entire written output, but more accurately designates those works of a distinct literary nature. The various genres identified by modern scholars are useful for categorizing texts, but may not have had the same significance to the ancient Egyptians, especially as several different genres may be combined in a single work, such as the TALE OF SINUHE.

Literature in the strict sense is first attested in the MIDDLE KINGDOM, a period that witnessed unsurpassed creativity and diversity in composition. Fictional works such as the TALE OF THE SHIPWRECKED SAILOR, the TALE OF THE ELOQUENT PEASANT, the TALES OF WONDER, and the undoubted masterpiece, the *Tale of Sinuhe*, testify to the storytelling and dramatic genius of their anonymous authors. Works dealing with the theme of 'national distress' and the darker side of life were a particularly characteristic product of the Middle Kingdom court. They include the PROPHECY OF NEFERTI, the ADMONITIONS OF IPUWER, the DISPUTE OF A MAN WITH HIS BA, and the extraordinary INSTRUCTION OF AMENEMHAT FOR HIS SON. In the NEW KINGDOM, literature began to be composed in the Late Egyptian phase of the LANGUAGE. Again, dramatic tales were popular, as represented by the *Tale of the Predestined Prince* and the TAKING OF JOPPA.

Works written in DEMOTIC first appear in the PTOLEMAIC PERIOD, and include outstanding examples of fictional narrative. At all periods, literature was written by and for a small literate group, and it is difficult to ascertain how widely known the most popular texts became. None the less, the literary achievements of the ancient Egyptians were considerable, even if they are often overshadowed by their ART and architecture.

lotus Term used (incorrectly) by Egyptologists to refer to the water-lily (*Nymphaea*) which was the emblem of UPPER EGYPT and played an important symbolic role in Egyptian RELIGION. Opening in the morning and closing again at night, the water-lily had strong solar connotations. According to one of the CREATION MYTHS, the sun god arose from a water-lily floating on the waters of NUN. Hence, the flower was a symbol of rebirth; Chapter 81 of the BOOK OF THE DEAD is a spell to help the deceased undergo transformation into a water-lily.

One of two 'heraldic pillars' erected by Thutmose III in the centre of Karnak temple is decorated with the so-called **lotus**, the emblematic plant of Upper Egypt.

Two varieties of water-lily, white and blue, were native to ancient Egypt. The blue form was prized for its fragrance, and was the emblem of NEFERTEM, 'lord of perfumes'. The Egyptians may have understood and used the narcotic effect obtained by soaking the petals and roots in alcohol. A third type of water-lily, the true lotus (*Nelumbo*), was introduced from India in the PERSIAN PERIOD.

Lower Egypt The northern half of the TWO LANDS, the duality that comprised the territory of ancient Egypt. Essentially synonymous with the NILE DELTA, Lower Egypt was associated in Egyptian ideology with the goddess WADJET, the red crown, and the SOULS OF PE. Its emblem was the PAPYRUS reed. For administrative purposes, Lower Egypt was divided into NOMES (twenty in the PTOLEMAIC PERIOD), although these were less fixed than in UPPER EGYPT. The first Lower Egyptian nome, the region around MEMPHIS, was viewed as a transitional area between Lower and UPPER EGYPT.

Luxor Temple Well-preserved monument on the east bank of the NILE at THEBES, begun by AMENHOTEP II and embellished by subsequent rulers. Called *ipet resyt*, 'the southern harem', it was a dependent institution to KARNAK; this is illustrated by the unusual orientation of the temple, northwards towards Karnak rather than westwards towards the river. It was dedicated to AMUN KAMUTEF and was built primarily as the setting for the annual OPET FESTIVAL, illustrated in reliefs in the processional colonnade.

*View of **Luxor Temple** looking south down the avenue of sphinxes towards the entrance pylon fronted by an obelisk and colossal statues of Ramesses II.*

Three chambers near the sanctuary housed the BARQUE SHRINES of AMUN, MUT and KHONSU during the festival. Another room has reliefs depicting the divine birth of Amenhotep III. A new forecourt, incorporating an earlier shrine of HATSHEPSUT and THUTMOSE III, was added to the temple by RAMESSES II. In front of the PYLON, decorated with scenes illustrating the Battle of KADESH, stood two massive seated statues of the king, and two OBELISKS; one of the latter now stands in the Place de la Concorde in Paris. The avenue of SPHINXES leading from Karnak was rebuilt by NECTANEBO I, and the main sanctuary of Luxor Temple by ALEXANDER THE GREAT. The Roman emperor Hadrian built a small shrine nearby, dedicated to SERAPIS.

Luxor Temple became a shrine of the imperial cult in the ROMAN PERIOD, the site of a church in the Christian period, and of a mosque after the Islamic conquest. An important collection of statues was discovered in 1989 during conservation work in the 18th Dynasty forecourt; the pieces are now exhibited in the Luxor Museum.

M

Maadi Site on the east bank of the NILE, about 5 km (3 miles) south of the centre of Cairo; today Maadi is a southern suburb of the city. Excavations have revealed an important settlement and cemetery of the early PRE-DYNASTIC PERIOD, characterized by POTTERY, black basalt jars, and other artifacts in a distinctive Lower Egyptian cultural tradition, termed the 'Maadi Culture'. A DONKEY grave suggests that trade caravans operated via the Wadi Digla. Maadi evidently maintained close contacts with PALESTINE since objects from the settlement included imported Palestinian pottery, copper ingots, and flint tools of Palestinian types. Subterranean dwellings in one part of the settlement appear to indicate a Palestininan element in the local population, living side by side with the Egyptian inhabitants. The cemeteries at Maadi and nearby Wadi Digla are characterized by simple burials with few, if any, FUNERARY GOODS. Children were often buried within the settlement. The community at Maadi was apparently abandoned in the middle of the fourth millennium BC, perhaps because of environmental factors, although some continuity of settlement is indicated by a small 1st Dynasty cemetery in the vicinity.

Maadi culture *see* Predynastic period

Maat Concept of cosmic order, truth and justice, personified as a goddess, which lay at the very heart of Egyptian morality and RELIGION. WISDOM LITERATURE of all periods stressed moderation and truthfulness in personal behaviour, while the WEIGHING OF THE HEART ceremony judged the actions of the deceased against the ideal of Maat. The VIZIER held the title 'priest of Maat', and was expected to dispense justice equally and without favour – as was the king, who, as upholder and defender of created order, was the supreme guardian of Maat. To emphasize this pre-eminent role of KINGSHIP, the coronation of HAT-SHEPSUT took place in the temple of Maat, within the precinct of MONTU at KARNAK; in the 20th Dynasty, the same location was used for the trial of those accused of robbing the royal tombs. AKHENATEN described himself as 'living by Maat' (an alternative translation is 'living on Maat'). The village of DEIR EL-MEDINA, which housed the workmen responsible for building the royal tombs, was known to the ancient Egyptians as the 'Place of Truth' (*set* Maat). As a goddess, Maat was

depicted as a seated woman with an ostrich feather on her head, or as the feather alone. Her cult is attested from the OLD KINGDOM onwards.

macehead Weapon for smiting, consisting of a discoid, biconical or pear-shaped piece of stone which was attached to a handle of wood, horn or

*Detail of a granite column from Tanis showing the image of the goddess **Maat** – a seated woman with a feather on her head, holding an ankh – being offered by Ramesses II.*

*Tutankhamun, holding a long staff, an ankh, and a mace with a pear-shaped **macehead**, is greeted by the goddess Nut, in a painting in the king's burial chamber in the Valley of the Kings.*

Magic *was an important element in ancient Egyptian religious practice; this wooden statuette was made for a chief magician, Hetepi, in the 11th Dynasty.*

Small ivory statuette from the Main Deposit *at Hierakonpolis; like many of the other objects found with it, this piece probably dates to the late Predynastic period or 1st Dynasty.*

ivory. Attested from the early PREDYNASTIC PERIOD, maceheads were important emblems of authority. As such, purely symbolic clay maceheads were often included among FUNERARY GOODS. The earliest maceheads from UPPER EGYPT, found in graves of the early fourth millennium BC, were disc-shaped, and were used for slashing and cutting as well as smiting. Biconical and piriform (pear-shaped) maceheads were introduced in the mid-fourth millennium, the latter perhaps from LOWER EGYPT: piriform maceheads were found in the upper level of the settlement at MERIMDA BENI SALAMA, possibly derived from Near Eastern prototypes. The piriform mace became closely associated with KINGSHIP towards the beginning of the 1st Dynasty, as attested in the giant ceremonial maceheads of SCORPION and NARMER from HIERAKONPOLIS. The quintessential motif of royal power, the king smiting his enemies with a mace was a characteristic element in Egyptian iconography from the early Predynastic period to the end of the ROMAN PERIOD.

magic The modern distinction between RELIGION, magic and MEDICINE would not have been recognized by the ancient Egyptians. Magical power, personified as the god Heka, could be invoked for a variety of purposes, including protection from malign forces and the curing of ailments. In private and state spheres, magic spells and curses were key elements of religious practice. Magical figurines were used to enhance fertility, and to guarantee success in childbirth; however, if deliberately mutilated, a figurine was believed to cause harm to the intended victim. AFTERLIFE BELIEFS similarly relied on magic to protect the deceased in the next world, and to guarantee eternal sustenance for the KA. The MIDDLE KINGDOM TALES OF WONDER (Papyrus Westcar) describe a number of magic acts, while a tomb of the same period, excavated beneath the RAMESSEUM, contained a collection of magical objects including an IVORY clapper, a statuette of a masked woman, various PAPYRUS documents, and a bronze wand in the shape of a SNAKE. The URAEUS was sometimes described as *weret hekau*, 'great of magic'.

magic bricks *see* funerary objects

Maiherpri Official of the mid-18th Dynasty. He grew up in the royal nursery and was fan-bearer on the king's right hand. His physical features suggest Nubian ancestry. His intact tomb in the VALLEY OF THE KINGS (KV36), probably dating to the reign of AMENHOTEP II or THUTMOSE IV, discovered in 1899, contained a range of fine FUNERARY GOODS, including a copy of the BOOK OF THE DEAD, leather quivers and loincloths.

Main Deposit Collection of VOTIVE objects excavated in 1900 in the early temple at HIERAKONPOLIS. It included important royal artifacts from the very beginning of Egyptian history, including the SCORPION MACEHEAD and NARMER PALETTE. The true date of the deposit and the precise circumstances in which it was found are unclear because of poor record-keeping at the time of discovery.

malachite Bright green copper ore, occurring in the Eastern Desert and the SINAI. Found in graves of the PREDYNASTIC PERIOD, it was a principal ingredient for KOHL (eye-paint) until the middle of the OLD KINGDOM, when green eye-paint was superseded by a black variety, based on GALENA. Malachite may also have been an ingredient in EGYPTIAN BLUE.

Malkata Site on the southern edge of western THEBES, where AMENHOTEP III built a ceremonial complex for the celebration of his SED FESTIVALS. Constructed in the 29th or 30th year of his reign (c. 1360 BC), the buildings comprise four palaces surrounded by kitchens, storerooms, and residential areas, including large houses for court officials. Fragments of painted plaster show the exuberant decoration of the palace apartments. The huge artificial harbour to the east of Malkata, the Birket Habu, was probably constructed at the same time to stage water-borne ceremonies.

mammisi Temple building in which the marriage of a goddess and the birth of her divine offspring were celebrated. Perhaps derived from earlier 'divine birth' chapels, such as those at DEIR EL-BAHRI and LUXOR TEMPLE, mammisis are known at DENDERA, EDFU and PHILAE. In the PTOLEMAIC PERIOD, they were usually orientated perpendicular to the main temple, and took the form of a small PERIPTERAL temple with a screen wall between the columns. The term mammisi, derived from Coptic, was coined by Jean-François Champollion (see EGYPTOLOGY), and is used interchangeably with 'birth-house'.

Mandulis (Merwel) Solar god of Lower NUBIA, usually known by the Greek version of his name. Although worshipped throughout Lower Nubia, he is best attested at KALABSHA where a temple (now re-erected

close to the ASWAN High Dam) was dedicated to him in the early ROMAN PERIOD. At PHILAE, a chapel of Mandulis names him as the companion of ISIS, and also associates him with the Greek sun god Helios; a late text equates Mandulis with HORUS and the Greek god Apollo, again emphasizing his solar connotations.

Mandulis was usually depicted as a man wearing a complex CROWN of ram-horns, sun discs and cobras, surmounted by tall plumes; he could also be shown as a human-headed bird wearing the same distinctive crown.

Manetho Egyptian priest of the early 3rd century BC from SEBENNYTOS, who was commissioned by Ptolemy II to write a HISTORY of Egypt from earliest times to the end of the 30th Dynasty. The work, entitled the *Ægyptiaca*, probably drew heavily on temple records; it has only survived in secondary sources, notably the writings of the Jewish historian Josephus and three early Christian authors (Julius Africanus, Eusebius and George, called Syncellus). Manetho is best known for devising the system of dynasties still used by Egyptologists.

map True maps, as opposed to diagrammatic representations of natural or urban landscapes, seem to have been relatively rare in ancient Egypt. PETROGLYPHS at three sites in the Eastern Desert (Wadi el-Atwani, Wadi Umm Salam and Wadi Abu Wasil) bear striking similarities to the local topography in each case, and may well be maps. Their age is difficult to determine, but they may date back as far as the PREDYNASTIC PERIOD. Imaginary maps of the underworld were sometimes painted on COFFINS in the MIDDLE KINGDOM and in later tombs. However, the earliest real-life map that can be dated with certainty is a 20th Dynasty PAPYRUS from the reign of RAMESSES IV which shows the siltstone quarries of the WADI HAMMAMAT and the nearby gold mines of Bir Umm Fawakhir. It was made either to facilitate or to commemorate a quarrying expedition. Another papyrus from the same reign shows a detailed plan of the tomb of Ramesses IV in the VALLEY OF THE KINGS.

Mariette, Auguste see Egyptology

marl see pottery

marriage An exclusive relationship with a person of the opposite gender seems to have been the ideal for adults in ancient Egypt, but there is little evidence for any formal institution or ceremony of marriage. A declaration of intent to live as husband and wife was probably made before one or more witnesses, but was largely a matter of recognition by the community. Divorce and remarriage were possible by similar means. Marriage did not, as in some other cultures, entail a woman losing her legal or property rights. On the contrary, the LAW guaranteed a woman's ownership of the property she brought into a marriage and, usually, a third of joint property. In the LATE PERIOD and PTOLEMAIC PERIOD, marriage contracts were drawn up to define the property rights of the two partners. The other legal implications of cohabitation are not fully understood.

Polygamy does not seem to have been illegal, but, instead, impractical and undesirable for most private individuals. The king was an exception, often taking multiple wives in order to cement alliances, especially with foreign powers. Likewise, in the NEW KINGDOM, brother–sister and father–daughter marriage are attested for kings, but not among ordinary citizens. The word *hemet* is usually translated 'wife' but probably meant simply 'female partner'. The male equivalent, *hi* ('husband'), is rarely attested, reflecting the male bias inherent in the ancient Egyptian written record.

mask In Egyptian ART, it is difficult to distinguish between humans wearing animal masks and anthropomorphic deities shown with animal-heads. A Predynastic PALETTE (now in the Manchester Museum) appears to show a man wearing an ostrich mask, next to a group of the birds; the jackal-headed human figure playing a reed flute, depicted on another palette (in the Ashmolean Museum, Oxford), is less certainly identified as a masked man. However, recent discoveries of POTTERY masks in Predynastic contexts at HIERAKONPOLIS clearly indicate that such objects played a part in early religious and funerary rituals. A CARTONNAGE lion mask from KAHUN (dating to the MIDDLE KINGDOM) and a pottery JACKAL mask of the LATE PERIOD are rare examples from later periods. A relief in the temple of HATHOR at DENDERA clearly shows a priest wearing a jackal mask, confirming the use of masks in temple rites, at least in the PTOLEMAIC and ROMAN PERIODS.

Funerary masks are better attested at all periods. Famous examples range from the gold masks of TUTANKHAMUN and PSUSENNES to the Roman 'mummy portraits' from HAWARA and the FAYUM. Whether in a funerary or religious context, the purpose of a mask was the same: to transform the wearer from a mortal to a divine state.

Maskhuta, Tell el- *see* Tell el-Maskhuta

Maspero, Gaston *see* Egyptology

mastaba Type of ancient Egyptian tomb with a mud-brick or stone rectangular superstructure, the walls of which taper slightly inwards. The term derives from the Arabic for 'bench', tombs of this type resembling the bench outside a typical Egyptian house. The royal tombs of the 1st and 2nd Dynasties are thought to have had mastaba superstructures, although they have not survived. Mastabas were built for private individuals throughout the EARLY DYNASTIC PERIOD and OLD KINGDOM. Some of the best examples, with elaborately decorated internal chambers, are at SAQQARA. The burial chamber and store rooms were located below ground, accessible via a shaft. In the MIDDLE KINGDOM, ROCK-CUT TOMBS replaced mastabas as the usual form for private funerary monuments, although mastabas continued to be built at sites in the MEMPHITE NECROPOLIS, such as ABUSIR. The architecture of NEW KINGDOM and LATE PERIOD tombs in LOWER EGYPT and at ABYDOS owed much to the mastaba tradition.

Mastabat el-Fara'un Stone funerary monument in the shape of a giant SARCOPHAGUS, built for SHEPSESKAF at southern SAQQARA.

mathematics The ancient Egyptians had advanced knowledge of numbers and geometry, as attested in various surviving mathematical texts, most notably the Rhind Papyrus, dating to the SECOND INTERMEDIATE PERIOD. Scribes would have learned mathematics by the repeated copying of examples. The numerical system itself was decimal, with signs for 1, 10, 100, and so on. Manipulation of numbers was based upon practical applications, rather than abstract mathematical theory; hence, the Egyptians do not seem to have devised complex formulae, instead relying on series of simpler calculations. Multiplication was achieved by a combination of doubling and addition, division by halving and subtraction. Fractions were generally confined to those with a numerator of one, together with commonly used fractions such as two-thirds and three-quarters; more complex fractions were expressed as combinations of simpler fractions. Methods were devised for calculating the volume of a cylinder and a pyramid, and the area of a circle; but the Egyptians do not seem to have been aware of *pi*.

Maxims of Ptahhotep Work of WISDOM LITERATURE, attributed to a VIZIER of the reign of ISESI, but more probably composed in the early MIDDLE KINGDOM. It survives in four copies from the Middle and New Kingdoms. A long text, it comprises 37 separate maxims, framed by a prologue and epilogue. The sayings touch on human relations, focusing on the virtues of self-control, moderation, generosity, and MAAT; some themes recur several times.

Maya Treasurer during the reign of TUTANKHAMUN. Maya's tomb, with finely executed reliefs and painted decoration, was rediscovered at SAQQARA in the 1980s.

Mazghuna Site on the west bank of the NILE, 4 km (2.5 miles) south of DAHSHUR. On the southernmost edge of the MEMPHITE NECROPOLIS, it was the site of two MIDDLE KINGDOM pyramids, both now destroyed. Some scholars have attributed the monuments to AMENEMHAT IV and SOBEKNEFERU, but they may date to the 13th Dynasty.

measurement *see* weights and measures

Medamud Site on the east bank of the NILE in the THEBAN region of UPPER EGYPT, about 5 km (3 miles) north of KARNAK. The major feature is a temple dedicated to the TRIAD of MONTU, Rattawy and HARPOCRATES. The oldest phase of the building, dating to the late OLD KINGDOM, was very different in plan from 'classic' Egyptian temples. It comprised an irregular, polygonal enclosure containing a grove of trees, surrounding a small mud-brick temple, at the rear of which two winding corridors led to small chambers, each covered by a mound of soil. Stone elements from the MIDDLE KINGDOM temple have survived; they name various 12th and 13th Dynasty kings, including SENUSRET III, SOBEKHOTEP III, UGAF and SOBEKEMSAF. The existing temple structure dates from the reigns of THUTMOSE III and AMENHOTEP II, with Ptolemaic and Roman additions. A smaller cult building dedicated to the bull manifestation of Montu lies nearby, as do the remains of two Coptic churches.

medicine Texts concerned with medical practices, and titles of medical practitioners, have survived from as early as the 3rd Dynasty. They give valuable insights

Painted limestone relief of **Maya** from his 18th Dynasty tomb at Saqqara, showing him with his hands raised in prayer; Maya served as treasurer during the reign of Tutankhamun.

into the level of medical knowledge in ancient Egypt. Doctors and dentists, surgeons and vets are all attested, indicating the existence of medical specialisms. From the LATE PERIOD onwards, sanatoria were often attached to temples, for example at DENDERA. In the PTOLEMAIC PERIOD, the Asklepieion at SAQQARA (the cult centre of the deified IMHOTEP) became a centre for healing, attracting pilgrims from far and wide. Treatments were based upon the observation of symptoms and previous experience, rather than theory, with MAGIC playing an important part. Indeed, many minor ailments were considered the result of malign influences and treated primarily with spells and AMULETS; in the NEW KINGDOM, those suffering from (cataract-induced) blindness often appealed to the god PTAH for a cure. However, knowledge of certain specific conditions was often advanced. A late MIDDLE KINGDOM papyrus lists conditions associated with heavy construction activity, such as broken bones and dislocations, confirming considerable experience of building-related injuries; it also demonstrates knowledge of a link between the HEART and the pulse. Three papyri of the Middle Kingdom and NEW KINGDOM deal with gynaecological concerns, including the earliest known pregnancy test using barley and emmer. Other texts record treatments for SNAKE bites and anal conditions. Despite the dissection of bodies for MUMMIFICATION, the Egyptians do not seem to have had a particularly good knowledge of anatomy or the function of internal organs.

Medinet el-Fayum Modern name for the town serving as the administrative capital of the FAYUM region. A settlement was probably established here in the EARLY DYNASTIC PERIOD, and the town became an important cult centre of the crocodile god SOBEK in the MIDDLE KINGDOM (hence the town's classical name Crocodilopolis). The earliest elements of the temple of Sobek date to the 12th Dynasty, but most of the structure was built in the PTOLEMAIC and ROMAN PERIODS, when Crocodilopolis was the capital of the province of Arsinoë. Most of the ancient remains are covered by the modern town.

Medinet Habu Site in western THEBES, dominated by the well-preserved mortuary temple of RAMESSES III. Earlier activity is represented by a small 18th Dynasty temple (dating to the reigns of HATSHEPSUT and THUTMOSE III), located inside the 20th Dynasty enclosure wall; it is dedicated to AMUN of LUXOR TEMPLE, whose cult image visited Medinet Habu every ten days. The temple of Ramesses III was originally connected to the NILE by means of a canal, and is surrounded by a massive mud-brick wall, with a fortified entrance tower designed to resemble a Syrian fortress (migdol). The rooms above the gateway were probably the king's private apartments; they are decorated with scenes showing Ramesses III and women of the royal HAREM. The temple itself was dedicated to a divine form of the king ('AMUN-RA United with Eternity'). Hence, its outer walls are adorned with the iconography of KINGSHIP: the exterior face of the First PYLON shows the king smiting his enemies, while the decoration of the northern wall includes scenes of the battle against the SEA PEOPLES.

In its basic plan, the temple copies the RAMESSEUM. The First Court contains a WINDOW OF APPEARANCE, connecting with a small royal palace behind, which may have been used by the king on important occasions. The Second Court has colourful scenes of religious FESTIVALS. The rear portions of the temple, including the HYPOSTYLE HALL, are now largely reduced to their lower courses of masonry. The walled temple enclosure was used as a place of safety in times of civil strife, the residents of DEIR EL-MEDINA moving there in the late 20th Dynasty. In the LATE PERIOD,

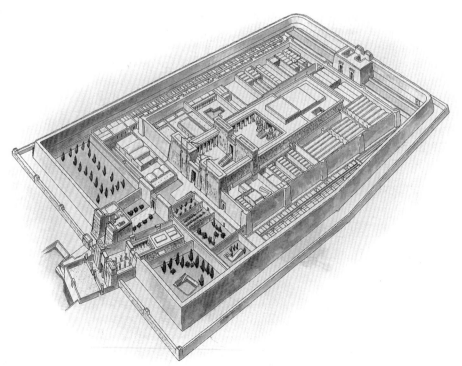

*Reconstruction drawing of the mortuary temple of Ramesses III at **Medinet Habu**, as it would have appeared when completed in the early 20th Dynasty.*

several holders of the office of God's Wife of Amun, notably Amenirdis (daughter of Kashta) and her successor Shepenwepet II, were buried in stone tombs in front of the temple. In the Ptolemaic period, the town of Djeme was built against the temple walls. The Second Court was used as a church in the Roman period.

Medinet Maadi Site on the south-western edge of the Fayum. The major monument is a well-preserved temple to the cobra goddess Renenutet, founded in the reigns of Amenemhat III and Amenemhat IV. The inner sanctuary comprises three chapels, dedicated to the goddess and the two royal builders. The temple was expanded in the Ptolemaic period with the addition of a kiosk, portico and transverse hall, the three elements forming a processional way. There are also Roman period remains at the site.

Medjay Nomadic people from the Eastern Desert of Egypt and Nubia. The Medjay are first attested in Egyptian texts of the late Old Kingdom; the inscription of Weni tells of them having served in an Egyptian military campaign. In the Middle Kingdom, Medjay served as garrison troops in the fortresses of Lower Nubia, helping to prevent attacks by their fellow tribespeople. (The fortress at Serra East was called 'Repressing the Medjay'.) From the Second Intermediate Period onwards, they were employed by the Egyptians as desert scouts; they are identified by some scholars with the Pan Grave culture. In the 18th Dynasty, they became a paramilitary police force, and the term Medjay was used throughout the New Kingdom to denote an occupation rather than an ethnic group. The term is not attested after the 20th Dynasty, although a people called the Meded who fought against Kush in the 5th and 4th centuries BC may be the same group.

Megiddo, Battle of Military encounter (c. 1457 BC) between the army of Thutmose III and forces loyal to the prince of Kadesh, probably supported by the Mitanni. Part of a wider Egyptian campaign to put down a rebellion of city states and secure their loyalty, the engagement took place early in Thutmose III's sole reign, at the site of Megiddo (now in Israel's Jezreel Valley). This was a strategically important location, controlling the main route from Egypt to the Levant. Thutmose III included a description of the battle in his Annals, inscribed on the walls of Karnak temple, and

The early 4th Dynasty pyramid at **Meidum** *suffered a series of disastrous collapses, leaving only the stepped masonry core standing above mounds of rubble.*

on a stela erected at Gebel Barkal. It is the earliest detailed account of a battle in history. According to the text, which was intended to extol the king's virtues, he ignored the advice of his generals and instead chose the most direct route to attack Megiddo, involving marching his army through a narrow pass. The strategy worked, and the Egyptians were able to take their enemy by surprise. The rulers of Kadesh and Megiddo fled to the city, where they were hauled onto the battlements by their garments. After a seven-month siege, Megiddo and its inhabitants were captured by the Egyptian forces.

Meidum Site on the west bank of the Nile, near the entrance to the Fayum, best known for its collapsed pyramid of the early Old Kingdom. The monument was begun as a step pyramid, and was later converted into a true, smooth-sided pyramid. New Kingdom graffiti at the site attribute the entire construction to the 4th Dynasty king Sneferu, although the earlier phase of the monument is sometimes associated with his predecessor Huni (though without direct evidence). Two uninscribed stelae were found in the mortuary temple against the eastern side of the pyramid. The valley temple has not yet been excavated. Surrounding the pyramid, to the east and north, are cemeteries for officials and royal relatives. They include the mastaba of Nefermaat, which contained a fine painted relief of geese (now in the Egyptian Museum, Cairo), and the tomb of Rahotep and Nofret, whose painted statues are early masterpieces of sculpture. Flinders Petrie (see Egyptology) found the earliest surviving mummy at Meidum, dated to the 5th Dynasty.

Meir Site on the west bank of the NILE in MIDDLE EGYPT. It is best known for a series of ROCK-CUT TOMBS, dating to the 6th and 12th Dynasties, built for the NOMARCHS of CUSAE (which lies 8 km (5 miles) to the east) and their families. The tomb-owners included Senbi, nomarch in the reign of AMENEMHAT I, and a number of individuals called Ukhhotep. The shaft tombs of attendants are cut into the nearby cliffs.

Meketaten Second daughter of the 18th Dynasty King AKHENATEN and his wife NEFERTITI, born in the king's fifth or sixth regnal year. She was buried in a chamber of the royal tomb at AMARNA; the wall decoration includes scenes of mourning at her death, and suggests that she may have died in childbirth.

Meketra High official of the 11th Dynasty who served as chancellor and steward of the palace in the reign of MENTUHOTEP II. Meketra's tomb near DEIR EL-BAHRI contained a remarkable collection of 24 wooden TOMB MODELS, ranging from individual offering bearers to boats, a model house, and a complex tableau showing the cattle count.

Memnon *see* Colossi of Memnon

Memphis Site on the west bank of the NILE, at the junction of UPPER and LOWER EGYPT, 24 km (15 miles) south of the centre of modern CAIRO. Occupying a strategic location between the Nile Valley and the DELTA, at a confluence of important trade routes, Memphis was known as 'the balance of the TWO LANDS'. It is said by HERODOTUS to have been founded by MENES at the beginning of the 1st Dynasty, although archaeological remains suggest that a settlement existed in the vicinity from the PREDYNASTIC PERIOD. Memphis was the capital of Egypt, at least for administrative purposes, throughout most of the pharaonic period. Its name in ancient Egyptian, *inebu-hedj* ('white walls'), referred to the whitewashed compound which housed the royal residence and the offices of government. Drill cores have established the location of the early city, which was a ribbon development between the western escarpment of SAQQARA and the river. In the EARLY DYNASTIC PERIOD, the Nile flowed considerably further to the west than it does today. As its course changed, the city of Memphis spread eastwards and southwards. The name Memphis is probably derived via Greek from the name of PEPI I's pyramid town, Men-nefer, which lay at the southern end of the present ruin field. The archaeological site of Memphis covers a large area, centred on the village of Mit Rahina, where parts of the MIDDLE KINGDOM city have been excavated. The most visible, and famous, remains are a fallen colossus of RAMESSES II and a TRAVERTINE SPHINX of the NEW KINGDOM. Other important features include palaces of MERENPTAH and APRIES; a building for embalming the APIS bulls, constructed during the 26th Dynasty; FAIENCE workshops dating to the ROMAN PERIOD; and two temples of PTAH. Memphis was the god's main cult centre throughout Egyptian history. With the foundation of ALEXANDRIA at the beginning of the PTOLEMAIC PERIOD, Memphis relinquished its role as capital city; in the medieval period, its monuments were heavily plundered for stone during the building of Fustat (Cairo).

Wooden model from the 11th Dynasty Theban tomb of **Meketra**, *showing him presiding over a census of cattle from the comfort of a shaded pavilion.*

Memphite Belonging to, or characteristic of, the site of MEMPHIS. The Memphite NECROPOLIS stretches along the edge of the Western Desert, from ABU RAWASH in the north to DAHSHUR in the south, taking in the sites of GIZA, ZAWIYET EL-ARYAN, ABU GHURAB, ABUSIR and SAQQARA.

menat Ancient Egyptian name for the counterpoise attached to a heavy beaded necklace, often decorated with an image of HATHOR.

Mendes (Tell el-Rub'a, Tell Timai) Site in the eastern central DELTA. Excavations have uncovered settlement remains from the PREDYNASTIC and EARLY DYNASTIC PERIODS, indicating the early importance of the town. In later periods it was the capital of the sixteenth Lower Egyptian NOME, the home town of SMENDES, and of NEPHERITES who was buried at the site. The town suffered destruction in the FIRST INTERMEDIATE PERIOD, and again at the beginning of the second PERSIAN PERIOD. The main local deity was originally the fish goddess Hat-Mehit, but her cult was eclipsed by the ram god BANEBDJEDET.

The surviving archaeological remains are concentrated in three areas. In the main temple precinct, built over an OLD KINGDOM cemetery, all that survives is a granite NAOS of AMASIS, although earlier construction work is known to have been carried out under THUTMOSE III and RAMESSES II. A rise to the east of the temple is yet to be fully investigated, while a large settlement to the south is thought to have been the main residential area. Mendes prospered in the early PTOLEMAIC PERIOD as a centre of WINE and perfume manufacture. However, when the local NILE branch began to weaken, the town declined; it had been largely abandoned by the middle of the ROMAN PERIOD.

Menes Legendary first king of Egypt, according to the 19th Dynasty KING-LISTS and later historical accounts. HERODOTUS credits him with founding MEMPHIS by diverting the course of the NILE. Egyptologists have argued whether Menes is to be equated with NARMER, AHA or a combination of the two.

Menkauhor (c. 2375 BC) Seventh king of the 5th Dynasty. The location of his pyramid complex is unknown, but may have been at SAQQARA or DAHSHUR. Texts also mention a SUN TEMPLE, as yet undiscovered. Foreign contacts are suggested by an inscription from

*Crystalline limestone colossus of Ramesses II from **Memphis**; now lying horizontally, the statue once towered in front of the temple of Ptah, chief deity of the ancient Egyptian capital.*

the LEVANT. Otherwise, little is known about the king or his reign.

Menkaura (Mycerinus) (c. 2500 BC) Fifth and penultimate king of the 4th Dynasty. The son of KHAFRA and grandson of KHUFU, he built the third pyramid at GIZA, although it was left unfinished at his death and completed by his successor SHEPSESKAF. It was cased in blocks of red granite, instead of the usual white limestone. TRIAD and dyad statues of the king (with deities, personifications of the NOMES, and his wife

Stone dyad of **Menkaura** and his principal wife; discovered at Giza in 1910, this beautiful composition ranks as one of the masterpieces of Egyptian sculpture.

Khamerernebty) were found in the pyramid temple, where his mortuary cult was maintained throughout the OLD KINGDOM. Details of Menkaura's life are recorded by HERODOTUS, but not in contemporary inscriptions.

Menna Inspector of estates in the reign of THUTMOSE IV (c. 1400–c. 1390). His tomb at SHEIKH ABD EL-QURNA includes important scenes of land survey and AGRICULTURE.

Mentuemhat High official from THEBES whose career spanned the transition from the 25th to the 26th Dynasties. He rose to power in the reign of TAHARQO, achieving the offices of 'prince of the city' and fourth prophet of AMUN. In this capacity, he oversaw additions to KARNAK, and controlled a huge temple estate stretching from ASWAN to HERMOPOLIS. Several

statues of Mentuemhat, of exceptional quality, have been found at Karnak. Despite the sacking of Thebes by the ASSYRIANS, Mentuemhat retained control of the region, and was described on an Assyrian cylinder-seal as 'king of Thebes'. His tomb at ASASIF comprised a huge stone and mud-brick building with columns and fine reliefs.

Mentuemsaf (throne name: Djedankhra) (late 17th century BC) Ephemeral king of the later SECOND INTERMEDIATE PERIOD (16th or 17th Dynasty), whose authority was probably confined to UPPER EGYPT.

Mentuhotep II ('MONTU is satisfied') (throne name: Nebhepetra) (c. 2010–c. 1960 BC) King of the 11th Dynasty who won the civil war against the royal house of HERAKLEOPOLIS and reunified Egypt. There is some disagreement over his regnal number, since he was named after the ancestor of the 11th Dynasty, Mentuhotep (father of INTEF I), who was only much later accorded royal titles (as Mentuhotep I). After the reunification, Mentuhotep II re-established the post of VIZIER to head the administration, and launched military campaigns against LIBYA, NUBIA and the bedouin of the Eastern Desert. He commissioned temple building at various sites in UPPER EGYPT, including DENDERA and GEBELEIN; but his major monument was his innovative mortuary complex at DEIR EL-BAHRI. Its novel architectural plan, combining elements from OLD KINGDOM and 11th Dynasty royal TOMBS, was the inspiration for HATSHEPSUT's neighbouring monument six centuries later. Finds from Mentuhotep's complex include a seated black statue of the king, equating him with OSIRIS, and the sarcophagi and other burial equipment of his six QUEENS.

Mentuhotep III (throne name: Sankhkara) (c. 1960–c. 1948 BC) Second king of the 11th Dynasty after the reunification of Egypt. He is credited with rebuilding the fortresses along the border of the eastern DELTA, and was later the focus of a cult at el-Khatana. Fine reliefs of the king have been recovered from temples in the THEBAN region, including EL-TOD. He also constructed a temple and SED FESTIVAL palace on top of Thoth Hill, overlooking western THEBES. He is often associated with an unfinished mortuary complex in a valley to the south of DEIR EL-BAHRI.

Mentuhotep IV (throne name: Nebtawyra) (c. 1948–c. 1938 BC) Third king of the post-reunification 11th

Dynasty. He reigned for less than a decade, and is best attested in a series of mining inscriptions from WADI EL-HUDI and WADI HAMMAMAT. The latter mention the VIZIER Amenemhat, who probably succeeded as AMENEMHAT I.

Mentuhotep V, VI, VII (throne names: Sewedjara, Sankhenra, Merankhra, respectively) (mid-18th century to late 17th century BC) Ephemeral kings who reigned during the 13th Dynasty and late SECOND INTERMEDIATE PERIOD (16th/17th Dynasties).

Merenptah (Merneptah) ('Beloved of PTAH') (throne name: Baenra-hetephermaat) (c. 1213–c. 1204 BC) Fourth king of the 19th Dynasty, who succeeded to the throne after twelve older brothers had pre-deceased their father RAMESSES II. The major event of his reign was an attack on Egypt by the Libyans, in alliance with the SEA PEOPLES. An account of the Egyptian victory was inscribed on the walls of KARNAK, and on a commemorative STELA which includes the earliest surviving Egyptian reference to ISRAEL (among a list of defeated enemies). The stela was discovered in Merenptah's mortuary temple in western THEBES, which reused many blocks from the nearby monument of AMENHOTEP III. Merenptah had a tomb built in the VALLEY OF THE KINGS (KV8), although his mummy was found in the cache in the tomb of AMENHOTEP II (KV35). His principal surviving monument is a palace at MEMPHIS.

Merenra (Nemtyemsaf) (c. 2270 BC) Third king of the 6th Dynasty, and the successor of PEPI I. Events from his six-year reign are described in the AUTOBIOGRAPHIES of WENI and HARKHUF. The king's pyramid is at SAQQARA.

Mereruka VIZIER, chief justice, and inspector of priests of the pyramid of TETI during the reigns of Teti and PEPI I. His high office was the result of his marriage to a member of the ROYAL FAMILY. He was buried, together with his wife and son, in an impressive MASTABA. Located near the pyramid of Teti, and next to the tomb of KAGEMNI, it is the largest OLD KINGDOM private burial at SAQQARA. Its decoration provides an important source of evidence for Old Kingdom culture, and includes scenes of craft activities and the attempted domestication of gazelles and hyenas.

Mereruka's funerary statue is located in a six-columned hall at the centre of his mastaba; it is posi-

Granite statue from Karnak of **Mentuemhat,** *mayor of Thebes during the transition from the 25th to the 26th Dynasty.*

tioned as though it is emerging from the tomb to receive offerings.

Meretseger Cobra goddess of THEBES, also known as 'the peak of the west', believed to dwell in the mountain overlooking the VALLEY OF THE KINGS. Her name means 'she who loves silence', and she was believed to punish wrongdoers with blindness. During the NEW KINGDOM, she was worshipped throughout western Thebes, especially at DEIR EL-MEDINA where many STELAE were dedicated to her. The decline in the importance of her cult mirrored the decline of the THEBAN NECROPOLIS after the 20th Dynasty.

Merikara (c. 2000 BC) King of the 9th/10th Dynasty, probably the last of his line before the reunification of Egypt under MENTUHOTEP II. An inscription in the FIRST INTERMEDIATE PERIOD tomb of Kheti II, NOMARCH of ASYUT, contains a hymn of praise to Merikara and an account of battles between the Herakleopolitan and THEBAN armies. The text known as the INSTRUCTION FOR MERIKARA is addressed to him and seems to refer to contemporary events. Merikara is known to have built a PYRAMID, but it has not been located.

Merimda Beni Salama

Merimda Beni Salama Site on the western edge of the DELTA, 60 km (37.5 miles) northwest of CAIRO. Excavations have uncovered the earliest evidence yet found in Egypt for fully sedentary village life. Approximately contemporary with the BADARIAN culture of UPPER EGYPT, the prehistoric settlement at Merimda comprised rows of windbreaks and huts, laid out as if along streets. This apparent town planning, together with the provision of communal granaries, indicates a degree of social organization. The community depended for its subsistence on fishing, AGRICULTURE, HUNTING and ANIMAL HUSBANDRY. Artifacts from the upper levels of the site include elaborate burnished POTTERY; figurines of humans and cattle; a pottery mask, perhaps depicting a deity; and pear-shaped MACEHEADS. Graves of children within the settlement were entirely devoid of FUNERARY GOODS. In the early fourth millennium BC, the site was used as a cemetery by people of the Lower Egyptian, MAADI cultural tradition. Displaying a combination of Near Eastern and African influences, Merimda seems to have been an important early centre of cultural development.

Meritaten Eldest daughter of the 18th Dynasty king AKHENATEN and NEFERTITI, born before the king's 5th regnal year. She may have borne him a daughter (Meritaten-ta-sherit) and was subsequently promoted to the position of 'great royal wife' at the end of Akhenaten's reign, perhaps to signify her status as heiress. She seems to have retained this role in the reign of Akhenaten's successor, SMENKHKARA.

Mermesha (throne name: Smenkhkara) (late 18th century BC) King (seventeenth or eighteenth) of the 13th Dynasty whose name means 'the general' and who may therefore have come to power as a military officer. His most important surviving monuments are two colossal statues, now in the Egyptian Museum, Cairo.

Merneferra Ay see Ay (I)

Merneith Mother of the 1st Dynasty king DEN, and probably regent during his minority. Because of her status, she was granted the privilege of a royal tomb, complete with subsidiary burials of retainers, in the royal NECROPOLIS at ABYDOS. Her funerary STELA is inscribed with her name, but omits the SEREKH which was reserved for a reigning king. The necropolis seal of Den names her as 'the king's mother', but she is omitted from a KING-LIST compiled at the end of the 1st Dynasty. Her period of office is the first attested occasion of a woman holding the reins of power in Egypt.

Merneptah *see* Merenptah

Meroë Site on the east bank of the NILE in the Butana region of Upper NUBIA (southern Sudan). Following the demise of NAPATA in the 5th century BC, Meroë became the capital of the kingdom of KUSH; the subsequent phase of Nubian culture is thus called the Meroïtic period. However, earlier monuments at the site include temples of ISIS and AMUN from the 7th century BC. The settlement, comprising palaces, work-

Funerary stela of **Merneith** *from the 1st Dynasty royal cemetery at Abydos; inscribed with the queen's name, this slab would have stood in front of her tomb on the Umm el-Qaab.*

Close cultural contact between **Mesopotamia** *and Egypt in the late 4th millennium BC is suggested by the motifs on this carved ivory knife handle from Gebel el-Arak; the man standing between two lions, well attested in contemporary Mesopotamian iconography, even wears a Sumerian-style turban.*

*Scene of **metalworking** in the 5th Dynasty tomb of Niankh-khnum and Khnumhotep at Saqqara; four men blow through pipes to heat a fire containing a crucible of molten metal, while the foreman on the right announces that the metal is nearly ready to be cast.*

shops and the remains of iron smelting, is accompanied by a series of cemeteries. Burials range from simple graves to the pyramid tombs of the Kushite royal family, Meroë having succeeded NAPATA as the principal royal NECROPOLIS in the mid-3rd century BC. At this time, a TEMPLE to the Nubian LION god Apedemak was built to the east of Meroë. The Kushite kingdom came to an end in AD 350, and Meroë had been entirely abandoned by the 5th century AD.

Meroïtic Belonging to, or characteristic of, the site of MEROË.

Mersa Matruh Site of the Ptolemaic city of Paraetoniuim, on the Mediterranean coast 200 km (125 miles) west of ALEXANDRIA; an island in the lagoon was a centre of NEW KINGDOM trade with the Aegean.

Merwel *see* Mandulis

Meryra Name of two high officials of the AMARNA period, buried in the Northern Tombs at Amarna. Meryra I was High Priest of the ATEN. Meryra II was steward of NEFERTITI; the decoration in his tomb shows the reception of foreign tribute in AKHENATEN's 12th regnal year, and Akhenaten's successor, SMENKHKARA, with the Great Royal Wife, MERITATEN.

Meshwesh *see* Libyans, Shoshenq

Meskhenet Goddess of childbirth who was believed to determine a child's destiny. She was also a funerary goddess, associated with the judgment and rebirth of the deceased. An important household deity in private RELIGION, she had no specific cult centre. She was represented as a birth-brick – the brick on which a mother gave birth – with a woman's head, or as a woman with a birth-brick or stylized uterus on her head.

Mesopotamia The land 'between the two rivers' Tigris and Euphrates, corresponding to modern Iraq. It was the location of the ancient states of Sumer, Akkad, Assyria and Babylonia. Mesopotamia's connections with Egypt were most prominent during the late PREDYNASTIC PERIOD, when the emerging elites of UPPER EGYPT copied and adapted Mesopotamian iconography and architecture – and perhaps also the idea of WRITING – to project their own authority. Sporadic trade between Mesopotamia and Egypt is attested at various periods, notably in LAPIS LAZULI. In the LATE PERIOD, the ASSYRIANS posed a real threat to Egypt, conquering it at the end of the 25th Dynasty.

metalworking While not a leading centre of metallurgy, ancient Egypt nevertheless developed technologies for extracting and processing most of the metals found within its own borders and in neighbouring lands. Moreover, in the specific area of GOLD working, the products of Egyptian craftsmen were perhaps unequalled in the ancient world.

Copper was the first metal to be exploited in Egypt. Small beads have been found in BADARIAN graves; larger items were produced in the later PREDYNASTIC PERIOD, by a combination of mould-casting, annealing and cold-hammering. Copper ore was imported from the Timna area of Palestine, via trading centres

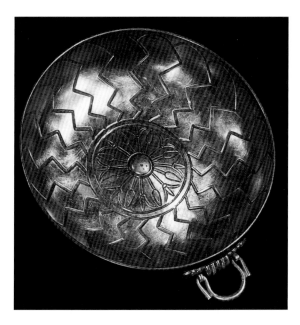

Ancient Egyptian **metalworking** was capable of producing masterpieces, such as this silver bowl from the 21st Dynasty tomb of Psusennes I at Tanis.

which time it had largely replaced copper; the introduction of bellows at the same period revolutionized metalworking in general.

Silver had to be imported from the LEVANT, and its rarity initially gave it greater value than gold (which, like ELECTRUM, was readily available within the borders of Egypt and Nubia). Early examples of silver working include the bracelets of HETEPHERES. By the MIDDLE KINGDOM, silver is more widely attested and seems to have become less valuable than gold, perhaps because of increased trade with the Near East. The treasure from el-TOD comprised a hoard of silver objects, probably made in the Aegean, while silver JEWELRY made for female members of the 12th Dynasty royal family was found at DAHSHUR and LAHUN. Silver was readily available in the New Kingdom, and was extensively used for the burial equipment of the 21st and 22nd Dynasty kings at TANIS. In Egyptian RELIGION, the bones of the gods were said to be made of silver, while their flesh was of gold.

Iron was the last metal to be exploited on a large scale by the Egyptians. Meteoritic iron was used for the manufacture of beads from the Badarian period, and iron ores such as haematite were important ingredients in cosmetic pigments. However, the advanced technology required to smelt iron was not introduced into Egypt until the Late Period. Before that, iron objects were imported, and consequently were highly valued for their rarity. The AMARNA LETTERS refer to diplomatic gifts of iron being sent by Near Eastern rulers, especially the HITTITES, to AMENHOTEP III and AKHENATEN. An iron dagger blade was included among TUTANKHAMUN'S FUNERARY GOODS. The earliest evidence for iron smelting dates to the 6th century BC, at NAUKRATIS. Only in the ROMAN PERIOD did iron tools and weapons become common in Egypt.

such as MAADI, and was also mined in the SINAI and the Eastern Desert. Evidence of copper smelting from Early Dynastic levels at BUHEN suggests that the exploitation of metal ores may have been one of the key motives for Egypt's early interest in NUBIA. In the NEW KINGDOM, Egypt controlled the mines at Timna and also obtained copper by trade from Cyprus. The production of copper artifacts peaked in the OLD KINGDOM when huge numbers of copper chisels were manufactured to cut the stone blocks for the PYRAMIDS. (Hard stone tools were generally used for this purpose in the Middle and New Kingdoms.) Scenes in the tombs of MERERUKA and TY show the various stages of copper working, including melting the ore in a crucible. The copper statues of PEPI I and MERENRA from HIERAKONPOLIS are rare survivors of large-scale metalworking.

Bronze, an alloy of copper and tin, is first attested in the 2nd Dynasty, in the form of vessels from the tomb of KHASEKHEMWY. Egypt probably obtained supplies of tin from Syria; ingots of the metal were among the cargo of the Bronze Age shipwreck recovered in the 1980s at Uluburun off the south coast of modern Turkey. The lost-wax process was used to cast bronze objects from the Old Kingdom onwards, and was employed to great effect in the LATE PERIOD for the mass production of bronze statuettes. The word for bronze is first attested in texts of the 18th Dynasty, by

Metjen Official whose career spanned the end of the 3rd Dynasty and beginning of the 4th Dynasty. His MASTABA (originally at SAQQARA, now in Berlin) is inscribed with an autobiographical text detailing his career within the government; it is an important source of evidence for administration in early Egypt. Metjen's statue has also survived, a fine example of early OLD KINGDOM SCULPTURE.

Middle Egypt Modern term for the central part of the Egyptian NILE Valley, from Beni Suef in the north to Sohag in the south. It corresponds broadly to the southern part of the Herakleopolitan realm during the

FIRST INTERMEDIATE PERIOD. Middle Egypt is characterized by ROCK-CUT TOMBS of the MIDDLE KINGDOM, and includes the archaeological sites of BENI HASAN, EL-BERSHA, MEIR and QAU. Despite these and other well-preserved monuments, the region is relatively little visited, and lacks the tourist infrastructure of CAIRO, LUXOR and ASWAN.

Middle Kingdom (c. 1975–c. 1650 BC) Phase of Egyptian history comprising the period from the reunification of the country under MENTUHOTEP II in the middle of the 11th Dynasty to the renewed political fragmentation of Egypt in the late 13th Dynasty. In common usage, the term is often synonymous with the 12th Dynasty. The Middle Kingdom was thus a period of strong central government following the divisions of the FIRST INTERMEDIATE PERIOD. It was also a period of great cultural achievement, when many of the masterpieces of Egyptian LITERATURE were composed, including the TALE OF SINUHE. A favourite theme in works of the time was 'national distress', reflected not only in literature but also in the royal SCULPTURE of SENUSRET III and AMENEMHAT III. Despite this brooding sense of unease, the 12th Dynasty was one of the most stable royal lines ever to rule Egypt, strengthened by the practice of CO-REGENCY.

Developments within Egypt during the Middle Kingdom included the foundation of a new royal capital at ITJ-TAWY, the rise of THEBES (accompanied by the earliest buildings at KARNAK), and an upsurge in activity in the FAYUM. Intensive exploitation of the desert regions involved frequent MINING AND QUARRYING expeditions to SINAI, WADI HAMMAMAT and WADI EL-HUDI. To secure its borders against foreign aggression, the Middle Kingdom state built a series of fortifications to defend the north-eastern DELTA, and numerous FORTRESSES in Lower NUBIA to maintain control of trade routes and counter the growing threat from the Kingdom of KUSH. OLD KINGDOM traditions were revived for the royal tombs, but the PYRAMIDS and other royal buildings of the Middle Kingdom have not survived particularly well. Much better preserved are the numerous private ROCK-CUT TOMBS in the provinces, reflecting strong local identities and the 'democratization of the afterlife'.

In the 13th Dynasty, a succession of ephemeral rulers weakened royal authority, a process exacerbated by increasing immigration into the Delta. The abandonment of the capital at Itj-tawy after the reign of Merneferra AY (I) effectively mark the end of the cen-

tralized state and the beginning of the SECOND INTERMEDIATE PERIOD.

Min Fertility god, and one of the most ancient members of the Egyptian pantheon. A cosmetic PALETTE inscribed with his distinctive symbol (variously interpreted as a thunderbolt, barbed arrow, door-bolt, or fossil), and colossal statues of an ITHYPHALLIC fertility god from COPTOS indicate that the cult of Min was already in existence in the PREDYNASTIC PERIOD. Coptos remained his primary cult centre, its location at the mouth of the WADI HAMMAMAT probably giving Min his secondary role as guardian of the Eastern Desert; he is depicted in PETROGLYPHS throughout the region. In the MIDDLE KINGDOM, Min became closely associated with HORUS, and in the NEW KINGDOM with the creator aspect of AMUN. The composite Amun-Min was worshipped at KARNAK. In later periods, the cult of Min was also practised at AKHMIM. He was depicted in distinctive form, as a mummiform male figure, grasping his erect penis in his left hand, and holding a flail aloft in his right. He was usually shown wearing a twin-plumed headdress, and often standing before a bed of lettuces; the cos lettuce, because of its milky white sap, resembling semen, was associated with Min from the

*Incised drawing of **Min** from the siltstone quarries in the Wadi Hammamat (reign of Sobekemsaf, 17th Dynasty); the fertility god Min was the local deity of Coptos, gateway to the Wadi Hammamat, and patron deity of the entire Eastern Desert.*

OLD KINGDOM. The SED FESTIVAL frequently included a festival of Min, to ensure the king's continued potency.

mining and quarrying From prehistoric times, the ancient Egyptians had a detailed knowledge of the geology of the NILE Valley and adjacent deserts. They exploited the varied and abundant stone and mineral resources for a range of purposes: architecture, SCULPTURE, JEWELRY, the manufacture of fine quality objects, and high value items for trade. Among the principal sites of mining and quarrying activity were: WADI MAGHARA and SERABIT EL-KHADIM in the SINAI (TURQUOISE); GEBEL ZEIT (GALENA); Wadi Dara in the Eastern Desert (copper); WADI HAMMAMAT (siltstone and GOLD); WADI EL-HUDI (amethyst); Wadi Allaqi and other areas of the Nubian desert (gold); TURA (limestone); HATNUB (TRAVERTINE); GEBEL EL-SILSILA (sandstone); ASWAN (granite); and the Western Desert near Toshka (diorite). The emerald mines in the Sikait-Zubara region of the Eastern Desert were worked from the PTOLEMAIC period, while imperial porphyry was quarried at MONS PORPHYRITES during the ROMAN PERIOD.

Inscriptions at mining and quarrying sites, such as the 12th Dynasty text of Horwerra at Serabit el-Khadim, give details of the composition of mining expeditions, which were organized along military lines. Study of the sites themselves (for instance the unfinished obelisk at Aswan) reveals the techniques used by the ancient Egyptians to extract stone and mineral-bearing ores. Both open and closed quarries are known. Sometimes, tunnels were needed to reach the best seams. Soft stones, such as limestone, could be cut using copper tools. The quarrying of hard stone required stone pounders in an even harder material, such as dolerite. The usual method was to cut trenches around, and partially beneath, the block to be extracted. The block would then be prised loose using wooden levers or wedges, inserted underneath and dampened with water to cause expansion. Repeated heating and cooling of the rock itself, using fire and water, could also be used to loosen a block. Rough blocks of stone were generally given an initial dressing at the quarry site, before being transported to the river's edge on sledges, and from there by barge to their final destination. Mineral ores were crushed, then either processed on site or taken to nearby smelting centres for purification.

Minshat Abu Omar Site in the north-eastern DELTA where excavations have uncovered a major cemetery of the PREDYNASTIC PERIOD and 1st Dynasty. The FUNER-

The sandstone quarries at Gebel el-Silsila preserve abundant evidence of **mining and quarrying**, including the chisel marks left by quarrymen as they extracted blocks of stone.

ARY GOODS suggest strong connections with UPPER EGYPT, and the local community seems to have owed its prosperity to the site's strategic location for trade with PALESTINE. Drill cores have revealed the location of the early settlement. The cemetery was reused for burials during and after the LATE PERIOD.

Mirgissa Site on the west bank of the NILE in Lower NUBIA, at the southern end of the Second CATARACT; it is now submerged beneath Lake Nasser. Mirgissa has been identified with the ancient Egyptian town of Iken which, according to MIDDLE KINGDOM inscriptions, held a monopoly on trade between Egyptian-controlled Lower Nubia and areas further south. The archaeology of the site confirms this identification. Two 12th Dynasty FORTRESSES were built to protect trade routes. Other features included granaries, an armoury for the manufacture and storage of WEAPONS, a quayside for BOATS, and a slipway for hauling boats around the nearby Kabuka rapids.

mirror Usually made of flat polished discs of copper or bronze, mirrors are attested in Egypt from the OLD KINGDOM onwards. Handles were generally modelled in the form of a PAPYRUS stem, the goddess HATHOR, or a nubile female figure. The last emphasized the mirror's erotic connotations.

Mitanni Kingdom which developed in northern MESOPOTAMIA, probably along the southern shore of the Caspian Sea, during the 16th century BC. It gradually expanded southwards into Syria, and became Egypt's main rival in the LEVANT during the 18th Dynasty. Known to the Egyptians as Nah(a)rin(a), the Mitanni fought the army of THUTMOSE I, and confronted the forces of THUTMOSE III at the Battle of MEGIDDO. Friendlier relations were established in due course, cemented by the diplomatic marriages of THUTMOSE IV and AKHENATEN to Mitannian princesses. The Mitanni were a useful ally of Egypt against the growing power of the HITTITES, but were eventually conquered and absorbed by the Hittite empire; Mitannian troops fought on the Hittite side at the Battle of KADESH. Mitannian territory was later conquered by the ASSYRIANS. Although the mass of the Mitannian population were Hurrians, the rulers spoke an Indo-European language; they may have been instrumental in introducing horsemanship and the CHARIOT to the Near East.

Mnevis (Mer-wer) Sacred BULL of HELIOPOLIS, regarded as the manifestation (BA) of the sun god RA. Like other sacred bulls, there was only one Mnevis bull at a time. It was required to be totally black. Each bull was given a lavish burial; those of the RAMESSIDE period are known from a site north-east of Heliopolis. Because of its solar connotations, the cult of the Mnevis bull was maintained during the reign of AKHENATEN. A boundary STELA at AMARNA mentions an as yet undiscovered Mnevis burial place 'in the eastern mountain of Akhetaten'. In ART, the Mnevis was depicted with the sun disc and URAEUS between its horns. The cow which gave birth to a Mnevis bull was worshipped in its own right as the goddess Hesat.

Moalla, el- Site on the east bank of the NILE in UPPER EGYPT, about 24 km (15 miles) south of LUXOR. The most famous tomb in the FIRST INTERMEDIATE

*An 18th Dynasty bronze **mirror**, its handle in the form of a naked girl with raised arms.*

Relief of Ankhtifi from his First Intermediate Period tomb at el-**Moalla**

PERIOD cemetery was built for ANKHTIFI, regional governor during the early stages of the civil war between the Herakleopolitan and THEBAN dynasties.

Mons Claudianus Site in the Eastern Desert where quarrying for granite and quartz diorite began in the reign of the Roman Emperor Augustus and continued until the 5th century AD. A fort, served by a well outside its walls, was built in the ROMAN PERIOD to guard the site.

Mons Porphyrites Site in the Red Sea hills of the Eastern Desert, 50 km (31 miles) north of MONS CLAUDIANUS. This was the only known ancient source of imperial porphyry, a purple rock highly prized for SCULPTURE and architecture in the Roman and Byzantine periods. Remains at the site date from the 1st to the 4th centuries AD, and include quarries, a fortified settlement with a temple to SERAPIS, and smaller settlements for the quarry workers. Mons Porphyrites controlled all quarrying and military activity in the surrounding area.

Montu War god of the Theban region. First attested in the late FIRST INTERMEDIATE PERIOD, he was originally the principal deity of THEBES, but was later supplanted in this role by AMUN. None the less, Montu continued to be associated with the military role of the

king. The BUCHIS bulls at ARMANT were regarded as manifestations of Montu. He was eventually fused with the sun god to form the compound deity Montu-Ra. Montu was depicted as a FALCON-headed man, usually wearing a sun disc and twin plumes. In religious texts, he is described as having four heads, controlling the four points of the compass, and referring to his four principal cult centres at ARMANT, KARNAK, MEDAMUD and EL-TOD.

moon *see* calendar, Khonsu, Thoth

mortuary temple *see* Medinet Habu, Ramesseum, temple

mummification Preservation of a body against decay by treatment with drying agents and a range of other procedures. In the PREDYNASTIC PERIOD, bodies buried in shallow pits dug in the surface sand would have been preserved by natural desiccation. The need to preserve the body swiftly became one of the Egyptians' core AFTERLIFE BELIEFS. Wrapping the deceased in resin-soaked bandages was already practised in the BADARIAN period, perhaps for ritual reasons, and is attested in Predynastic graves at HIERAKONPOLIS and ADAIMA. When the greater use of brick-lined burial chambers and coffins in the late Predynastic period prevented natural drying from occurring, artificial

methods of preservation were developed. In the 2nd Dynasty, entire bodies were wrapped from head to toe in resin-soaked bandages. Although the body inside swiftly decayed, the outward appearance was maintained by the wrappings. The first true mummy – a word derived from *mummia* ('tar'), owing to the blackened appearance of many specimens – was probably made in the early OLD KINGDOM. The removal of the internal organs, a key procedure for preventing decay, is attested in the early 4th Dynasty burial of HETEPHERES, while the earliest excavated mummy, from MEIDUM, dates to the 5th Dynasty.

Details of the mummification process can be ascertained from studying mummies themselves, and from a textual account in the writings of HERODOTUS. First, the body was washed in a bath of NATRON, to purify it. The viscera were then removed through a slit made in the abdomen or, a cheaper option, through the anus. With the exception of the HEART, which was returned to the body, the other organs were generally cleaned, preserved in natron and placed in special CANOPIC JARS; however, in the THIRD INTERMEDIATE PERIOD, all the viscera were usually returned to the body at the end of the mummification process. From the beginning of the MIDDLE KINGDOM, the brain was removed through the nasal cavity, using a sharp, hooked instrument. The body itself was then dried, by packing dry natron around and inside it. Once this procedure was

The final stages of **mummification** *can be seen in reverse order by unwrapping the mummy of Wah, an 11th Dynasty estate manager.*

Unusual scenes (read from bottom to top) showing the body of the deceased undergoing **mummification**, on the Late Period painted coffin of Djedbastiufankh from el-Hiba.

finished, the body cavity was treated with aromatic substances before the incision was sewn up; in the NEW KINGDOM and 21st Dynasty, packets of straw or resin-soaked linen bandages were often placed inside the body cavity to plump it out and preserve a more lifelike appearance. Finally, the whole body was wrapped in linen bandages, soaked with resin and other unguents. Many metres of wrappings were needed, and the process must have taken several days. AMULETS were placed among the bandages to provide magical protection for the body. According to the accounts of Classical authors, the whole mummification process usually took around seventy days, with rituals accompanying every stage. Being so time-consuming and costly, it was originally restricted to the elite, but became more widespread in the PTOLEMAIC and ROMAN PERIODS. The mummification of animals was a common practice in the sacred ANIMAL CULTS of the LATE PERIOD. Mummies are one of the most distinctive products of ancient Egyptian culture, and continue to exercise a powerful grip on the imagination. *See also* the OPENING OF THE MOUTH.

mummy *see* mummification

Music and dance played an important part in ancient Egyptian religious ritual, as shown by the decoration of a sandstone relief block from the Red Chapel of Hatshepsut at Karnak, which includes a harpist, sistrum-players, acrobats and dancers.

Muqdam, Tell el- *see* Leontopolis

music On secular and religious occasions, music played an important part in celebrations. Musicians, playing instruments such as the castanets and flute, are depicted on objects from the PREDYNASTIC PERIOD. A wide range of percussion, wind and string instruments were known to the ancient Egyptians. They include rattles, clappers, drums, tambourines and the SISTRUM; pipes, flutes and trumpets; and harps (particularly popular at feasts). The lyre and lute were introduced from the LEVANT. Musical notation is not attested until the early PTOLEMAIC PERIOD. Groups of musicians, either mixed gender or female only, are known from the OLD KINGDOM. Women singers and sistrum-players had an important role in temple cults, especially those of HATHOR and ISIS. TOMB DECORATION from all periods indicates that, as today, groups of workers sang to generate a sense of solidarity and to maintain their enthusiasm.

Mut Goddess worshipped in the THEBAN area as the wife of AMUN and mother of KHONSU. Her cult is first attested in the late MIDDLE KINGDOM, when she replaced an earlier consort of Amun. She was closely linked with another female deity, SEKHMET, both goddesses being regarded as the daughter and eye of RA, sent to terrorise the earth. The leonine statues in the Mut complex at KARNAK stress this aspect of Mut. By contrast, she also had a protective role as the king's divine mother; AMULETS often showed her suckling a child on her lap. In ART, she is depicted as a woman holding a PAPYRUS sceptre, and wearing a long dress and a VULTURE headdress topped by the white crown or double crown. The GOD'S WIFE OF AMUN was regarded as Mut's earthly incarnation.

Mutemwia Wife of THUTMOSE IV and mother of AMENHOTEP III. A relief in LUXOR TEMPLE shows her conceiving her son by means of a union with the god AMUN.

***muu* dancers** Ritual dancers who performed alongside funeral processions. Often depicted in TOMB DECORATION, especially in the MIDDLE KINGDOM, they are identified by their distinctive kilts and reed crowns.

Mycenaean Belonging to, or characteristic of, the site of Mycenae on the Aegean coast of the Peloponnese peninsula, Greece. Contacts between Egypt and

*Painted relief of the goddess **Mut** from the mortuary temple of Ramesses III at Medinet Habu; Mut rose to prominence in the New Kingdom as consort of the state god Amun.*

Mycenae are best attested in the NEW KINGDOM. Mycenaean pottery has been found at 18th Dynasty Egyptian sites, notably AMARNA. A fragmentary PAPYRUS from the city suggests that Mycenaean soldiers may have served as mercenaries in AKHENATEN's army. Mycenae and the surrounding region seem to have replaced Minoan CRETE as Egypt's major trading partner in the Aegean in the later New Kingdom.

Mycerinus *see* Menkaura

mythology Knowledge of the stories which underpinned ancient Egyptian RELIGION is derived mainly from fragmentary references on stelae and papyri, and in temple inscriptions. Among the best attested are the various CREATION MYTHS, AFTERLIFE BELIEFS, and myths connected with KINGSHIP. The 12th Dynasty stela of IKHERNOFRET contains a detailed account of the OSIRIS Mysteries, re-enactments of mythological episodes in the life and death of the god which took place at ABYDOS in the MIDDLE KINGDOM. The RAMESSEUM DRAMATIC PAPYRUS likewise contains various mythological episodes which may have been performed at specific occasions. A few, more extensive, narrative myths are preserved in literary form; they include the *Contendings of Horus and Seth* and the *Tale of Isis and the Seven Scorpions*.

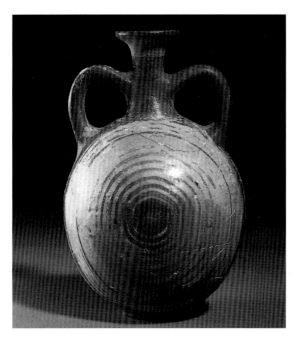

Mycenaean *pilgrim flask from an 18th Dynasty house at Amarna; it was probably used as a container for valuable oil.*

N

Nabta Playa Site in the south-eastern part of the Western Desert, west of ABU SIMBEL. Excavations have revealed remains of prehistoric activity around the shores of a seasonal lake (*playa*), long since dried up. Notable features include a series of megalithic structures and alignments, dating from *c.* 4500 to 4000 BC. Most striking are a stone circle oriented to the midsummer sunrise and a huge buried monolith, deliberately shaped and resembling a cow. Cattle burials reinforce the impression of a people for whom cattle were a vital resource. The evidence from Nabta indicates advanced architectural and social developments at a surprisingly early period.

Nagada (Naqada) Site on the west bank of the NILE in UPPER EGYPT, 27 km (17 miles) north of LUXOR, best known for its settlements and extensive cemeteries of the PREDYNASTIC PERIOD. When Flinders Petrie (*see* EGYPTOLOGY) first encountered Predynastic material at Nagada, he wrongly assigned it to the FIRST INTERMEDIATE PERIOD, but subsequently realized its true age and significance. The Predynastic cultural tradition of Upper Egypt is named the 'Nagada Culture' after the site. A scatter of small, desert-edge villages was replaced in the middle of the fourth millennium BC by a larger settlement closer to the floodplain, probably reflecting a shift in subsistence patterns from ANIMAL HUSBANDRY to AGRICULTURE. The walled South Town, one of the earliest substantial settlements yet discovered in Egypt, was the site of administrative activities associated with the local ruling elite. Their tombs were located in a special burial-ground (Cemetery T), separate from the cemeteries of the general population. FUNERARY GOODS in all classes of burial illustrate the increasing wealth and stratification of Predynastic Upper Egyptian society.

Nagada's particular prosperity seems to have been based on controlling access to the GOLD reserves in the WADI HAMMAMAT: the ancient name of Nagada, Nubt, means 'golden'. In the 1st Dynasty, two large royal tombs were built at Nagada, one of them for queen NEITHHOTEP. The site remained important in the EARLY DYNASTIC PERIOD, a small STEP PYRAMID being erected at nearby Tukh at the end of the 3rd Dynasty. In the OLD KINGDOM and later periods, however, the importance of Nagada as a regional centre was eclipsed by other nearby towns, especially COPTOS, DENDERA and THEBES.

Nagada remained a cult centre of SETH; his temple was periodically embellished in the pharaonic period.

Nagada Culture *see* Predynastic period

Naga el-Deir Site on the east bank of the NILE in UPPER EGYPT, near ABYDOS. Located opposite the presumed location of THIS, Naga el-Deir served as the town's principal cemetery, with burials of nearly every period from the Predynastic to the present day. The earliest graves contained well-preserved organic remains, including human bodies. Important small finds include a stamp seal imported from MESOPOTAMIA, some of the earliest gold JEWELRY from Egypt, cylinder seals of the EARLY DYNASTIC PERIOD, button seals and textiles of the OLD KINGDOM.

Nag Hammadi Town on the west bank of the NILE in UPPER EGYPT, upstream of ABYDOS. It is best known for the discovery made nearby, in 1945, of thirteen PAPYRUS codices (twelve of them intact). Dating to the 4th century BC, they are extremely important for the early history of Christianity, since they include myths and doctrines belonging to the movement known as Gnosticism, which were rejected by the orthodox churches.

Nakht SCRIBE and astronomer of AMUN in the mid-18th Dynasty (probably the reign of THUTMOSE IV), whose tomb at SHEIKH ABD EL-QURNA has fine decoration, including scenes of AGRICULTURE and entertainment at a banquet.

Nakhtmin Son of AY and heir during his brief reign. Nakhtmin never succeeded to the throne (which passed instead to HOREMHEB).

names The choice of names, for kings, private individuals or even buildings, was hugely symbolic in ancient Egypt, and carried great importance. A person's name was assigned immediately after birth, and was regarded as an essential element of his or her identity. Names could be simple adjectives (such as Nofret, 'beautiful') or more complex sentences (such as ANKHESENAMUN, 'she lives for AMUN'). From the OLD KINGDOM, it was not uncommon for individuals to have two names, a longer formal one and a shorter nickname. Changing fashions in naming conventions often reflected religious and political developments. Hence many individuals, especially kings, were given theophorous names, that is, a name incorporating the name of a favoured deity. Examples include Amenemhat ('AMUN is at the fore'), SOBEKHOTEP ('SOBEK is satisfied'), HOREMHEB ('HORUS is in festival'), and RAMESSES ('it is RA who bore him'). Similarly, private individuals might be named after the reigning king, such as Pepinakht-Heqaib (after PEPI II), Khakheperra-seneb (after

The Neolithic stone circle at **Nabta Playa** *in Egypt's southwestern desert suggests advanced astronomical knowledge and a complex society among desert cattle-herders as early as the 5th millennium BC.*

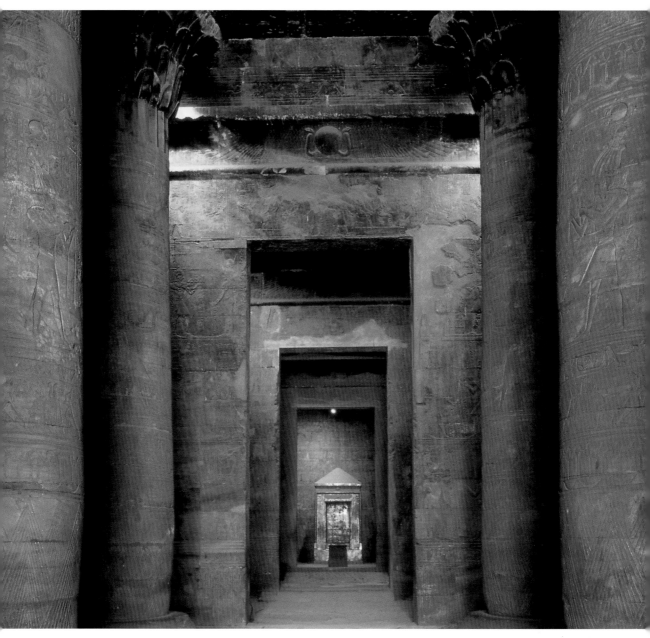

*View through the columns of the inner hall and sanctuary to the **naos** in the innermost part of the Ptolemaic temple of Horus at Edfu. The naos would have contained the cult image or barque shrine of a deity.*

Khakheperra, the throne name of SENUSRET II), and AHMOSE SON OF ABANA (after AHMOSE). A king's full royal titulary comprised five distinct titles and names, each emphasizing a different aspect of KINGSHIP.

To know a person's name was to have power over them, hence the lists of enemies inscribed on EXECRA-TION TEXTS. Survival in the afterlife depended upon one's 'good name' being remembered and spoken by others. Adding one's own name to a monument effectively appropriated its power. Conversely, obliteration of a name from the written record signified annihilation. THUTMOSE III erased HATSHEPSUT's name from her monuments, perhaps because a female king was seen as an offence against MAAT; likewise, AKHENATEN's followers erased the name of Amun and other deities from temples throughout Egypt because, in the king's new religion, ATEN was the sole god.

naos The innermost part of a TEMPLE or shrine, more specifically the rectangular box-shaped container housing the cult image or BARQUE SHRINE of a deity. A popular form of statue ('naophorous') showed an individual holding a *naos*, with the cult image sometimes depicted inside.

Napata District spanning both sides of the NILE along the Dongola Reach in Upper NUBIA, southwest of the Fourth CATARACT. The main site, to the south of the river, comprises a cemetery, a little-known settlement, and a possible palace; north of the river is the sacred site of GEBEL BARKAL. Strategically located at the junction of two important desert routes (north to Kawa and south to MEROË), Napata was first settled in the early 18th Dynasty as an outpost of Egyptian-controlled Nubia. It came to prominence as the capital of the kingdom of KUSH in the first millennium BC. Although eventually supplanted as the capital by Meroë, it remained an important centre for many centuries. The greater Napata district also includes the royal burial-grounds of EL-KURRU and NURI, and a settlement and cemetery site at Sanam.

Naqada *see* Nagada

Narmer (c. 2950 BC) King at the very beginning of Egyptian history, whom scholars place either at the end of the PREDYNASTIC PERIOD or at the start of the 1st Dynasty. He was certainly regarded by subsequent kings of the 1st Dynasty as the first of their line, and may therefore be equated with the legendary MENES. Although his name is conventionally read as Narmer, this is almost certainly incorrect. Two chambers on the UMM EL-QAAB at ABYDOS (B17 and B18) have been identified as his TOMB; nearby chambers may originally have formed part of a larger burial complex. A label from the tomb shows an envoy from the LEVANT stooping and paying homage, although it is difficult to establish if this records a real or idealized episode. Narmer's name is attested in southern PALESTINE, the Eastern Desert, and at sites throughout Egypt. The most famous artifacts from his reign are a ceremonial MACEHEAD and PALETTE from HIERAKONPOLIS.

Narmer Palette Ceremonial palette of siltstone, discovered in the MAIN DEPOSIT at HIERAKONPOLIS. An icon of early Egypt, it illustrates the codification of the principles of Egyptian royal ART at the outset of the pharaonic period. The decoration concerns the activities of KINGSHIP, either real or ritual. On one side, NARMER is shown wearing the white CROWN and

*The early 1st Dynasty **Narmer Palette** from the temple of Horus at Hierakonpolis shows the formalization of Egyptian court art and the central importance of royal iconography at the very beginning of pharaonic history.*

smiting a captive identified as an inhabitant of the 'PAPYRUS land' – probably LOWER EGYPT or the region immediately to the east; a recently discovered label of Narmer appears to record the same event. On the other side, the king wears the red crown and, accompanied by attendants and royal standards, inspects two rows of decapitated enemies. The whole composition, which has been linked to the unification of Egypt, is presided over by two figures of the goddess BAT. Significant are the inclusion of the SERPOPARD motif, adopted from MESOPOTAMIA, and the use of HIEROGLYPHS to label the main figures.

natron Naturally occurring mixture of sodium carbonate, sodium bicarbonate and other impurities. A drying agent, it was a key ingredient in purification rituals and MUMMIFICATION. It was also used in place of soap for daily hygiene; and, as an alkaline substance, in the manufacture of GLASS and glazes. Deposits are known

Granite funerary stela of **Nebra** from Memphis; originally it would have marked the location of the king's tomb at nearby Saqqara.

at ELKAB and in LOWER EGYPT, but the main source in ancient times was the Wadi Natrun in the Western Desert. Natron was the subject of a royal monopoly in the PTOLEMAIC PERIOD.

Naukratis (Kom Gi'eif) Site in the northwestern DELTA, 80 km (50 miles) south-east of ALEXANDRIA. In ancient times, it lay close to the Canopic branch of the NILE, and was connected to the river by a canal. This strategic location gave Naukratis an important role in trade, and it was an important commercial centre during the LATE PERIOD and PTOLEMAIC PERIOD. Silver and bronze coins struck at Naukratis are among the rare examples of coinage known from pharaonic Egypt. From the early 26th Dynasty, the city was settled by Greeks, perhaps originally mercenaries who had served in the ARMY of PSAMTIK I. According to HERODOTUS, AMASIS allowed Greek merchants to settle and trade there, and granted them land so that they could build temples to their gods. Cult buildings include temples of Apollo, Aphrodite and Hera, while NECTANEBO I built a temple to NEITH in the Egyptian quarter of the city. Naukratis declined in importance following the foundation of ALEXANDRIA, but remained one the of three principal Greek cities in Egypt.

navy *see* army, boats and ships, Nekau, Sea Peoples

Near East *see* Levant

Nebirierau (mid to late 17th century BC) Name of one or two ephemeral kings of the later SECOND INTERMEDIATE PERIOD, whose authority was probably confined to UPPER EGYPT.

Nebra (Raneb) (c. 2725 BC) Second king of the 2nd Dynasty. A granite funerary STELA, inscribed with the king's SEREKH, was found near MEMPHIS; it probably came from SAQQARA, where a series of underground galleries near the pyramid of UNAS has been identified as his tomb. The name of Nebra has also been found inscribed on the cliffs of the Western Desert behind ARMANT. Otherwise, he is sparsely attested.

Necho *see* Nekau

necropolis (from the Greek for 'city of the dead'; pl. necropoleis) Large burial-ground, usually comprising more than one individual cemetery.

Nectanebo I (Nakhtnebef) (throne name: Kheperkara) (380–362 BC), the founder of the 30th Dynasty, was born into a military family and rose to power as ruler of SEBENNYTOS in the DELTA. He seized power after the death of HAKOR, and finally became king after NEPHERITES II was deposed. Nectanebo I successfully repelled an invading Persian army and, perhaps to emphasize indigenous Egyptian culture in the face of growing foreign threats, promoted sacred ANIMAL CULTS. He also undertook a major building programme at temples throughout Egypt, including KARNAK (where he built the First PYLON) and PHILAE.

Nectanebo II (Nakhthorheb) (throne name: Senedjemibra) (360–343 BC) was the last native ruler of Egypt until modern times. Enjoying the support of the ARMY, he deposed his uncle TEOS while the latter was on campaign abroad. Nectanebo built a huge temple to ISIS at Behbeit el-Hagar in the DELTA, and carried out work in the sacred animal necropoleis at ARMANT, BUBASTIS and SAQQARA (the SERAPEUM). He retained control of UPPER EGYPT following a Persian invasion, but eventually capitulated to the forces of ARTAXERXES III and fled Egypt.

Neferefra (c. 2390 BC) Fifth king of the 5th Dynasty. His PYRAMID, completed as a MASTABA, has been located and excavated at ABUSIR. Fragments of the king's mummy were found in the burial chamber.

Neferhotep Name borne by three kings of the late MIDDLE KINGDOM and SECOND INTERMEDIATE PERIOD. In the middle of the 13th Dynasty, Neferhotep I (throne name: Khasekhemra) (early 17th century BC) formed a mini-dynasty with his brothers SAHATHOR and SOBEKHOTEP IV. A dyad of Neferhotep I, based on a similar statue of AMENEMNAT III from HAWARA, is now in the Egyptian Museum, CAIRO.

Neferirkara (Kakai) (c. 2400 BC) Third king of the 5th Dynasty. In his PYRAMID complex at ABUSIR archaeologists found a collection of PAPYRUS documents (the 'Abusir Papyri'), detailing the practice of the royal mortuary cult.

Nefertari ('Beautiful companion') Principal wife of RAMESSES II who held an unusually prominent position at court during her husband's reign. A letter from her to the HITTITE king was preserved in CUNEIFORM in

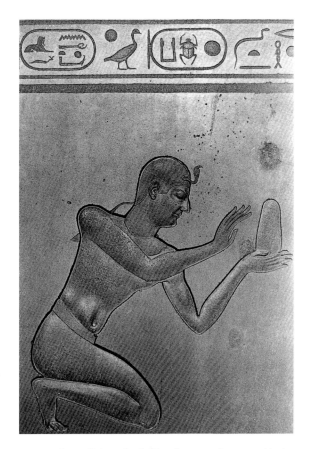

Nectanebo I offering a loaf of bread, on a 30th Dynasty black basalt screen wall from Alexandria; the king's prominent hooked nose suggests an attempt at true portraiture.

*Upper part of a statuette of **Neferefra**, discovered in the ruins of his pyramid at Abusir; the falcon god Horus enfolds the king with his wings in a protective gesture.*

the archive at Hattusas (Boghazköy), the Hittite capital. Ramesses II gave prominence to Nefertari in the decoration of the smaller temple at ABU SIMBEL; he also built for her one of the largest and most beautifully decorated tombs in the VALLEY OF THE QUEENS (QV66).

Nefertem God associated with the blue water-lily, and hence with the sun god which was believed to have risen from a LOTUS flower. He was worshipped at MEMPHIS as the son of PTAH and SEKHMET, and at BUTO as the son of WADJET. He was also linked with royal and cult monuments, and bore the epithet 'protector of the TWO LANDS'. He is depicted as a young man wearing a water-lily headdress, sometimes with twin plumes and counterpoises.

Ramesses II's favourite wife **Nefertari** *presents offerings to the goddess Isis, in a scene from Nefertari's sumptuous tomb in the Valley of the Queens.*

Nefertiti ('The beautiful one is come') Principal wife of AKHENATEN in the late 18th Dynasty. Her family background is uncertain: some scholars have speculated that she was a princess of MITANNI, but it is more likely that she was related to the family of YUYA, TUYU and AY. Her sister MUTNODJMET is probably identical with the woman of the same name who became the principal wife of HOREMHEB. Nefertiti bore Akhenaten six daughters, and played an unusually prominent role in the politics and RELIGION of his court. A formal CO-REGENCY may have been established between Nefertiti and Akhenaten late in his reign. In ART, she was often depicted as equal in status to the king, even being shown in the traditional pose of smiting a foreign captive. The theory that Nefertiti reigned for a brief period after Akhenaten's death as king in her own right – under the name Neferneferuaten – is meeting with increasing support. Nefertiti's burial has not been located, but may have been at THEBES. The most famous depiction of Nefertiti is the painted bust found in the workshop of the sculptor THUTMOSE at AMARNA in 1912 (now in the Egyptian Museum, Berlin); it has always been regarded as an icon of female beauty.

negative confession In AFTERLIFE BELIEFS of the NEW KINGDOM and later periods, the declaration of innocence which a newly deceased person was required to make in order to gain admission to the afterlife. Described in the BOOK OF THE DEAD, the confession took place before a panel of 42 judges; the deceased had to declare that he/she had not committed a specified list of misdemeanors.

Nehesy (throne name: Aasehra) (c. 1640 BC) King of the 13th or 14th Dynasty whose name means 'the Nubian', perhaps referring to his dark complexion rather than his ancestry. A statue of Nehesy, usurped by MERENPTAH, was found at LEONTOPOLIS. Nehesy is

*Painted wooden bust found in the tomb of Tutankhamun depicting the young king as the god **Nefertem**, emerging from a water-lily.*

*Painted limestone bust of **Nefertiti** from the workshop of the sculptor Thutmose at Amarna; probably a sculptor's model, the piece was unfinished but still stands as an icon of female beauty.*

also attested at AVARIS in the DELTA, which may have been his power-base.

Neith Goddess of warfare and hunting. One of the most ancient of Egyptian deities, her cult is attested from the beginning of the 1st Dynasty. She seems to have had a close connection with the ROYAL FAMILY, as

Painted relief of the goddess **Neith,** *goddess of war and hunting, but also of protection, from the 19th Dynasty tomb of Nefertari in the Valley of the Queens.*

indicated by the theophorous NAMES of the 1st Dynasty royal women NEITHHOTEP, HERNEITH and MERNEITH; a label of AHA records a royal visit to the temple of Neith, identified by her symbol of shield and crossed arrows. By the OLD KINGDOM, she was regarded as the consort of the god SETH and mother of the crocodile god SOBEK. Her maternal, protective aspect was stressed over her warlike character. In a funerary context, she was one of the four goddesses (with ISIS, NEPHTHYS and SELKET) who protected the COFFIN and the CANOPIC JARS. She was associated with the east side of the coffin, and with one of the SONS OF HORUS called Duamutef. In ART, Neith is usually depicted as a woman wearing the red crown. From the earliest times, her principal cult centre was at SAIS. It rose to particular prominence in the 26th Dynasty, whose kings originated from the town. Because of her warlike aspect, Neith was identified by the Greeks with their goddess Athena.

Neithhotep Important female member of the ROYAL FAMILY at the very beginning of Egyptian history. She was probably the wife of NARMER and the mother of AHA. Her tomb, at NAGADA, was a large MASTABA decorated in the PALACE-FAÇADE style. Her name indicates the importance of the cult of NEITH in the 1st Dynasty.

Nekau I (Necho I) of SAIS (672–664 BC) was nominally the founder of the 26th Dynasty, although he came to power as vassal ruler of Egypt, following the Assyrian conquest of Egypt in 671 BC. He was probably killed in battle against TANUTAMANI in 664 BC, and was succeeded by his son PSAMTIK I.

Nekau II (Necho II) (throne name: Wehemibra) (610–595 BC) was Psamtik I's son, and hence the third king of the 26th Dynasty. He took advantage of a decline in ASSYRIAN power, wresting control of the kingdoms of ISRAEL and Judah, and re-establishing an Egyptian empire in the LEVANT. His military successes, which included a campaign into NUBIA, depended heavily on Greek and Carian mercenaries, with whom he also staffed the first proper Egyptian navy. He encouraged Greek traders to settle in the DELTA, and founded a new city at TELL EL-MASKHUTA in connection with the excavation of a canal along the WADI TUMILAT, to link the NILE with the Red Sea.

Nekhbet Vulture goddess of ELKAB. From the 1st Dynasty, she was also regarded as the patron deity of

UPPER EGYPT; with her Lower Egyptian counterpart WADJET, she formed the TWO LADIES symbolizing the duality of the Egyptian state. The PYRAMID TEXTS associate her with the white CROWN, and she was also believed to have the role of nursing the king (hence her later identification with Eileithyia, the Greek goddess of childbirth). Usually depicted in art as a VULTURE, she could also be represented as a COBRA, as in the double URAEUS worn by 18th Dynasty queens.

Nekhen *see* Hierakonpolis

nemes *see* headdresses

Nepherites I (Nefaarud) (throne name: Baenra-merynetjeru) (399–393 BC), from MENDES, usurped the throne in 399 BC to found the 29th Dynasty, deposing AMYRTAEOS; he reigned for just six years, was buried at Mendes, and was succeeded by the ephemeral Psammuthis.

Nepherites II (380 BC) was the fourth and last king of the 29th Dynasty who reigned for less than a year before NECTANEBO I seized the throne.

Nephthys Goddess whose origins and precise role are poorly understood. A member of the ENNEAD of HELIOPOLIS, she was the sister-wife of SETH, but her role as sister of ISIS was more important. The two goddesses together acted as protectors of the dead, Nephthys guarding the head of the COFFIN and Isis the foot. Nephthys was associated with Hapi (one of the four SONS OF HORUS) and, in the LATE PERIOD, with ANKET. In later tradition, Nephthys was also regarded as the mother of ANUBIS and she is often shown in scenes of the judgment of the dead. She is depicted as a woman wearing on her head the HIEROGLYPHS for her name (which means 'lady of the mansion'). No cult centre is known for Nephthys.

Netjerikhet *see* Djoser

New Kingdom (c. 1539–c. 1069 BC) One of the major periods into which Egyptologists divide ancient Egyptian history, comprising the 18th, 19th and 20th Dynasties of kings, from the reign of AHMOSE to the reign of RAMESSES XI. It was a period of strong central government, and a golden age of achievement in ART and architecture. It is also one of the best attested periods of Egyptian history, especially in the sphere of daily life.

The expulsion of the HYKSOS at the end of the SECOND INTERMEDIATE PERIOD brought about a revival of Egyptian autonomy and confidence, and also began Egypt's involvement in the geopolitics of the LEVANT. The New Kingdom witnessed the creation of an Egyptian 'empire' in Syria-Palestine, defended by frequent military campaigns against a succession of competing foreign powers, notably the MITANNI and HITTITES. Egypt also annexed and colonized a large part of NUBIA, exploiting the area's GOLD reserves and founding a series of new towns and temples.

Although MEMPHIS remained the main administrative capital of Egypt throughout the New Kingdom (with the possible exception of the AMARNA period), the architectural and archaeological records are dominated by the monuments of THEBES. On the east bank, great temples were erected at LUXOR and KARNAK, the priesthood of AMUN-RA becoming an economically and politically powerful force. On the west bank, the kings built their mortuary temples and inaugurated the

The goddess **Nephthys**, sister of Isis, identified by the hieroglyphs on her head, depicted on the sarcophagus of Thutmose IV. The two goddesses acted as protectors of the dead.

VALLEY OF THE KINGS as the principal royal NECROPOLIS; the VALLEY OF THE QUEENS accommodated the tombs of other members of the ROYAL FAMILY. The village of DEIR EL-MEDINA was founded to house the workmen engaged in the construction of the royal tombs, while the various cemeteries of western Thebes provided space for the TOMBS OF THE NOBLES.

The 18th Dynasty royal line comprised a series of kings mostly called AMENHOTEP and THUTMOSE; an important figure is the female king HATSHEPSUT. Towards the end of the 18th Dynasty, the reign of AKHENATEN marked a striking departure from the conventions of art and RELIGION. He founded a new capital at AMARNA and elevated the ATEN to the position of sole god. After the restoration of the pre-Amarna traditions, the last surviving member of the 18th Dynasty royal family, HOREMHEB, adopted a fellow army officer as his heir, inaugurating the RAMESSIDE period; the 19th Dynasty was overtly militaristic in character. A major development within Egypt was the foundation of PER-RAMESSES. In the 20th Dynasty, a series of ephemeral kings weakened the institution of KINGSHIP. Finally, in the reign of RAMESSES XI, Egypt was divided for administrative purposes, ushering in the political fragmentation of the THIRD INTERMEDIATE PERIOD.

Niankh-khnum and Khnumhotep Two manicurists dating to the reign of NIUSERRA (5th Dynasty), buried

*Roman **nilometer** on the island of Elephantine; the carved notches next to the staircase allowed the height of the annual Nile flood to be measured, primarily for taxation purposes.*

in a joint MASTABA at SAQQARA, decorated with fine reliefs; it is sometimes known as the Tomb of the Two Brothers.

Nile One of the longest rivers in the world, the Nile is fed by Lake Victoria and by rainfall over the Ethiopian Highlands. The river flows in a generally northward direction through NUBIA and Egypt to the Mediterranean Sea, a distance of more than 6,600 km (4,125 miles). In its Nubian stretch, the Nile's course is interrupted by a number of rocky barriers (CATARACTS), creating hazards for shipping. None the less, the Nile was the main artery of transport and communication in ancient times.

It was and remains the principal geographical feature of Egypt and Nubia, defining a narrow strip of fertile floodplain running through an otherwise arid region. Within this floodplain, the course of the main river channel has moved considerably over time. The Nile was known to the ancient Egyptians as *iteru* ('the river'); its life-giving potential was worshipped as the god HAPY. Until modern times, the annual INUNDATION, when the Nile burst its banks, renewed the fertility of the soil and gave Egypt its prosperity. Disastrously high or low floods could cause FAMINE, straining social and political structures.

nilometer Device for measuring the height of the NILE, especially the maximum level reached during the INUNDATION. Ancient nilometers comprised a series of steps leading down to the water level; examples survive at ELEPHANTINE, and at the temples of DENDERA, EDFU, ESNA, KOM OMBO and PHILAE. A nilometer of the Islamic period at Cairo uses a pillar instead of steps.

Nine Bows Ancient Egyptian term for the enemies of Egypt; the bow was a symbol of hostility and the number nine signified 'many'. The Nine Bows were a popular motif on royal objects, especially footstools, throne bases and sandals, so that the king could symbolically trample his enemies underfoot. The precise composition of the enemies represented by the Nine Bows varied over time, but generally included Nubians and Libyans.

Ninetjer (c. 2725 BC) Third king of the Second Dynasty. His tomb at SAQQARA comprised a series of underground galleries and a now-vanished superstructure, which was presumably cleared to make way for

DJOSER'S STEP PYRAMID (the chambers under the Step Pyramid contained reused stone vessels of Ninetjer). Private tombs from the reign of Ninetjer are known at Saqqara and GIZA. A statuette of the king is one of the earliest examples of royal SCULPTURE.

Nitiqret (Nitocris) Name of two prominent women at very different periods of Egyptian history. The TURIN CANON and MANETHO list a female king called Nitiqret at the end of the 6th Dynasty (c. 2175 BC), perhaps in succession to PEPI II, but she is not mentioned in contemporary OLD KINGDOM records. The second Nitiqret was the daughter of PSAMTIK I in the early 26th Dynasty; to cement Psamtik's control of THEBES, she was adopted as the eventual successor to Shepenwepet II and Amenirdis II as GOD'S WIFE OF AMUN.

Nitocris *see* Nitiqret

Niuserra (Ini) (c. 2385 BC) Sixth king of the 5th Dynasty and builder of a pyramid complex at ABUSIR.

nomarch Governor of a NOME or province. The term is a translation of the Egyptian title 'great chief of a nome', first attested in the 6th Dynasty. Although, in theory, all governors were appointed by the king, in practice the office of nomarch was often hereditary within families.

nome Administrative province of Egypt. The Greek term, introduced in the PTOLEMAIC PERIOD, corresponded to the ancient Egyptian *sepat*, which originally referred to an area of irrigated land, perhaps one of the natural IRRIGATION basins into which the NILE Valley was divided for taxation purposes.

Nomes are first attested in the EARLY DYNASTIC PERIOD. For most of the pharaonic period, UPPER EGYPT was divided into 22 such provinces, with relatively fixed boundaries; LOWER EGYPT into 20, which were much more fluid. The nome capitals moved over time, according to central government policy. Each nome had its own sign or standard. In royal mortuary temples, especially of the OLD KINGDOM, nomes personified as women were often shown bringing offerings for the royal cult, symbolizing the involvement of the entire country.

Nubia The southern stretch of the NILE Valley, from the First to the Sixth CATARACTS, together with its bordering desert regions. In modern terms, it comprises

Glazed faience tile from the palace of Ramesses III in his mortuary temple at Medinet Habu, Thebes; the captive from **Nubia** *is shown with jet-black skin and characteristic dress.*

the southernmost part of Egypt, and Sudan. The area between the First and Second Cataracts is generally known as Lower Nubia (corresponding to the ancient Egyptian WAWAT), the area between the Second and Sixth Cataracts as Upper Nubia (KUSH). As well as being a crucial route for trade with sub-Saharan Africa, Nubia was also the source of prestigious raw materials, such as ebony and IVORY, copper and GOLD. Egypt therefore took a keen interest in its southern neighbour, conquering it at various periods.

Nubian influences on Predynastic Egyptian culture can be traced in styles of POTTERY and in shared traits such as cattle burials. Towards the end of the PREDYNASTIC PERIOD, centres of political power developed in Lower Nubia, notably at Seyala and Qustul. Their advanced culture is termed the A-Group. However, as Egypt moved towards a unified state, its rulers began to impose their authority on Nubia by military means. Campaigns are suggested by inscriptions at Gebel Sheikh Suleiman in the Second Cataract region, and by references on 1st Dynasty labels to Ta-Sety ('land of the bowmen'), the earliest Egyptian name for Nubia. At the same time, the A-Group disappears from the archaeological record, presumably extinguished by repeated Egyptian attacks.

Comparatively little is known about Egyptian–Nubian relations during the EARLY DYNASTIC PERIOD and OLD KINGDOM, apart from periodic trade expeditions. In the 6th Dynasty, the government official WENI recounts how he conscripted large numbers of Nubians to serve in an Egyptian campaign against Palestine, while the tomb inscription of HARKHUF illuminates the political developments that were taking place in Lower Nubia at the time. These can be equated with the cultural manifestation termed the C-Group, which remained the dominant culture of Lower Nubia until the beginning of the NEW KINGDOM. (The existence of an intermediate cultural stage between the A-Group and C-Group, termed the B-Group, has now been discredited. The objects previously assigned to the B-Group are thought to belong to a late stage of the A-Group.) The C-Group population seems to have followed a pastoral lifestyle, based upon ANIMAL HUSBANDRY, even though the Nubian Nile Valley was amenable for AGRICULTURE.

Nubian soldiers played an important role in the THEBAN armies during the civil war of the FIRST INTERMEDIATE PERIOD. However, following the reunification of Egypt under MENTUHOTEP II, the Egyptian attitude to its southern neighbour changed markedly.

The MIDDLE KINGDOM is characterized by the construction of a series of fortresses, within signalling distance of one another, throughout Lower Nubia, and the fortification of the border at SEMNA. The background seems to have been an increasing threat from the Kingdom of KUSH, centred at KERMA in Upper Nubia. The Egyptians' fears seem to have been well founded: recent evidence has come to light for a major Kushite invasion of Egypt during the SECOND INTERMEDIATE PERIOD, laying waste sites in Upper Egypt and perhaps reaching as far north as CUSAE; while the STELA of KAMOSE records a military alliance between Kush and the HYKSOS. However, another Nubian group, the MEDJAY, served as mercenaries in the Egyptian army. Their distinctive PAN GRAVES have been found at sites throughout UPPER EGYPT and Lower Nubia.

Following the expulsion of the Hyksos, the 18th Dynasty kings lost no time in conquering Kush and formally annexing Nubia as far as the Fourth Cataract (GEBEL BARKAL). New towns and temples were founded along Egyptian lines; Nubia was governed by a VICEROY OF KUSH, appointed by the king; the large-scale Egyptianization of Nubia began in earnest. However, Nubian autonomy was not permanently extinguished. Following the collapse of the New Kingdom state, local rulers regained control and began to expand their authority.

In a reversal of the usual process, the descendants of the Kushite kings conquered Egypt and ruled as the 25th Dynasty. Their home town of NAPATA was adorned with monuments. The rulers themselves adopted Egyptian BURIAL CUSTOMS, building pyramid C-style tombs at el-KURRU, and later, following their retreat back to their Nubian heartland, at NURI and MEROË. In the LATE PERIOD and following eras, as Egypt was conquered by successive foreign powers, Nubia retained a vibrant indigenous tradition, represented by the Meroïtic and X-Group (c. AD 350–700) cultures.

Archaeological interest in Nubia reached a peak in the 1960s, as a UNESCO-sponsored international rescue mission sought to save the monuments of Lower Nubia from the rising waters of Lake Nasser, following the construction of the Aswan High Dam. In the decades since, scholars have began to look at Nubia not simply as a southern extension of ancient Egypt (which seems to have been the ancient Egyptians' own preferred view), but as a vibrant and dynamic series of cultures in its own right.

Nun God of the watery abyss believed to have existed before the time of creation, and from which the PRIMEVAL MOUND appeared. A member of the OGDOAD of HERMOPOLIS, Nun was generally regarded negatively, as a formless void in which the souls of stillborn babies and unrighteous individuals would dwell for eternity. The wavy courses of bricks ('pan bedding') favoured for temple enclosure walls may have symbolized the waters of Nun being kept at bay outside the sacred area.

Nuri Site on the left/east bank of the NILE in the Fourth CATARACT region of Upper NUBIA, a few kilometres north-east of NAPATA. It was the burial-ground of the rulers of KUSH from the middle of the 7th century to the early 3rd century BC, after the abandonment of EL-KURRU. The NECROPOLIS comprises at least nineteen royal burials, including the PYRAMID tombs of TAHARQO – the first king to be buried at the site – and his successors of the 25th Dynasty; the monuments can be seen from the summit of GEBEL BARKAL. The tombs of QUEENS are located in a separate area. Nuri was succeeded by MEROË as the principal necropolis of the Kushite royal family.

Nut Sky goddess. Perhaps originally identified with the Milky Way, she was believed to arch over the earth, her body forming the vault of heaven, and her limbs extending to the four points of the compass. In a similar vein, she was identified with the COFFIN lid that covered and protected the body of a deceased person. In the Heliopolitan CREATION MYTH, she was the daughter of SHU and TEFNUT. She also played a crucial role in the solar cycle, swallowing the setting sun every evening and giving birth to it again every morning; in temple and tomb reliefs the sun disc is shown travelling through her body. This association with daily rebirth gave her important funerary associations, and the PYRAMID TEXTS mention her in connection with the king's resurrection.

Usually depicted in human form, she could also be shown as a cow. As a celestial, universal deity, Nut had no particular cult centre, but chapels to her were built in the temples of ESNA and EDFU; the ceiling of the HYPOSTYLE HALL at DENDERA carries a huge depiction of Nut.

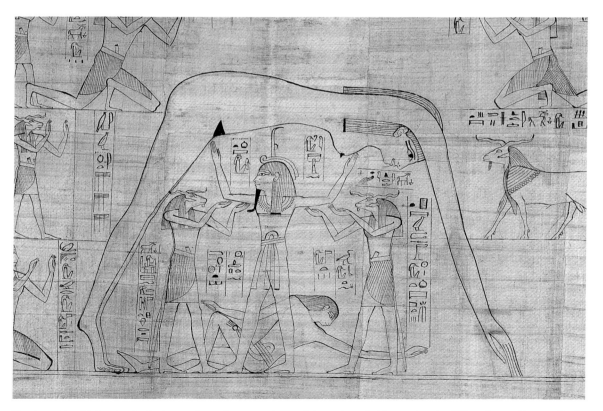

The sky goddess **Nut** *arches her body over the earth, surrounded by divine and magical figures, in a detail from the 21st Dynasty* Book of the Dead *(funerary papyrus) of Nesitanebasharu from Deir el-Bahri.*

Granite **obelisk** of Thutmose I in the temple of Amun-Ra at Karnak; another obelisk erected by his daughter Hatshepsut is just visible behind the palm tree.

Four **offering table**s piled high with provisions, in a detail from the 21st Dynasty funerary papyrus of the priestess Here-ubekhet from Deir el-Bahri.

O

oasis Fertile area of low-lying land surrounded by desert, where the water table lies close enough to the surface to allow permanent vegetation. The Western Desert of Egypt contains a series of oases, stretching in a line parallel with the NILE Valley. They were exploited throughout Egyptian prehistory and history. The principal oases are (north to south) SIWA, BAHARIYA, FARAFRA, DAKHLA and KHARGA.

obelisk Tall, needle-shaped stone monument, gently tapering upwards from the base to the tip. The point was carved to resemble a PYRAMIDION, and was frequently gilded to reflect the rays of the sun, emphasizing the obelisk's strong solar connotations. The first obelisk may have been erected in the temple of RA at HELIOPOLIS; the earliest surviving example, from the reign of SENUSRET I, still dominates the site. As early as the OLD KINGDOM, obelisks were also associated with TOMBS. A large, squat obelisk of solid masonry was the principal architectural feature of the SUN TEMPLE of NIUSERRA. In the NEW KINGDOM, pairs of obelisks were often set up in front of temple PYLONS, such as the obelisks of HATSHEPSUT at KARNAK, and the obelisks of RAMESSES II at LUXOR TEMPLE (one of which is now in Paris). The quarrying and transport of obelisks represented considerable feats of technology and engineering. Hatshepsut boasted of her own achievement in transporting and erecting obelisks in scenes and texts on her Red Chapel at Karnak, and in her mortuary temple at DEIR EL-BAHRI. An unfinished obelisk in the granite quarries at ASWAN shows that extraction was carried out using channels cut in the surrounding rock, wooden levers and basalt pounders. From the LATE PERIOD onwards, AMULETS in the shape of obelisks were made for funerary use. In late antiquity, several Egyptian obelisks were removed to Rome; in modern times several have been transported to major world capitals, including London and Paris.

obsidian Black volcanic glass. From the PREDYNASTIC PERIOD onwards, it was imported into Egypt from the regions bordering the Red Sea, and used for inlays and small objects.

offering formula Standard prayer used in a funerary context to request offerings to sustain the KA of the deceased in the afterlife. First attested on FALSE DOORS in the EARLY DYNASTIC PERIOD, the formula remained in continual use throughout the pharaonic, PTOLEMAIC and ROMAN PERIODS on COFFINS and funerary STELAE. It was designed to magically ensure a perpetual supply of offerings, should the actual supplies of FOOD AND DRINK cease. The prayer opens with an appeal to the king to make offerings to a funerary god (OSIRIS or ANUBIS) so that he, in turn, may give offerings to the deceased. This emphasizes the role of the king as intermediary, and illustrates the system of redistribution characteristic of the Egyptian state economy. The middle part of the formula lists the types and quantities of offerings being requested, headed by BREAD and BEER, and often including oxen, fowl, ALABASTER and CLOTHING. The prayer ends with the titles and name of the deceased. An extra feature, present in some instances, is the 'appeal to the living', which asks visitors to the tomb to recite the formula and so give effect to its magic.

offering table Small stone table on which FOOD AND DRINK offerings were placed for the benefit of a tomb owner or deity. In a funerary setting, the offering table was an important feature of private burials throughout Egyptian history. It was located in the publicly accessible part of the tomb, so that relatives of the deceased or funerary PRIESTS could leave regular offerings. Early tables were one-legged and circular; later models were shaped like the HIEROGLYPH for 'offering' (a loaf of bread on a mat). The upper surface was often carved with channels for liquid offerings; and with images of food and drink, lists of offerings, or a copy of the OFFERING FORMULA, to act as magical substitutes. Funerary STELAE often show the deceased seated in front of a table piled high with offerings. The SOUL HOUSES of the MIDDLE KINGDOM were variants of the basic offering table. In a cultic setting, offering tables were used in the open courts of the ATEN temples at AMARNA.

ogdoad Group of eight deities. The most prominent ogdoad featured in the CREATION MYTH of HERMOPOLIS. It comprised four pairs of deities that were believed to have existed at the time of creation and brought the PRIMEVAL MOUND into being. Each pair, consisting of a FROG god and a SNAKE goddess, symbolized a different creative force, a different aspect of the primeval waters: NUN and Naunet embodied formlessness; AMUN and Amaunet, hiddenness; Heh and Hauhet, infinity; and Kek and Kauket, darkness.

Old Kingdom (c. 2575–c. 2125 BC) The broad phase of ancient Egyptian history between the EARLY DYNASTIC PERIOD and the FIRST INTERMEDIATE PERIOD. Corresponding to the Pyramid Age, it is generally held to comprise the 4th to the 8th Dynasties, although some scholars include the 3rd Dynasty (c. 2650–c. 2575 BC), and others conclude the Old Kingdom at the end of the 6th Dynasty (c. 2175 BC). The Old Kingdom was a period of strong central control during which court culture reached unprecedented heights, as exemplified by the Great PYRAMID of KHUFU at GIZA, and the richly decorated TOMBS of high officials at SAQQARA. These and other architectural wonders dominate our view of the period; by contrast, textual evidence is sparse and knowledge of historical events limited. In the 5th Dynasty, greater local autonomy is suggested by the appearance of ROCK-CUT TOMBS throughout the provinces. However, there is no consensus about the causes behind the collapse of the Old Kingdom centralized state. Economic, environmental and political factors are all likely to have played a part.

Omari, el- *see* Helwan

onomastica (sing. onomasticon) Ancient texts consisting of lists of words, probably composed as works of reference, and used in scribal training. Examples include lists of plants, animals, cities and professions.

Onuris (Anhur) God of war and hunting. Originally from the region of THIS, his main cult centre in later periods was SEBENNYTOS, where a temple of Onuris-SHU was built by NECTANEBO II. According to one legend, Onuris travelled to NUBIA to bring back the EYE OF RA. He was also linked with HORUS. In ART, Onuris is depicted as a standing bearded male with a short wig, surmounted by two or four tall plumes. His right hand is raised as if ready to throw a spear, and he often holds a length of rope in his left hand.

opening of the mouth Ceremony for bringing to life the dead and their funerary statues. (It could even be performed on entire temples.) First attested in the 4th Dynasty, it probably existed much earlier, since examples of the ritual flint knife (*peshes-kef*) used in the ceremony are known from the PREDYNASTIC period. A similar ceremony is described in the PYRAMID TEXTS, but most of the evidence for the Opening of the Mouth dates to the NEW KINGDOM, when the rites comprised 75 separate elements. The 18th Dynasty tomb of

Wall painting of Horus performing the **opening of the mouth** ceremony on the mummy of the deceased, in the 20th Dynasty tomb of Inherkha at Deir el-Medina.

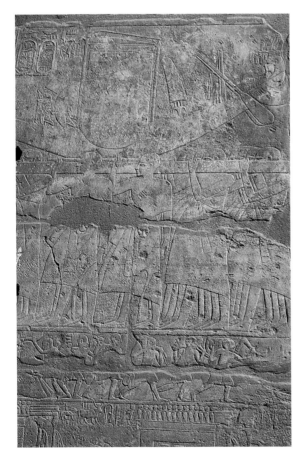

Relief of the **Opet Festival** at Luxor Temple, dating to the reign of Tutankhamun; priests carry the sacred barques of Amun, Mut and Khonsu to the quayside at Karnak for their river journey to Luxor.

REKHMIRA contains the earliest full copy of the ceremony, which included purification, censing, anointing, and incantations. The most important acts involved touching various parts of the mummy or statue with special instruments, some made of meteoritic iron, in order to open the mouth and restore the senses. In this way, the mummy and statues would become suitable homes for the dead person's KA. Ideally, the ceremony was carried out by the heir of the deceased, to legitimize his inheritance. For this reason, AY had himself depicted opening the mouth of TUTANKHAMUN's mummy in the latter's tomb.

Opet Festival Annual religious festival, staged at THEBES, and best attested during the NEW KINGDOM. Lasting from two to four weeks, it centred on the procession of the BARQUE SHRINES of AMUN, MUT and KHONSU from KARNAK to LUXOR TEMPLE, which was built primarily as a setting for the festival. Reliefs in the temple's colonnade depict the procession in detail. In the early 18th Dynasty, the cult images travelled overland along the avenue of SPHINXes, borne aloft on the shoulders of priests, and resting at way-stations along the route. By the late 18th Dynasty, they were taken by barge up the NILE. Above all, the festival celebrated the myth of the royal KA which lay at the heart of KINGSHIP ideology. At the end, the king would enter the sanctuary of Luxor Temple and commune with the royal ka, immanent in the cult image of Amun. He would then emerge into the forecourt of the temple to great acclaim, transfigured into 'foremost of all the living kas'. HOREMHEB scheduled his coronation to coincide with the Opet Festival in order to give his accession added legitimacy.

oracles The practice of asking a deity to approve an important decision or answer a question probably dates back to the MIDDLE KINGDOM or earlier, but first became popular in the NEW KINGDOM. The inhabitants of DEIR EL-MEDINA made frequent recourse to an oracle of the deified AMENHOTEP I to settle disputes. Further oracles could be consulted if a favourable decision was not obtained at first. ALEXANDER THE GREAT visited the oracle of Ammon in the SIWA OASIS to confirm his legitimacy as king of Egypt. In a temple context, the decision of an oracle might be communicated by movement, orally, or by drawing lots. FESTIVALS provided a good opportunity for ordinary people to seek an oracular judgment: PRIESTS carrying the BARQUE SHRINE of a deity in procession would tilt one way or another to indicate yes or no. In the LATE PERIOD and PTOLEMAIC PERIOD, an alternative practice was to sleep on sacred ground in order to receive an oracle in a dream. In the THIRD INTERMEDIATE PERIOD, oracular amuletic decrees were a popular form of protection; an AMULET, consisting of a small cylinder containing a divine decree said to have been issued by an oracle, was worn to ward off harm.

Orion Constellation which played an important role in early AFTERLIFE BELIEFS, and frequently mentioned in the PYRAMID TEXTS. One of the 'star shafts' in the Great Pyramid of KHUFU seems to have been oriented toward Orion. The constellation, or one of its constituent stars (Rigel), was worshipped by the Egyptians as the god Sah, often in a TRIAD with SOPDET and SOPDU.

Osireion Cult building at ABYDOS, behind the temple of SETI I. Constructed of huge granite blocks, it was once thought to date to the OLD KINGDOM but is now dated to the reigns of Seti I and MERENPTAH; the architecture is thought to have been a deliberate attempt at archaizing, to recall the monuments of the 4th Dynasty and so give the impression of great antiquity. It is built in the shape of a royal tomb in the VALLEY OF THE KINGS, with a long descending corridor decorated with scenes from the *Book of Gates*, and a transverse hall with excerpts from the BOOK OF THE DEAD. At the centre of the monument is a hall of red granite with ten pillars, and two platforms surrounded by a water-filled moat, symbolizing the PRIMEVAL MOUND. The precise purpose of the building remains unclear, but it is believed to have been intended as a CENOTAPH for the god OSIRIS.

Osirid pillar Architectural feature, common in royal MORTUARY TEMPLES of the NEW KINGDOM, consisting of a square stone pillar, one side of which is carved as a colossal figure of the god OSIRIS, associated with the dead king. Well-preserved porticoes of Osirid pillars are found at HATSHEPSUT's monument at DEIR EL-BAHRI, and in the second court of the RAMESSEUM.

Osiris God of death, resurrection and fertility. Probably in origin an underworld deity, embodying the fertility of the soil, Osiris gradually absorbed attributes from other gods, such as SOKAR and KHENTIAMENTIU, as his cult grew in popularity from the late OLD KINGDOM onwards. According to Egyptian theology, Osiris was a member of the ENNEAD of HELIOPOLIS, linking him with the most popular of the CREATION MYTHS. A series of stories surrounding the god himself

*Painted relief of **Osiris** from the 18th Dynasty tomb of Horemheb in the Valley of the Kings; swathed in mummy wrappings, the god holds the crook and flail, signifying his role as king of the dead.*

developed by the late Old Kingdom, and his myth was to remain popular throughout the pharaonic period; a full account is preserved in the writings of the Greek historian Plutarch. At the core of the myth was the murder of Osiris by his brother SETH, who proceeded to dismember the body and scatter its pieces throughout the land. Osiris's widow, ISIS, gathered the pieces together, made the first mummy, and then aroused Osiris sufficiently to be impregnated, conceiving

travelled through the underworld led to a merger of the solar and Osirian concepts of the afterlife during the NEW KINGDOM. Osiris was also believed to act as judge of the dead, presiding over the WEIGHING OF THE HEART ceremony and welcoming the righteous into a blessed afterlife. He was generally depicted as a male mummy, his hands projecting through the mummy wrappings and holding the characteristic ROYAL REGALIA of the crook and flail (to symbolize his roles as a dead king, and king of the dead). The god's skin could be coloured white, green (symbolic of vegetation and rebirth), or black (symbolic of the earth), and he was usually shown wearing the *atef* CROWN (a combination of the white crown with a plume on either side, and sometimes with the addition of ram's horns). The main cult centre of Osiris was at ABYDOS. In the MIDDLE KINGDOM, the 1st Dynasty tomb of DJER was identified as the tomb of Osiris, and became a place of pilgrimage. An annual festival of Osiris took place at Abydos, during which his cult image took part in a grand procession, and episodes from his myth were re-enacted. In the 19th Dynasty, the temple of SETI I at Abydos included a chapel to Osiris, and the OSIRIEION was built as a focus of his cult. Osiris was also worshipped at BUSIRIS in the DELTA.

Osiris bed Item of funerary equipment found in royal tombs of the NEW KINGDOM; it comprised a wooden frame in the shape of the god OSIRIS which was filled with soil and sown with barley seeds. The germination of the barley in the tomb symbolized the triumph of Osiris – as god of fertility, vegetation and resurrection – and the promise of rebirth. Only seven examples have survived, one from the tomb of TUTANKHAMUN. A later development of the Osiris bed was a ceramic brick with the figure of Osiris carved into the upper surface.

Osorkon Libyan name held by five kings of the 21st, 22nd and 23rd Dynasties. Their precise relationship to each other, regnal numbers, place within the order of succession, and the overall chronology of the THIRD INTERMEDIATE PERIOD have all been much debated.

Osorkon the Elder (Osorchor) (throne name: Aakheperra-setepenra) (*c.* 975–*c.* 970 BC). He was the son of a Libyan chief and became king (21st Dynasty) in succession to AMENEMOPE.

Osorkon I (throne name: Sekhemkheperra-setepenra) (*c.* 925–*c.* 890 BC) Successor of SHOSHENQ I, and the

Osiris bed *from Tutankhamun's tomb; the ritual object, symbolic of regeneration, comprises a wooden frame in the shape of the god Osiris, filled with Nile silt and seed; the seed germinated to make a 'corn mummy', emphasizing the triumph of life over death.*

HORUS. In due course, the son avenged his father and won the KINGSHIP from Seth. The myth thus combined AFTERLIFE BELIEFS and kingship ideology, the two most powerful elements of Egyptian RELIGION. By the FIRST INTERMEDIATE PERIOD, Osiris had become the quintessential god of resurrection, with whom every deceased person wished to be identified. Moreover, the identification of Osiris with the night sun as it

second king of the 22nd Dynasty. He built a temple to ATUM and extended the temple of BASTET at BUBASTIS.

Osorkon II (throne name: Usermaatra-setepenamun) (c. 875–c. 835 BC) was the son and successor of TAKELOT I (22nd Dynasty). His authority in UPPER EGYPT was challenged by the High Priest of AMUN, HARSIESE. After Harsiese's death, Osorkon appointed one of his own sons as High Priest, allowing him to reassert royal control over the THEBAN region. However, late in his reign, a subsequent holder of the priestly office, TAKELOT II, claimed ROYAL TITLES and effectively founded a rival dynasty in Upper Egypt. Osorkon II built a tomb within the temple precincts at TANIS.

Osorkon III (c. 780–c. 750 BC) was a king of the 23rd Dynasty ruling from the Theban region, where he had previously served as High Priest of AMUN and was involved in a prolonged power struggle with rival factions (recorded in the inscription known as the CHRONICLE OF PRINCE OSORKON). His daughter Shepenwepet I became GOD'S WIFE OF AMUN.

Osorkon IV (throne name: Aakheperra-setepenamun) (c. 735–c. 715 BC) was the last king of the 22nd Dynasty, ruling over a limited area of the DELTA around BUBASTIS and TANIS. During his reign, Egypt was conquered by PIYE, the ruler of KUSH.

ostraca (sing. ostracon) Sherds of pottery or flakes of limestone which were used for WRITING short texts or for drawings. Ostraca were much more readily available than PAPYRUS, and were used in particular by the inhabitants of DEIR EL-MEDINA for a wide variety of jottings and correspondence. The hundreds of examples which have survived provide insights into daily life, HUMOUR AND SATIRE, not attested in the official record.

Oxyrhynchus (el-Bahnasa) Site on the west bank of the Bahr Yusuf channel in MIDDLE EGYPT, named by the Greeks after the sacred fish worshipped locally. The site is first mentioned in an inscription of PIYE, and in the 26th Dynasty became the capital of the nineteenth Upper Egyptian NOME. It was important in the ROMAN PERIOD, with close economic links to the BAHARIYA OASIS. Oxyrhynchus is famous for the discovery of thousands of Greek papyri, dating from the PTOLEMAIC PERIOD to the early Islamic period. The collection includes LITERATURE, biographies, private and official correspondence, and important early Christian texts.

P

Paentjeni (throne name: Sekhemra-khutawy) (late 17th century BC) Ephemeral king of the SECOND INTERMEDIATE PERIOD known only from a single STELA (now in the British Museum, London). His name, which means 'the one of THIS', suggests that his authority may have been restricted to the area around This and ABYDOS.

Paheri Official of the 18th Dynasty, whose tomb at ELKAB contains important inscriptions and finely executed decoration, including agricultural scenes showing the stages of the harvest.

Pakhet Lioness goddess, regarded as a fierce hunter who terrified her enemies; she thus shared many of the traits of other lioness goddesses, especially SEKHMET. Pakhet is first attested in the MIDDLE KINGDOM, when COFFIN TEXTS refer to her as a nocturnal hunter 'with sharp claws' (her name means 'she who scratches/tears'). In the early NEW KINGDOM, a small temple to Pakhet was built by HATSHEPSUT and THUTMOSE III at SPEOS ARTEMIDOS. A cemetery of sacred CATS was located nearby, and the region as a whole seems to have been the centre of Pakhet's cult.

In the Egyptian pantheon, Pakhet was linked with a form of HORUS as her divine consort; the Greeks associated her with their goddess of hunting, Artemis (hence the name given to her temple, Speos Artemidos, 'the cave of Artemis'). Only rarely depicted in Egyptian ART, Pakhet was shown as a woman with the head of a lioness. AMULETs of Pakhet were worn for protection.

palace From the late PREDYNASTIC PERIOD, there was a close symbolic association between the palace and its inhabitant, the king. The SEREKH or rectangular frame enclosing the king's primary name depicted a section of PALACE-FAÇADE, and this distinctive architectural style carried powerful royal connotations. In the 18th Dynasty, the term for palace (per-aa, 'great house') began to be applied to the person of the king, and is the origin of the word PHARAOH.

Built in mud-brick, relatively few palaces have survived, and it is not always easy now to identify the original purpose of royal buildings. Major residences are represented by a section of an early palace gateway at HIERAKONPOLIS, remains at AVARIS, as well as the North Riverside Palace at AMARNA. Buildings used for ceremonial purposes – such as the SED FESTIVAL, royal appearances, or the reception of foreign dignitaries – include MALKATA, the Great Palace and King's House at Amarna, and the palace of SETI I at QANTIR. Temporary royal residences – used for HUNTING expeditions, during visits to temples, or on campaign – have been excavated at Kom el-Abd in southern THEBES, MEDINET HABU, DEIR EL-BALLAS, and in NUBIA. Palaces seem to have been brightly decorated with a mixture of natural and ideological motifs on walls, ceiling and floors. In the NEW KINGDOM, many palaces incorporated a WINDOW OF APPEARANCE.

palace-façade Style of architectural decoration, characterized by alternating niches and buttresses, giving a panelled appearance. Imitating the façade of the early royal palace (confirmed by the excavation of an early palace gateway at HIERAKONPOLIS), the style had strong symbolic associations with KINGSHIP. The SEREKH represented a section of palace-façade. The same architectural style was also used for the outer walls of high status MASTABAS in the EARLY DYNASTIC PERIOD, and in later periods for the exterior decoration of royal COFFINS and SARCOPHAGI.

Ceremonial **palette** of the late Predynastic period, decorated with motifs associated with the triumph of order over chaos; the central well indicates its original function as a grindstone for cosmetics.

Palermo Stone Name given to the largest surviving fragment of an ancient ANNALS stone, now housed in the Archaeological Museum in Palermo. The stone is a large slab of basalt, inscribed on both sides with salient events of the reigns of each king from the beginning of the 1st Dynasty to the latter part of the 5th Dynasty. The annals are arranged in a series of registers and compartments, each compartment corresponding to a single year. Most of the original slab is now missing, although six smaller fragments from the same or similar stones survive. The slab would originally have been set up in a temple context, to emphasize the continuity of the royal succession, and the events recorded are primarily concerned with the ritual duties of KINGSHIP. The stone is thus of limited use for HISTORY, although similar sources were probably used by MANETHO.

Palestine Term used by archaeologists for the area corresponding to modern Israel, the Gaza Strip and the West Bank. It is part of the wider geographical region termed Syria-Palestine or the LEVANT. The term 'Palestine' is used interchangeably with 'Canaan', which also refers more specifically to one of the three divisions of the NEW KINGDOM empire in the Near East.

palette Term applied to two distinct kinds of artifact from ancient Egypt. The cosmetic palette is a flat piece of stone, most commonly siltstone from the WADI HAMMAMAT, used for grinding mineral pigments (such as GALENA and MALACHITE) to make eye-paint and other cosmetics. Such palettes were common FUNERARY OBJECTS in the PREDYNASTIC PERIOD, and were carved in a wide variety of shapes, from simple lozenges to elaborate animal forms. During the transition to the 1st Dynasty, larger ceremonial cosmetic palettes were produced with complex scenes celebrating KINGSHIP; the most famous example is the NARMER PALETTE. The scribal palette, which formed the basis of the HIEROGLYPH for 'SCRIBE' and 'WRITING', consisted of a rectangular piece of wood with a central groove to hold reed brushes and pens, and one or two circular wells at one end for cakes of pigment.

pan bedding *see* Nun

Pan Grave Term applied to a group of semi-nomadic people from eastern NUBIA who are attested in Egypt during the late MIDDLE KINGDOM and SECOND INTER-

MEDIATE PERIOD. Their culture is represented by distinctive artifacts and BURIAL CUSTOMS, including handmade POTTERY with incised decoration; bracelets and other JEWELRY made from strips of Red Sea shell; CLOTHING, notably leather kilts; FUNERARY GOODS, including horns and painted skulls of gazelles, sheep and cattle; and characteristic, shallow, circular graves, known as pan graves, after which the group is named, and which are known from sites throughout UPPER EGYPT and Lower Nubia. All these features suggest contacts with the C-Group and KERMA cultures of Nubia, the nomads of the Eastern Desert, and the ancient Egyptians. The Pan-Grave people have therefore been identified with the MEDJAY.

papyrus The reed *Cyperus papyrus*, once common along the banks of the NILE and its tributaries, was the emblematic plant of LOWER EGYPT. In RELIGION, it was associated with the watery conditions believed to have existed at the time of creation. Hence, columns in temples were often carved to resemble the papyrus reed, singly in its closed or open (flowering) form, or as bundles of stalks tied together. The plant itself was used for making a paper-like writing material. To make the paper, the plant stems were first peeled and the pith was cut into strips which were then placed on top of each other in two layers, at right angles. After beating, compressing with a heavy weight, and drying, the resulting sheet of interlocked fibres was polished with a pebble to produce a smooth surface for writing.

The inside of a roll of papyrus (recto) was written on first, while the outside (verso) was often left blank. The earliest surviving (miniature) roll of papyrus was found, uninscribed, in the 1st Dynasty TOMB of Hemaka at SAQQARA. Papyrus remained the main writing material for official documents until cloth paper was introduced in the 8th to 9th centuries AD. Reused papyrus was a principal ingredient in the manufacture of CARTONNAGE. Papyrus reeds were also used to make baskets and simple BOATS (skiffs).

Pasebakhaenniut *see* Psusennes I, II

pat Ancient Egyptian word denoting the members of the ruling elite, in contrast to the REKHYT or common people. The term probably originated as a designation for the small group of royal relatives, belonging to a single, hereditary ruling family, from which all high officials were drawn. The title *iri-pat* ('member of the pat') was commonly held by officials in the EARLY DYNASTIC PERIOD, and continued in use, perhaps with a less specific meaning, in later periods.

Pedubast Name of two kings of the THIRD INTERMEDIATE PERIOD. Pedubast I (c. 825–c. 800 BC) was based at THEBES and claimed ROYAL TITLES in direct opposition to TAKELOT II, with whom he waged a civil war for two decades, receiving support from the king in TANIS SHOSHENQ III. Pedubast II (c. 735–c. 725 BC), based at Tanis, was an ephemeral successor of SHOSHENQ V.

Peftjauawybast (c. 735–c. 725 BC) King of the late THIRD INTERMEDIATE PERIOD who ruled the northern part of UPPER EGYPT until it was conquered by PIYE.

Pepi I (throne name: Meryra) (c. 2310 BC) Second king of the 6th Dynasty. He reigned for at least forty years and commissioned temple buildings at ABYDOS,

*Calcite statue of the infant **Pepi II**, of the 6th Dynasty, on the lap of his mother, Ankhnesmerira II; the boy king is shown as a miniature adult.*

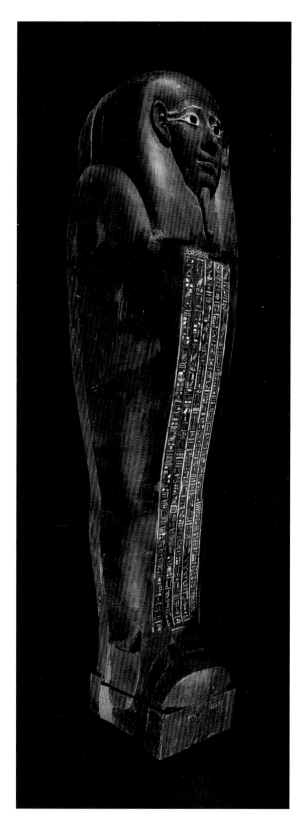

Wooden inner coffin of **Petosiris**, *from his tomb at Tuna el-Gebel, dating to the early Ptolemaic period; the hieroglyphs in five vertical columns down the front are inlaid in coloured glass.*

BUBASTIS, DENDERA and ELEPHANTINE; however, few significant monuments survive from his reign. A life-size copper statue of the king was found in the sanctuary of the temple of HORUS at HIERAKONPOLIS. His pyramid complex at south SAQQARA, which includes a version of the PYRAMID TEXTS, was called Men-nefer ('established and beautiful'), thought to be the origin for the name MEMPHIS.

Pepi II (throne name: Neferkara) (c. 2265 BC) Fourth king of the 6th Dynasty, in succession to his half-brother MERENRA. Pepi II was a child at his accession; a letter from the young king in which he expresses his eaagerness to see a dwarf that the governor of ASWAN was bringing him is transcribed on the façade of the tomb of HARKHUF at QUBBET EL-HAWA. The king probably reigned for over ninety years; his death seems to have caused a crisis in the royal succession, since most of the obvious heirs seem to have predeceased him. His PYRAMID complex at south SAQQARA includes a relief showing the king as a SPHINX, trampling his enemies, directly copied from the pyramid complex of SAHURA at ABUSIR.

peret see calendar

Peribsen (c. 2700 BC) King of the late 2nd Dynasty. Uniquely among Egyptian rulers, he replaced the usual HORUS FALCON atop his SEREKH with the animal of the god SETH. The reasons behind this striking theological change are not known, but may have been connected with the internal political situation. He reinstated ABYDOS as the royal NECROPOLIS, modelling his tomb closely on those of the early 1st Dynasty kings. The absence of contemporary inscriptions from LOWER EGYPT mentioning Peribsen is striking, although, in the early OLD KINGDOM, his mortuary cult was celebrated at SAQQARA.

At the same site, inscriptions have been found mentioning a king with the HORUS NAME Sekhemib-Peren-maat. The same ruler is also named on seal impressions from the entrance to Peribsen's tomb, and from ELEPHANTINE. Most scholars therefore identify the two kings as one and the same individual. It is possible that the two different names were used at different stages of his reign, or in different parts of the country.

peripteral Architectural term for a building surrounded by an external colonnade.

peristyle Open courtyard with an internal colonnade on all four sides, such as the Second Court of RAMESSES III's mortuary temple at MEDINET HABU.

Per-Ramesses (Qantir) Settlement on the Pelusiac branch of the NILE in the north-eastern DELTA, adjacent to AVARIS. Although the earliest levels date to the 18th Dynasty, the site was traditionally founded by SETI I to mark the ancestral home of the 19th Dynasty royal family. It was subsequently developed by RAMESSES II into a royal residence and major city. Excavations have uncovered the remains of palaces, army barracks, chariot stables and workshops, a shrine of ASTARTE, and evidence for communities of HITTITES and Mycenaeans. Texts indicate that the city was a flourishing port, with harbour facilities on the river and temples to the major state gods of the RAMESSIDE period. Per-Ramesses declined in importance after the end of the 20th Dynasty and was eventually abandoned; most of its statues and the stonework from its temples were moved to TANIS and BUBASTIS during the THIRD INTERMEDIATE PERIOD.

Persian period Term applied to two phases of Egyptian history when the country was controlled by the Achaemenid empire. The first Persian period, corresponding to the 27th Dynasty, began after the invasion of CAMBYSES in 525 BC and lasted until the restoration of Egyptian self-rule in 404 BC. It seems to have been a period of relative prosperity. The traditional Egyptian cults continued to be observed, and a new temple of AMUN was built at HIBIS in the KHARGA OASIS. Details of the period have been gleaned from the inscribed statue of Wadjhorresnet, originally set up in the temple of NEITH at SAIS. The second Persian period, also known as the 31st Dynasty, lasted from the death of NECTANEBO II in 343 BC to the conquest of ALEXANDER THE GREAT in 332 BC. Numerous documents in DEMOTIC and Arabic have survived from both periods.

Petosiris High Priest of THOTH at HERMOPOLIS at the beginning of the PTOLEMAIC PERIOD. The tomb he built for himself, his father and his brother at TUNA EL-GEBEL shows a mixture of Egyptian and Greek influences in its architecture and decoration.

Petrie, Flinders *see* Egyptology

petroglyph Rock carving. Petroglyphs from all periods of prehistory and history are common on the

cliffs bordering the NILE Valley, and in the Eastern and Western Deserts.

pets The ancient Egyptians kept a variety of animals as companions or for amusement. A CAT buried in a human grave of the BADARIAN period may have been a

Pets were popular among all social classes in ancient Egypt; the little golden shrine from the tomb of Tutankhamun shows the king's pet, a young lion, leashed under the royal stool during a hunting excursion.

Predynastic petroglyphs in the heart of the Eastern Desert depict the domesticated animals that once grazed the area after the summer rains.

pet; pet cats are certainly shown in TOMB DECORATION from the MIDDLE KINGDOM onwards. DOGS, especially greyhounds and other breeds suitable for HUNTING, are attested from the PREDYNASTIC PERIOD. In the NEW KINGDOM, popular pets included vervet monkeys, gazelles, and even leopards; while, at all periods, kings kept wild animals such as LIONS and ELEPHANTS in their own private zoos.

pharaoh The term used for the ancient Egyptian king. The word is derived via Greek from the ancient Egyptian word *per-aa* ('great house', palace). Originally applied to the royal residence, it was used from the 18th Dynasty to refer to the king himself. Hence, the use of 'pharaoh' for Egyptian rulers before the NEW KINGDOM is strictly anachronistic and best avoided.

Philae Island in the NILE just south of ASWAN. The original island of Philae is now submerged, following the construction of the Aswan High Dam; in the 1970s its monuments were dismantled and re-erected on the neighbouring island of Agilqiyya. This latter island is now generally referred to as Philae. A few sherds of MIDDLE KINGDOM POTTERY have been found at Philae, but it is best known for the temple of ISIS which dominates the island.

Reused blocks from the reign of TAHARQO indicate cult activity in the 25th Dynasty, while 26th Dynasty remains include a KIOSK of PSAMTIK II, and blocks from a shrine of AMASIS. However, the surviving temple dates from the 30th Dynasty (reign of NECTANEBO I) to the ROMAN period. A smaller temple to the Nubian god ARENSNUPHIS forms part of the complex. The cult of Isis at Philae survived into the Christian period, when the island was the last outpost of pharaonic culture. It was finally abandoned around AD 535. Philae is also important as the location of the last surviving inscription in Egyptian HIEROGLYPHS, dated to 24 August AD 394.

Philistines *see* Sea Peoples

Phoenicians Semitic-speaking people who displaced the Canaanites to occupy the coastal area of modern Lebanon during the 1st millennium BC. Successful sailors and traders, they founded the port cities of Sidon and Tyre. Egyptian texts, such as the TALE OF SINUHE, refer to them as Fenekhu.

phoenix *see benu* bird

phyle Greek word, a translation of the Egyptian *sa* ('watch'), denoting a group of priests or workmen serving for a designated period as part of a roster system.

Piankhy *see* Piye

pig Swine had an ambiguous status in ancient Egypt. An enigmatic pottery statuette, dated to the PREDYNASTIC PERIOD, depicts a pig goddess, perhaps suggesting an early pig cult. However, in later periods, the pig was associated with the god SETH, making it the subject of certain TABOOS. None the less, bones found on settlement sites, and the pig pens in the workmen's village at AMARNA, indicate that pork formed an important part of the diet. A scene in the 6th Dynasty tomb of KAGEMNI may show a farmer giving a piglet milk from his own tongue; however, pigs were rarely depicted in ART because of their association with Seth. Similarly, although the major temples owned herds of pigs, they were never presented as offerings. By the time HERODOTUS wrote his account of Egypt, swineherds were evidently considered an underclass in Egyptian society.

Pimay (c. 785–c. 775 BC) King of the late 22nd Dynasty. He was the son of SHOSHENQ III.

Pinedjem Name of two High Priests of AMUN during the 21st Dynasty (c. 1069–c. 945 BC). Pinedjem I, who probably came to power during the latter part of RAMESSES XI's reign, combined the offices of High Priest and ARMY commander. He effectively controlled UPPER EGYPT south of EL-HIBA during the reign of Smendes (probably his uncle), and used ROYAL TITLES at THEBES where he was effectively recognized as the local king. His daughter Maatkara became GOD'S WIFE OF AMUN, while his son acceded to the throne as PSUSENNES I. Pinedjem II was the grandson of Pinedjem I and the nephew of Psusennes I. During the reign of SIAMUN, Pinedjem II was replaced as High Priest of AMUN by his son, who subsequently became king as PSUSENNES II.

Piramesse *see* Per-Ramesses

Pithom *see* Atum

Piye (Piankhy, Piya) (throne name: Usermaatra) (c. 747–c. 715 BC) Ruler of KUSH in succession to ALARA

*The temple buildings on the island of **Philae** were removed to the nearby island of Agilqiyya to save them from the rising waters after the construction of the Aswan High Dam.*

and KASHTA, and regarded as the first king of the 25th Dynasty in Egypt. Building on his father's successful expansion into Lower NUBIA, Piye took control of UPPER EGYPT and had his sister Amenirdis I adopted as the next GOD'S WIFE OF AMUN by the incumbent, Shepenwepet I. This guaranteed eventual control of the THEBAN region.

In 728 BC, to counter an alliance led by TEFNAKHT, Piye swept northwards and crushed the rebels. He celebrated his victory on a STELA, copies of which were erected at GEBEL BARKAL, KARNAK and MEMPHIS. In its style, the inscription consciously imitated earlier models, beginning the archaizing trend so characteristic of 25th Dynasty court culture. After a reign of more than thirty years, Piye was buried in the Kushite royal cemetery at el-KURRU, in a pyramid-style tomb.

police *see* Medjay

Place of Truth *see* Deir el-Medina

pottery On settlement and cemetery sites throughout Egypt, from early Predynastic times onwards, pottery is by far the most common type of artifact, due to its ability to survive in most conditions and over long periods. Pottery vessels were used for a wide variety of purposes, including storage, eating, drinking and cooking. For the PREDYNASTIC PERIOD, the study of pottery and its stylistic changes over time has allowed Egyptologists to devise a CHRONOLOGY without written evidence (SEQUENCE DATING); in later historic periods, too, pottery styles provide useful dating evidence, in addition to, or in the absence of, inscriptions. Ceramicists who specialize in the study of pottery classify Egyptian wares according to the internationally recognized Vienna System, which allows comparisons between different sites and periods.

The most important criterion is fabric, either the readily available, alluvial NILE clay, or the rarer, calcareous desert marl. Nile wares, which fire to a red-brown colour, are the most common at all periods and could

*Decorated **pottery** vessels from the 18th Dynasty (top) and the Predynastic period (bottom) illustrate the technical and artistic skill of potters throughout ancient Egyptian history.*

be produced with relatively simple technology. Marl wares required more specialist knowledge; fired at a much higher temperature, they produce characteristic buff-coloured pottery. Criteria for more detailed classification include the kind of tempering agent used, technology, and surface treatment.

The earliest pottery was entirely handmade. A turning device was used at Buto in the early 4th millennium BC for the local manufacture of Palestinian-style pottery, but was not adopted for the production of pottery in the indigenous, Egyptian tradition until much later. The true potter's wheel was only introduced in the late OLD KINGDOM, while the foot-operated kick-wheel did not appear until the PERSIAN or PTOLEMAIC PERIOD.

Decorated pottery of all kinds (burnished, polished, painted) was popular in the Predynastic Period. Thereafter, wares tended to be simpler and more utilitarian, with the exception of the blue-painted pottery characteristic of the late 18th Dynasty. In periods of strong central control, such as the Old, Middle and New Kingdoms, pottery styles tended to be dictated by the court, and hence generally homogeneous throughout the country. At other periods, local traditions flourished, giving rise to distinct regional styles. The study of imported pottery provides evidence for trade between Egypt and other lands.

Predynastic period (c. 5000–c. 2950 BC) The later phase of Egyptian prehistory, beginning in the sixth millennium BC and ending with the unification of Egypt at the beginning of the 1st Dynasty (c. 2950 BC). It was a period of great innovation and development, when the seeds of classic Egyptian civilization were sown. Spanning some three thousand years, it is subdivided by archaeologists for convenience into subphases or 'cultures', based upon changes in the style of POTTERY and other artifact types.

For much of the Predynastic period, different cultural traditions seem to have existed in UPPER EGYPT and LOWER EGYPT (although this perception is perhaps the result of the different types of evidence – mainly cemeteries in Upper Egypt, mainly settlements in Lower Egypt), necessitating different terminologies. The Upper Egyptian sequence is better known and begins with the BADARIAN culture. This is followed by three phases named by Flinders Petrie after the sites where they were first identified: Amratian, after el-Amra, near ABYDOS; Gerzean, after Gerza near TARKHAN; and Semainean, after Semaina, near DIO-

POSOLIS PARVA. Modern scholars have renamed them the NAGADA Culture – divided into Nagada I (*c.* 4000–3600 BC), Nagada II (*c.* 3600–3200 BC) and Nagada III (*c.* 3200–2950 BC) – after the important Predynastic site in Upper Egypt. Nagada III is also termed the 'Protodynastic', since it corresponds to the period of state formation when many of the features of dynastic Egypt, including KINGSHIP ideology, were rapidly developing.

The Lower Egyptian sequence includes many diverse cultural traditions from different regions. The FAYUM A culture, from the shores of Lake Fayum, represents the earliest agricultural settlements. Other important Lower Egyptian sites of the fifth millennium BC include MERIMDA BENI SALAMA and el-OMARI. The main phase of Predynastic Lower Egyptian culture is named after the site of MAADI ('Maadi culture' or occasionally 'BUTO-Maadi culture'), and is roughly contemporary with the Nagada I and early Nagada II phases in Upper Egypt. During the latter half of the Nagada II phase, Upper Egyptian cultural traits and technological innovations, especially in pottery manufacture, spread northwards. This brought about a cultural unification of Egypt some centuries before the political unification.

prenomen (throne name) *see* royal titles

priests Those who served the cults of Egyptian deities, and the mortuary cults of deceased kings and private individuals, bore a range of different titles, reflecting their widely varying roles. The basic Egyptian term for a temple priest was *hem-netjer* ('god's servant'). More specialized tasks are indicated by such terms as 'purifier', 'lector-priest' and 'stolist' (one who clothed the cult image of a deity); the higher ranks of the priesthood bore titles such as 'second prophet' (often responsible for temple administration), 'first prophet', and 'chief priest'. In the EARLY DYNASTIC PERIOD, the title *zekhenu-akh* designated a priest serving the royal mortuary cult.

Prior to the NEW KINGDOM, most priests were not full-time professionals, but were drawn from the local community and served on a rota according to the PHYLE system. Female members of the ruling elite might serve as priestesses of HATHOR and, at other

*Shaven-headed **priests** dressed in robes take part in a religious procession in a scene from the first court of Ramesses III's mortuary temple at Medinet Habu.*

periods, as temple dancers and musicians. In the New Kingdom, the professionalization of the priesthood was accompanied by an increase in their political and economic influence as the major state temples, notably the temple of AMUN-RA at KARNAK, began to control ever larger estates.

At all periods, only the most senior priests would have come into contact with the cult image of the deity. The chief priest carried out his role on behalf of the king. In theory, all priests were confirmed in office by royal appointment; in practice, however, many offices, particularly in the provinces, became hereditary at certain periods of Egyptian history. A particular case of a priestly office carrying real political power was the GOD'S WIFE OF AMUN, a title first attested in the New Kingdom and from the 20th Dynasty on traditionally bestowed on the king's daughter. The main function of the god's wife was to act as the consort of Amun in religious ceremonies.

Priests also had to abide by certain rules, codes of conduct and TABOOS; for example, in the New Kingdom, shaven heads were required as a sign of ritual purity. According to HERODOTUS, priests were circumcised and had to abstain from sexual intercourse while in office. Certain priests wore particular garments, such as the leopard skin worn by the *sem*-priest (an office closely associated with the heir to the throne). As a reward for service, priests would generally receive a share of the goods presented to a temple or mortuary cult, according to the system of 'reversion of offerings'.

primeval mound In Egyptian RELIGION, the first area of dry land that emerged from the watery abyss at the time of creation. Personified as the god Tatenen, it was a powerful symbol both of creation and of resurrection, and as such influenced the design of Egyptian TOMBS and TEMPLES.

The 1st Dynasty tomb of DJET at ABYDOS contained a hidden mound to assist the king's rebirth. Likewise, the forms of the MASTABA and PYRAMID deliberately recalled the primeval mound. According to CREATION MYTHS, a reed which grew on the mound provided a perch for a FALCON god and hence served as the prototype for all temples.

From an early period, temples were founded on a mound of pure clean sand, recreating the primeval mound. In temples of the NEW KINGDOM and later periods, the columns of the HYPOSTYLE HALL symbolized the reed marshes of creation. The primeval mound

came to be associated with the cult of OSIRIS (as god of fertility and regeneration), hence the symbolic island at the centre of the OSIRIEION.

Prophecy of Neferti Work of LITERATURE set in the reign of SNEFERU but composed in the early 12th Dynasty. Various NEW KINGDOM copies are preserved on papyri, writing boards and OSTRACA. The work recounts how a wise man, Neferti, is summoned by the king to entertain him with speeches, and prophesies a future of civil disorder and strife, brought to an end by a 'saviour from the south' called Ameny (assumed to refer to AMENEMHAT I). The work is a fine example of the theme of 'national distress', popular in the 12th Dynasty.

Psammetichus *see* Psamtik I, II, III

Psammuthis (throne name: Userra-setepenptah) (393 BC) Ephemeral second king of the 29th Dynasty, in succession to NEPHERITES I. He reigned for less than a year and was succeeded by HAKOR.

Psamtik I (throne name: Wahibra) (664–610 BC) Effectively the first king of the 26th Dynasty, although preceded in later KING-LISTS by his father, NEKAU I of SAIS. In theory, Psamtik was a vassal of the ASSYRIANS, but he took control of the DELTA with the assistance of Greek and Carian mercenaries. By his ninth year, the kings of KUSH had retreated from UPPER EGYPT and Psamtik was recognized as ruler of the whole country, abandoning any pretence of loyalty to Assyria. In time-honoured fashion, he had his daughter NITIQRET adopted as the next GOD'S WIFE OF AMUN, to secure his control over the THEBAN region. His reign marked something of a renaissance in Egyptian culture: he maintained the archaizing style of the 25th Dynasty, and inaugurated the sacred ANIMAL CULTS that were such a distinctive feature of religion in the LATE PERIOD. He was succeeded by NEKAU II.

Psamtik II (throne name: Neferibra) (595–589 BC) Fourth king of the 26th Dynasty, the son and successor of NEKAU II. His name is well attested on monuments, and his foreign mercenaries left graffiti at ABU SIMBEL. To curb the power of the kings of KUSH, he sent an army deep into NUBIA. One of his generals, AMASIS, eventually deposed Psamtik II's son and successor, APRIES.

Detail of the gold funerary mask of **Psusennes I**, from his tomb at Tanis; surpassed in quality only by the mask of Tutankhamun, this fine example of the goldsmith's craft has inlays of lapis lazuli and glass; it was found in situ, covering the face of the royal mummy.

Psamtik III (throne name: Ankhkaenra) (526–525 BC) The seventh and last king of the 26th Dynasty, the son and successor of AMASIS. He reign of just six months was brought to an abrupt end by the invasion of CAMBYSES; Psamtik was executed by the victorious Persians.

Psusennes I (Pasebakhaenniut) (throne name: Aakheperra-setepenamun) (c. 1040–c. 985 BC) Third king of the 21st Dynasty. He ruled only LOWER EGYPT, but maintained good relations with the THEBAN rulers of UPPER EGYPT: his daughter married a Theban High Priest, and he may himself have been the son of the High Priest of AMUN, PINEDJEM I. Psusennes was buried at TANIS, his power base, with magnificent FUNERARY GOODS, including a gold MASK, gold vessels and elaborate JEWELRY.

Psusennes II (Pasebakhaenniut) (throne name: Titkheperura-setepenra) (c. 950–c. 945 BC) Seventh and last king of the 21st Dynasty, in succession to SIAMUN. He was probably the son of the THEBAN High Priest PINEDJEM II, whom he succeeded in that office before becoming king. After his death, or possibly during his lifetime, the Libyan rulers of the 22nd Dynasty took power in LOWER EGYPT, OSORKON I marrying the daughter of Psusennes II.

Relief block from the 18th Dynasty temple of Hatshepsut at Deir el-Bahri, recording an expedition to **Punt***; the ruler of Punt (right) is followed by his obese wife (centre) and an attendant (left).*

Ptah Memphite god of craftsmen and creation. First attested in the 1st Dynasty, his cult acquired national importance because of the status of MEMPHIS as capital city. For example, Ptah is one of the four state gods depicted in the sanctuary of RAMESSES II's temple at ABU SIMBEL. According to the CREATION MYTH developed by the priests of Memphis – the 'Memphite theology' – Ptah brought the world into being by his thoughts and spoken words. He was worshipped in a TRIAD with SEKHMET and NEFERTEM, but also became closely linked with another Memphite deity, the underworld god SOKAR, and with OSIRIS. From the 18th Dynasty, the APIS bull was regarded as the BA of Ptah. Worshippers at the Ptah temple at Memphis left ear-STELAE – stelae decorated with images of human ears and dedicated to 'Ptah of the hearing ear' – as VOTIVE offerings. The name of one of the temples at Memphis, Hut-ka-Ptah ('mansion of the KA of Ptah'), is thought to be the origin of the Greek word 'Aigyptos', modern 'Egypt'.

Ptah was depicted as a standing male figure with a tight-fitting robe, and a skull-cap exposing his ears; his hands protruded from his robe and held a staff combining the ANKH, DJED PILLAR and WAS SCEPTRE. From the MIDDLE KINGDOM onwards, Ptah was shown with a straight beard.

Ptah-Sokar-Osiris Compound funerary god, resulting from the SYNCRETISM of PTAH with two underworld deities, SOKAR and OSIRIS. First attested in the LATE PERIOD, Ptah-Sokar-Osiris was depicted as a standing male mummy. Private burials of the period often included a wooden Ptah-Sokar-Osiris statuette, on a hollow pedestal sometimes ornamented with FALCONS, and containing a corn mummy or a copy of the BOOK OF THE DEAD.

Ptah-Tatenen Compound deity, a fusion of PTAH with another MEMPHITE god, Tatenen. The latter was an earth and vegetation god, who represented the PRIMEVAL MOUND emerging from the waters of NUN.

Ptolemaic period (332–30 BC) The phase of Egyptian history spanning the three centuries from the conquest of ALEXANDER THE GREAT to the death of CLEOPATRA VII. Strictly speaking, the reigns of Alexander, his half-brother Philip Arrhidaeus and his son Alexander IV should be classified separately as the Macedonian period (332–309 BC). The Ptolemaic dynasty was founded by Ptolemy I Soter, one of Alexander's gener-

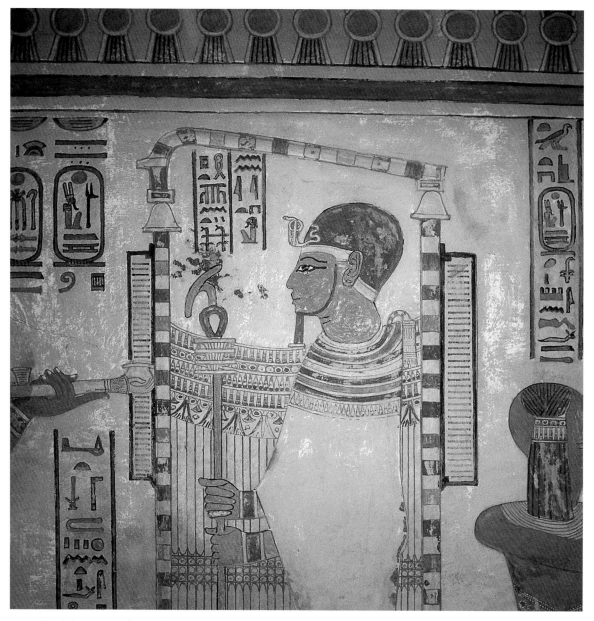

*The god **Ptah** depicted standing inside his shrine, in a painted relief from the 20th Dynasty tomb of prince Amenherkhepeshef in the Valley of the Queens.*

als, who continued the policy of honouring Egyptian RELIGION, inaugurating the cult of SERAPIS. In his reign and those of his successor kings, all named Ptolemy, many temples were rebuilt or extended. The Ptolemies retained the system of NOMES for administrative purposes, and over thirty new towns were founded in the FAYUM. Periodic revolts against Ptolemaic rule broke out in the THEBAN region, remote from the capital city at ALEXANDRIA. Increasing involvement with Rome ultimately spelled the end of the Ptolemaic dynasty, and the beginning of the ROMAN PERIOD.

Ptolemy *see* Ptolemaic period

Punt (Pwene) Land to the south of Egypt, to which the Egyptians sent trading expeditions from the OLD KINGDOM to the end of the NEW KINGDOM. The earliest reference to Punt in an Egyptian text occurs in the inscription from the tomb of HARKHUF, which tells of a DWARF having been brought from Punt in the reign of ISESI. Some expeditions from Egypt travelled overland, but the more usual route was by sea from the Red Sea coast.

The precise location of Punt has not been established, but it is likely to have been in East Africa, probably in the vicinity of modern Eritrea and eastern Sudan. It was famed as the source of exotic products, notably INCENSE trees, but also ebony, IVORY, and monkeys. In this context, it is mentioned in the TALE OF THE SHIPWRECKED SAILOR. Famous reliefs in the temple at DEIR EL-BAHRI record an expedition to Punt in the reign of HATSHEPSUT. They show a Puntite village with beehive-shaped dwellings on stilts, set among palm trees; the local flora and fauna; and the wife of the ruler of Punt, depicted as grotesquely obese.

Puyemra Second prophet of AMUN in the reigns of HATSHEPSUT and THUTMOSE III, buried in a finely decorated tomb at ASASIF in the THEBAN NECROPOLIS.

Pwene *see* Punt

pygmy *see* dwarf

Entrance **pylon** *of the Ptolemaic temple of Horus at Edfu; as in other temples of the New Kingdom and later periods, the two tapering towers, joined by a gateway, formed a monumental rendition of the hieroglyph for 'horizon', the place of sunrise and sunset.*

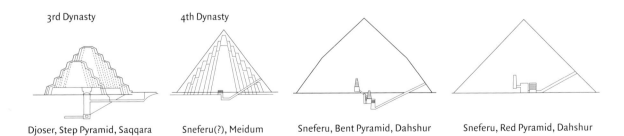

3rd Dynasty   4th Dynasty

Djoser, Step Pyramid, Saqqara   Sneferu(?), Meidum   Sneferu, Bent Pyramid, Dahshur   Sneferu, Red Pyramid, Dahshur

Throughout the Old Kingdom, the **pyramid** *was the characteristic royal mortuary monument; a sequence of cross sections illustrates the evolution of the form.*

pylon Ceremonial gateway of an Egyptian temple or temple-style tomb. Formed of two tapering towers, each surmounted by a cornice, joined by a less elevated section enclosing the entrance doorway, a pylon mimicked the HIEROGLYPH for 'horizon', which was a schematic depiction of the two hills between which the sun rose and set. It thus played a crucial role in the symbolic architecture of a cult building, associating it with the place of recreation and rebirth. Rituals to the sun god were often carried out on the top of temple pylons. Pylons were usually filled with a solid core of rubble, but might also contain internal stairways and rooms. Vertical grooves on the exterior face were designed to hold flag poles, kept in place with giant clamps projecting from the pylon. The pylon was the public face of a cult building, visible to the general population. Hence, in temples, they were often decorated with reliefs proclaiming royal power, such as scenes of the king smiting his enemies or performing other ritual duties. The oldest intact pylons belong to mortuary temples of the RAMESSIDE period. The most important temples, such as KARNAK, comprised a series of pylons and courts.

pyramid Monument rising from a square base to a pointed apex, with four triangular sides. It was the form generally adopted for the royal tomb from the beginning of the 3rd Dynasty to the end of the MIDDLE KINGDOM, and again in the 25th Dynasty; and, on a much smaller scale, for the superstructure of some private tombs in the NEW KINGDOM. The best-known examples, the pyramids of GIZA, are the only surviving Wonder of the Ancient World, and have become emblematic of ancient Egyptian civilization as a whole.

The earliest pyramid, the STEP PYRAMID of DJOSER, developed from the MASTABA. Subsequent royal tombs

of the 3rd Dynasty were also built as step pyramids, although none was completed. Several small step pyramids were built at the end of the 3rd or beginning of the 4th Dynasty as markers of the royal cult. The true pyramid, with smooth sides, was an innovation of the reign of SNEFERU, who filled in the steps of the pyramid at MEIDUM. Sneferu ushered in the greatest age of pyramid building, constructing two further, gigantic monuments at DAHSHUR. His son, KHUFU, built the largest ever pyramid, the Great Pyramid at Giza. In its size, the precision of its alignment to the compass points, and its complex series of internal chambers, it represents the ultimate expression of royal power, architectural sophistication and technical accomplishment. A pyramid nearly as large was built at Giza by Khufu's second successor, KHAFRA; but, thereafter, royal pyramids tended to be considerably smaller, and less carefully constructed. The pyramids of the 5th Dynasty placed greater emphasis on the decoration of other parts of the mortuary complex, and PYRAMID TEXTS were introduced into some of the subterranean chambers in the reign of UNAS.

After the hiatus of the FIRST INTERMEDIATE PERIOD, the pyramid form was re-adopted for royal tombs at the beginning of the 12th Dynasty. However, unlike their Old Kingdom predecessors which were solid masonry constructions, Middle Kingdom pyramids were built around a core of stone or mud-brick rubble, making them far more prone to collapse. Royal pyramids at all periods were cased with dressed blocks of stone: usually fine white limestone from TURA but, in the case of the MENKAURA's pyramid, blocks of red granite from ASWAN.

Pyramid building required not only architectural and technical expertise, but also the mobilization and organization of a large workforce. This was achieved

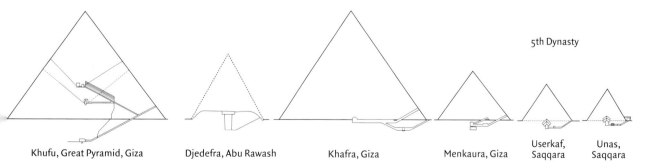

Khufu, Great Pyramid, Giza   Djedefra, Abu Rawash   Khafra, Giza   Menkaura, Giza

5th Dynasty

Userkaf, Saqqara   Unas, Saqqara

Black granite **pyramidion** from the 12th Dynasty pyramid of Amenemhat III at Dahshur; the capstone is inscribed with the king's names and titles, and solar symbols.

by the system of CORVÉE LABOUR, supplemented by a smaller, permanent group of personnel. Pyramids were probably laid out using observation of the stars. Blocks were hauled from the quarries to the building site using sledges and ropes. The construction ramps required to reach the higher levels of a pyramid would have been massive feats of engineering in their own right.

A typical royal pyramid complex of the Old and Middle Kingdom comprised several distinct elements: on the low desert, the pyramid itself, containing the burial chamber within or below the superstructure; an adjacent mortuary temple (or pyramid temple), for the celebration of the royal cult; a causeway leading from the mortuary temple down to the floodplain; and at the lowest point of the complex, a VALLEY TEMPLE, next to the river, accessible by canal during the INUNDATION. Around the main pyramid, smaller, subsidiary pyramids might be provided for the king's KA and/or his

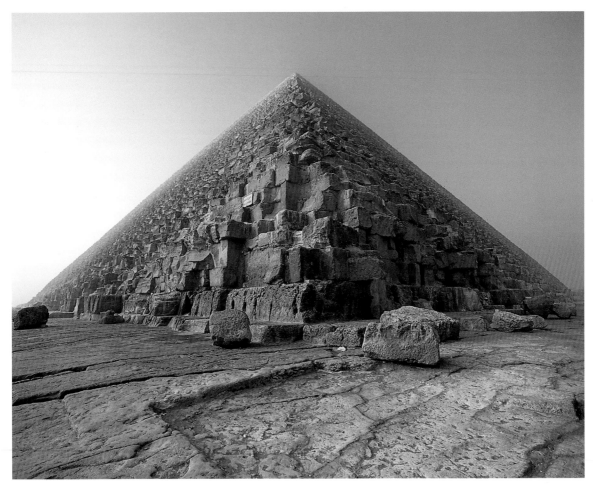

The Great **Pyramid** of Khufu at Giza represents the high point of monumental funerary architecture; it was the tallest building in the world from the time of its completion until the 19th century AD.

wives. One or more BOAT BURIALS (either actual craft or boat-shaped pits) often completed the provision for the king's afterlife.

pyramidion Capstone at the top of a PYRAMID. Called *benbenet* in ancient Egyptian, it associated the pyramid as a whole with the sacred BENBEN STONE. Pyramidions may have been covered in gold leaf to reflect the rays of the sun; in the MIDDLE KINGDOM, they were often inscribed with ROYAL TITLES and religious symbols. The black granite pyramidion of AMENEMHAT III from his monument at DAHSHUR is one of a number of pyramidia now in the Egyptian Museum in Cairo.

Pyramid Texts The earliest collection of religious writing from Egypt, inscribed inside the burial chambers and corridors of nine royal pyramids of the late OLD KINGDOM. The earliest set is in the 5th Dynasty PYRAMID of UNAS, the latest in the 8th Dynasty pyramid of King IBI. The texts comprise nearly a thousand individual 'utterances' – spells, prayers and longer passages – although no single pyramid contains a complete set. They concern the king's resurrection into the afterlife and his destiny among the gods. The various utterances were probably composed at different periods; they certainly reflect different AFTERLIFE BELIEFS.

Some sections are likely to have been handed down by oral tradition; the 'Cannibal Hymn', in which the king is said to feast on the bodies of the gods, may already have been very ancient by the time it was written down. Later sections, composed in the late Old Kingdom, show the rise of the cult of OSIRIS. During the process known as the 'democratization of the afterlife', selections of Pyramid Texts were adapted for use in private burials, where they formed the basis of the COFFIN TEXTS.

*The walls of Teti's burial chamber at Saqqara are inscribed with extracts from the **Pyramid Texts**, sacred writings intended to assist the king in his resurrection and afterlife.*

Q

Qaa (c. 2800 BC) Eighth and last king of the 1st Dynasty. His reign may have been a long one, as an inscription mentions a second SED FESTIVAL, a festival generally held to mark the thirtieth anniversary of a king's succession, and as more than one tomb in the elite cemetery at north SAQQARA is dated to his reign. These graves contain numerous POTTERY vessels imported from the LEVANT, suggesting flourishing contacts with the region, while an IVORY gaming rod from the king's tomb at ABYDOS shows the figure of a bound Asiatic captive. The architecture of Qaa's tomb suggests a continuation of the practice of HUMAN SACRIFICE. Seal impressions confirm that his burial was overseen by his successor, HETEPSEKHEMWY. The walls of the Coptic village of Deir Sitt Damiana probably incorporate the remains of Qaa's funerary enclosure at Abydos. An inscription mentioning Qaa has also been discovered in the Wadi Hellal near ELKAB.

Qadesh (Qedeshet, Qudshu) Syrian goddess associated with sacred ecstasy and sexual pleasure, whose cult reached Egypt in the 18th Dynasty. She was worshipped in a TRIAD with MIN and RESHEP, and was also linked with HATHOR, and the other Near Eastern goddesses ANAT and ASTARTE. She was usually

The upper part of the 19th Dynasty stela of Qeh from Deir el-Medina shows the Asiatic goddess **Qadesh** flanked by Min (left) and Reshep (right).

depicted naked, standing on a LION, holding flowers and SNAKES.

Qadesh, Battle of see Kadesh, Battle of

Qahedjet see Huni

Qantir see Per-Ramesses

Qasr el-Sagha Site in the northern part of the FAYUM depression. Archaeological remains include traces of a settlement close to the shore of Lake Fayum (Birket Qarun) and, further into the desert, an unfinished and uninscribed stone temple. Dated to the late MIDDLE KINGDOM, the temple was probably built to provide magical protection against the hostile forces believed to inhabit the desert regions.

Qasr Ibrim Site in Lower NUBIA, 238 km (149 miles) south of ASWAN; it was originally located on the east bank of the NILE, but, since the construction of the Aswan High Dam, occupies a headland in Lake Nasser. Due to its elevated position, it is the only significant site in Lower Nubia to have escaped permanent flooding, and is remarkable for the exceptional preservation of organic remains, including textiles, basketry, leather and wood. Qasr Ibrim was first occupied in the NEW KINGDOM; monuments from this period include four rock-cut shrines. Later activity is attested by temples from the 25th Dynasty to the MEROÏTIC period, including one built by TAHARQO; cemeteries from the Meroïtic period onwards; extensive material from Roman military occupation; and an 8th century AD Nubian cathedral. The site was abandoned only in the 19th century AD.

Qau (Qau el-Kebir, Antaeopolis) Site on the east bank of the NILE in MIDDLE EGYPT, best known for a series of imposing tombs built for three successive NOMARCHS of the 12th Dynasty (Wahka I, Ibu and Wahka II). Other remains include tombs of the late OLD KINGDOM, LATE PERIOD, and PTOLEMAIC and ROMAN periods; quarries used from the NEW KINGDOM onwards; and the site of a destroyed Ptolemaic period temple.

Qebehesenuef see Sons of Horus

Qedeshet see Qadesh

Qila el-Dabba see Dakhla Oasis

quarrying *see* mining and quarrying

Qubbet el-Hawa Site on the west bank of the NILE opposite ASWAN, comprising a series of ROCK-CUT TOMBS hewn into the cliffs, and a NECROPOLIS of smaller tombs at the foot of the escarpment, extending northwards over the low desert. From the late OLD KINGDOM to the MIDDLE KINGDOM, the governors of Aswan were buried in decorated rock-cut tombs overlooking Aswan and ELEPHANTINE. Most famous are those of HARKHUF (with its autobiographical inscription) and Sarenput, governor of Aswan in the reign of SENUSRET I. The most important tombs had a forecourt, connected to the river by a causeway running up the cliff face. There are also a few NEW KINGDOM tombs.

Qudshu *see* Qadesh

queens Although kings' wives were often important individuals with considerable political influence, the ancient Egyptian LANGUAGE had no word for 'queen'. Rather, royal women were generally designated according to their relationship with the reigning monarch: as 'great royal wife' (principal queen, a title introduced in the late 12th Dynasty), 'royal wife' (secondary queen), or 'king's mother'. Particularly in the NEW KINGDOM, the great royal wife played a role in politics and RELIGION second only to the king.

Some holders of the office, such as NEFERTITI and NEFERTARI, were powerful figures in their own right. As in other African monarchies, the king's mother enjoyed high status in ancient Egypt, beginning with MERNEITH in the 1st Dynasty and including such figures as AHMOSE NEFERTARI and TIYE in the 18th Dynasty. However, most royal spouses are less well attested. Secondary wives, including those from diplomatic marriages, may have lived in the HAREM, with their own courtiers and servants.

The potential for political conspiracy must always have existed in such institutions, as different wives vied to see their son succeed to the throne. Examples of queens plotting against their husbands are known from the 6th and 20th Dynasties. The term 'queen' is not strictly applicable to female monarchs: HATSHEPSUT, for instance, generally presented and styled herself as male in order to conform to the principles of MAAT. Hence, the term 'female king' is preferable.

Qurna Modern village at the northern end of the THEBAN NECROPOLIS which has lent its name to the nearby mortuary temple of SETI I.

Qurnet Murai Small hill in the southern part of the THEBAN NECROPOLIS, behind the mortuary temple of AMENHOTEP III. The earliest burials are 11th Dynasty SAFF TOMBS, but the majority of interments date to the late 18th Dynasty, including tombs of several VICEROYS OF KUSH. It is thought that AMENHOTEP SON OF HAPU may have been buried here.

The popularity of the site during the 18th Dynasty was no doubt influenced by the proximity of Amenhotep III's monuments, including MALKATA. The cemetery saw limited use during the RAMESSIDE period. In the Christian period, the site was dominated by the monastery of St Mark.

Qustul *see* Nubia

*The unfinished 12th Dynasty temple at **Qasr el-Sagha** in the Fayum was never decorated and its original dedication remains uncertain.*

*Some of the rock-cut tombs in the cliffs at **Qubbet el-Hawa** opposite Aswan had long causeways leading down to the river. The tombs date mostly to the Old and Middle Kingdoms.*

R

Ra Sun god, and perhaps the most important deity in the Egyptian pantheon. The cult of Ra is first attested in

The sun god Ra enthroned, in a wall painting from the late 18th Dynasty Theban tomb of Roy, royal scribe and steward of the estates of Horemheb and Amun.

the 2nd Dynasty; the construction in the reign of DJOSER of a shrine at HELIOPOLIS, the principal cult centre of Ra, is evidence of the growing importance of solar religion in the 3rd Dynasty. By the beginning of the OLD KINGDOM, Ra had risen to prominence as the supreme god, reflected in the adoption of 'son of Ra' as one of the ROYAL TITLES. The kings of the 5th Dynasty lavished as much or more attention on SUN TEMPLES as they did on their pyramids, marking a high point of solar worship. In subsequent periods of Egyptian history, the cult of Ra absorbed other important gods by SYNCRETISM, giving rise to compound deities such as Ra-Horakhty (the morning sun, a fusion of Ra and HORUS), Ra-ATUM (the evening sun), and AMUN-Ra, king of the gods.

In the FIRST INTERMEDIATE PERIOD, the increasing popularity of the OSIRIS myth led to the identification of Ra with the god of the dead during the sun's nocturnal passage through the underworld. There, Ra was believed to bring new life to the deceased and fight against the serpent APOPHIS to defend created order. The promise of daily rebirth inherent in the myth of the solar cycle assured its dominance in AFTERLIFE BELIEFS. In the NEW KINGDOM, it featured prominently in the decoration of the royal tombs in the VALLEY OF THE KINGS. In the reign of AKHENATEN, the sun god – worshipped as the solar disc or ATEN – was promoted to the position of sole deity, to the exclusion of all other cults. At other periods, Ra was depicted as a man with a

Egyptian art clearly distinguished people of different race, as shown by this group of Nubian tribespeople in the Theban tomb of Huy, viceroy of Nubia in the reign of Tutankhamun.

Painted relief from the tomb of **Ramesses I** *in the Valley of the Kings, showing the king kneeling in jubilation between the animal-headed souls of Pe (right) and Nekhen (left), representing Lower and Upper Egypt.*

FALCON's head wearing a solar disc. In his underworld aspect he could be shown with the head of a ram.

race The modern concept of race is not easily applied to the population of ancient Egypt. The Egyptians recognized different skin colours, and were careful in their ART to distinguish themselves from black-skinned Nubians and the pale-skinned inhabitants of the LEVANT. However, such differences were considered subordinate to cultural considerations: if a foreigner adopted Egyptian culture, he was considered Egyptian and could achieve high office. It is likely that the indigenous inhabitants of ancient Egypt, like their modern descendants, exhibited a broad spectrum of racial characteristics, from more Mediterranean in the DELTA to more African in southern UPPER EGYPT. This range is already apparent in the Predynastic population. The theory that a 'dynastic race' of eastern invaders was responsible for the foundation of ancient Egyptian civilization lacks any archaeological evidence and is now almost totally discredited. It was originally the product of a colonial, European world-view which thought the continent of Africa incapable of producing an advanced civilization without external influence.

Radjedef *see* Djedefra

Ra-Horakhty *see* Horus, Ra

Rahotep (throne name: Sekhemra-wahkhau) (late 17th century BC) Ephemeral king of the later SECOND INTERMEDIATE PERIOD (16th or 17th Dynasty), whose authority was probably confined to UPPER EGYPT. A STELA of Rahotep, now in the British Museum, London, records the refurbishment of the OSIRIS temple at ABYDOS.

ram *see* Amun, Banebdjedet, Herishef, Khnum

Ramesses I ('It is RA who bore him') (throne name: Menpehtyra) (c. 1292–c. 1290 BC) First king of the 19th Dynasty. An officer in the Egyptian ARMY, from the eastern DELTA, he was adopted as heir by HOREMHEB, during whose reign he served as VIZIER. The accession of Ramesses, and his reign of barely two years, mark the beginning of the RAMESSIDE period. His building projects included temples at ABYDOS and BUHEN, and completing the construction of the second PYLON at KARNAK. His small tomb in the VALLEY OF THE KINGS (KV16) is beautifully decorated with scenes from the *Book of Gates*. He was succeeded by his son SETI I.

Ramesses II (throne name: Usermaatra-setepenra) (c. 1279–c. 1213 BC) Third king of the 19th Dynasty and one

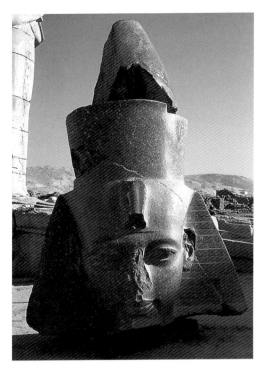

Head from a colossal statue of **Ramesses II**, also often known as 'Ramesses the Great', in his mortuary temple at Thebes, the Ramesseum.

Vignette from the 20th Dynasty Great Harris Papyrus depicting **Ramesses III** in long, flowing robes. The early part of his reign was taken up with battles against the Sea Peoples.

of the most famous of all Egyptian rulers. Sometimes dubbed 'Ramesses the Great', his reign of more than sixty years was characterized by a huge building programme. He completed the HYPOSTYLE HALL at KARNAK, and at LUXOR TEMPLE added a courtyard and PYLON in front of the late 18th Dynasty temple. He also built temples at ABYDOS and MEMPHIS, while his constructions in NUBIA included the imposing monuments at ABU SIMBEL. He commissioned large numbers of colossal statues of himself, and usurped many buildings from earlier reigns, making his name one of the most common on Egyptian monuments. In western THEBES, he built an impressive mortuary temple, the RAMESSEUM; a tomb for one of his principal queens, NEFERTARI, in the VALLEY OF THE QUEENS (QV66); a tomb for himself (KV7), and another for his many sons who predeceased him (KV5), both located in the VALLEY OF THE KINGS. The tomb for his sons followed an entirely new plan and is the largest in Egypt. At PER-RAMESSES in the DELTA, he transformed the city founded by his father SETI I into a new royal residence, with temples, palaces and industrial areas.

The major event of Ramesses II's reign was the Battle of KADESH; presented as a great victory for the king, it was celebrated in text and relief on his most important temples, including the Ramesseum, Luxor and Abu Simbel. The long-term result of the battle was a peace treaty with the HITTITES, and two diplomatic marriages to Hittite princesses. The king is also known to have taken at least four other principal wives, including Istnofret and three of his own daughters. Ramesses II was eventually succeeded by his thirteenth son, MERENPTAH.

Ramesses III (throne name: Usermaatra-meryamun) (c. 1187–c. 1156 BC) Second king of the 20th Dynasty, the son and successor of SETHNAKHT. In his ROYAL TITLES, his building projects and his military campaigns, he seems to have intended to emulate his predecessor RAMESSES II. The first decade of his reign was characterized by a series of campaigns to halt the infiltration of migrants from LIBYA, and by the great battle against the SEA PEOPLES. The next two decades were peaceful, although failure to pay the workmen at DEIR EL-MEDINA led to the first recorded strike in history, in the 29th year of the king's reign. His major monuments are his mortuary temple at MEDINET HABU and his tomb in the VALLEY OF THE KINGS (KV11). The circumstances surrounding the death of Ramesses III are uncertain. His mummy shows no signs of violence, but a papyrus records the trial of plotters in a HAREM conspiracy, in which a wife of the king sought to kill him and place her own son on the throne. Ramesses III is generally regarded as the last of the great NEW KINGDOM rulers.

Ramesses IV (throne name: Heqamaatra-setepenamun) (c. 1156–c. 1150 BC) Third king of the 20th Dynasty, the son and successor of RAMESSES III. At the time of his accession, the Great Harris PAPYRUS, the largest surviving papyrus roll, was drawn up to catalogue the various lands and endowments owned by temples. Despite this impressive administrative feat, Ramesses IV's reign marks the beginning of a decline in royal authority under a series of increasingly weak kings. There was often greater continuity among officials: in the first year of his reign, Ramesses IV appointed a high priest who served six consecutive kings, dying in the reign of RAMESSES IX. Ramesses IV doubled the workforce at DEIR EL-MEDINA to ensure completion of his tomb in the VALLEY OF THE KINGS (KV2), but his mortuary temple was never finished. His principal accomplishment was sending mining expeditions to the WADI HAMMAMAT to bring back fine-grained siltstone for SCULPTURE.

Ramesses V (throne name: Usermaatra-sekheperenra) (c. 1150–c. 1145 BC) Fourth king of the 20th Dynasty, the son of RAMESSES IV. He has left few monuments and failed to finish his tomb in the VALLEY OF THE KINGS (KV9); it was completed by his uncle and successor, RAMESSES VI, and served the two rulers as a joint burial. Two well-known documents written during the reign of Ramesses V are the Wilbour Papyrus (a land survey) and the will of Naunakhte (a legal document drawn up by a woman living at DEIR EL-MEDINA, disinheriting some of her children in favour of those whom she considered to have treated her well in her old age; the will demonstrates that WOMEN in ancient Egypt were free to dispose of their property as they wished).

Ramesses VI (throne name: Nebmaatra-meryamun) (c. 1145–c. 1137 BC) Fifth king of the 20th Dynasty. A younger son of RAMESSES III, he succeeded his nephew RAMESSES V who died without issue; he completed the latter's tomb in the VALLEY OF THE KINGS (KV9). Ramesses VI has left few traces, but was the last king for whom an inscription records an expedition to the SINAI.

Ramesses VII (throne name: Usermaatra-setepenra-meryamun) (c. 1137–c. 1129 BC) Sixth king of the 20th Dynasty, the son of RAMESSES VI. He began work on a tomb in the VALLEY OF THE KINGS (KV1), but otherwise very little is known about his brief reign. He died without issue.

Ramesses VIII (throne name: Usermaatra-akhenamun) (c. 1129–c. 1126 BC) Seventh king of the 20th Dynasty. A younger son of RAMESSES III, he succeeded his nephew RAMESSES VII. Probably very elderly at his accession, Ramesses VIII reigned for little more than a year and has left few traces. He is the only ruler of the RAMESSIDE period without a tomb in the VALLEY OF THE KINGS.

Ramesses IX (throne name: Neferkara-setepenra) (c. 1126–c. 1108 BC) Eighth king of the 20th Dynasty, the nephew of RAMESSES VIII. Despite a reign of eighteen years, he carried out no significant building projects, apart from a limited amount of work at KARNAK. He built a tomb in the VALLEY OF THE KINGS (KV6) for himself and a son who predeceased him.

Ramesses X (throne name: Khepermaatra-setepenra) (c. 1108–c. 1099 BC) Ninth and penultimate king of the 20th Dynasty. Probably a younger son of RAMESSES IX, virtually nothing is known about his brief reign. He began a tomb in the VALLEY OF THE KINGS (KV18) which was never finished or used.

Ramesses XI (throne name: Menmaatra-setepenptah) (c. 1099–c. 1069 BC) Tenth and last king of the 20th Dynasty, and the last ruler of the NEW KINGDOM. Probably a son of RAMESSES X, he reigned for nearly three decades, the longest reign since that of RAMESSES III. However, he was unable to emulate his precedessor's achievements, largely because of internal political difficulties. After the High Priests of AMUN effectively seized control of THEBES, law and order deteriorated, and the RAMESSEUM was looted. In response, it seems that Ramesses XI appointed the VICEROY OF KUSH, Panehsy, to rule UPPER EGYPT under martial law. Panehsy may have used his position to attempt a coup, but was defeated. In his place, the king appointed HERIHOR as Viceroy of Kush and governor of Upper Egypt, while SMENDES assumed similar powers over LOWER EGYPT.

To mark this decisive break with the past, Ramesses named his 19th regnal year (c. 1080 BC) 'the first year of

*A group of Osirid pillars in the ruined court of the **Ramesseum**, the mortuary temple of Ramesses II at western Thebes.*

the renaissance', and documents at Thebes were dated according to this new era until the end of the reign. In reality, it marked not a renaissance but the beginning of the formal division of Egypt and the collapse of central royal authority. Ramesses XI's tomb in the VALLEY OF THE KINGS (KV4) was never finished, and he may have been buried at PER-RAMESSES. However, the city was abandoned shortly after his death and its monuments transferred to TANIS.

Ramesseum Mortuary temple of RAMESSES II in western THEBES. Built in the style of a traditional NEW KINGDOM temple, it comprised a series of PYLONS and courts, leading to a HYPOSTYLE and thence to the sanctuary at the rear of the building. The inside face of the first and second pylons was decorated with scenes from the Battle of KADESH. The First Court was originally dominated by a huge seated statue of the king, carved in granite, and provided with its own chapel. Fallen and broken, it provided the inspiration for Shelley's famous poem *Ozymandias*, following the Roman historian Diodorus, who described the temple as the tomb of Ozymandias (a corruption of Ramesses II's throne name, Usermaatra).

Around the stone temple, numerous mud-brick subsidiary buildings were arranged within an outer enclosure wall. They included a royal palace, store rooms, and well-preserved granaries with vaulted roofs. With such facilities, the Ramesseum served as an administrative centre for western Thebes in the 20th Dynasty. However, it was partly dismantled by RAMESSES III who reused some of the blocks in the construction of his own mortuary temple at MEDINET HABU. At the end of the 20th Dynasty, the temple was stripped of its ornamentation by robbers, and despoiled.

Ramesseum Dramatic Papyrus Document discovered in the tomb of a 13th Dynasty lector priest beneath the RAMESSEUM. One of a collection of papyri belonging to the tomb owner, presumably for his professional use, the text records the details of various rituals connected with KINGSHIP. They are dedicated to SENUS-RET I and may have been performed at his coronation or SED FESTIVAL. For each ritual act, dramatizing a different mythological episode, the document gives a brief description, records the speeches given by the priests performing the roles of different deities, and notes the objects used and the place in which the ritual was imagined to take place. The different episodes are depicted in a series of illustrations at the bottom of the papyrus roll.

Ramesside Period from the accession of RAMESSES I to the end of the reign of RAMESSES XI, from the 19th and 20th Egyptian dynasties (*c*. 1292–*c*. 1069 BC).

Ramose VIZIER under AMENHOTEP III and AMEN-
HOTEP IV. His beautiful, though unfinished, tomb at
SHEIKH ABD EL-QURNA contains decoration in both
traditional and AMARNA period styles, illustrating the
rapidity with which AKHENATEN's new artistic conventions were adopted throughout Egypt early in his reign.

Ramses *see* Ramesses

Re *see* Ra

red crown *see* crowns

Red Pyramid *see* Dahshur

Rekhmira VIZIER in the reigns of THUTMOSE III and
AMENHOTEP II. His tomb at SHEIKH ABD EL-QURNA is
one of the best surviving examples from the 18th
Dynasty. The TOMB DECORATION includes scenes of
craftsmen at work, and peoples from NUBIA, Syria and
CRETE bringing tribute. Accompanying texts describe
the installation of the vizier, his duties, and the moral
code by which he was expected to act.

rekhyt Ancient Egyptian word for the general popu-
lace, as distinct from the ruling elite (PAT). Connotations of subservience are reinforced by the
HIEROGLYPH for *rekhyt*, which shows a lapwing with its
wings pinioned behind its back. On the late Predynastic SCORPION MACEHEAD, lapwings are shown
hanging by ropes from standards, symbolizing the
dependence of the people on the king, and their subject
status. In later periods, the *rekhyt* hieroglyph was commonly used in temple decoration as part of a motif that
could be read 'all people adore [the king]'.

religion It is perhaps misleading to refer to 'ancient
Egyptian religion' as a single entity, since for most, if
not all, of Egyptian history there was a marked difference between the myths and practices associated with
state ideology, and those belonging to the sphere of
private, non-royal individuals.

   State religion was explicitly and predominantly
concerned with the eternal struggle between order and
chaos, and with the role of the king in preserving MAAT
(harmony). At the core of state religion was the belief
in a contract between the gods and the Egyptian
people, in which the king was the channel of communication, duty bound to maintain the cults of the gods
in order to retain their active support. Hence, reliefs in

state TEMPLES always showed the king performing the
daily rituals, even if, in practice, this was delegated to
PRIESTS. Embedded within state theology were CRE-
ATION MYTHS, and AFTERLIFE BELIEFS concerned with
the final destiny of the king. These various strands,
especially the ideology of KINGSHIP which lay at the
heart of state religion, were essential elements running
throughout Egyptian court culture, manifested in ART
and architecture. By contrast, private religion, as practised by the majority of the population – in their houses
and at small community shrines – was concerned with

The 18th Dynasty vizier **Ramose** *and a male companion at a
banquet, in a finely carved relief from Ramose's tomb in western
Thebes.*

In Egyptian hieroglyphs, the lapwing symbolized the **rekhyt** *or
common people, and was often shown adoring the name of the
reigning king, as in this Ramesside relief from Karnak.*

*Limestone **reserve head** from Giza, 4th Dynasty; the function of these extraordinary sculptures is still unclear. They are found exclusively in tombs of the 4th Dynasty, placed close to the body of the deceased.*

fundamental, universal concerns such as fertility, childbirth, and protection from bites, stings and other afflictions. The devices employed to secure a desired outcome included spells, incantations, charms, and a whole range of practices often labelled as MAGIC, even though the modern distinction between religion, magic and medicine would not have been recognized by the ancient Egyptians.

Egyptian religion comprised a complex web of myths and beliefs, some of them apparently contradictory, and was characterized by a huge number of deities and DEMONS. However, the system was far from static. It was always open to new beliefs and cults – such as those imported from the LEVANT in the NEW KINGDOM, or the ANIMAL CULTS popular in the LATE PERIOD – even if these were outwardly presented as conforming to long-established traditions. The inherent conservatism of Egyptian ART and WRITING masks a dynamic religion which successfully adapted to changing circumstances, and remained at the core of Egyptian society for more than three thousand years.

Renenutet Cobra goddess worshipped as protector of the king, his linen garment, and, by extension, mummy wrappings. She was also associated with fertility, corn and the harvest. Her various roles connected her with a number of other deities, including WADJET, ISIS and SOBEK. In the BOOK OF THE DEAD, she was said to be the mother of HORUS from a union with ATUM. She was depicted as a cobra or a woman with a cobra's head. Her cult was particularly popular at MEDINET MAADI, and an annual festival of Renenutet was celebrated in the FAYUM.

reserve head Type of funerary SCULPTURE found in MEMPHITE tombs of the 4th Dynasty. Some thirty examples are known, all dating to the reigns of KHUFU and KHAFRA. Each comprises a human head carved in limestone, often with the ears left unsculpted or deliberately removed. Many also show lines carved around the neck and on the back of the head. Reserve heads were placed in the burial chamber, close to the body of the deceased. Their precise purpose remains unclear. They may have been intended as substitute ('reserve') heads in case the actual body was destroyed. Alternatively, they may have had more complex connotations of neutralizing the potentially dangerous power of the deceased in the afterlife.

Reshep (Reshef, Reshpu) War god of the Amorites, whose cult was introduced to Egypt during the 18th Dynasty as a result of Egyptian military involvement in the LEVANT. Sharing several traits in common with the THEBAN war-god MONTU, Reshep became absorbed into Egyptian RELIGION, and was depicted on STELAE and in bronze statuettes. He is usually depicted as a bearded man wearing the white crown, which has a gazelle's head instead of the usual URAEUS, and a ribbon hanging down the back. He is sometimes shown holding a mace or spear, to emphasize his martial nature.

Rhind Papyrus *see* mathematics

rishi see coffin

rock-cut tombs Funerary monuments hewn into a cliff face began to be popular in the early OLD KINGDOM. The burial chamber was usually located beneath the tomb chapel, reached by a vertical shaft, but in some cases was entirely separate. A hall with columns or pillars became a common feature of rock-cut tomb chapels from the late Old Kingdom onwards. During the FIRST INTERMEDIATE PERIOD and MIDDLE KINGDOM, rock-cut tombs for NOMARCHS and other high officials were constructed at sites throughout

*Late Period stone statuette of the Syrian god **Reshep**, in characteristic pose with a spear and shield and wearing a white crown adorned with a gazelle's head.*

Egypt, often displaying local traditions of architecture and TOMB DECORATION. Examples include the tombs at ASYUT, BENI HASAN, EL-BERSHA, MEIR and QAU in MIDDLE EGYPT. In the NEW KINGDOM, huge numbers of rock-cut tombs were built in the THEBAN NECROPOLIS for officials (TOMBS OF THE NOBLES), members of the royal family (VALLEY OF THE QUEENS) and monarchs (VALLEY OF THE KINGS). Rock-cut tombs continued to be built after the New Kingdom, but in much fewer numbers.

Roman period (AD 30 BC–395) The phase of Egyptian history spanning the four centuries from the death of CLEOPATRA VIII and her son Ptolemy Caesarion in 30 BC, to the formal division of the Roman Empire in AD 395. Egypt's involvement with Rome began in the late PTOLEMAIC PERIOD, when the Roman general Pompey was appointed as guardian to Cleopatra VII. A series of ill-fated alliances culminated in her suicide and the murder of her son, following the defeat of Mark

The **Rosetta Stone** *bears an inscription in three scripts recording a decree issued by Ptolemy V in 196 BC; it was instrumental in the decipherment of hieroglyphics.*

Antony's forces by Octavian at the Battle of Actium. Octavian subsequently declared himself emperor, took the name Augustus, and proclaimed himself PHARAOH. He and his successors treated the country as a private, imperial estate, rather than as a province. It was administered on the emperor's behalf by prefects based in ALEXANDRIA, although the traditional system of NOMES was retained for convenience. Greek remained the official LANGUAGE. Large numbers of troops were garrisoned throughout Egypt and Lower NUBIA, to maintain internal security, and guard quarries and other strategic sites. A series of fortresses in the Eastern Desert, for example DAYDAMUS, was constructed to protect trade routes to the Red Sea. Egypt was also valued as a major supplier of wheat to the Roman Empire.

Although Roman emperors continued to sponsor temple construction projects, and had themselves depicted in ART as traditional pharaonic rulers, they showed relatively little interest in Egypt, visiting only occasionally. An exception was Hadrian, who founded the city of ANTINOÖPOLIS in honour of his drowned lover, Antinous. Egyptian RELIGION, especially the cult of ISIS, spread throughout the Roman empire, becoming influential and popular. However, for the majority

A tablet from a private house at Amarna shows the **royal family** *– Akhenaten, Nefertiti and their three eldest daughters – under the protective rays of the Aten.*

of the Egyptian population, Roman rule was harsh. The emperor Caracalla went so far as to ban all Egyptians from Alexandria, while Diocletian persecuted the Egyptian followers of the new Christian faith. Such conditions led to the depopulation of Roman Egypt and its economic decline. Towards the end of the Roman period, the rise of Christianity marked a new era in Egyptian culture. The emperor Theodosius ordered the closure of all temples in AD 384, although traditional religion survived in some areas for a considerable time. At the division of the Roman Empire, Egypt became part of the eastern province, Byzantium.

Rosetta Stone Black granite STELA, discovered by the Napoleonic expedition to Egypt in 1799 near the village of Rosetta (el-Rashid), where it had been reused in the walls of a medieval fort. The stone was subsequently surrendered to British forces, and was sent to the British Museum in London where it has remained ever since. It is inscribed with a royal decree, issued at MEMPHIS on 27 March 196 BC, the anniversary of the coronation of Ptolemy V Epiphanes. The fact that the same inscription is written in three scripts, HIERO-GLYPHIC, DEMOTIC and Greek (the last of which could be read by 19th-century scholars), made the Rosetta Stone a key artifact in the decipherment of hieroglyphic WRITING by Jean-François Champollion (see EGYPTOLOGY).

royal family In the EARLY DYNASTIC PERIOD, it is likely that royal relatives – members of the PAT – held all the major positions in the government. Although the great offices of state were opened up to persons of non-royal birth in later periods, the king's relatives maintained their important political and religious roles throughout Egyptian history. This was particularly true of QUEENS, who embodied the female principle to complement the king's own mythological role. At certain periods, the practice of CO-REGENCY was adopted to ensure a smooth succession. To the same end, in the NEW KINGDOM and THIRD INTERMEDIATE PERIOD, the king's eldest son was often placed in charge of the ARMY or appointed High Priest of one of the major cults, especially that of PTAH at MEMPHIS. However, other male relatives were generally less visible, and were perhaps deliberately barred from positions of influence to prevent them becoming serious rivals for the throne. In the early New Kingdom, kings often married their own sisters in order to emphasize their difference from ordinary people and their own quasi-

divine status, the king and his sister-wife re-enacting the roles of SHU and TEFNUT.

royal regalia In ancient Egypt, as in other monarchies throughout history, a range of different symbolic objects carried strong royal associations and were used in iconography to denote and proclaim KINGSHIP in the public sphere. Although very few of the artifacts themselves have survived, representations abound in Egyptian ART. Two early ceremonial objects which depict the king wearing the full range of regalia are the SCORPION MACEHEAD and the NARMER PALETTE. Foremost among royal accoutrements were the various CROWNS and HEADDRESSES, each of which carried particular connotations. From early in the PREDYNASTIC PERIOD, the symbol of authority *par excellence* was a staff or stick. As a mark of office, this is already attested in a prehistoric grave at el-OMARI. The staff was so closely associated with status that the HIEROGLYPH of a man carrying a long straight stick was used to write the word 'official'. In a royal context, the simple staff evolved into a number of different sceptres, notably the *kherep* sceptre (signifying 'control') and the curiously shaped WAS SCEPTRE. The latter seems to have derived from the practice of ANIMAL HUSBANDRY, as do two other quintessential symbols of kingship, the crook and flail (or goad). Both are attested in the Predynastic period and signified the king's role in, respectively, restraining and encouraging his people, as a herdsman would his livestock. The BULL's tail, worn suspended from the belt of the king's kilt, likewise harked back to a period of cattle-herding, and imbued the king with the strength, virility and fecundity of a wild bull. The king's sandals, from late Predynastic times entrusted to a sandal-bearer, were symbolic of the monarch's superiority and inevitable triumph over the enemies of Egypt. Hence, on a victory STELA of KHASEKHEM, the king is referred to by the epithet 'effective sandal against the foreign land'. A similar, but more overtly militaristic message was conveyed by the final item of royal regalia, the pear-shaped macehead. The image of the king holding a mace in his upraised arm to smite a defeated captive was employed as the single most powerful and eloquent expression of kingship from the early Predynastic period until the end of the ROMAN PERIOD, a span of some 4,000 years.

royal titles The classic titulary of an Egyptian king comprised five distinct titles and NAMES, each expressing a different aspect of KINGSHIP ideology. Earliest

*The gold inner coffin of Tutankhamun depicts the king with the full panoply of **royal regalia**: the crook and flail, the nemes headdress adorned with a vulture and uraeus serpent, and the divine beard.*

*Detail of an inscription from the 12th Dynasty White Chapel of Senusret I, Karnak, with one of the most important **royal titles**: the nesut-bity title ('he of the sedge and bee') which signified the many dualities brought together in the office of kingship.*

and always pre-eminent was the HORUS title, first attested in the late PREDYNASTIC PERIOD. It was adopted at a king's accession, and proclaimed him as the earthly incarnation of the FALCON god. The accompanying Horus name, written inside a SEREKH surmounted by a figure of Horus, described the particular aspect or attribute of the god that the king wished to stress at the beginning of his reign. In the early 1st Dynasty, two further elements of the royal titulary were introduced. Again, both were adopted by a king at his accession. The first is the TWO LADIES title and name, expressing the king's role as unifier of the TWO LANDS of UPPER and LOWER EGYPT, represented by their patron deities NEKHBET and WADJET. The second is the complex title *nesut bity* ('he of the sedge and bee'), with its accompanying name. This seems to have emphasized the many different kinds of DUALITY inherent in the role of the king, although in the PTOLEMAIC PERIOD its Greek translation was simply 'King of Upper and Lower Egypt'. From the middle of the OLD KINGDOM, the name which accompanied this title was customarily written in a CARTOUCHE and, as the throne name (prenomen), became one of the principal names used on royal monuments. A fourth royal title, the Horus of Gold, is also first attested in the EARLY DYNASTIC PERIOD. Its precise meaning is uncertain, but it may have alluded to the mythological triumph of Horus (in this context equated with the king) over SETH, since another name for Seth was 'the one of Nubt', or 'the golden one'. The fifth and final element of the royal titulary was the title 'son of RA', introduced by DJEDEFRA in the early 4th Dynasty. It emphasized the king's position as son and heir of the supreme god, and introduced the king's birth name (nomen), written in a cartouche. Although all five titles and names had thus appeared on royal monuments by the early OLD KINGDOM, the final form of the complete five-fold titulary was not established until the MIDDLE KINGDOM. Great care was taken with the choice of royal names. Since royal titles both expressed and conferred legitimacy, foreign rulers took pains to adopt a full complement, and to follow established naming traditions.

Rudamun (Amunrud) (c. 755–c. 735 BC) King of the 23rd Dynasty. A son of OSORKON III, he seems to have been recognized jointly with PIYE as king at THEBES. After his death, control of the Theban region effectively passed to the KUSHITE 25th Dynasty. His sister, Shepenwepet I, was GOD'S WIFE OF AMUN before adopting Piye's own sister, Amenirdis I, as her successor.

S

sa Egyptian word for 'protection', written with the sign of a rolled-up and folded reed mat. This HIEROGLYPH was commonly used as an AMULET and on MAGIC objects, especially in the MIDDLE KINGDOM. In the NEW KINGDOM it was generally depicted together with other amuletic signs, notably the ANKH and the DJED PILLAR.

sacred animals *see* animal cults, Apis, Buchis, Mnevis

sacred lake Artificial pool within a temple enclosure, fed by ground water. Attested from the EARLY DYNASTIC PERIOD onwards, such pools were used for a variety of purposes connected with TEMPLE RITUAL: they provided a ready source of fresh water for libations; homes for sacred animals, such as geese or CROCODILES; and settings for ceremonies involving sacred barques. Lined with stone, and provided with several flights of steps leading down to the water, sacred lakes were usually rectangular, but could also be irregular in shape, such as the horseshoe-shaped feature in the MUT complex at KARNAK.

saff tomb Type of ROCK-CUT TOMB with a broad, open forecourt and a T-shaped covered section consisting of a transverse corridor with a pillared façade and, perpendicular to it, another corridor leading back into the cliff. The external appearance of the tomb is thus of a row of pillars, hence the name *saff* (from the Arabic for 'row'). It was a popular form for tombs in the THEBAN area during the FIRST INTERMEDIATE PERIOD; the three best-known examples were built at EL-TARIF for the first three kings of the 11th Dynasty (the Saff el-Dawaba for INTEF I, the Saff el-Kisasiya for INTEF II, and the Saff el-Baqar for INTEF III). There are also private *saff* tombs at DENDERA and ARMANT.

Sah *see* Orion

Sahathor (Sihathor) (throne name: Menwedjara) (early 17th century BC) King of the mid-13th Dynasty in succession to his brother NEFERHOTEP I. He was succeeded, in turn, by a second brother, SOBEKHOTEP IV.

Sahura (c. 2425 BC) Second king of the 5th Dynasty, and the first to construct a mortuary complex at ABUSIR. His pyramid and associated buildings are well preserved. The mortuary temple was paved with black basalt blocks, contrasting with a colonnade of sixteen red granite columns. The walls were decorated with painted reliefs, including a scene of the king smiting his enemies.

Sais (Sa el-Hagar) Site in the western DELTA. It was the capital of the fifth Lower Egyptian NOME, the principal cult centre of the goddess NEITH, and the power base of the 24th and 26th Dynasties (the latter known as the Saite period). Textual references, from the 1st Dynasty

View north-westwards across the **sacred lake** at Karnak, which would have played an important role in cultic activities in the temple of Amun-Ra.

onwards, confirm that Sais was one of the most important Delta towns throughout Egyptian history. However, few archaeological remains are visible, and none earlier than the RAMESSIDE period; most are covered by the modern village and surrounding fields, or were destroyed in the 19th century AD, the core of the site now being a large lake. Recent work has revealed traces of occupation dating back to the PREDYNASTIC PERIOD, including evidence for ANIMAL HUSBANDRY and early cereal cultivation.

Saite Belonging to, or characteristic of, the site of SAIS. The term 'Saite period' is used to describe the 26th Dynasty (664–525 BC), whose kings originated from Sais.

Salitis According to MANETHO, the first HYKSOS king of the 15th Dynasty.

Sanakht (Zanakht) (c. 2600 BC) King of the 3rd Dynasty whose precise position in the order of succession remains uncertain. He was probably the fourth king, the predecessor of HUNI. Two rock-cut scenes at WADI MAGHARA show Sanakht carrying out ritual actions (including smiting a foreign captive), and contain the earliest known reference to TURQUOISE in an Egyptian text. A seal impression with the king's name from ELEPHANTINE suggests that there was a building on the island connected with the administration of a royal estate. Another seal impression, from a 3rd Dynasty MASTABA at BEIT KHALLAF, shows the SEREKH of Sanakht facing the base of a CARTOUCHE (the earliest example of the latter); the name in the cartouche has been reconstructed as Nebka, a ruler of the

Granite block from the 5th Dynasty pyramid temple of **Sahura** at Abusir engraved with the king's name and title.

3rd Dynasty known from later KING-LISTS. Hence, Sanakht and Nebka are generally regarded as one and the same person. No funerary monument has been identified for Sanakht, unless it was the structure known as el-Deir at ABU RAWASH.

Saqqara Area of the MEMPHITE NECROPOLIS, on the west bank of the NILE, which has perhaps the greatest concentration of funerary monuments anywhere in Egypt, spanning the entire sweep of Egyptian history from the 1st Dynasty to the Christian period. The EARLY DYNASTIC PERIOD, OLD KINGDOM, NEW KINGDOM and LATE PERIOD are particularly well represented. On the whole, there are few monuments at Saqqara from the MIDDLE KINGDOM, when activity was concentrated further south at the sites of DAHSHUR and LISHT. Occupying a vast stretch of desert, Saqqara is divided for convenience into five bands, north to south.

The most northerly part, bordering ABUSIR, includes the earliest tombs; they are located on the edge of the escarpment, overlooking the site of ancient MEMPHIS. Decorated in the distinctive PALACE-FAÇADE style, these huge and imposing MASTABAS were built for members of the ruling elite during the Early Dynastic period. Further into the desert are elaborately decorated Old Kingdom tombs, built for high officials such as TY; and the sacred animal necropolis, including the SERAPEUM. North central Saqqara is dominated by the PYRAMID complex of TETI and the adjacent mastabas of KAGEMNI and MERERUKA. The nearby cliff face is studded with ROCK-CUT TOMBS of the AMARNA period and late 18th Dynasty, including those of AKHENATEN's vizier APER-EL, and TUTANKHAMUN's wet-nurse, Maya.

The central part of the Saqqara necropolis contains a notable concentration of royal funerary monuments. Most impressive is the 3rd Dynasty STEP PYRAMID complex, with the 5th Dynasty pyramids of USERKAF and UNAS at its northeastern and southwestern corners, respectively. The causeway of the Unas complex overlies the substructures of two 2nd Dynasty royal tombs, probably part of a more extensive royal burial-ground that originally stretched for some distance north and south. The superstructures of these early royal tombs were probably dismantled for reuse in (or to make way for) the construction of DJOSER's monument. Mastabas of 5th Dynasty officials and members of the ROYAL FAMILY cluster around the Unas causeway, which leads from a VALLEY TEMPLE at the foot of the escarpment to the pyramid on the desert

*The vast necropolis of **Saqqara** comprises monuments from most periods of ancient Egyptian civilization, including the 3rd Dynasty Step Pyramid of Djoser (left) and the ruined 5th Dynasty pyramid of Userkaf (right).*

plateau. Some distance further west are the remains of the unfinished step pyramid complex of SEKHEMKHET; the mysterious GISR EL-MUDIR, dating to the Early Dynastic period; and an even more enigmatic enclosure, most clearly visible in aerial photographs. The location of these monuments, deep in the desert, may indicate that access to the Saqqara necropolis was originally from the north, via the Wadi Abusir, rather than from the east, as it was in later periods. Several LATE PERIOD shaft tombs are located in central Saqqara, especially in the areas of the mortuary temples of Userkaf and Unas. Other tombs of the Late Period and PTOLEMAIC PERIOD lie around the Teti pyramid and along the route to the Serapeum.

The area to the south of the Unas causeway was an important court cemetery during the New Kingdom, with large numbers of imposing, temple-style tombs facing each other along 'streets'. Significant rediscoveries in this part of Saqqara include the tomb built for HOREMHEB before he became king, and other tombs from the reign of Tutankhamun. Nearby is a major monument of the Christian period, the monastery of Apa Jeremias. South Saqqara, bordering DAHSHUR, is characterized by another concentration of royal mortuary complexes, spanning the whole of the Old Kingdom. Notable monuments include the 4th Dynasty MASTABAT EL-FARA'UN of SHEPSESKAF, the 5th Dynasty pyramid of ISESI, the 6th Dynasty pyramids of PEPI I and PEPI II, and the 8th Dynasty pyramid of IBI.

Despite over a century of intensive archaeological excavation, Saqqara continues to reveal new surprises almost every year, and it is certain that many more tombs remain to be discovered.

sarcophagus Stone chest (from the Greek for 'flesh eating') which contained one or more wooden coffins protecting the body in a burial. The earliest examples have been found in 3rd Dynasty step PYRAMIDS; stone sarcophagi were a royal prerogative during the NEW KINGDOM and THIRD INTERMEDIATE PERIOD.

Sarenput *see* Qubbet el-Hawa

Satet (Satis) Goddess closely associated with the island of ELEPHANTINE. She is mentioned in the PYRAMID TEXTS, and was regarded as the guardian of Egypt's southern border. She was also associated with the INUNDATION, since the rushing waters of the annual flood first became audible at Elephantine. An early shrine on the island, located between natural granite boulders, was dedicated to Satet from the OLD

*Sandstone **sarcophagus** of Thutmose III in his tomb in the Valley of the Kings; in common with the burial chamber itself, the sarcophagus is shaped like a cartouche.*

KINGDOM. In the NEW KINGDOM, the goddess was worshipped in a TRIAD with KHNUM and ANKET.

Satire of the Trades Work of LITERATURE dated to the MIDDLE KINGDOM but preserved on various papyrus copies from the 18th and 19th Dynasties. The text is presented as an instruction from a man called Duakhety to his son Pepi, as he takes him to school. The office of SCRIBE is praised, while all other occupations are ridiculed and belittled. For this reason, the work remained popular for scribal training.

Satis *see* Satet

scarab Dung beetle associated with the rising sun, because the insect's habit of rolling a ball of dung was

*Lapis lazuli **scarab** on a bracelet from the burial of Tutankhamun; the beetle was a potent symbol of rebirth, and was a major element in the writing of the king's throne name, hence its frequent occurrence in his ceremonial jewelry.*

*Detail from the ceremonial macehead of the late Predynastic King **Scorpion** (although the scorpion hieroglyph in front of his face may have been a royal epithet rather than a name).*

seen as a metaphor for the god KHEPRI pushing the sun into the heavens at the beginning of each day. The emergence of young beetles from the dung ball was also equated with the sun's promise of daily rebirth from the decay of death. The scarab was a very popular form for AMULETS and JEWELRY from the OLD KINGDOM to the PTOLEMAIC PERIOD. In the MIDDLE KINGDOM, scarab seals were also produced, their flat undersides being ideal for inscriptions. AMENHOTEP III issued a series of commemorative scarabs to celebrate major events of his reign. A specialized form of scarab was the 'HEART scarab', usually made of a green stone, and inscribed with Chapter 30b of the BOOK OF THE DEAD; it was placed on the body of the deceased, over the heart, in burials from the late Middle Kingdom onwards. The largest known example of a scarab is the stone sculpture next to the sacred lake at KARNAK.

sceptre *see* royal regalia

science *see* astronomy and astrology, mathematics, medicine

scorpion An ever-present danger to those living or working on the desert edge, scorpions were objects of fear and reverence from an early period. Small FAIENCE scorpions were deposited in early temples as VOTIVE objects, probably to afford magical protection against stings. AMULETS in the shape of scorpions were made for the same reason. The scorpion was worshipped as the goddess SELKET and also as the god Shed. Scorpions and other harmful creatures were commonly depicted on CIPPUS plaques of the LATE PERIOD.

Scorpion Name conventionally attributed to one or more kings of the late PREDYNASTIC PERIOD. The scorpion was clearly a metaphor of royal power, and as such occurs in various contexts, including a victory scene at Gebel Sheikh Suleiman in Lower NUBIA. Some of the POTTERY vessels from tomb U-j at ABYDOS, the Predynastic grave of a powerful ruler (c. 3150 BC), are inscribed with the figure of a scorpion, interpreted by some as the tomb owner's name. Likewise, the image of a scorpion on a stick on a MACEHEAD from HIERAKONPOLIS (c. 3000 BC) denotes the royal figure performing an IRRIGATION ritual; whether it signifies his name, title or some other attribute of KINGSHIP remains open to debate. The same king may also be identified by a potmark from MINSHAT ABU OMAR which consists of a SEREKH containing a scorpion.

scribe Term for any member of the literate ruling class in ancient Egypt. Throughout the pharaonic period, literacy was probably restricted to under 10 percent of the population, and was an almost exclusively male preserve. Female literacy is attested in the NEW KINGDOM, but there is no certain occurrence of a word for 'female scribe' until the 26th Dynasty. The ability to read and write brought with it authority and access to the highest offices of the land. Hence, scribes enjoyed great prestige, reflected in works of LITERATURE such as the SATIRE OF THE TRADES, and in SCULPTURE. From the OLD KINGDOM onwards, members of the elite often had themselves depicted in a scribal pose, sitting cross-legged with a roll of papyrus on their lap. Scribes were trained in schools attached to temples (HOUSE OF LIFE). The HIEROGLYPH for 'scribe' showed the scribal equipment of PALETTE, water pot and reed pens.

sculpture The quality of the statuary produced in ancient Egypt reached a level arguably unsurpassed in any other civilization, ancient or modern. The sheer quantity of surviving sculpture testifies to its importance in pharaonic culture and is indicative of Egypt's prosperity and stability over a long period of time; the quality of the workmanship demonstrates the skill and imagination of Egyptian craftsmen, honed under royal patronage over countless generations.

Sculpture was made primarily for religious reasons, to give permanence to an ideal, rather than to record actuality. Hence statues of kings generally presented them as youthful and muscular, irrespective of their true age; departures from this tradition, for example the statues of SENUSRET III with their careworn expression and the androgynous features on those of AKHENATEN, were also dictated by particular ideological motives. A private individual, if a man, might have himself depicted in the pose of a SCRIBE (signifying membership of the ruling elite that came with literacy), or as a corpulent (hence prosperous and contented) elder of the community; statues of women are less common, but generally show an idealized feminine beauty.

The religious purpose of sculpture allowed little room for unlicensed innovation, and works were never ascribed to individual artists; indeed, most were probably team efforts, produced by a group of assistants following the guidelines laid down by a master sculptor. The idealizing nature of sculpture also made most subjects anonymous – true portraiture was exceedingly rare – with identity only ascribed later by means of an inscription. The human figure was portrayed in a variety of poses, including standing, sitting and kneeling, or in a squatting position with the knees drawn up beneath the chin so as to confine the body within a tight sculptural unit (the 'block statue'). A pair statue

Painted limestone statue of a seated **scribe**, *dated to the early 4th Dynasty. He has a roll of papyrus on his lap and would have held a stylus for writing in his hand.*

A distinct form of Egyptian **sculpture** *appearing in the early 18th Dynasty was the block statue, which provided a greater area for inscriptions; this one of Sennefer is from the reign of Thutmose III.*

(dyad) was a common form for a husband and wife, or for a king and a deity; group statues comprising three figures (TRIADS) are also well attested. When sculpting a human figure, the stone between the limbs was often left uncarved rather than being removed, to provide greater rigidity; the back pillar of standing statues served a similar purpose. As well as statues of humans and deities, animal sculpture was a particular skill of Egyptian craftsmen, with fine examples surviving from the PREDYNASTIC PERIOD onwards.

STONE was the most prized material for sculpture, because of its immutability; stone statues were made to last for eternity and were probably a royal prerogative, granted to private individuals as a token of special favour. Different types of stone carried particular symbolic associations (for example, red granite and quartzite had solar connotations because of their COLOUR). Sculpture in metal or wood was probably quite common, but is rather sparsely attested because it has survived less well. Other materials used include clay, IVORY and FAIENCE. Finished pieces were commonly painted; those of the highest quality might be provided with inlaid eyes of rock crystal and OBSIDIAN, and with eyebrows and other features in silver or GOLD.

Sea Peoples Name given to a diverse group of migrant peoples whose attempts to settle along the shores of the eastern Mediterranean in the 13th and 12th centuries BC caused widespread conflict and destruction throughout the LEVANT. Egyptian and Near Eastern records give the names of various constituent groups within the Sea Peoples. Attempts have been made to identify them with known historical places or peoples, for example the Ekwesh with the Achaeans, the Lukka with the Lycians, the Sherden with Sardinia, and the Shekelesh with Sicily. However, such linkages remain speculative. While it is clear that at least some of the Sea Peoples came from the Aegean and Asia Minor, their precise geographical origins remain obscure, as do the reasons behind their sudden appearance as a hostile force. Clearly possessing an advanced culture, with excellent seafaring skills, they seem to have come in three successive waves. At first, various groups launched sporadic raids on coastal settlements: the Lukka are mentioned in the AMARNA LETTERS, while the Sherden attacked the DELTA early in the reign of RAMESSES II. Captives from the latter group were conscripted into the Egyptian ARMY and took part in the Battle of KADESH.

Ramesses II built a series of fortresses along the Delta coastline, for example at ZAWIYET UMM EL-RAKHAM, in an attempt to protect Egypt from further attacks. However, early in the reign of his successor MERENPTAH, the Sea Peoples formed an alliance with the Libyans and attempted once again to invade Egypt. Their defeat was celebrated on the ISRAEL STELA. The final, and most celebrated, military encounter took place in the eighth year of RAMESSES III's reign (c. 1180 BC). After destroying the HITTITES and various coastal states in the Levant, an alliance of peoples including the Peleset (Philistines) attacked Egypt on two fronts: a land-based invasion via the northern SINAI, including whole families travelling by ox-cart; and a naval battle off the Delta coast. Both were defeated, and the Egyptian victory was celebrated in reliefs on the exterior walls of Ramesses III's mortuary temple at MEDINET HABU.

sebakh Ancient mud-brick removed from archaeological sites for use as fertilizer.

Sebennytos (Samannud) Site in the northern central DELTA which was the home town of NECTANEBO I and MANETHO; the local temple archives probably provided a major source of information for the latter's history of Egypt. The archaeological remains at the site, principally belonging to a temple to ONURIS-SHU, date from the 30th Dynasty and PTOLEMAIC PERIOD.

Second Intermediate Period (c. 1650–c. 1539 BC) The phase of ancient Egyptian history between the collapse of the MIDDLE KINGDOM administration in the late 13th Dynasty and the re-establishment of central authority and national unity at the beginning of the NEW KINGDOM. The intervening period of about a century and a half was characterized by political frag-

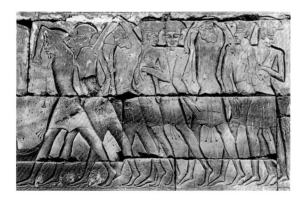

Relief from the mortuary temple of Ramesses III at Medinet Habu showing captured **Sea Peoples** after their attempted invasion was successfully repulsed by Egyptian forces.

mentation and, especially, by the migration into the DELTA of large numbers of people from the LEVANT. In the face of such pressure, the MEMPHITE royal court abandoned the capital of ITJ-TAWY, leaving the Delta to be ruled by a series of local rulers, grouped together as the 14th Dynasty. They were replaced, in turn, by a line of foreign kings, ruling from AVARIS, whose authority extended over the whole of LOWER EGYPT and northern UPPER EGYPT. These were the HYKSOS (c. 1630–c. 1520 BC), vilified in later Egyptian tradition. While they ruled in the north of the country, the south was under the control of various local rulers (identified by some as the 16th Dynasty). A particularly powerful line emerged at THEBES (the 17th Dynasty). Eventually, civil war broke out as the Thebans under TAA I and II attempted to expel the Hyksos and reunify the country. The fight continued for several generations, through the reigns of KAMOSE and AHMOSE. With the aid of Nubian mercenaries (identified archaeologically as the PAN GRAVE people), the Theban forces eventually prevailed against a coalition of Hyksos and KUSHITE power, thus inaugurating a period of renewed centralized government.

Sedeinga Site in Upper NUBIA, just north of SOLEB; its temple dedicated to TIYE was restored by TAHARQO.

***sed* festival** Jubilee celebration, usually staged to mark a king's thirtieth year on the throne. It was one of the most important rituals of Egyptian KINGSHIP, symbolizing the interrelationship between the king, the gods and the people, and is first attested in the early 1st Dynasty. One of the key elements of the festival was the ceremony of 'encompassing the field', whereby the king strode or ran between pairs of territorial markers to signify the renewal of his authority over the whole country. Reliefs of DJOSER from his STEP PYRAMID show the king performing this ritual. This theme of rejuvenation was echoed in the ceremony at the heart of the *sed* festival: the king's re-enthronement as ruler of UPPER EGYPT and of LOWER EGYPT. This took place on a special dais with two thrones and two flights of steps, a representation of which was used as the HIEROGLYPH for *sed* festival. An actual example of such a dais has been preserved in the *sed* festival court complex of Djoser at Saqqara, which was intended to provide a permanent set for the eternal celebration of the festival. The ceremonial buildings required for the festival, which in reality would have been temporary structures of wood and matting, are replicated in stone. They include a series of shrines to house the cult images of

Egypt's various provincial deities, gathered together to pay homage to the king, and he to them. The king would also receive delegations of officials and people, once again to renew the bonds of loyalty that lay at the heart of the Egyptian monarchy. The *sed* festival of AMENHOTEP III comprised a number of other rituals, including elaborate, water-borne processions on the huge artificial harbour (the BIRKET HABU) excavated for the occasion. Although translated into Greek as 'thirty year festival', it is clear that the *sed* festival was sometimes celebrated by kings who had not yet reached such a milestone; for example, Akhenaten's *sed* festival seems to have been staged early in his reign.

Sehel Island in the NILE, in the First CATARACT region, to the south of ELEPHANTINE. Its rocks are covered with numerous inscriptions, dating from the MIDDLE KINGDOM to the PTOLEMAIC PERIOD, many of them dedicated to the local goddess ANKET. Most famous is the 'Famine STELA' which purports to date to the reign of DJOSER but is in fact Ptolemaic. SOBEKHOTEP III erected a small shrine on the island, while a temple of Ptolemy IV is known from reused blocks. Inscriptions record the excavation of a canal near Sehel in the reign of PEPI I, to assist shipping through the Cataract; SENUSRET III had it dredged and widened to facilitate his military campaign against NUBIA.

Seila Site at the entrance to the FAYUM, 18 km (11 miles) west of MEIDUM. The principal monument is a small

*The granite boulders on the island of **Sehel**, south of Elephantine in the First Cataract region, are covered with inscriptions from many periods of ancient Egyptian history.*

One of hundreds of granite statues of the lioness goddess **Sekhmet** erected at Karnak during the reign of Amenhotep III in the 18th Dynasty.

Gilded wooden statuette of **Selket** from Tutankhamun's tomb; the scorpion goddess was one of four protective deities who guarded the king's canopic shrine.

step PYRAMID, dated to the reign of SNEFERU. It was probably a marker of the royal cult, since it lacks any burial. An altar of TRAVERTINE was found on the north side of the pyramid.

Sekenenra Taa II *see* Taa

Sekerher (c. 1620 BC) King of the HYKSOS 15th Dynasty, almost certainly the predecessor of KHYAN. Sekerher was the last 15th Dynasty ruler to style himself *heka-khasut* ('ruler of foreign lands') rather than adopting the full ROYAL TITLES of an Egyptian king. A door-jamb of Sekerher has been discovered at Ezbet Helmi, part of the site of AVARIS.

Sekhemib(-Perenmaat) *see* Peribsen

Sekhemkhet (c. 2625 BC) Probably the second king of the 3rd Dynasty. He built an unfinished step PYRAMID complex at SAQQARA, to the south-west of DJOSER's monument. A graffito on the enclosure wall of Sekhemkhet's complex names IMHOTEP, suggesting that the same architect may have been responsible for both projects. Finds from the underground chambers include a TRAVERTINE sarcophagus (empty when it was discovered) and a fine set of gold JEWELRY. Sekhemkhet is also attested in a rock-cut scene in the WADI MAGHARA and on a seal impression from ELEPHANTINE.

Sekhmet Lioness goddess who personified the aggressive aspects of female deities and was propitiated as the bringer of pestilence. The numerous statues of Sekhmet erected by AMENHOTEP III in the MUT complex at KARNAK, and at his mortuary temple in western THEBES, may have been an act of appeasement designed to protect Egypt against plague. Sekhmet was usually depicted as a woman with a lioness's head.

Selket (Selkis, Serket) SCORPION goddess, often invoked in prayers to protect against or cure stings and bites. Her cult is attested as early as the 1st Dynasty, and she is mentioned in the PYRAMID TEXTS. In funerary beliefs, Selket was one of the four goddesses who protected the corners of the COFFIN and the CANOPIC JARS; she was associated with the FALCON-headed Qebehsenuef. She is usually depicted as a woman with a scorpion on her head; the creature is often shown without legs or sting, to render it harmless. The title 'priest of Selket' may have designated someone skilled in the treatment of scorpion stings, rather than a religious office.

Semainean *see* Predynastic period

Semerkhet (c. 2825 BC) Seventh and penultimate king of the 1st Dynasty. His reign was probably brief; he is the only 1st Dynasty ruler not represented among the high status tombs of north SAQQARA. Semerkhet's own tomb, at ABYDOS, was surrounded by subsidiary tombs, covered by the same superstructure as the royal burial chamber itself: a clear indication of retainer sacrifice. The only object of note to survive from Semerkhet's reign is a black granite funerary STELA, one of a pair that originally stood in front of the royal tomb.

Semna Site in the Second CATARACT region of NUBIA, commanding a strategically important gorge which guarded the approaches to Lower Nubia. SENUSRET I founded a fortified town at Semna, while SENUSRET III erected a STELA at the site, formally establishing it as Egypt's southern border and exhorting future generations to defend it. Four FORTRESSES were built in close proximity (Semna, Semna South and Uronarti on the west bank; Kumma on the east), to protect the frontier and supervise shipping. PAPYRUS reports on surveillance operations, carried out by Egyptian troops in Lower Nubia and sent back to the garrison headquarters at THEBES, are known as the Semna Despatches.

Sened (c. 2700 BC) Ephemeral and poorly attested king of the 2nd Dynasty.

Senenmut High official of the early 18th Dynasty who served as chief steward of AMUN during the reign of HATSHEPSUT. Of humble background from ARMANT, he began his career at the royal court under THUTMOSE II. His influence grew and he became tutor to Hatshepsut's daughter, Neferura; many of Senenmut's numerous statues show him cradling the girl in his lap. Some scholars have speculated that he may have been Hatshepsut's lover, but there is no firm evidence for this. As royal architect, he oversaw state building projects at THEBES, including the temple at DEIR EL-BAHRI, where he left his mark by having himself depicted in a relief, albeit in a hidden location behind doors. He may also have been responsible for the quarrying and transportation of Hatshepsut's obelisks, erected at KARNAK. He built two monuments for himself in the THEBAN NECROPOLIS: a funerary chapel at SHEIKH ABD EL-QURNA, and a rock-cut burial-place at Deir el-Bahri; the latter was never finished. After Neferura's possibly premature death, Senenmut largely disappears from the record. It is not certain if he outlived Hatshepsut.

*Painted wooden statue of **Senusret I** from his pyramid complex at Lisht; the king wears the white crown and a simple linen kilt, and carries a staff of authority.*

senet *see* games

Sennefer High official of the 18th Dynasty who was mayor of THEBES during the reign of AMENHOTEP II. The burial chamber of his tomb at SHEIKH ABD EL-QURNA is famous for its painted ceiling, decorated to resemble a vine with bunches of grapes.

Senusret I (throne name: Kheperkara) (c. 1918–c. 1875 BC) Second king of the 12th Dynasty, the son of AMEN-EMHAT I, with whom he ruled in a CO-REGENCY for up to ten years. LITERATURE from his reign, notably the TALE OF SINUHE and the INSTRUCTION OF AMENEMHAT I FOR HIS SON, suggests that Senusret I may have succeeded to the throne following the murder of his father in a court conspiracy. He continued the policy of expanding Egyptian control in Lower NUBIA, building a series of FORTRESSES within signalling distance of each other from the First CATARACT to BUHEN. He also undertook building programmes at the temple of HELIOPOLIS, where his obelisk still stands; at COPTOS; and at ABGIG in the FAYUM. At KARNAK, he built the exquisite 'White Chapel', one of the finest surviving examples of 12th Dynasty relief decoration. His pyramid complex at LISHT followed the model established by his father, but with an unparalleled number of pyramids of his wives and daughters surrounding the main monument. Sculpture found at Lisht includes a series of life-size limestone statues, and two fine wooden statues of the king. Hence, in his surviving monuments, Senusret I is one of the best-attested rulers of the MIDDLE KINGDOM.

Senusret II (throne name: Khakheperra) (c. 1842–c. 1837 BC) Fourth king of the 12th Dynasty, who succeeded AMENEMHAT II perhaps after a short CO-REGENCY. His major surviving monument is the pyramid complex at LAHUN, with its accompanying town at KAHUN. The location of the king's mortuary complex indicates the high degree of interest shown by the 12th Dynasty in the FAYUM.

Senusret III (throne name: Khakaura) (c. 1836–c. 1818 BC) Fifth king of the 12th Dynasty, and one of the most important rulers of the MIDDLE KINGDOM. Within Egypt, he reorganized provincial administration, reducing the power of NOMARCHS, and appointed three VIZIERS with responsibility over LOWER EGYPT, UPPER EGYPT and NUBIA respectively. He vigorously pursued SENUSRET I's programme of military control

over Lower Nubia, launching a series of campaigns to quell resistance, assisted by the widening of the canal near SEHEL island to permit larger fleets of warships to bypass the First CATARACT. Egyptian subjugation of Lower Nubia was reinforced by the construction of new fortresses in strategic locations, and the establishment of a heavily fortified border at the SEMNA gorge. He was later deified and worshipped in Nubia, and the memory of his actions preserved in the legend of 'High Sesostris'. In the LEVANT, he waged a campaign against 'Sekmem' (probably the site of Shechem in modern ISRAEL). His building programme included work at the temple of MEDAMUD; a pyramid complex at DAHSHUR, modelled on the STEP PYRAMID of DJOSER; and a mortuary complex at south ABYDOS which was either a CENOTAPH or the king's actual burial place. The distinctive portrayal of the king in sculpture – with brooding, hooded eyes, large protruding ears and grim expression – has been interpreted as a depiction of world-weariness, and as an image of determined despotism; it may have been a conscious attempt at archaizing, harking back to the reign of Djoser and an earlier model of KINGSHIP.

Senusret IV (throne name: Sneferibra) (mid to late 17th century BC) Ephemeral king of the later SECOND INTERMEDIATE PERIOD (16th or 17th Dynasty), whose authority was probably confined to UPPER EGYPT.

Senwosret *see* Senusret I, II, III, IV

Seqenenra Taa II *see* Taa

sequence dating System developed by the British archaeologist Flinders Petrie (1853–1942) for assigning relative dates to Predynastic graves, largely on the basis of their POTTERY. The system was based upon the study of FUNERARY GOODS from the cemeteries at NAGADA, Ballas and DIOSPOLIS PARVA. It relied on the assumption that certain classes of pottery underwent gradual but continuous stylistic change, and hence that graves containing similar types of pottery are close in date.

Serabit el-Khadim Site in the mountains of southwestern SINAI, 29 km (18 miles) east of the Gulf of Suez. It was the focus of TURQUOISE mining expeditions from the early MIDDLE KINGDOM to the late NEW KINGDOM; the surrounding hills were known as the 'turquoise terraces'. Remains of mining activity

Granite head of **Senusret III** from Medamud; the heavily lidded eyes and brooding expression are typical and distinctive features of this king's statuary.

include mines cut deep into the rock, and miners' huts. A temple to HATHOR, 'lady of turquoise', includes numerous rock-cut and free-standing STELAE which were dedicated by members of mining expeditions to Hathor and to SOPDU, 'guardian of the desert ways'. SCARABS and jugs of TELL EL-YAHUDIYA ware from the SECOND INTERMEDIATE PERIOD levels at Serabit el-Khadim indicate continued activity at the site during the HYKSOS period. Examples of Proto-Sinaitic script (a rudimentary alphabetic writing system) have been found in the vicinity.

Serapeum Underground catacombs at SAQQARA used from the late 18th Dynasty to the end of the PTOLEMAIC PERIOD for the burials of the mummified APIS bulls (identified with SERAPIS in the Ptolemaic period). Opening off long galleries, the burial chambers of the 26th Dynasty and later each contained a huge granite SARCOPHAGUS, weighing as much as eighty tons. In the 30th Dynasty, a sacred avenue of SPHINXES was built as an approach to the Serapeum; it ran from MEMPHIS up onto the Saqqara plateau. The name 'Serapeum' was also applied to the cult centre of Serapis at ALEXANDRIA, sacked by Christians in the late ROMAN PERIOD.

Serapis God of fertility and corn, formed through SYNCRETISM from the cults of OSIRIS and APIS, influenced by the solar, funerary and healing attributes of the Greek gods Zeus, Helios, Hades, Asklepios and Dionysos. Serapis is first attested in the early PTOLEMAIC PERIOD. His main cult centre was the SERAPEUM at ALEXANDRIA, renowned as a centre of learning, where he was worshipped together with his consort ISIS. The cult of Serapis was adopted by the Romans and became popular throughout the Roman world; texts mention a temple of Serapis in Britain.

serdab Room in an OLD KINGDOM MASTABA which contained the KA-statue of the deceased. It was often provided with a narrow slit or pair of eye-holes in the wall, through which the ka could leave and enter the room, and offerings could be made. The earliest *serdab* (from the Arabic for 'cellar') is situated on the north side of DJOSER'S STEP PYRAMID and contained a life-size statue of the king.

serekh Rectangular frame which enclosed the king's HORUS name. Representing a section of the royal PALACE-FAÇADE, and surmounted by a FALCON, it sym-

The temple of Hathor at **Serabit el-Khadim** in the southwestern Sinai; monuments were dedicated by members of the many turquoise-mining expeditions that worked nearby.

bolized the belief, central to KINGSHIP ideology, that the king was the earthly incarnation of the Horus, and that the god was resident in the palace in the person of the king.

Serket *see* Selket

serpent *see* snake

serpopard Name given to a mythical creature with four legs and a long serpentine neck, depicted on ceremonial objects of the late PREDYNASTIC PERIOD and early 1st Dynasty. The motif was borrowed from MESOPOTAMIA. A pair of serpopards frame the central well of the NARMER PALETTE, perhaps symbolizing the DUALITY that characterized the ancient Egyptian world-view.

Sesebi Site in Upper NUBIA between the Second and Third CATARACTS. Founded by AKHENATEN, it comprises a walled town, which probably housed a specialized state-run community; and a large temple dedicated to the Theban TRIAD, built at the beginning of the king's reign.

Seshat Goddess of writing and measurement. From an early period, she was closely associated with temple-foundation ceremonies, assisting the king in the ritual of 'stretching the cord' (laying out the temple); she is shown in this context on a decorated block from HIERAKONPOLIS dating to the reign of KHASEKHEMWY. In the OLD KINGDOM and MIDDLE KINGDOM, her role also extended to recording the numbers of foreign captives and the amount of plunder carried off during military campaigns. In the NEW KINGDOM, she became closely associated with the SED FESTIVAL, and was often shown in temple reliefs allotting the king his given span of years and recording his NAMES on the leaves of the sacred ISHED TREE. Seshat is depicted as a woman wearing a long panther-skin dress and a HEADDRESS consisting of a band topped by a seven-pointed star and bow. As a universal deity, she had no particular cult centre.

Sesostris *see* Senusret I, II, III, IV

Seth God of confusion and disorder with an ambiguous role in ancient Egyptian RELIGION. He is one of the earliest attested deities, his cult at NAGADA having been celebrated from Predynastic times. In the EARLY DYNASTIC period, he played an important role in

The name of the 1st Dynasty king Djet, written in a **serekh** surmounted by the falcon god, dominates the decoration of this ivory comb from his tomb at Abydos.

A 19th Dynasty relief from Luxor Temple showing the goddess **Seshat** writing the number of years of the king's reign on a notched palm-rib (the hieroglyph for 'year').

KINGSHIP ideology; the ruler was revered as the incarnation of both HORUS and Seth. PERIBSEN elevated Seth to the status previously enjoyed by the FALCON god, placing him atop his SEREKH. Seth was an important member of the ENNEAD of HELIOPOLIS. However, with the rise of the OSIRIS myth in the OLD KINGDOM, Seth's role as Osiris's murderer caused him to be regarded as disruptive and subversive, his image too dangerous to depict on temple walls, even as a HIEROGLYPH. Yet in solar religion, he was seen as an important ally of the sun god RA in the eternal struggle against chaos. Standing on the prow of the SOLAR BARQUE, it was Seth who speared the serpent APOPHIS, hence directing his aggression against the enemy of creation. Seth was associated with deserts and foreign lands, both places of hostility in the Egyptian worldview. He was also the god of storms, identified with the Asiatic and Greek storm gods BAAL and Typhon.

The RAMESSIDE period was characterized by a renewed reverence for Seth, as demonstrated by such royal NAMES as Seti and Sethnakht. However, in the LATE PERIOD, opinion swung against Seth once more; he was seen as the embodiment of evil, and many of his statues were recarved to resemble other, more benign deities. His primary cult centre throughout the pharaonic period was at Nagada, although his similarity to the Asiatic god Baal made him a popular deity in the eastern DELTA. (This explains his importance to the 19th Dynasty royal family, which originally came from the area.)

Seth was depicted as a curious beast with a long snout, tall erect ears with squared ends, and a forked tail. He could also be shown as a man with the head of this so-called 'Seth-animal'. It has been variously identified as a pig, dog, ass, or aardvark, but was probably a composite mythical animal, reflecting Seth's disruptive nature and his close association with the deserts (believed to be the home of mythical creatures). In mythology, the HIPPOPOTAMUS could also be seen as an embodiment of Seth – hence the act of harpooning one was a metaphor for the defeat of disorder.

Sethnakht (throne name: Userkhaura-meryamun) (c. 1190–c. 1187 BC) First king of the 20th Dynasty. He came to power after the dynastic strife which characterized the end of the 19th Dynasty, but reigned for only two years. His ancestry is not clear; before claiming the KINGSHIP, he may have been an army general, based in the eastern DELTA. He legitimized his accession by an ORACLE of the god SETH, delivered in the god's temple at PER-RAMESSES. He was succeeded by his son RAMESSES III.

Sethos see Seti I, II

Seti I (Sethos) ('The one of SETH') (throne name: Menmaatra) (c. 1290–c. 1279 BC) Second king of the 19th Dynasty, who succeeded his father RAMESSES I, probably after a CO-REGENCY. He continued the militaristic nature of the 19th Dynasty, launching a series of campaigns against LIBYA and the LEVANT, recorded in reliefs at KARNAK. He was also one of the most prolific builders of the RAMESSIDE period. Perhaps to reinforce the legitimacy of the new dynasty, he erected a beautifully decorated temple at ABYDOS, its KING-LIST emphasizing the unbroken line of succession from MENES to Seti himself and his son RAMESSES II.

At Karnak, Seti began work on the magnificent HYPOSTYLE HALL. His tomb in the VALLEY OF THE KINGS (KV17), famous for its astronomical ceiling, is probably the most spectacular of all NEW KINGDOM

Granite statue of Ramesses III being greeted by the gods Horus (left) and **Seth** (right), the two gods whose mutual opposition is reconciled in the person of the king.

royal tombs. The king's mummy, one of the best preserved of all royal mummies, was found reburied in the cache at DEIR EL-BAHRI.

Seti II (Sethos) (throne name: Userkheperura-setepenra) (c. 1204–c. 1198 BC) Sixth king of the 19th Dynasty. His reign was interrupted by a usurper, AMENMESSE, who ruled in UPPER EGYPT and NUBIA. Seti II undertook building work at KARNAK and the RAMESSEUM, but never finished his tomb in the VALLEY OF THE KINGS (KV15). He was succeeded by SIPTAH, with TAWOSRET (Seti's widow) acting initially as regent.

sexuality The ancient Egyptians had a relatively relaxed and open attitude to sexual matters. Sexuality and fertility were major concerns of private RELIGION; from the early PREDYNASTIC PERIOD, sexual symbolism was important in a funerary context because of its connotations of rebirth. BULLS and rams alike were revered for their fecundity and virility, while the fertility god of COPTOS (MIN) is one of the earliest attested deities in the Egyptian pantheon. Sexual activity outside marriage and homosexuality seem to have been regarded as departures from ideal behaviour, and the INSTRUCTION OF ANI counsels against involvement with prostitutes. However, there is no evidence for such activities being punishable by LAW. For reasons of ritual purity, PRIESTS were expected to abstain from sexual activity during their period of temple service.

Seyala *see* Nubia

Shabaqo (throne name: Neferkara) (c. 715–c. 702 BC) Second king of the 25th Dynasty. He succeeded his

Mummy of **Seti I**, found reburied in a cache of royal mummies at Deir el-Bahri; the king's body is particularly well preserved, a testament to the skill of the 19th Dynasty embalmers.

The scenes on a 19th Dynasty erotic papyrus suggest a relatively robust and uncomplicated attitude to **sexuality** on the part of the ancient Egyptians.

Wooden **shabti** box and figurines of Henutmehit from her 19th Dynasty tomb in western Thebes. The shabtis were intended to act as substitutes for the deceased in the afterlife.

A man uses a **shaduf** to raise water from a canal to irrigate a garden plot, in a scene from the 19th Dynasty tomb of Ipui at Deir el-Medina.

brother PIYE and completed the task of bringing the whole of Egypt under central control by defeating BAKENRENEF, the last king of the 24th Dynasty. Shabaqo undertook numerous building projects, including additions to temples at MEMPHIS, ABYDOS and ESNA. The best-known artifact from his reign is the 'Shabaqo Stone', a basalt slab inscribed with a version of the MEMPHITE creation myth ('the Memphite theology') that claimed to be a copy of an OLD KINGDOM original. It illustrates the archaizing tendency so characteristic of 25th Dynasty court culture. Shabaqo was buried in a PYRAMID-style tomb in the Kushite royal cemetery at el-KURRU.

Shabitqo (Shebitku) (throne name: Djedkaura) (c. 702–690 BC) Third king of the 25th Dynasty, in succession to his uncle SHABAQO.

shabti (shawabti, ushabti) Funerary figurine, the purpose of which was to act as a substitute for the deceased when he was called upon to perform agricultural work or CORVÉE LABOUR in the afterlife. The ancient Egyptian word ushabti means 'answerer' and it was the *shabti*'s duty to answer the call to work on the tomb owner's behalf. Shabtis evolved in the MIDDLE KINGDOM from the servant statues included among FUNERARY GOODS. The earliest examples were crude statuettes in wax, clay or wood; later, they were fashioned as mummiform figures and, from the end of the 12th Dynasty, were customarily inscribed with the 'shabti text', Chapter 6 of the BOOK OF THE DEAD which specifies the *shabti*'s duties. From the middle of the 18th Dynasty, *shabtis* were shown carrying agricultural tools; after the AMARNA period, they were shown in everyday dress. Shabtis first appeared in a royal context in the early 18th Dynasty and became a key part of a king's funerary equipment. The ideal number came to be regarded as 401 – one for each day of the year, together with an overseer for each group of ten – but the tomb of SETI I was provided with as many as 700 *shabtis*. In the THIRD INTERMEDIATE PERIOD and LATE PERIOD, vast numbers of figurines were manufactured for royal and private burials alike. Some were finely executed in wood or stone; but most were mass-produced in FAIENCE. Shabtis are thus one of the most common types of artifact from ancient Egypt. Their use finally died out in the PTOLEMAIC period.

shaduf Irrigation device used for lifting water from the NILE or a canal on to fields. It comprised a long horizontal pole, with a bucket at one end and a counter-weight at the other, mounted on a vertical stake. Introduced in the 18th Dynasty, it is first depicted in tombs of the AMARNA period.

shawabti *see shabti*

Shebitku *see Shabitqo*

Sheikh Abd el-Qurna Area of the central THEBAN NECROPOLIS between el-KHOKHA and QURNET MURAI. The earliest tombs, built for governors of THEBES and VIZIERS, date to the early MIDDLE KINGDOM. There are also a few tombs of the RAMES-SIDE period. However, the cemetery's heyday was the 18th Dynasty (up to the reign of AMENHOTEP IV) when it was the most popular part of the Theban necropolis for high status burials. Important tombs include those of SENENMUT, REKHMIRA, KENAMUN and RAMOSE.

Sheikh el-Beled ('headman of the village') Nickname given to a near life-size statue of the chief lector priest Ka-aper from SAQQARA. He is depicted as a slightly corpulent middle-aged man, carrying a staff and sceptre to symbolize authority. Made from sycamore wood, it is one of the finest examples of OLD KINGDOM sculpture and has been tentatively dated to the late 4th Dynasty.

shemu *see calendar*

shen HIEROGLYPH of a circle of rope, knotted at the bottom, which symbolized eternity and protection. It was often shown in reliefs, being offered to the king by HORUS or NEKHBET. The CARTOUCHE which enclosed the king's name was an elongated version of the *shen*.

Shepenwepet *see Osorkon, Piye, Rudamun*

Shepseskaf (c. 2475 BC) Sixth and last king of the 4th Dynasty. For his tomb, he departed from the tradition of a pyramid, constructing instead a unique, SARCOPHAGUS-shaped funerary monument at south SAQQARA, known as the MASTABAT EL-FARA'UN.

Shepseskara (Izi) (c. 2390 BC) Sixth king of the 5th Dynasty.

Sherden *see Sea Peoples*

The life-size wooden statue of Ka-aper was nicknamed **Sheikh el-Beled** *because its portly figure reminded the workmen who discovered it of their village headman.*

Sheshi (throne name: Maaibra) (late 17th century BC) King of the SECOND INTERMEDIATE PERIOD (14th or 15th Dynasty), of Asiatic origin, attested on numerous SCARAB seals from the LEVANT and the fortress of Uronarti in NUBIA.

Sheshonq *see* Shoshenq

Gold funerary mask of the 22nd Dynasty king **Shoshenq II** from his tomb at Tanis.

Ivory headrest from the tomb of Tutankhamun, with the god **Shu** between the 'lions of yesterday and tomorrow'; the symbolism of this object identified the king, when he used it, with the sun god Ra.

shesmet **girdle** Belt from which a bead apron was suspended. It was part of the royal costume in the EARLY DYNASTIC PERIOD (for example on the NARMER PALETTE), and was also worn by certain deities.

ships *see* boats and ships

Shoshenq Libyan name held by six or seven kings of the 22nd and 23rd Dynasties. Their precise relationship to each other, their regnal numbers, their place within the order of succession, and the overall chronology of the THIRD INTERMEDIATE PERIOD have all been much debated.

Shoshenq I (throne name: Hedjkheperra-setepenra) (c. 945–c. 925 BC) was a descendant of the Libyan great chiefs of the Meshwesh and nephew of OSORKON the Elder, who rose to power as army general under PSUSENNES II (to whom he was related by marriage). Shoshenq I's accession marked the beginning of the Libyan 22nd Dynasty. To reassert royal control in UPPER EGYPT, he appointed his son as High Priest of AMUN, in combination with the office of army commander. He launched a military campaign to restore Egyptian authority in Palestine, defeating the kingdoms of ISRAEL and Judah, and commemorating his victory on the 'Bubastite Portal' at KARNAK. He is probably to be equated with the biblical Shishak. His reign marks something of a high point in the Third Intermediate Period.

Shoshenq II (throne name: Heqakheperra-setepenra) (c. 890 BC) was the son of OSORKON I, and ruled with him in a CO-REGENCY. However, he predeceased his father and so never reigned as sole king in his own right. His silver COFFIN was found in the tomb of Psusennes I at TANIS.

Shoshenq III (c. 835–c. 795 BC) was the successor, and presumably the son, of OSORKON II. Ruling from Tanis, his authority seems to have been widely recognized throughout the DELTA. He was succeeded by the obscure Shoshenq IV (c. 795–c. 785 BC).

Shoshenq V (throne name: Aakheperra) (c. 775–c. 735 BC) was the penultimate king of the 22nd Dynasty. His long reign, of nearly forty years, is well attested in the archaeological record, especially in his home town of Tanis. Monuments include a temple to the Theban TRIAD and a chapel to celebrate the king's SED FESTIVAL.

Shoshenq VI, VII Two further kings named Shoshenq (VI and VII) (c. 800–c. 780 BC and c. 725–c. 715 BC) are attested from the 23rd Dynasty.

shrine *see* temple

Shu God of air and sunlight. According to the CRE-ATION MYTH of HELIOPOLIS, Shu was the son of ATUM and one half of the first divine couple (with his sister-wife TEFNUT). He is attested in the PYRAMID TEXTS and COFFIN TEXTS, but was not the focus of a separate cult until the NEW KINGDOM. Uniquely, his name and image escaped persecution during the AMARNA period because of Shu's strong connection with sunlight; according to the formal titles given to the ATEN, Shu was said to 'dwell in the sun disc'. In the LATE PERIOD, he and Tefnut were worshipped in leonine form at LEONTOPOLIS. Shu is usually depicted as a man wearing a plume on his head, lifting up the sky goddess NUT to separate her from the earth god GEB.

Shunet el-Zebib Mud-brick funerary enclosure of KHASEKHEMWY at ABYDOS. Situated on the low desert, facing the town, it proclaimed its royal status by means of PALACE-FAÇADE architecture. It is one of the earliest surviving buildings in Egypt and remains a dominant feature at Abydos. The preparations for the king's funeral probably took place here, and it subsequently served as the main location of his mortuary cult. It is closely linked, in form and function, to the contemporary 'Fort' at HIERAKONPOLIS. A fleet of twelve boats unearthed in recent years beside the enclosure, but perhaps belonging to the nearby enclosure of DJER, reflects an aspect of early royal AFTERLIFE BELIEFS. The Arabic name of the building – meaning 'storehouse of raisins'– reflects its more recent use.

Siamun (throne name: Netjerkheperra-setepenamun) (c. 970–c. 950 BC) Sixth and penultimate king of the 21st Dynasty, who carried out building works at TANIS. One of his daughters may have been given in marriage to King Solomon of Israel.

sidelock of youth Characteristic hairstyle of children and used in Egyptian ART to denote childhood (and, by association, the child god KHONSU). It involved shaving the hair, leaving only a single, plaited lock hanging down the side of the head. Actual examples of

*The niched eastern façade of the **Shunet el-Zebib**, the late 2nd Dynasty funerary enclosure of Khasekhemwy at Abydos. Constructed of mud-brick, it is one of the earliest surviving buildings in Egypt.*

One half of a double cartouche-shaped cosmetic box from the tomb of Tutankhamun shows the young king wearing his hair in the distinctive **sidelock of youth**.

sidelocks have been found in OLD KINGDOM graves of children at Mostagedda in MIDDLE EGYPT.

Sihathor *see* Sahathor

silver *see* metalworking

Sinai Mountainous peninsula bordering Egypt to the north-east. Jutting into the Red Sea, it forms a land bridge between the continents of Africa and Asia. The Sinai's northern, Mediterranean coastal strip ('the Ways of HORUS') was used as the main overland route between Egypt and the LEVANT from prehistoric times; it was fortified under RAMESSES II. Egyptian involvement in the Sinai focused on the mining of TURQUOISE and COPPER, especially at the south-western sites of WADI MAGHARA, Wadi Kharit and SERABIT EL-KHADIM. Frequent mining expeditions, especially in the MIDDLE KINGDOM, brought Egyptians into contact with the native inhabitants who shared cultural traits with their Palestinian neighbours. A number of

inscriptions have been found in the Sinai and Levant, written in 'Proto-Sinaitic'; derived from HIEROGLYPHS, this script represents an early stage in the development of an alphabetic writing system. Sites with BIBLICAL CONNECTIONS in the Sinai include Mount Sinai and St Catherine's Monastery (said to house the Burning Bush).

Sinuhe *see* Tale of Sinuhe

Siptah ('Son of PTAH') (throne name: Akhenra-setepenra) (c. 1198–c. 1193 BC) Seventh king of the 19th Dynasty, who succeeded to the throne as a boy on the death of SETI II. His parentage is uncertain, but it is possible that he was a son of AMENMESSE. Siptah's tomb in the VALLEY OF THE KINGS (KV47) was never finished. During his short reign of six years, power seems to have been exercised principally by the high official BAY and the queen TAWOSRET, Seti II's widow; the latter proclaimed herself pharaoh after Siptah's death.

Sirius *see* Sopdet

sistrum (pl. sistra) Rattle used in religious ceremonies, especially temple rituals, and usually played by WOMEN. It was closely associated with HATHOR in her role as 'lady of MUSIC', and the handle was often decorated with a Hathor head. Two kinds of sistrum are attested, NAOS-shaped and hoop-shaped; the latter became the more common.

Siwa Oasis Most northerly and westerly of the OASES of the Libyan Desert, situated about 560 km (350 miles) west of Cairo. Its archaeological remains, the earliest dating to the 26th Dynasty, include temples of AMUN founded by AMASIS and NECTANEBO II. ALEXANDER THE GREAT is said to have visited the oracle of Ammon (Amun) at Siwa in 332 BC, receiving recognition as the god's son and thus legitimate king of Egypt.

skiff *see* boats and ships, papyrus

slaves Despite the popular (though entirely incorrect) notion that the PYRAMIDS were built by gangs of slaves, slavery was very rare in ancient Egypt before the PTOLEMAIC PERIOD. Major construction projects were carried out by CORVÉE LABOUR; MINING AND QUARRYING by conscripted workers, convicts and – from the MIDDLE KINGDOM onwards – prisoners of war.

Although not free to return to their country of origin, prisoners of war were nevertheless able to own property and many were eventually allocated land-holdings, allowing them to settle permanently in Egypt. Documents from DEIR EL-MEDINA indicate that some households had individuals who were required to carry out menial tasks; but such people do not appear to have been slaves in the classical sense of the word.

Smendes (Nesbanebdjedet) (throne name: Hedjkheperra-setepenra) (c. 1069–c. 1045 BC) First king of the 21st Dynasty. After the death of RAMESSES XI, Egypt was effectively divided into two states. Smendes, perhaps Ramesses XI's son-in-law, ruled LOWER EGYPT from TANIS, while UPPER EGYPT was ruled by the High Priest of AMUN, PINEDJEM I. Smendes is mentioned in the tale of WENAMUN. He was succeeded by PSUSENNES I, Pinedjem I's son.

Smenkhkara (throne name: Ankhkheperura) (c. 1336–c. 1332 BC) Eleventh king of the 18th Dynasty, in succession to AKHENATEN. His brief reign holds many unsolved mysteries. Smenkhkara was previously assumed to have been Akhenaten's son, the older brother of TUTANKHAMUN; he was identified with the mummy of a young man found reburied in the VALLEY OF THE KINGS (tomb KV55). However, some scholars identify Smenkhkara with NEFERTITI, reigning in male guise as king in her own right following her husband's death.

snake An ever-present threat to people and livestock, snakes were regarded with fear and awe in ancient Egypt. Their dangerous nature made them a natural metaphor for evil, the serpent APOPHIS representing the very antithesis of created order. However, the Egyptian pantheon also contained many snake deities whose powers could be used to good ends and who, if suitably propitiated, were believed to offer protection against snake-bites. Most snake deities were female, such as MERETSEGER, RENENUTET, the royal URAEUS and WADJET (the last two depicted as cobras); but the PYRAMID TEXTS also mention a snake god, Nehebkau. Snakes were associated with the primeval waters of NUN and with the underworld: the four goddesses of the Hermopolitan OGDOAD were depicted with snakes' heads; the tomb of SETI I shows a huge snake, perhaps the creature whose coils were believed to circle the universe, symbolizing the balance between existence and non-existence. Snakes were also closely associated

with magic. A 13th Dynasty magician's wand from the RAMESSEUM is shaped like a snake, while CIPPUS plaques of the LATE PERIOD showed the infant HORUS holding snakes and other dangerous creatures. Medical papyri include treatments for snake-bites, showing that the Egyptians had detailed knowledge of the various species of snake and the effects of their venom.

Sneferu (c. 2575 BC) First king of the 4th Dynasty. He was the son of HUNI and queen Meresankh, and the father of KHUFU. His reign marks the high point of pyramid construction: Sneferu built – or at least completed – the pyramid at MEIDUM, as well as two further, massive pyramids at DAHSHUR. A small step PYRAMID

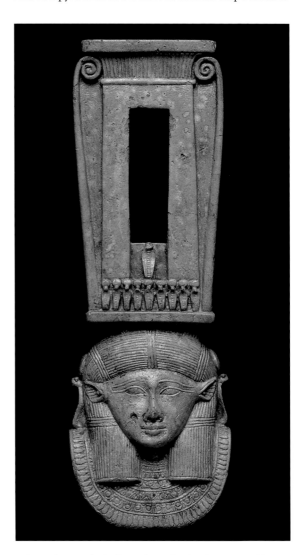

Faience **sistrum** in the form of a Hathor-head surmounted by a naos, 26th Dynasty. Sistra were rattles played during religious ceremonies and could also be hoop-shaped.

at SEILA has also been attributed to him. His VALLEY TEMPLE at Dahshur contained reliefs depicting offering bearers and personifications of the NOMES, signifying the involvement of the whole country in supplying the king's mortuary cult. A rock-cut inscription from the SINAI indicates mining activity during Sneferu's reign.

Snofru *see* Sneferu

Sobek CROCODILE god, associated with water and fertility. His main early cult centre, attested from the 1st Dynasty, was at MEDINET EL-FAYUM (known to the Greeks as Crocodilopolis). In later periods, a major temple to Sobek was built at KOM OMBO. Both sites may have had sacred lakes containing crocodiles. There were also smaller shrines at many other sites. The cult of Sobek rose to particular prominence in the MIDDLE KINGDOM, associated with increased activity in the FAYUM as a whole, and reflected in the names of several late Middle Kingdom rulers (such as SOBEKNEFERU and SOBEKHOTEP). In the NEW KINGDOM, Sobek became assimilated into the cult of AMUN, and was closely identified with the sun god as SOBEK-RA. This explains why the Greeks associated Sobek with their

*Relief of the crocodile god **Sobek** on the walls of the late Ptolemaic temple at Kom Ombo which was dedicated to the deity. The temple may have had a sacred lake containing crocodiles.*

own sun god, Helios. Sobek was depicted either as a crocodile, perched on a shrine; or as a man with a crocodile's head, wearing a headdress comprising a horned sun disc and feathers.

Sobekemsaf Name of two kings of the late SECOND INTERMEDIATE PERIOD. One is known to have been the father of INTEF V and INTEF VI.

Sobekhotep Name held by eight, mostly ephemeral, kings of the late MIDDLE KINGDOM and SECOND INTERMEDIATE PERIOD. Sobekhotep II (throne name: Sekhemra-khutawy) (c. 1700 BC) undertook temple building at MEDAMUD and DEIR EL-BAHRI. An important pair of PAPYRUS documents from the reign of Sobekhotep III (throne name: Sekhemra-swadjtawy) (c. 1680 BC) give details of income and expenditure in the royal court at THEBES. Sobekhotep IV (throne name: Khaneferra) (c. 1660 BC) formed a mini dynasty with his two brothers NEFERHOTEP I and SAHATHOR. He added to several temples, and commissioned colossal statues, some of which survive.

Sobekneferu (throne name: Sobekkara) (c. 1760–c. 1755 BC) Eighth and last ruler of the 12th Dynasty. She was the daughter of AMENEMHAT III and, according to MANETHO, the sister of AMENEMHAT IV whom she succeeded. Her reign of about three years is the first securely attested instance in ancient Egyptian history of a woman ruling in her own right. A flood level at the fortress of Kumma in Lower NUBIA is dated to her reign, and she may have been responsible for finishing the mortuary temple of Amenemhat III at HAWARA. Her tomb has not been identified with certainty, but may have been one of the pyramids at MAZGHUNA.

Sokar God of the MEMPHITE NECROPOLIS. The Festival of Sokar, attested from the beginning of Egyptian history, involved dragging the god's sacred barque around a ritual circuit; it remained a prominent festival in the religious calendar, and was illustrated on the walls of RAMESSES III's mortuary temple at MEDINET HABU. Sokar was probably in origin an earth deity, but by the OLD KINGDOM had become associated with OSIRIS, and hence with AFTERLIFE BELIEFS. Sokar is mentioned in funerary contexts in the PYRAMID TEXTS and the COFFIN TEXTS, while the silver coffin of SHOSHENQ II from TANIS was modelled to resemble Sokar. His cult became closely intertwined, through SYNCRETISM, with that of another Memphite god,

PTAH; Ptah-Sokar is attested in the Old Kingdom, and PTAH-SOKAR-OSIRIS in the MIDDLE KINGDOM. Sokar was depicted as a low mound surmounted by a boat containing a FALCON's head, or as a mummiform figure with a falcon's head.

solar barque In Egyptian RELIGION, the boat in which the sun god and his attendants travelled. It had a distinctive shape, with an upturned prow and incurved stern. The journey across the heavens was made in the morning barque, the voyage through the underworld in the evening barque. Full-size versions of both were buried next to the pyramid of KHUFU at GIZA, for the king's use in the afterlife.

Soleb Site on the west bank of the NILE in the Third CATARACT region of Upper NUBIA. Its principal monument is a temple of AMENHOTEP III, dedicated to AMUN-RA of KARNAK and a deified version of the king himself, 'Nebmaatra Lord of Nubia'. The temple was a setting for his SED FESTIVAL celebrations. The adjacent town became the capital of the Egyptian province of KUSH in the late 18th Dynasty. Its cemeteries include burials of the NEW KINGDOM and MEROÏTIC period.

Songs of the Harper Genre of text characterized by a sceptical view of the afterlife and a corresponding exhortation to enjoy earthly existence. Such lyrics, associated with harp-players, may have originated as songs sung at feasts. They have been found in tombs of the MIDDLE KINGDOM and NEW KINGDOM.

Sons of Horus The four supernatural beings who protected the mummified internal organs of the deceased in their CANOPIC JARS. They are first mentioned in the PYRAMID TEXTS, where they assist the king's journey to the heavens. Their more characteristic role became an important feature of AFTERLIFE BELIEFS from the late 18th Dynasty, when the lids of the canopic jars began to be modelled as the heads of the four Sons of Horus. The four genii continued to be depicted on FUNERARY GOODS as late as the ROMAN PERIOD. The human-headed Imsety guarded the liver, was associated with the south, and protected by ISIS. The baboon-headed Hapi guarded the lungs, was associated with the north, and protected by NEPHTHYS. The jackal-headed Duamutef guarded the stomach, was associated with the east, and protected by NEITH. The falcon-headed Qebehsenuef guarded the intestines, was associated with the west, and protected by SELKET.

Sopdet (Sothis) Goddess who personified the dog-star Sirius. She is attested from the early 1st Dynasty – depicted as a cow with a plant between her horns – suggesting that the connection between the HELIACAL RISING of Sirius and the beginning of the CALENDAR year may already have been established at this early period. She was more usually represented as a woman with a star on her head, or a woman wearing a tall crown with horns at the side and surmounted by a star. Sopdet was worshipped in a TRIAD with Sah (ORION) and SOPDU.

Sopdu FALCON god who, as 'Lord of the East', personified Egypt's eastern frontier with PALESTINE. His main cult centre was at Per-Sopdu in the eastern DELTA, and he was also worshipped at SERABIT EL-KHADIM in the SINAI. He was associated with HORUS and, in the PYRAMID TEXTS, with the king's teeth (a play on the name Sopdu, which means 'sharp'). He was depicted as a crouching falcon; or as a bearded man wearing a SHESMET GIRDLE and a headdress of two falcon's feathers, carrying a WAS SCEPTRE, ANKH and battle axe.

Sothic cycle *see* chronology

Sothis *see* Sopdet

The 4th Dynasty cedarwood **solar barque** *discovered dismantled in a pit next to the Great Pyramid of Khufu at Giza is a remarkable example of early boat-building.*

soul house Form of OFFERING TABLE produced during the FIRST INTERMEDIATE PERIOD and MIDDLE KINGDOM, ranging in complexity from a simple pottery tray to a model of a house and courtyard filled with food offerings (such as a foreleg of beef). Soul houses are particularly characteristic of the FUNERARY GOODS from Deir Rifeh in MIDDLE EGYPT.

souls of Pe and Nekhen In Egyptian RELIGION, the sacred spirits associated with the Predynastic rulers of LOWER EGYPT and UPPER EGYPT respectively. (Pe was the ancient Egyptian name for BUTO, Nekhen the name for HIERAKONPOLIS.) They were believed to assist the living king and serve the dead king. The souls of Pe were represented as FALCON-headed, the souls of Nekhen as JACKAL-headed. Together they were often shown kneeling, greeting the rising sun or taking part in royal rituals (for example, in the tomb of RAMESSES I, where they greet the king's reborn BA).

speos A small rock-cut temple (from the Greek for 'cave').

Speos Artemidos Rock-cut temple located in a dry valley on the east bank of the NILE, just south of BENI HASAN in MIDDLE EGYPT. Dedicated to the lioness goddess PAKHET, it was built by the female king HATSHEPSUT, completed by her successor THUTMOSE III, and later usurped by SETI I. A vestibule of eight HATHOR-headed columns leads, via a short corridor, to the sanctuary.

The temple is most famous for the inscription on its upper façade, in which Hatshepsut claimed to have liberated Egypt from the HYKSOS (ignoring the four reigns separating the end of the SECOND INTERMEDIATE PERIOD from her accession).

sphinx Mythical beast comprising a LION's body with a man's head. Versions are also known with the head of a ram (CRIOSPHINX) or FALCON (hieracosphinx), while a sphinx with the tail of a CROCODILE is attested at the mortuary temple of AMENHOTEP III. The sphinx was a pre-eminent symbol of royal power, and as such was often shown wearing the *nemes* HEADDRESS, or trampling foreign enemies underfoot. The sphinx also had strong solar connotations, associating the king with the sun god. The earliest known sphinx statue dates to the reign of the OLD KINGDOM king DJEDEFRA; only the head survives. Later in the 4th Dynasty, the Great Sphinx at GIZA was carved from a knoll of bedrock, to

The Great **Sphinx** has guarded the Giza necropolis since the 4th Dynasty and continues to inspire awe and speculation; it is generally believed to have been carved in the reign of Khafra.

act as guardian of the royal NECROPOLIS; its age and purpose are still the subject of speculation, especially by unorthodox writers. In the NEW KINGDOM, the sphinx was worshipped as the god Horemakhet, and also associated with Hauron, the Canaanite desert god. Processional avenues of sphinxes were common features at major sacred sites in the New Kingdom and later periods, notably at KARNAK, LUXOR TEMPLE and the SERAPEUM. The word 'sphinx' may be a Greek corruption of the Egyptian phrase *seshep ankh* ('living image').

stars *see* astronomy and astrology, calendar, Orion, Sopdet

stela (stele) (pl. stelae) Upright tablet of stone or wood, often with a curved top, painted or carved with text and pictures. Numerous examples were produced throughout Egyptian history for a variety of purposes, including funerary, VOTIVE and commemorative. Funerary stelae, attested from the early 1st Dynasty, typically bore the name and titles of the deceased. This basic form, which served to identify the tomb owner, evolved into a key component of the funerary equipment with a magical function. Hence, from the 2nd

Dynasty onwards, the owner was usually shown seated before an OFFERING TABLE piled with food and drink; in the MIDDLE KINGDOM, the OFFERING FORMULA was generally inscribed along the top of the stela. Both were designed to ensure a perpetual supply of offerings in the afterlife. Votive stelae, inscribed with prayers to deities, were dedicated by worshippers seeking a favourable outcome to a particular situation. In the Middle Kingdom, many hundreds were set up by pilgrims on the 'terrace of the great god' at ABYDOS, so that they might participate in the annual procession of OSIRIS. One particular variety of votive stela common in the NEW KINGDOM was the ear stela, inscribed with images of human ears to encourage the deity to listen to the prayer or request.

Commemorative stelae were produced to proclaim notable achievements (for example, the stela of Horwerra, recording a mining expedition to SERABIT EL-KHADIM, and the Restoration Stela of TUTANKHAMUN, celebrating the restoration of the traditional cults at the end of the AMARNA period); to celebrate military victories (for instance, the ISRAEL Stela of MERENPTAH); and to establish frontiers (for example the SEMNA stela of SENUSRET III and the boundary stelae around Amarna).

The **Step Pyramid** of Djoser at Saqqara is the oldest pyramid in Egypt, dating to the beginning of the 3rd Dynasty, and one of the earliest structures to be built of dressed stone on a monumental scale.

Step Pyramid Funerary monument of Netjerikhet (DJOSER) at SAQQARA. Since its initial excavation in the early 20th century AD, it has been restored and reconstructed under the direction of the French architect Jean-Philippe Lauer (1902–2001), who dedicated his entire adult life to the monument. It still dominates the Saqqara plateau and the surrounding floodplain, as it would have done in antiquity. Attributed to the architect IMHOTEP, it was one of the earliest buildings to make extensive use of dressed stone. It also represented a major innovation in mortuary architecture, combining the two elements of the royal burial – the tomb and the funerary palace – in a single monument. At the heart of the complex is the PYRAMID itself, originally designed as a MASTABA, then enlarged in two successive changes of plan to a pyramid of four, and finally of six, steps. Its subterranean chambers are decorated with blue FAIENCE tiles, symbolizing the watery abyss of the underworld, and with relief panels showing the king carrying out royal rituals.

The pyramid is surrounded by an extensive complex of buildings, each designed to perform a specific function in the afterlife. The South Tomb, built within the thickness of the enclosure wall, provided a final resting-place for the king's KA, and was thus a precursor of the satellite pyramids in 4th Dynasty royal mortuary complexes. The enclosure wall itself was decorated in the PALACE-FAÇADE style, proclaiming the royal ownership of the monument. Inside, a dummy royal palace was provided to serve the king for eternity, while a large courtyard in front of the pyramid with an elevated dais served as an eternal arena for the rituals of KINGSHIP. In particular, two pairs of horseshoe-shaped markers denoted the ritual area in which the king would inspect prisoners, and around which he would stride or run to assert his territorial claim over Egypt. A smaller courtyard, along the eastern edge of the complex, was provided as a setting for the SED FESTIVAL. It is lined with dummy chapels, for the deities of UPPER and LOWER EGYPT, and contains a double throne-platform, a representation of which was used as the HIEROGLYPH for 'sed festival'. Two buildings known as the 'House of the North' and 'House of the South' represent the tented structures in which the king would have robed, disrobed and received guests during the ceremonies. On the northern side of the pyramid, a SERDAB housed the king's statue, and an unfinished court with a large altar was probably intended for offerings to the royal funerary cult. The western side of the complex is filled by a huge masonry structure, overlying a series of underground galleries that may have been earlier, 2nd Dynasty royal tombs. Certainly, the chambers beneath the step pyramid itself were filled with stone vessels usurped from 1st and 2nd Dynasty burials.

Subsequent kings of the 3rd Dynasty also built step pyramids, although none on the same scale as Djoser's monument. These later examples include unfinished step pyramids at Saqqara and ZAWIYET EL-ARYAN, built, respectively, by SEKHEMKHET and an unknown king, most probably KHABA; and a series of small step pyramids, dated to the reign of HUNI or SNEFERU, at ELEPHANTINE, EDFU, el-Kula (near HIERAKONPOLIS), Sinki (near ABYDOS), ZAWIYET EL-AMWAT and SEILA. Remains that may belong to a further monument in the series have recently come to light at ATHRIBIS. The pyramid at MEIDUM was originally built as a stepped structure, before being converted into a true pyramid.

stone The ancient Egyptians made full use of the wide range of different stones available in the NILE Valley and adjacent deserts. The cliffs bordering the floodplain provided abundant supplies of limestone; the white variety from the quarries at TURA was particularly prized, and was used for the casing blocks of PYRAMIDS and for other architectural uses. In southern UPPER EGYPT, the predominant geology changes, limestone giving way to sandstone; this was another important material for construction and SCULPTURE, and was most extensively quarried at GEBEL EL-SILSILA. The area around ASWAN was exploited for its outcrops of granite, used for buildings, OBELISKS, and statuary. Basalt, found in the deserts, was occasionally used for pavements, especially in the pyramid complexes of the OLD KINGDOM.

Many other types of stone were extracted in smaller quantities to make statues, vessels and other small objects. Varieties included breccia; siltstone from the WADI HAMMAMAT; flint from MIDDLE EGYPT; TRAVERTINE from HATNUB; and diorite from the Western Desert of Lower NUBIA, including a famed variety from quarries at Gebel el-Asr, used for the seated statues of KHAFRA found in his VALLEY TEMPLE, and again extensively in the MIDDLE KINGDOM. In the ROMAN PERIOD, imperial porphyry from MONS PORPHYRITES was especially highly valued. Throughout most of Egyptian history, MINING AND QUARRYING of stone seems to have been a royal monopoly, although individuals may have procured small quantities for private use. Stone was a material with strong royal connotations, whether used for sarcophagi or in a temple context. The earliest architectural use of stone is dated to the 1st Dynasty, although advanced knowledge of stone-working is already attested at NABTA PLAYA in the prehistoric period.

stretching the cord *see* Seshat

Sumerian The language and culture of southern MESOPOTAMIA in the 4th and 3rd millennia BC, until the incorporation of Sumer into the AKKADIAN empire (c. 2300 BC). The Sumerian language has no known cognates. It was the first to be written, using the CUNEIFORM script which was subsequently adopted by other languages in the region. Sumer was the cradle of civilization in the Near East; cities with sophisticated architecture and administration were founded at sites such as Uruk and Ur. Outposts of Sumerian culture in northern Mesopotamia may have facilitated the spread of Mesopotamian ideas and motifs to Egypt during the late PREDYNASTIC PERIOD.

sun *see* Aten, Atum, Ra, sun temple

sun temple Stone monument where daily rites were carried out to express royal devotion to the sun god RA. Sun temples were a particular feature of state religion in the 5th Dynasty, and are known to have been built by six kings. Only two have been excavated: those of USERKAF, at ABUSIR, and NIUSERRA, at ABU GHURAB. The latter is better preserved and shows the main features of such a monument. At its centre was a large squat obelisk of solid masonry, designed to resemble the BENBEN STONE. In front, a large courtyard contained a stone altar where FOOD AND DRINK offerings were presented; large numbers of cattle were slaughtered at the site for this purpose. The internal rooms of the complex were decorated with scenes illustrating the ideology of KINGSHIP.

syncretism Theological practice of combining two or more deities into a single focus of worship, such as AMUN-RA and PTAH-SOKAR-OSIRIS. A characteristic feature of Egyptian RELIGION, it allowed connections to be made between members of a hugely diverse pantheon.

Syria-Palestine *see* Levant

T

Taa Name of two kings at the end of the 17th Dynasty (c. 1550 BC). Taa I (throne name: Senakhtenra) was succeeded by Taa II (throne name: Seqenenra), who led the THEBAN opposition to HYKSOS rule. Taa II was probably killed in battle against the Hyksos forces since his skull shows a deep wound caused by a Palestinian-style axe-blade. He was succeeded by KAMOSE.

taboo Egyptian RELIGION identified certain practices, foods and days as detrimental to MAAT, and therefore best avoided. It was regarded as particularly important for PRIESTS to maintain their ritual purity by being shaven headed and abstaining from sexual activity. Such taboos are reflected in ART produced for religious reasons, even if they were not always observed in daily life. Hence, PIGS (because of their association with SETH) and fish (because of their role in the OSIRIS myth) were regarded as ritually unclean, and rarely feature in temple decoration, although they remained important as part of the daily diet. Taboos varied from place to place, and over time.

Taharqo (Taharqa) (throne name: Khura-nefertem) (690–664 BC) Fourth king of the 25th Dynasty, the son of PIYE, younger brother and successor of SHABITQO. He reigned for 26 years, during which time he undertook numerous building projects, notably in the First Court at KARNAK and at MEDINET HABU. He also campaigned extensively in the LEVANT, repelling an attempted invasion by the ASSYRIANS under their king Esarhaddon. However, a subsequent invasion reached

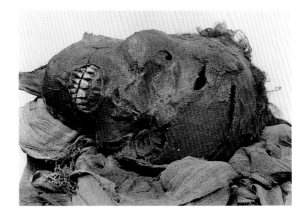

The mummified head of Seqenenra **Taa** *II clearly shows the fatal wounds inflicted by an axe-blade, suggesting that the king died in combat, perhaps against the Hyksos.*

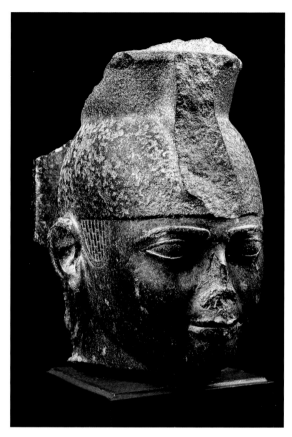

*Granodiorite head of **Taharqo** from Thebes; the rounded face, broad nose and thick neck are characteristic of 25th Dynasty royal sculpture.*

MEMPHIS, while the army of Esarhaddon's successor, Ashurbanipal, penetrated as far south as THEBES, forcing Taharqo to retreat to NUBIA. The KUSHITES regained power briefly following the withdrawal of the Assyrian army. Taharqo recorded events from the beginning of his reign on a series of STELAE erected in the temple of KAWA in Upper Nubia. He died at NAPATA, and was buried in a pyramidal tomb in the Kushite royal cemetery at NURI.

Takelot Libyan name borne by three kings of the THIRD INTERMEDIATE PERIOD.

Takelot I (c. 890–c. 875 BC) The successor of OSORKON I (22nd Dynasty) and father of OSORKON II, but little is known about his reign.

Takelot II (c. 840–c. 815 BC) Rose to power as High Priest of AMUN in the reign of OSORKON II, and imitated previous holders of the office by claiming ROYAL TITLES, effectively founding a rival dynasty based at THEBES (the 23rd Dynasty). In turn, he had to deal with a rival claimant (PEDUBAST I) with whom he fought a civil war for two decades. Details of the struggle are recorded in the CHRONICLE OF PRINCE OSORKON, commissioned by Takelot II's son and inscribed at KARNAK.

Takelot III (c. 750–c. 735 BC) Ruled first in a CO-REGENCY with his father OSORKON III (23rd Dynasty) after the latter had been sole king for more than two decades. He was succeeded by his brother RUDAMUN.

Taking of Joppa Work of LITERATURE, preserved on a RAMESSIDE PAPYRUS and dated to the late NEW KINGDOM. The story is set in the reign of THUTMOSE III, and concerns the Egyptian army's successful attempt to capture the city of Joppa (modern Jaffa, on the outskirts of Tel Aviv) by means of a clever ruse. The ruler of Joppa is plied with drink to render him defenceless. Then, pretending to have surrendered, the Egyptians send baskets into the city, ostensibly as booty. In fact, the baskets conceal Egyptian soldiers who, once inside Joppa, capture it. Joppa is listed among Thutmose III's conquests during his first campaign in the LEVANT, so the story may have some basis in historical fact.

talataat Small sandstone blocks used for the rapid construction of buildings at KARNAK during the reign of AKHENATEN, subsequently dismantled and reused as fill for later monuments. Numerous examples have been found in the Ninth and Tenth PYLONS at Karnak (built by HOREMHEB), and at LUXOR TEMPLE and MEDAMUD. Similar blocks, derived from buildings at AMARNA (but not strictly *talataat*, which is a Theban term), have come to light at ASYUT and HERMOPOLIS. Many of the blocks are decorated; careful work to reassemble complete scenes has provided an important artistic source for the Amarna period. The term *talataat* may refer to the regular dimensions of the blocks ('three hand-widths' in Arabic) or may be a corruption of the Italian *tagliata* ('cut blocks').

Tale of Sinuhe Famous text composed in the early 12th Dynasty and considered the greatest surviving masterpiece of ancient Egyptian LITERATURE. It is a sophisticated work, combining different literary forms. It was viewed as a classic, remained highly popular for centuries, and survives in numerous copies. The fictional work is set in the reign of SENUSRET I (c. 1918–c. 1875 BC), and is presented as the autobiography of a court official, Sinuhe, who flees Egypt on hearing the news of AMENEMHAT I's death. After spending time in the LEVANT among the local Palestinian population, Sinuhe eventually receives a pardon from the king and returns to Egypt to end his days in his home country.

Tale of the Eloquent Peasant Work of LITERATURE composed in the MIDDLE KINGDOM but set in the earlier times of the FIRST INTERMEDIATE PERIOD. The story concerns a peasant who is robbed on his way to market, and pleads for justice before the High Steward. So impressive is the peasant's speech, that he is goaded into more and more pleading, until, exhausted, he finally receives justice. The work illustrates the high status in which public speaking was held in ancient Egypt; the tension between the silence of the official and the peasant's increasing desperation gives the text its dramatic impact.

Tale of the Shipwrecked Sailor Vivid work of fiction of the MIDDLE KINGDOM, in which a despondent official, returning home after an unsuccessful mission, is urged by one of his attendants to consider how disaster may be turned to success; the attendant relates a story that happened to him when he was shipwrecked on a fantasy island inhabited by a giant SNAKE.

Tales of Wonder (Papyrus Westcar) Work of LITERATURE composed in the MIDDLE KINGDOM and preserved on a single papyrus dating to the HYKSOS period. The text originally comprised at least five magical tales, set in the 3rd and 4th Dynasties, of which three are substantially preserved. In the first tale, the fictional narrator is Prince Bauefra, son of KHUFU. He recounts a story set at the court of SNEFERU, in which the king orders a crew of young women to row on a lake for his amusement. When one of the rowers drops a piece of her JEWELRY in the water, a lector priest, Djadjaemankh, is brought to retrieve it. By magic, he folds one half of the water on top of the other half, and so fetches the jewel for its owner. The second and third tales, narrated by Prince Hordedef (another of Khufu's sons), are set at Khufu's own court. A magician, Djedi, is summoned to court to demonstrate his abilities. Asked to reattach the severed head of a human prisoner (showing Khufu's reputation as a tyrant in later tradition), Djedi protests, and instead performs his magic on birds and an ox. He goes on to prophesy the wondrous birth of three brothers who will succeed as the first three kings of the 5th Dynasty.

Tanis (San el-Hagar) Site in the north-eastern DELTA which rose to prominence as a royal residence in the THIRD INTERMEDIATE PERIOD. Earlier blocks and statuary were brought to the site from nearby PER-RAMESSES at the end of the NEW KINGDOM. The main monuments at Tanis date to the 21st and 22nd Dynasties. They include a temple of AMUN and several royal tombs, constructed within the temple precincts. PSUSENNES I inaugurated the new royal burial-ground, and was interred in a granite SARCOPHAGUS originally made for MERENPTAH. His tomb, with spectacular FUNERARY GOODS, was discovered in the late 1930s. Other kings buried in the vicinity included AMENEMOPE, OSORKON II, SHOSHENQ II and SHOSHENQ III. In the LATE PERIOD, Tanis was the capital of the nineteenth Lower Egyptian NOME. Additions to the temple were carried out by NECTANEBO I, and a temple of ASTARTE was built at the site by Ptolemy IV. In the ROMAN PERIOD, the port of Tanis silted up, leading to the town's decline and eventual abandonment.

Tanutamani (throne name: Bakara) (664–657 BC) Fifth and last king of the 25th Dynasty. His brief reign was dominated by the growing power of the ASSYRIANS. Defeating the Assyrian-backed NEKAU of SAIS (nominally first king of the 26th Dynasty) in 664 BC, Tanutamani was recognized as king by the DELTA princes. However, after just one year, he was overthrown by an Assyrian invasion led by Ashurbanipal, and retreated southwards; monuments in the THEBAN region continued to be dated to Tanutamani's reign for another six years, while LOWER EGYPT was ruled by the Assyrian vassal PSAMTIK I. Tanutamani died in NUBIA and was buried in a pyramid-style tomb at el-KURRU. His other major monument was a stela, erected in the temple at GEBEL BARKAL.

Tarif, el- Northernmost area of the THEBAN NECROPOLIS, about 5 km (3 miles) north of SHEIKH ABD EL-QURNA. The earliest archaeological remains from the Theban region have been found here, comprising flint tools and POTTERY from a hunter-gatherer culture (termed the Tarifian), dated to the 6th millennium BC. Predating the BADARIAN culture by as much as a thousand years, it is the earliest pottery yet discovered in the NILE Valley. A settlement of the 4th millennium BC has also been excavated at el-Tarif. Tombs at the site include 4th Dynasty MASTABAS, the SAFF TOMBS of the 11th Dynasty kings INTEF I, II and III, and some MIDDLE KINGDOM private tombs.

Tarkhan Site on the west bank of the NILE, 30 km (19 miles) south of MEMPHIS, near the entrance to the FAYUM. An extensive NECROPOLIS on the desert edge contain numerous tombs of the late PREDYNASTIC PERIOD and 1st Dynasty, together with later interments of the ROMAN PERIOD. The 'valley cemetery' comprises mostly smaller, poorer graves; the surrounding 'hill cemeteries', larger, wealthier tombs, including a few MASTABAS decorated in the PALACE-FAÇADE style. The burials at Tarkhan are important for charting cultural changes that accompanied the unification of Egypt at the beginning of the pharaonic period. A mud-brick temple at the nearby site of Kafr Ammar dates to the THIRD INTERMEDIATE PERIOD.

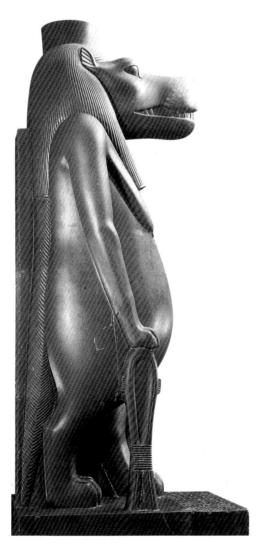

*Statue of the goddess **Taweret** from the 26th Dynasty chapel of Osiris-Pededankh at Karnak; the protector of women in childbirth is shown as a pregnant hippopotamus.*

Tatenen, Tatjenen *see* Ptah-Tatenen

Tausert *see* Tawosret

Taweret Goddess who protected pregnant women and young children. She was one of the most popular deities in private RELIGION, and was often depicted on objects associated with childbirth, such as magic wands, headrests and birthing beds. Her protective qualities made her an ideal subject for AMULETS, attested from the OLD KINGDOM onwards. She also featured in the decoration of the palace at MALKATA, and on the astronomical ceiling in the tomb of SETI I, where she was associated with the northern sky. She was depicted as a pregnant HIPPOPOTAMUS with pendulous breasts, the legs of a LION, and the tail of a CROCODILE (or, alternatively, a crocodile perched on her back). She was often shown holding the HIEROGLYPH for 'protection' (*sa*). A household deity, she had no formal cult temples.

Tawosret (Tausret, Twosret) (throne name: Satra-meritamun) (*c*. 1198–*c*. 1190 BC) Eighth and last ruler of the 19th Dynasty. The widow of SETI II, she ruled at first as regent for the young king SIPTAH, then as PHARAOH in her own right after his death. The tomb she began in the VALLEY OF THE KINGS (KV14) was usurped by her successor, SETHNAKHT.

taxation From the late PREDYNASTIC PERIOD onwards, taxation underpinned the functioning of the ancient Egyptian state. Ink inscriptions from the threshold of the 1st Dynasty suggest that tax was already levied separately on UPPER EGYPT and LOWER EGYPT, for administrative efficiency. In a non-monetary economy, taxation took the form of a percentage of agricultural produce. During the EARLY DYNASTIC PERIOD and OLD KINGDOM, a biennial census of Egypt's natural resources (recorded on the PALERMO STONE) allowed the state to assess the correct level of taxation, based on areas of landholdings and numbers of livestock. Tax revenue was collected by government representatives, and brought together in central stores. It was redistributed to finance royal building projects, pay state employees, and alleviate shortages in times of poor harvests. Non-payment of taxes was a serious offence, punishable by beatings. However, individuals and institutions could be exempt from paying tax by royal decree.

*Painted relief from the burial chamber of **Tawosret** in the Valley of the Kings, showing the course of the sun (as a child, scarab, solar disc and ram-headed bird); the triangles symbolize the darkness and watery abyss of the underworld through which the sun travels each night.*

Tebtunis Site at the southern edge of the FAYUM. Probably founded in the MIDDLE KINGDOM, it became a major administrative, economic and religious centre in the PTOLEMAIC and ROMAN PERIODS; life at this time has been illuminated by a vast collection of PAPYRUS documents discovered at the site. Other archaeological remains include a Roman KIOSK and associated cult buildings dedicated to the local CROCODILE god. Tebtunis was abandoned by the mid-13th century AD.

Tefnakht (*c.* 730–*c.* 720 BC) Founder and first king of the 24th Dynasty. Ruling from SAIS, he was one of PIYE's main opponents during the latter's attempt to bring the whole of Egypt under KUSHITE control.

Tefnut Goddess of moisture. A member of the ENNEAD of HELIOPOLIS, she was the daughter of ATUM and the sister-wife of SHU, and hence one half of the first divine couple. As a universal deity, she had no principal cult centre, although at LEONTOPOLIS she was identified as one of the EYES of RA and worshipped in the form of a lioness. She was also associated with the URAEUS and appears as a SNAKE in the PYRAMID TEXTS.

tekenu Figure of obscure significance, sometimes shown taking part in the funeral ceremonies of private individuals, especially in the early NEW KINGDOM. Resembling a sack with a human head (or a human in a sack), it was usually shown on a sledge being drawn by people or cattle. It has been suggested that the *tekenu* was a collection of the body parts of the deceased that were not mummified or placed in the CANOPIC JARS, but which were still necessary for rebirth in the afterlife.

Tell Atrib *see* Athribis

Tell Basta *see* Bubastis

Tell el-Amarna *see* Amarna

Tell el-Balamun Site in the central DELTA where excavations in the late 20th century AD uncovered temple FOUNDATION DEPOSITS of the LATE PERIOD and elite tombs of the 22nd Dynasty.

Tell el-Daba *see* Avaris

Tell el-Fara'in *see* Buto

Tell el-Maskhuta Site in the eastern DELTA, near the WADI TUMILAT. Strategically located for trade routes to Arabia and the Horn of Africa, the settlement was first founded during the HYKSOS period. It was then abandoned from the 18th to the 26th Dynasties, before being refounded under NEKAU II as a control point and trade centre on the canal which was built to connect the

NILE and the Red Sea. Tell el-Maskhuta then remained inhabited until the ROMAN PERIOD.

Tell el-Muqdam *see* Leontopolis

Tell el-Yahudiya Site in the eastern DELTA, 20 km (12.5 miles) northeast of Cairo, controlling the strategic route from the SINAI to MEMPHIS via the WADI TUMILAT. The principal feature is a series of massive earthworks forming a rectangular enclosure, associated with the HYKSOS. The site has given its name to a distinctive type of small black POTTERY jug, with incised geometric patterns filled with white pigment. Vessels of 'Tell el-Yahudiya ware' have been found throughout the eastern Delta and eastern Mediterranean, and are a characteristic feature of Hyksos culture. Other remains at Tell el-Yahudiya include a temple of RAMESSES III, and a settlement and temple founded by an exiled Jewish priest in the PTOLEMAIC PERIOD.

temenos Sacred precinct surrounding the cult centre of a deity, usually applied to the area bounded by a temple enclosure wall.

temple Building in which the cult of a deity or king was celebrated. There were two basic types of temple in ancient Egypt: cult temples, built for the worship of one or more deities; and mortuary temples, dedicated to maintaining the cult of a deceased individual, usually a king. In the NEW KINGDOM, royal mortuary temples were officially dedicated, not to the deceased king, but to a form of AMUN-RA, thus blurring the distinction between god and king. The Egyptian term for temple was *hut-netjer* ('mansion of the god'), and this conveyed its essential function, to house and nourish the deity dwelling within. Hence, TEMPLE RITUAL focused on sustaining the cult image of the deity, treating it as a living being. The earliest religious buildings were probably fairly flimsy constructions of wickerwork and wood, identified by a flag-pole (which was the HIEROGLYPH for 'god'). Community shrines were doubtless modest affairs in mud-brick, with stone used only for important architectural elements such as doorways. The involvement of the state in temple construction began in earnest in the MIDDLE KINGDOM, giving rise to enduring stone monuments such as the earliest temple at KARNAK and the enigmatic building at QASR ES-SAGHA. At the same time, temples became buildings with restricted access, and the general population was barred from entry by high walls. Only during FESTIVALS might ordinary people penetrate inside the temple buildings, and then never beyond the outermost courtyard.

The greatest period of temple building was the New Kingdom, spectacularly attested in the monuments of THEBES. A typical temple of the period was laid out as a series of PYLONS and courtyards, interspersed with features such as OBELISKS, all arranged along a ceremonial axis, reflecting the importance of processions in cult activity. A SACRED LAKE was often provided within the temple precinct. Each architectural element of the building was resonant with symbolism, empha-

*Cut-away drawing of a typical Egyptian **temple** of the New Kingdom, showing the entrance pylon, peristyle forecourt, hypostyle hall, transverse hall and inner chambers.*

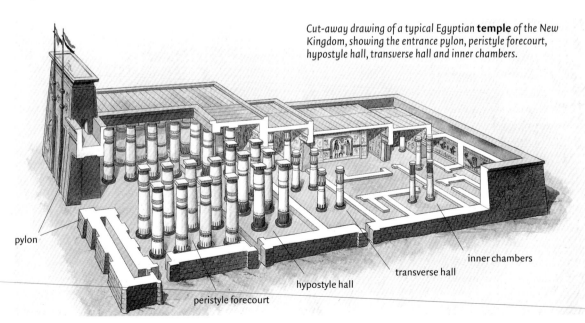

pylon

inner chambers

transverse hall

hypostyle hall

peristyle forecourt

sizing the temple's overarching role as a microcosm of the universe, where created order was maintained and chaos kept at bay. Hence, the shape of the pylon deliberately resembled the HIEROGLYPH for 'horizon', the place where the sun was reborn each day, defying death. The HYPOSTYLE HALL represented the reed marsh of creation, growing on the banks of the PRIMEVAL MOUND, with which the sanctuary itself was associated. To this end, the innermost part of the temple which housed the cult image of the deity was usually built upon a mound of clean sand, raised above the surrounding rooms. The outer walls of the temple were decorated with scenes of the king smiting his enemies, in accordance with his role as champion of MAAT. The enclosure wall surrounding the temple precinct formed a barrier against the forces of chaos; in the LATE PERIOD, pan bedding (see NUN) was employed to recall the watery abyss of creation.

Although, in practice, the daily ritual in a temple was delegated to PRIESTS, in theory it was the king who maintained the cults of the gods and was represented carrying out these duties on temple reliefs. The king's role was part of the contract between the human and divine spheres that ensured Egypt's continued prosperity and security. Beyond their primary religious function, temples were important in many other areas of Egyptian life. Many were institutional land owners (in the New Kingdom, at least), controlling vast estates throughout Egypt. They housed libraries, schools for scribal training (HOUSES OF LIFE), and workshops for craft production. They held large stores of grain, engaged in trade, and were an integral part of the Egyptian state-controlled economy.

temple ritual Evidence for the rites carried out in temples is scant before the NEW KINGDOM. The ABUSIR PAPYRI document the daily activities of priests in the mortuary temple of NEFERIRKARA; by contrast, there are few inscriptions or reliefs relating to cult temples in the Old and Middle Kingdoms. From the 18th Dynasty onwards, the evidence is much more substantial, with scenes on temple walls providing a fairly detailed account of daily ritual. Cult activity focused on the divine image of the deity, housed in the temple's innermost sanctuary. The image was regarded as a living being (the temple was its house), and as such required daily attention by PRIESTS. It would be undressed, washed, anointed with perfumed oils, and re-clothed. Priests would present FOOD AND DRINK offerings (later redistributed among the temple

employees) to nourish the deity. In some temples, the image of the deity was taken up to the roof each day at sunrise, to receive the life-giving rays of the sun. The axial layout of New Kingdom temples indicates that processions were an important part of ritual activity, the cult image being carried from place to place in its BARQUE SHRINE. At FESTIVALS, the divine image would leave its own temple to visit other sacred sites in the neighbourhood.

Teos (Tachos, Djeho, Djed-her) (throne name: Irmaatenra) (365–360 BC) Second king of the 30th Dynasty, who reigned briefly in succession to NECTANEBO I. After leading a campaign in the LEVANT, Teos was deposed by his nephew NECTANEBO II. Teos then fled to the Persian court.

Teti (c. 2325 BC) First king of the 6th Dynasty. His pyramid complex at SAQQARA revived 4th Dynasty practice by including two satellite pyramids for his QUEENS. The king's burial chamber beneath the main pyramid is inscribed with a copy of the PYRAMID TEXTS, and contained a grey basalt SARCOPHAGUS. The mortuary complex is surrounded by the MASTABAS of Teti's high officials, including his son-in-law MERERUKA. MANETHO states that Teti was murdered; he may have been succeeded by an ephemeral usurper, Userkara, before the next legitimate king, PEPI I, came to the throne.

Tetisheri Wife of TAA I and mother of TAA II. She was an influential woman at court, and was worshipped after her death as the ancestress of the 18th Dynasty. Her grandson AHMOSE established a CENOTAPH and funerary estate for her at ABYDOS.

Theban Belonging to, or characteristic of, the site of THEBES.

Thebes Site in UPPER EGYPT covering a vast area on both banks of the NILE. The main settlement and cult temples are located on the east bank, the NECROPOLIS and mortuary temples on the west bank. Thebes was the capital of the fourth Upper Egyptian NOME from the OLD KINGDOM onwards, but first came to prominence at the beginning of the MIDDLE KINGDOM as the home town of the 11th and 12th Dynasties. So began a programme of royal construction projects that continued, with only brief interruptions, throughout the Middle Kingdom, NEW KINGDOM and LATE PERIOD.

Thebes was transformed into the most important city of Upper Egypt, reflected in the great abundance of monuments from all periods – especially the New Kingdom, since the 18th Dynasty also came from Thebes.

On the east bank, little remains of the ancient city of Thebes, now covered by the modern buildings of Luxor. The dominant monument is the great temple of KARNAK, with its numerous PYLONS, courtyards and shrines. To the south, once connected by an avenue of SPHINXES, is LUXOR TEMPLE. The west bank is divided for convenience into different geographical areas, comprising, from north to south, EL-TARIF, QURNA, DRA ABU EL-NAGA, the VALLEY OF THE KINGS, DEIR EL-BAHRI, ASASIF, el-KHOKHA, SHEIKH ABD EL-QURNA, QURNET MURAI, DEIR EL-MEDINA, the VALLEY OF THE QUEENS and MALKATA. Notable monuments and col-lections of TOMBS include the SAFF TOMBS of the 11th Dynasty kings; the mortuary temple of MENTUHOTEP II; the TOMBS OF THE NOBLES, dating from the 4th to the 26th Dynasties; the royal tombs of the New Kingdom, and the village for the workers involved in their construction; and the royal mortuary temples of the 18th to 20th Dynasties, including such spectacular buildings as the temple of HATSHEPSUT, the RAMESSEUM, and the mortuary temple of RAMESSES II at MEDINET HABU. In the Late Period, Thebes lost its position as a key administrative centre, but retained its role as one of the most important sacred sites in Egypt. It was known to the ancient Egyptians as Waset, but was called Thebes by the Greeks after their own city of the same name. Today the Theban monuments constitute one of Egypt's greatest tourist attractions.

*Aerial view of **Thebes**, with the western necropolis in the distance, on the far side of the Nile, and the Karnak temple complex in the foreground.*

Thinis *see* This

Thinite Belonging to, or characteristic of, the site of THIS. The term Thinite period is used to describe the 1st and 2nd Dynasties (c. 2950–c. 2650 BC), many of whose rulers were buried in the Thinite royal cemetery at ABYDOS.

Third Intermediate Period (c. 1069–664 BC) The phase of Egyptian history between the NEW KINGDOM and the LATE PERIOD. A period of political fragmentation and concurrent rulers in different parts of the country, it began with the break-up of the New Kingdom state following the death of RAMESSES XI, and ended with the reunification of the country at the beginning of the 26th Dynasty. Some scholars include the 25th Dynasty within the Late Period.

The Third Intermediate Period was characterized by a north–south split, powerful DELTA families ruling LOWER EGYPT from sites such as TANIS, BUBASTIS, LEONTOPOLIS and SAIS; and the High Priests of AMUN at THEBES exercising control over UPPER EGYPT. It was also a period in which rulers of foreign origin (especially Libyan and Kushite) occupied the throne of Egypt. The internal chronology of the Third Intermediate Period, particularly the precise relationship between the numerous kings and rival dynasties, is still hotly disputed.

This (Thinis) Town on the west bank of the NILE in northern UPPER EGYPT, mentioned in texts from the EARLY DYNASTIC PERIOD. Its precise location has not been established, but the remains are presumed to lie under the modern city of Girga, or the nearby village of el-Birba. According to MANETHO, the kings of the 1st and 2nd Dynasties came from This. The town's main cemeteries were located at ABYDOS, a few kilometres to the south, and at NAGA EL-DEIR, on the opposite bank of the Nile. The presence at Abydos of high status, even royal, tombs dating to the late PREDYNASTIC PERIOD suggests that the rulers of This were major players in the process of national unification, eventually winning control over the whole country at the beginning of the 1st Dynasty. The town of This was subsequently the capital of the eighth Upper Egyptian NOME.

Thoëris *see* Taweret

Thoth God of WRITING and knowledge, regarded as the patron deity of SCRIBES. Thoth had varied roles in ancient Egyptian RELIGION. In KINGSHIP ideology, he was one of the deities (along with SESHAT) who wrote the king's NAMES on the leaves of the sacred ISHED TREE; in AFTERLIFE BELIEFS, Thoth noted the outcome of the WEIGHING OF THE HEART ceremony and was regarded as the guardian of the deceased in the underworld. Thoth was also closely identified with the moon, while in the myth of HORUS and SETH he acted as an intermediary between the quarrelling gods. His cult attracted royal patronage in the 18th Dynasty, as reflected in the names of the four kings called THUTMOSE ('Thoth is born'). The major cult centre of Thoth was at HERMOPOLIS (the Greeks identified him with their god Hermes), and he was also worshipped in the DAKHLA OASIS and in the DELTA. He was depicted in both IBIS and baboon form, most frequently as a ibis-headed man holding a scribal PALETTE. His lunar connections were reflected in his special headdress, combining a full and a crescent moon.

The ibis-headed god **Thoth** *purifying king Hatshepsut (whose figure has been deliberately excised) in a painted relief from an 18th Dynasty chapel at Karnak.*

throne name (prenomen) *see* royal titles

Thutmose Royal sculptor and 'master of works' at AMARNA during the reign of AKHENATEN. His house and workshop were excavated by a German expedition in 1912. Finds included many trial pieces, plaster casts and SCULPTURE in various stages of completion; most famous is the painted bust of NEFERTITI now in Berlin.

Thutmose I ('THOTH is born') (throne name: Aakheperkara) (c. 1493–c. 1481 BC) Third king of the 18th Dynasty. A skilled military leader, he conducted numerous campaigns in the LEVANT to secure Egyptian trade routes, creating the first extensive Egyptian 'empire' in the process. He claimed to have erected a STELA on the far bank of the River Euphrates in MESOPOTAMIA. He also extended Egyptian control of NUBIA as far south as the Fourth CATARACT. He built the earliest tomb in the main VALLEY OF THE KINGS (KV20, subsequently usurped by his daughter HATSHEPSUT), while a second tomb (KV38) may have been built by THUTMOSE III for the earlier king's reburial.

Thutmose II (throne name: Aakheperenra) (c. 1481–c. 1479 BC) Fourth king of the 18th Dynasty, the son and successor of Thutmose I by a lesser wife Mutnofret. His reign is rather poorly attested, apart from a victory STELA erected at ASWAN in his first year to commemorate a campaign which successfully crushed a rebellion in NUBIA. He built a mortuary temple in western THEBES, but the location of his tomb is not certain. He was succeeded by his widow, HATSHEPSUT, first as regent for the young THUTMOSE III, then as king in her own right.

Thutmose III (throne name: Menkheperra) (c. 1479–c. 1425 BC) Fifth king of the 18th Dynasty, regarded as one of the greatest rulers of the NEW KINGDOM. He was the son of THUTMOSE II by a minor wife, Isis, and succeeded to the throne when he was still a child. In the early part of his reign, effective power was exercised by his step-mother, HATSHEPSUT, acting as regent; after seven years, she assumed full royal titles and proclaimed herself king. Only after her death, twenty years later (c. 1458 BC), did Thutmose III assume power as sole ruler. He embarked on a major policy of military campaigns in the LEVANT, probably a deliberate attempt to emulate the achievements of his grandfather THUTMOSE I. Accounts of the battles, including the famous Battle of MEGIDDO, were inscribed on the walls of KARNAK; Thutmose III added considerably to the temple there, constructing the lavishly decorated 'Festival Hall' with its 'Botanical Garden' reliefs depicting the unusual plants encountered on his Near Eastern campaigns. He also undertook building projects at DEIR EL-BAHRI and MEDINET HABU in western THEBES, at BUTO and elsewhere in the DELTA, and at sites throughout NUBIA. His tomb in the VALLEY OF THE KINGS (KV34) has a CARTOUCHE-shaped burial chamber, its walls decorated to resemble sheets of unrolled PAPYRUS, illustrated with scenes from the AMDUAT. Late in his reign, Thutmose III began a systematic programme of removing Hatshepsut's name and image from her monuments. Interpreted by some scholars as an act of personal revenge, this policy may, rather, have been motivated by a desire to expunge an episode – the reign of a female king – that was seen as an affront against royal tradition.

Thutmose IV (throne name: Menkheperura) (c. 1400–c. 1390 BC) Eighth king of the 18th Dynasty and son of AMENHOTEP III. His Dream STELA, set up between the paws of the Great Sphinx at GIZA, claims that he was offered the KINGSHIP in a dream, if he cleared away the sand to reveal the sphinx. In foreign relations, he pursued a policy of peaceful contacts with the LEVANT, marrying a daughter of the king of the MITANNI, but he engaged in military action against NUBIA. His monuments at THEBES include a mortuary temple on the west bank, and a tomb in the VALLEY OF THE KINGS (KV43); the king's FUNERARY GOODS included part of a CHARIOT.

titulary *see* royal titles

Tiye Principal wife of AMENHOTEP III. The daughter of YUYA and TUYU (and perhaps the sister of AY), she was a powerful figure at court during the reigns of her husband (c. 1390–c. 1353 BC) and son AKHENATEN (c. 1353–c. 1336 BC), who seems to have planned to bury his mother alongside himself in the main chamber of the royal tomb at AMARNA. Some of her FUNERARY GOODS were discovered in a tomb (KV55) in the VALLEY OF THE KINGS, perhaps reburied there after being removed from AMARNA. She has been identified by some scholars as the 'elder lady', one of a cache of mummies reburied in the tomb of AMENHOTEP II. A lock of Tiye's hair was found in a miniature COFFIN in the tomb of her grandson TUTANKHAMUN.

Statue of **Thutmose III** from the temple of Amun-Ra at Karnak; the symmetry, balance and beautifully rendered details of the wig, beard and kilt make this one of the masterpieces of Egyptian sculpture.

Tod, el- Site on the east bank of the NILE in UPPER EGYPT, 20 km (12.5 miles) south of Luxor. Surviving remains date from the OLD KINGDOM to the Islamic period, and include a ROMAN PERIOD KIOSK. The most significant monument is the temple to MONTU, begun by MENTUHOTEP II, embellished by subsequent kings of the 11th, 12th and 18th Dynasties, and rebuilt in the PTOLEMAIC PERIOD.

Beneath the floor of the MIDDLE KINGDOM temple at the site, archaeologists discovered four bronze chests inscribed with the CARTOUCHE of AMENEMHAT II and containing a hoard of valuable objects. This so-called 'Tod treasure' comprised silver vessels from the Aegean or Anatolia, cylinder seals of LAPIS LAZULI from MESOPOTAMIA and GOLD ingots, and indicates the extent of long-distance trade during the 12th Dynasty.

tomb decoration Like the FUNERARY GOODS interred with the deceased, the decoration of a tomb served a wholly religious purpose, ensuring that the tomb owner achieved a successful rebirth and a comfortable afterlife. The earliest known example of tomb decoration was found in a grave of the PREDYNASTIC PERIOD (tomb T100) at HIERAKONPOLIS. The scenes showed a procession of boats, and other elements of early royal iconography, designed to maintain the status of the deceased for eternity. From the 3rd Dynasty, tombs of high-status private individuals were provided with a painted offering chapel, which then became the focus of the decoration. (The burial chamber was usually undecorated.) The most frequent motifs include FOOD AND DRINK offerings; offering bearers bringing further supplies; and scenes of food production and craft activity, to guarantee eternal provision in case the funerary goods themselves were destroyed. (This function was largely transferred to TOMB MODELS in the FIRST INTERMEDIATE PERIOD and early MIDDLE KINGDOM.) Other

*Head from a statuette of **Tiye**, found in the harem palace at Abu Gurob; this masterpiece of small-scale sculpture is made from yew wood, with the addition of inlays and gold foil.*

*The 19th Dynasty burial chamber of Pashedu at Deir el-Medina provides a good example of private **tomb decoration**, with two crouching figures of the jackal god Anubis guarding the entrance.*

genres of tomb decoration likewise fulfilled a religious purpose, for example the pilgrimage to ABYDOS frequently depicted in Middle Kingdom tombs. Scenes of HUNTING, in the marshes or in the desert, were metaphors for the triumph of order over chaos, and hence of life over death; certain elements, such as the spearing of fish or the catching of ducks, also had strong sexual connotations, considered beneficial for rebirth in the tomb. Scenes of the owner carrying out his duties were designed to reflect and, more importantly, to perpetuate his social status; HIERARCHICAL SCALING was used to reinforce the primacy of the deceased.

Close inspection reveals that so-called 'scenes of daily life' record a highly idealized view of life, free from dirt and disease, and lifted out of space and time. Subsidiary figures – including members of the tomb owner's family – are shown in subordinate roles; even if children were grown up at the time a tomb was built, they were none the less depicted as children, since that was their relationship to the deceased. The decoration of private tombs in the AMARNA period departs markedly from tradition; depictions focus on the activities of the king and ROYAL FAMILY, in line with AKHEN-ATEN's religious reforms. A greater emphasis on overtly religious scenes characterizes the decoration of private tombs in the LATE PERIOD. The royal tombs of the NEW KINGDOM in the VALLEY OF THE KINGS were burial chambers without tomb chapels (the public role of the latter being carried out by the MORTUARY TEMPLES near the cultivation). Hence, their decoration focuses on mythological scenes and texts from the BOOK OF THE DEAD and other afterlife books to assist the king's resurrection.

tomb models A key feature of Egyptian AFTERLIFE BELIEFS was the notion that objects could magically come to life in the tomb and hence act as substitutes for the thing or person depicted. For this reason, models were included among the FUNERARY GOODS from the PREDYNASTIC PERIOD onwards. The simplest models depicted items of FOOD AND DRINK, together with pottery vessels and granaries; beds, houses and boats were also quite common. In the OLD KINGDOM, servant statuettes were often included in high-status burials, to carry out menial tasks in the afterlife. Single figures were gradually replaced by more complex scenes of food preparation, craft production and farming. Group models of this kind became common in the FIRST INTERMEDIATE PERIOD and early MIDDLE KINGDOM. Elaborate boats were also included in

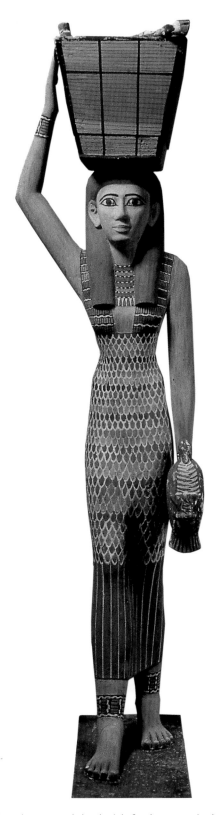

The 11th Dynasty Theban burial of Meketra contained a large number of **tomb models,** *including this painted wooden statue of a female servant carrying provisions.*

burials, to allow the deceased to participate in an after-life pilgrimage to ABYDOS. The most famous collection of tomb models was found in the tomb of MEKETRA at THEBES. Tomb models declined in popularity in the later Middle Kingdom, their functions largely usurped by SHABTI figurines.

tombs At all periods of prehistory and history, the most basic type of tomb consisted of a simple pit, cut into the ground and perhaps marked on the surface by a low mound. In the late PREDYNASTIC PERIOD, more complex tombs, lined with mud-brick and divided into two or more separate chambers, first appeared, marking a trend of increasing wealth differentiation between different social groups. Henceforth, the size and elaboration of a tomb reflected the status of its owner. Geological factors were also important in determining the architecture of a tomb, with ROCK-CUT TOMBS being favoured in many areas, notably MIDDLE EGYPT. Stone-lined chambers first appeared in the 1st Dynasty, and at this early period the emphasis seems to have been on the substructure. However, in the 3rd Dynasty, the focus shifted to the chambers above ground, housed within the MASTABA superstructure. In particular, the offering chapel, where FOOD AND DRINK were brought for the deceased, became the most important element in a tomb. A FALSE DOOR was provided, so that the tomb owner might communicate with the outside world, and the offering chapel was often decorated with elaborate scenes to provide magical sustenance in the afterlife.

The royal tomb – the most important construction project of any reign and a public manifestation of KINGSHIP ideology – underwent its own sequence of development, reflecting religious changes and security concerns. In the 1st Dynasty, the king's mortuary complex comprised two separate elements: the burial itself and the enclosure for the funerary cult (both of which were often surrounded by tombs of royal retainers). The STEP PYRAMID of DJOSER combined these two elements in a single monument, establishing the model for subsequent pyramid complexes of the OLD KINGDOM and MIDDLE KINGDOM.

In the NEW KINGDOM, the desire to thwart tomb robbers elevated security above visibility in the design of the royal tomb. Long narrow corridor tombs were therefore cut into the cliffs of the VALLEY OF THE KINGS, while mortuary temples on the low desert provided a more public face for the royal mortuary cult. In the THIRD INTERMEDIATE PERIOD and LATE PERIOD, royal tombs were generally built within temple precincts for added protection.

Tombs of the Nobles Collective name given to the decorated ROCK-CUT TOMBS built for high officials of the NEW KINGDOM in the NECROPOLIS of western THEBES, especially at DRA ABU EL-NAGA, DEIR EL-BAHRI, KHOKHA, ASASIF, SHEIKH ABD EL-QURNA and QURNET MURAI.

towns and cities The picture of urbanism in ancient Egypt is still partial, because relatively few settlements have been excavated compared with the number of tombs and temples. In recent years, archaeologists have increasingly turned their attention to towns and cities, producing important results at sites such as AVARIS, Balat in the DAKHLA OASIS, BUTO, ELEPHANTINE and PER-RAMESSES. At all periods, the process of

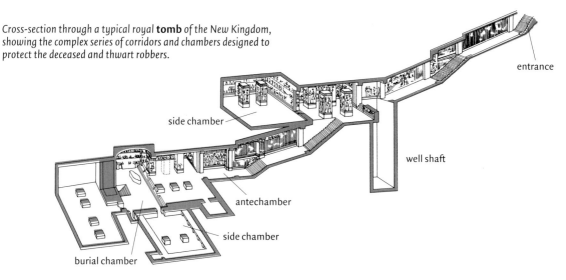

Cross-section through a typical royal **tomb** of the New Kingdom, showing the complex series of corridors and chambers designed to protect the deceased and thwart robbers.

entrance

side chamber

well shaft

antechamber

side chamber

burial chamber

urbanism was heavily influenced by geographic and political factors. The earliest towns developed in strategic locations for the exploitation of trade routes and resources. Hence, walled settlements grew up at Nagada and Hierakonpolis in the late Predynastic period, replacing earlier clusters of dwellings on the desert edge. There seems to have been a hierarchy of settlements along the Nile Valley, comprising royal and religious capitals, regional towns and smaller rural villages. However, ancient Egypt may have lacked the large numbers of dense urban communities found in other parts of the Near East.

The settlements that have been intensively excavated are probably unrepresentative, comprising mostly pyramid towns (such as Kahun) and workmen's villages (such as Deir el-Medina), their state planning evident from their rectangular plans and grid-systems of streets. Even Amarna was founded as a royal city and constructed very rapidly. Settlements that developed organically, over time, are comparatively poorly attested.

toys Given their love of games, it is highly likely that the ancient Egyptians also had children's toys, but they are exceptionally difficult to identify with certainty in the archaeological record. Small figurines and models found in tombs are usually interpreted as ritual objects; those from settlement sites are more easily labelled as toys; they include spinning tops, balls of string, and wooden models of animals with movable parts.

transliteration The rendition into the Roman alphabet – with some additional special signs and accents – of ancient Egyptian words. The standard system used by all Egyptologists allows ancient Egyptian words to be written when a hieroglyphic font is not available, and to be 'pronounced' following certain conventions.

travertine Translucent, yellow or light-brown rock, often banded, which was frequently used for stone vessels, sculpture and small architectural elements. The material is often, though erroneously, called '(Egyptian) alabaster'; it is also, more correctly, described as calcite. It was mined at sites throughout Egypt, most notably Hatnub.

triad A group of three. The term refers either to a statue comprising three individuals (such as the famous group statues of Menkaura from his pyramid temple); or to a group of three gods, linked by theology to form

a typical family unit of father, mother and child. Divine triads were a particular feature of state religion in the New Kingdom, and helped to rationalize the otherwise diverse and complex Egyptian pantheon. Examples include the Theban triad of Amun, Mut and Khonsu, and the triad of Khnum, Anuket and Satet worshipped in the First cataract region.

Tukh el-Qaramus Site in the eastern Delta, north of Bubastis, comprising secular and sacred buildings. It served as a military post to defend Egypt's northeastern frontier. It was inhabited during the New Kingdom and Third Intermediate Period, refounded in the early Ptolemaic period, and abandoned in the Roman period. The site is best known for a hoard of gold jewelry and silver temple plate dating to the early Ptolemaic period.

*Greywacke **triad** of Menkaura flanked by the goddess Hathor and the female personification of the jackal nome, from the king's mortuary temple at Giza.*

Tuna el-Gebel Site on the west bank of the NILE in MIDDLE EGYPT, situated along the desert edge to the west of HERMOPOLIS (which it served as the principal cemetery from the LATE PERIOD onwards). One of the boundary STELAE demarcating the city of AMARNA was erected at Tuna el-Gebel in the reign of AKHENATEN. There are also extensive cemeteries, including the tombs of high officials; the best-known tomb is that of PETOSIRIS. Other remains at the site include sacred animal burials, especially of IBISES and baboons (sacred to THOTH), dating to the LATE PERIOD and early PTOLEMAIC PERIOD; and a ROMAN PERIOD town.

Tura Site on the east bank of the NILE, opposite MEMPHIS, 14 km (9 miles) south-southeast of central Cairo. Extensive cemeteries include burials of the late PREDYNASTIC and EARLY DYNASTIC periods, the LATE PERIOD, and PTOLEMAIC and ROMAN periods. The site is best known for its quarries, where finest quality white limestone was extracted for royal monuments, especially the casing blocks of PYRAMIDS.

Turin Canon *see* king-lists

turquoise Opaque, pale blue or greenish blue semi-precious stone, highly valued by the ancient Egyptians (who called it *mefkat*). It was used for JEWELRY from the PREDYNASTIC PERIOD onwards, and became closely associated with the goddess HATHOR. State-sponsored expeditions to mine turquoise, at sites in the southwestern SINAI, began in the 3rd Dynasty and reached a peak in the 12th Dynasty. FAIENCE may have been developed as a cheap imitation of turquoise.

Tutankhamun ('Living image of AMUN') (throne name: Nebkheperura) (c. 1332–c. 1322 BC) Twelfth king of the 18th Dynasty. Born during the reign of AKHENATEN, he was originally named Tutankhaten ('Perfect image of ATEN'), in honour of the sun disc. He was probably Akhenaten's son, by a secondary wife, KIYA, and went on to marry his half-sister, Ankhesenpaaten (ANKHESENAMUN). After the demise of SMENKHKARA, Tutankhaten came to the throne, still only a boy of eight or nine. He changed his name to Tutankhamun, reflecting the restoration of the old cults dominated by the THEBAN god AMUN. This decisive act was recorded in a Restoration STELA, erected at KARNAK. Tutankhamun also carried out the decoration of the colonnade at LUXOR TEMPLE. He is assumed to have begun work on a tomb (KV23) in the western branch of the VALLEY OF THE KINGS, later usurped by AY, but was interred in a much smaller tomb in the main valley (KV62) that was probably never intended to house a royal burial. It appears that this latter tomb was pressed into service following Tutankhamun's premature death on the threshold of adulthood. This has suggested to some scholars that the young king was murdered on Ay's orders. However, a CT scan of Tutankhamun's mummified body in 2005 found no evidence of a violent death. Despite Tutankhamun's brief reign, and his exclusion from later KING-LISTS because of his association with the 'heretical' AMARNA period, he has achieved considerable fame through the discovery in 1922 of his near-intact tomb and its sumptuous FUNERARY GOODS. His gold funerary MASK has become an icon of ancient Egypt.

Tuthmoside Belonging to the early 18th Dynasty, beginning with the reign of THUTMOSE I (c. 1493 BC) and ending with the death of THUTMOSE IV (c. 1390 BC).

Tuthmosis *see* Thutmose I, II, III, IV

Tuyu Wife of YUYA and mother of TIYE, the principal wife of AMENHOTEP III. She held the priestly office of 'chief lady of the HAREM of AMUN' and was buried with her husband in a tomb in the VALLEY OF THE KINGS, furnished with FUNERARY GOODS of the finest quality.

Two Ladies The two deities NEKHBET and WADJET were the patron (or 'tutelary') goddesses of UPPER EGYPT and LOWER EGYPT respectively and symbolized the geographic DUALITY of the Egyptian state. Their role in the ideology of KINGSHIP, more specifically as one of the ROYAL TITLES, emphasized the position of the king as unifier.

Two Lands The two halves of the country of Egypt, namely UPPER EGYPT and LOWER EGYPT. They were conceived as a geographic DUALITY, a pair of contrasting opposites which together formed a harmonious whole. The term 'Two Lands' is a literal translation of the ancient Egyptian word *tawy*.

Twosret *see* Tawosret

Ty High official of the 5th Dynasty, he was overseer of the pyramid complexes and SUN TEMPLES of NEFERIRKARA and NIUSERRA, and of the sun temples of SAHURA and NEFEREFRA. His well-preserved and

*Gold funerary mask of **Tutankhamun**, from his burial in the Valley of the Kings; the mask is inlaid with coloured glass and semi-precious stones and originally covered the face of the king's mummy; gold was regarded as 'the flesh of the gods', hence the mask stressed Tutankhamun's rebirth as a deity.*

beautifully decorated MASTABA at SAQQARA contains important scenes of craftsmen at work, AGRICULTURE, ANIMAL HUSBANDRY, HUNTING the HIPPOPOTAMUS, and fowling in the marshes. Ty's KA statue was found in the SERDAB.

tyet girdle Also known as the 'knot of ISIS', a sacred symbol attested from the OLD KINGDOM. In shape, it was similar to the ANKH sign, but with the horizontal arms folded down at the sides. Closely associated with the goddess Isis, it was often used in combination with the DJED PILLAR (associated with her brother-husband OSIRIS). It was also linked with the goddess HATHOR, and with the COLOUR red. Hence, AMULETS of the *tyet* girdle were generally made from CARNELIAN, red FAIENCE or GLASS.

U

Uadji *see* Djet

Udimu *see* Den

Ugaf (Wegaf) (c. 1750 BC) King (perhaps the first) of the 13th Dynasty. Little is known about his brief reign.

Ukhhotep Name of several NOMARCHS of the 12th Dynasty buried in sumptuous tombs at MEIR.

Umm el-Qaab Area of the NECROPOLIS at ABYDOS where the Predynastic rulers of THIS and their successors, the kings of the 1st Dynasty and the last two kings of the 2nd Dynasty, built their tomb complexes. It may have been chosen as a royal burial-ground because of its alignment with a prominent cleft in the cliffs, identified in later periods as an entrance to the underworld. The Arabic name for the area means 'mother of pots', referring to the vast quantities of broken pottery littering the surface which were left as VOTIVE material by pilgrims visiting the supposed tomb of OSIRIS (actually the tomb of DJER).

The area known as the **Umm el-Qaab** ('mother of pots') at Abydos was chosen by Egypt's early kings for their burials; the ground is covered by pottery fragments left by later worshippers.

Unas (Wenis) (c. 2350 BC) Ninth and last king of the 5th Dynasty. His pyramid at SAQQARA, just to the south of the STEP PYRAMID enclosure wall, was the first to be inscribed with a copy of the PYRAMID TEXTS. Reliefs from the causeway leading to the VALLEY TEMPLE include scenes of granite columns for the temple being transported from ASWAN; there are also famous reliefs of FAMINE victims and of traders from the LEVANT arriving in Egypt by boat.

Upper Egypt The NILE Valley, from just south of MEMPHIS to the First CATARACT. (Sometimes the term MIDDLE EGYPT is used for the northern half of the Nile Valley, while UPPER EGYPT refers only to the stretch from ASYUT to ASWAN.) In ancient times, it was divided for administrative purposes into 22 NOMES. The topography of Upper Egypt, a narrow strip of flood-plain bordered by deserts on either side, was in marked contrast to the wide green expanse of the DELTA. Hence, in Egyptian thought, it was one half of the TWO LANDS (the DUALITY that comprised Egypt as a whole). In iconography and mythology it was associated with the white CROWN, the water-lily and the souls of Nekhen (*see* SOULS OF PE AND NEKHEN).

At the end of the PREDYNASTIC PERIOD, FIRST INTERMEDIATE PERIOD and SECOND INTERMEDIATE PERIOD the impetus for national (re-)unification came from Upper Egypt. The region is famous for its magnificent standing monuments, and until recently has been much more intensively investigated than LOWER EGYPT. This bias in the evidence, rather than any historical reality, may account for the apparent dominance of Upper Egypt throughout much of Egyptian history.

Jewelled **uraeus** of gold, lapis lazuli, carnelian and amazonite, found in the pyramid complex of Senusret II at Lahun; it probably adorned the king's crown or wig.

Upuaut *see* Wepwawet

uraeus Cobra (from the Egyptian *iaret*) figure worn on the brow by kings, QUEENS and certain deities to provide magical protection. It was believed to spit fire at the wearer's enemies. As an item of ROYAL REGALIA, it is first attested in the reign of DEN (1st Dynasty). From the OLD KINGDOM onwards, the WINGED DISC was usually shown with a pair of uraei flanking the solar orb. The uraeus was closely linked with the goddess WADJET, who was also depicted as a striking cobra.

Userkaf (c. 2450 BC) First king of the 5th Dynasty. His pyramid complex at SAQQARA was built at the north-eastern corner of the STEP PYRAMID complex; the location may have been chosen to associate Userkaf with the founder of the 3rd Dynasty, DJOSER. Userkaf inaugurated the 5th Dynasty tradition of building a SUN TEMPLE, although his monument, mentioned in texts, has not been located.

ushabti see shabti

Uweinat (Gebel Uweinat) Mountain massif in the remote south-western corner of Egypt's Western Desert, straddling the border with Libya and Sudan. The region is best known for its dramatic geological formations and its prehistoric rock art.

V

Valley of the Kings Area of the THEBAN NECROPOLIS in the hills behind DEIR EL-BAHRI which served as the principal burial-ground for Egyptian kings during the NEW KINGDOM. The site seems to have been chosen for its geology, symbolism and security. The local rock is of good quality, stable and easy to carve; the main valley is dominated by a pyramid-shaped peak, which perhaps suggested funerary connotations; and the area is relatively isolated and easy to guard, thus providing some protection for the tombs against robbery and desecration. The necropolis actually comprises two connected dry valleys: the main valley, containing the majority of the royal tombs, and the Western Valley, containing the remote tombs of AMENHOTEP III and AY. Tombs are numbered from 1 to 62, with the prefix KV (King's Valley) or WV (Western Valley). Archaeologists have also discovered twenty unfinished pits and shafts.

The earliest tomb (probably KV20) was prepared for THUTMOSE I, although another (KV39) located above the valley floor, near the path from DEIR EL-MEDINA, has been identified by some scholars as the tomb of AMENHOTEP I. The last in the series (KV4) was prepared for RAMESSES XI. Arguably the finest tomb in the valley is that of SETI I (KV17), with its elaborate astronomical ceiling; it epitomizes the characteristic style of a New Kingdom royal tomb, with a series of chambers and descending corridors cut deep into the mountainside. The tomb of TUTANKHAMUN, discovered almost intact with its spectacular FUNERARY GOODS, is undoubtedly the most famous in the valley, even though it is one of the smallest and was probably never intended to house a royal burial. The tomb of RAMESSES II's sons (KV5), located near the valley entrance, is the largest and most elaborate in the valley and, indeed, in the whole of Egypt. There also remains the possibility of a hitherto undiscovered royal tomb dating to the end of the AMARNA period.

Among the few individuals of non-royal birth granted the privilege of a tomb in the valley were the parents-in-law of Amenhotep III, YUYA and TUYU, and

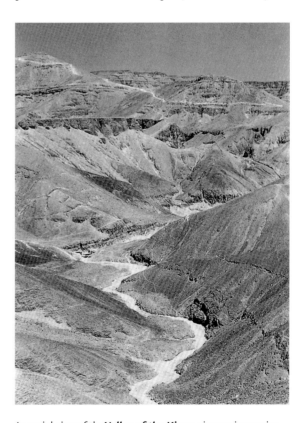

An aerial view of the **Valley of the Kings** *gives an impression of how the area would have looked in antiquity, before the advent of mass tourism.*

the late 19th Dynasty chancellor, BAY. In the 21st Dynasty, the royal mummies were moved from their own burial chambers to two secret caches, in an attempt to protect them from further desecration. One group was re-interred in the tomb of AMENHOTEP II, the second group in the tomb of the High Priest PINEDJEM II near DEIR EL-BAHRI. The Valley of the Kings remains one of Egypt's prime attractions, the splendid TOMB DECORATION in the royal burials providing a hint of the riches that must once have been interred at the site.

Valley of the Queens Area of the THEBAN NECROPOLIS, about 1 km (0.6 miles) north-west of MEDINET HABU, where the tombs of royal wives and other close royal relatives were clustered during the RAMESSIDE period. Although shaft tombs date from the early 18th Dynasty, the earliest inscribed tomb was prepared for the wife of RAMESSES I, and the surrounding area was used for burials throughout the 19th and 20th Dynasties. (By contrast, some 18th Dynasty QUEENS were interred with their husbands in the VALLEY OF THE KINGS.) The valley contains about eighty tombs in total, 21 of them inscribed. Most famous is the tomb of NEFERTARI, principal wife of RAMESSES II, during whose reign a village was built in the middle of the valley to accommodate the workmen. The mummies from the Valley of the Queens were removed to a safer location following a spate of tomb robberies in the late 20th Dynasty. The tombs were subsequently reused in the THIRD INTERMEDIATE PERIOD, LATE PERIOD and ROMAN PERIOD.

valley temple Element of a PYRAMID complex situated on the floodplain, and connected to the buildings on the desert plateau (the mortuary temple and the pyramid itself) by means of a sloping causeway. The best-preserved example is the valley temple of KHAFRA at GIZA. Valley temples are thought to have been accessible by boat during the INUNDATION, by means of a canal or quay connected to the NILE. It is likely that some of the funeral ceremonies, and perhaps certain stages of the MUMMIFICATION process, took place in the valley temple.

Viceroy of Kush (King's Son of Kush) Governor of NUBIA during the NEW KINGDOM. The post was established under KAMOSE or AHMOSE, originally with military responsibilities. However, these were delegated in the early 18th Dynasty to a 'Battalion Commander of KUSH', leaving the Viceroy as the principal administrator of NUBIA, appointed by the king and reporting directly to him. In the reign of AMENHOTEP III, responsibility for the GOLD mines of southern Nubia was also transferred to the Viceroy, giving him considerable economic as well as political power.

At the end of the 20th Dynasty, the Viceroy PANEHSY may have used his influence to attempt a coup against RAMESSES XI. The tombs of the Viceroys during the late 18th Dynasty (such as Amenhotep, who served AKHEN-

Pectoral of gold and inlays, representing the **vulture** goddess Nekhbet wearing the **atef** crown, from the treasure found in the tomb of Tutankhamun in the Valley of the Kings.

ATEN and TUTANKHAMUN) have provided evidence for the post's main responsibilities: the collection of taxes and tribute, and the organization of gold mining. In administrative affairs, the Viceroy was assisted by two deputies, one responsible for Kush proper (Upper Nubia), the other for WAWAT (Lower Nubia).

vignette *see* Book of the Dead

vizier The most senior official in the ancient Egyptian administration. The Egyptian term for the office of vizier is *taity zab tjaty*, sometime abbreviated to *tjaty*, first attested in the early 3rd Dynasty. The full, tri-partite, title signifies a role combining courtly, judicial and administrative responsibilities. The vizier served as the king's representative in most areas of GOVERN-MENT, apart from military and religious matters. The creation of an executive position at the head of the government was probably necessitated by the inauguration of monumental construction projects, and hence the requirement for a well-run and efficient bureaucracy. At first, viziers were generally royal princes; the office was opened up to non-royal holders in the 5th Dynasty. In periods of political instability, especially the 13th Dynasty, viziers seem to have provided a degree of continuity in government, counteracting the negative effects of a rapid succession of ephemeral kings. Although in theory every vizier was appointed by the king, in practice the office became quasi-hereditary at certain times. In the reigns of PEPI II and SENUSRET I, and again in the 18th Dynasty, the office of vizier was split in two along geographical lines. The southern viziers, based at THEBES, are generally better attested than their northern counterparts, based at MEMPHIS. The tomb of REKHMIRA contains an important series of texts describing the duties of the vizier.

votive Dedicated to a deity or given in a cult setting to express a prayer or a wish.

vulture Two species of this large scavenging bird were known in ancient Egypt: the griffon vulture and the Egyptian vulture. The griffon vulture is the more commonly depicted. As a HIEROGLYPH, it was used to write the word *mut* ('mother'). In Egyptian ART, it could serve as a representation of NEKHBET or MUT, while vultures with outspread wings were a popular protective motif for the ceilings of palace and temple buildings. The Egyptian vulture was the hieroglyph for the letter corresponding to the Hebrew *aleph* (usually rendered as an English 'a').

W

Wadi el-Hudi Area of the Eastern Desert, about 35 km (22 miles) south-east of ASWAN, where amethysts were mined from the MIDDLE KINGDOM onwards. Mining expeditions have left traces throughout the area, including inscriptions from the reign of MENTUHOTEP IV.

Wadi Hammamat Dry valley running from east to west across the Eastern Desert from the NILE Valley in the vicinity of COPTOS to the Red Sea coast. The shortest route across the Eastern Desert, it was a major thoroughfare from early Predynastic times; BADARIAN artifacts and numerous Predynastic PETROGLYPHS attest to its early importance. The wadi led to a major source of GOLD reserves, which were probably controlled by NAGADA during the PREDYNASTIC PERIOD. The oldest surviving MAP, dating to the RAMESSIDE period, shows the geology and topography of the principal gold-mining area in the Wadi Hammamat. The wadi also gave access to the 'Black Mountains', the principal source of fine-grained siltstone rock in Egypt. The main quarry was exploited from the Badarian period, and the stone used for cosmetic PALETTES, statuary and other artifacts.

The rock face surrounding the quarry on the south side of the wadi is covered with over 400 inscriptions, dating from the late OLD KINGDOM to the end of the ROMAN PERIOD; they record details of quarrying expeditions, and prayers to MIN, god of the Eastern Desert. Of particular historic importance are the inscriptions of MENTUHOTEP IV, which constitute the primary source for his reign. On the north side of the wadi, remains of ancient quarrying activity include a series of stone-built miners' huts, and an abandoned stone SAR-COPHAGUS, half-way up the cliff face.

Wadi Maghara Site in the south-western SINAI, 19 km (12 miles) east of the Gulf of Suez. It was known to the ancient Egyptians as 'the turquoise terraces', and was the focus of TURQUOISE mining from the EARLY DYNASTIC PERIOD onwards, with periods of particular activity during the OLD KINGDOM and MIDDLE KINGDOM. There are rock inscriptions at the site dating from the reigns of DJOSER, SEKHEMKHET, SANAKHT, SNEFERU and KHUFU. Other remains include traces of an Old Kingdom miners' settlement and evidence for copper smelting.

Wadi Tumilat Dry valley running west–east from the edge of the DELTA (about 20 km (12.5 miles) east of BUBASTIS) to Lake Timsah (modern Ismailiya, at the southern end of the Suez Canal). It was an important trade route from prehistoric times, linking LOWER EGYPT, the SINAI and southern PALESTINE. Recent excavations have uncovered evidence of large-scale Predynastic activity at Kafr Hassan Daoud. In the 26th Dynasty, NEKAU II built a canal along the route of the Wadi Tumilat to provide ships with direct access from the NILE to the Red Sea.

Wadjet Cobra goddess, closely linked with the URAEUS. Her main cult centre was at BUTO, and from the 1st Dynasty, she was regarded as the patron deity of

The goddess Isis holding a **was** sceptre, an emblem of authority carried by deities and kings, in a wall painting from the 19th Dynasty tomb of Nefertari in the Valley of the Queens.

LOWER EGYPT. In KINGSHIP ideology, she was one of the TWO LADIES, together with her Upper Egyptian counterpart NEKHBET. Usually portrayed as a rearing cobra, Wadjet could also be depicted as a lioness-headed goddess, linking her with other female deities such as SEKHMET.

Wadji *see* Djet

wadj-wer (Great Green) Term of uncertain meaning, perhaps referring to the lakes of the DELTA or to the Mediterranean or the Red Sea. It could be personified as a figure with watery skin. Curiously, some texts of the RAMESSIDE period refer to the *wadj-wer* being traversed on foot.

warfare *see* weapons and warfare

was sceptre Emblem of authority, carried by deities and the king, comprising a tall staff with two prongs at the base and the head of an unidentified animal at the top. It probably derives from an implement used in ANIMAL HUSBANDRY, although it has also been identified as a dried bull's penis. It had powerful protective connotations, especially in funerary contexts. The sceptre became the HIEROGLYPH for 'dominion' and, adorned with a streamer and feather, the emblem of the Theban NOME.

Wawat Ancient Egyptian name for Lower NUBIA, comprising the stretch of NILE Valley and adjacent deserts from the First to the Second CATARACTS. In the NEW KINGDOM, Wawat was governed by one of two deputies reporting to the VICEROY OF KUSH.

Ways of Horus *see* Sinai

weapons and warfare Some of the oldest artifacts from Egypt are weapons. Flint arrowheads and spearpoints occur in prehistoric contexts, and the bow had already been invented by Palaeolithic times. Objects and PETROGLYPHS from the PREDYNASTIC PERIOD show hunters armed with bows and arrows, lances, javelins and simple fighting sticks. Other weapons included throw-sticks, slings, clubs and maces. The piriform (pear-shaped) MACEHEAD became indelibly associated with authority, the motif of the ruler smiting his enemies with a mace becoming the quintessential image of KINGSHIP. OLD KINGDOM reliefs show the use of battle axes, with flint or copper blades. The development of more advanced METALWORKING during the MIDDLE KINGDOM enabled the production of more sophisticated daggers, for hand-to-hand combat. The sword was introduced in the NEW KINGDOM; reliefs on the walls of RAMESSIDE temples often show AMUN presenting the king with a curved sword. Also in the New Kingdom, the simple bow, carved from a single piece of timber, was replaced by the more advanced composite bow, of laminated wood, horn and sinew. Defensive weaponry included parrying sticks, shields, helmets and coats of mail with bronze scales. Full body armour was only introduced by Greek mercenaries in the 26th Dynasty.

Warfare was an important theme in Egyptian ideology, and a recurrent fact throughout Egyptian history. The unification of the state, at the beginning of the 1st Dynasty, is likely to have come about, at least in part, by a series of military conquests. A recently discovered rock inscription at GEBEL TJAUTI may record one such incident. Once the TWO LANDS had been unified, Egypt's neighbours were considered, in theory and in practice, as enemies of the state. Military action against LIBYA, NUBIA and PALESTINE is depicted and recorded in early royal art. During the Old Kingdom, and throughout pharaonic history, periodic campaigns were launched to keep in check troublesome peoples on Egypt's borders, and to maintain Egyptian access to trade routes. For such operations, troops were levied, on a local basis, from the general population, supplemented very often by mercenaries from Nubia and elsewhere. From the Middle Kingdom onwards, veterans could be rewarded with grants of land and other property. The bodies of Egyptian soldiers who died abroad were generally repatriated for burial.

Warfare within Egypt was a feature of the FIRST INTERMEDIATE PERIOD and Second Intermediate Period, while in the New Kingdom the creation of an Egyptian empire in the LEVANT necessitated concerted military action to maintain control over conquered territory, and hence the creation of a professional standing ARMY for the first time. THUTMOSE I and THUTMOSE III undertook scores of campaigns in the Near East, as did RAMESSES II. Major pitched battles between well-matched forces were relatively infrequent. Most famous are the Battle of MEGIDDO and the Battle of KADESH. Military tactics included siege warfare and assaulting enemy towns with battering rams. To demoralize the enemy forces and force a surrender, local crops might be deliberately burned, and the civilian population killed or taken captive as prisoners of war. Campaigns against Nubia were generally conducted in the cooler months of winter and spring, while action in the Levant took place in the summer.

***wedjat* eye** The (left) eye of HORUS that was lost during his confrontation with SETH, then magically restored by HATHOR. It was a powerful symbol of wholeness (the meaning of *wedjat*) and well-being, and hence a popular form for AMULETS. In the FIRST INTERMEDIATE PERIOD and MIDDLE KINGDOM, coffins were often decorated with a pair of *wedjat* eyes on the outside at the head end, to enable the deceased to look out towards the rising sun. In hieroglyphic WRITING, the elements of the *wedjat* eye were used to denote different fractions.

Wegaf *see* Ugaf

weighing of the heart In Egyptian RELIGION, the ceremony which took place at the entrance to the underworld, when the heart of the deceased was weighed against the feather of MAAT to determine fitness for the afterlife. If the heart weighed less, signalling a righteous life, the deceased was escorted by ANUBIS into the presence of OSIRIS, and welcomed into the underworld. If the heart weighed more, signalling unrighteousness, the deceased would be consumed by the monster AMMUT waiting nearby. The outcome of the weighing was recorded in writing by THOTH, who presided over the ceremony. In the NEW KINGDOM, it was popular to include an illustration of the weighing of the heart ceremony in a papyrus copy of the BOOK OF THE DEAD. Occasionally, Anubis is shown adjusting the scales to guarantee a favourable outcome for the deceased.

*Electrum pectoral from Dahshur (12th Dynasty), showing the goddess Bat, flanked by Horus and Seth, under the protection of a solar disc and a pair of **wedjat** eyes.*

weights and measures The principal unit of weight in ancient Egypt was the *deben*, equal to 93.3 grams. It was divided into 10 *kite*, these smaller units being used in the weighing of silver and GOLD. The value of non-metal goods could also be expressed as an equivalent of so many *deben* and *kite* (of copper), thus providing a system of 'prices' for use in barter and trade. Measurement of length was generally expressed in terms of the cubit (52.4 cm, corresponding to a man's forearm), and its subdivisions; a cubit comprised seven palm-widths, each of four fingers. Slightly different lengths of cubit were used at different periods: until the 26th Dynasty, artists' grids were laid out according to the 'short cubit' of six palm-widths; during the PERSIAN PERIOD, a 'royal Persian cubit' was occasionally used. For longer measurements, a unit of length called an *iteru* ('river') was used; comprising 20,000 cubits, it corresponded to the distance a boat might be towed along the NILE in a day.

Land-surveying employed a 100-cubit measure (*ta*, *meh-ta* or *khet*), and the double *remen*, one *remen* being the length of the diagonal of a square measuring one cubit by one cubit. The basic unit of land area was the *setjat* (*aroura* in Greek), equal to 10,000 square cubits. The unit of capacity/volume was the *khar* ('sack', bushel), equal to about 75.2 litres, and divided into 16 *heqat*, each of 10 *hinu*; the *hin* was further subdivided into thirds (*khay*) and units of 1/32.

In the excavation of tombs, a unit of volume was employed called the *denit*, corresponding to one cubic cubit. Stone, pottery and bronze weights dating from the PREDYNASTIC PERIOD onwards have survived, as

have wooden measuring rods, often marked with additional information.

Wenamun Central character in a text called the *Report of Wenamun*. The text survives in a single papyrus copy dating to the THIRD INTERMEDIATE PERIOD, although it may originally have been composed at the very end of the NEW KINGDOM. Scholars disagree over whether the text is purely fictional, or a story based on historical events. The narrative recounts the journey of Wenamun, a priest of AMUN, who is sent by the High Priest HERIHOR to the coast of Syria to procure new supplies of timber to refurbish the BARQUE SHRINE of Amun. He visits SMENDES in TANIS en route. Much of the interest in the story concerns Wenamun's difficulties in the LEVANT and CYPRUS, reflecting a political situation where Egypt had lost much of its former prestige and influence.

Weneg (*c.* 2700 BC) Ephemeral and poorly attested king of the 2nd Dynasty.

Weni High official of the 6th Dynasty. At the peak of his career, which spanned the reigns of TETI, PEPI I and MERENRA, Weni was governor of UPPER EGYPT. The autobiographical inscription from his tomb at ABYDOS is a major source for the internal politics and foreign relations of the late OLD KINGDOM. It includes a reference to a court conspiracy led by women of the royal HAREM; details of campaigns against the 'sand dwellers' of southern PALESTINE; and relations with NUBIA.

Vignette from the 19th Dynasty funerary papyrus of Hunefer depicting the **weighing of the heart**, *described in Chapter 125 of the* Book of the Dead.

Wenis *see* Unas

Wennefer Epithet of OSIRIS, meaning 'eternally incorruptible' – referring to his resurrection from the dead.

Wepwawet (Upuaut) JACKAL god, whose Egyptian name means 'opener of the ways'. Attested from the very beginning of the 1st Dynasty, his role was to precede the king, opening the way for him. By extension, he was associated with royal conquests; in the PYRAMID TEXTS, he is said to perform the OPENING OF THE MOUTH ceremony and lead the king into the afterlife, hence opening the way to immortality.

Wepwawet was depicted as a jackal on a standard, or as a man with the head of a jackal, and was closely linked with another canine god, Sed. His main cult centre was at ASYUT (known in Greek as Lykopolis, 'wolf city'), but he was also worshipped as a funerary god at ABYDOS.

Wepwawetemsaf (throne name: Sekhemra-neferkhau) (late 17th century BC) Ephemeral king of the SECOND INTERMEDIATE PERIOD known only from a single STELA (now in the British Museum, London), which has close stylistic similarities to that of another ephemeral king of the period, PAENTJENI. Wepwawetemsaf's authority may also have been restricted to the area around ABYDOS.

white crown *see* crowns

Wilkinson, John Gardner *see* Egyptology

window of appearance Ceremonial window in a royal building leading to a balcony where the king appeared in a highly ritualized setting to show himself before the people, reward loyal servants, and receive foreign dignitaries. It was an important feature of royal palaces in the NEW KINGDOM. Actual examples have survived in the King's House at AMARNA, and in the temple of RAMESSES III at MEDINET HABU. Reliefs in the tombs of courtiers at Amarna commonly show AKHENATEN and NEFERTITI at the window of appearance, distributing the GOLD of honour.

wine A prestigious drink, reserved for the wealthier members of society, wine was consumed at all periods of ancient Egyptian civilization and was also used as an offering to deities. The FUNERARY GOODS interred in the recently discovered tomb of a late Predynastic ruler at ABYDOS (tomb U-j) included hundreds of pottery wine jars imported from the LEVANT. Egyptian vineyards, located in the DELTA, are attested from the 1st Dynasty. Other wine-producing areas included the DAKHLA OASIS, KHARGA OASIS, and the ASYUT region of the NILE Valley. Private TOMB DECORATION from the MIDDLE KINGDOM and NEW KINGDOM includes scenes of wine production.

After picking, grapes were pressed, either in a cloth twisted between poles or by trampling with the feet. The juice was then poured into vats to ferment, and finally decanted into pottery vessels where it was left to age. Both red and white wines were made in this way, sometimes flavoured with added ingredients. The Egyptians also made alcoholic drinks from fermented dates, figs and pomegranates. The shoulder of a wine

Scene of **wine** *production in the 18th Dynasty tomb of Nakht at Thebes; each stage of the process is shown, from the harvest (right) to the pressing of the grapes in a vat (left) and the stoppered wine vessels (centre).*

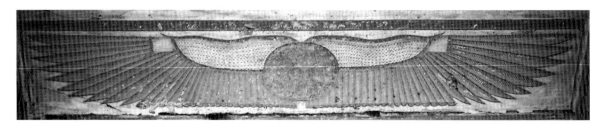

*A **winged disc** adorns a painted ceiling in the mortuary temple of Ramesses III at Medinet Habu.*

jar was usually inscribed with details of the wine inside, including variety, vineyard, date, production manager and owner.

winged disc The motif of the sun disc with a pair of wings was originally the symbol of HORUS of Behdet (a site in the eastern DELTA). From the OLD KINGDOM onwards, the disc was usually shown with a URAEUS on either side. The winged disc was thought to represent the outstretched wings of the celestial FALCON, symbolizing the vault of heaven. The motif had strong protective connotations; hence, in the NEW KINGDOM, it was often depicted on the ceilings of temples and ceremonial gateways.

wisdom literature Texts with an explicitly didactic purpose comprise one of the most distinctive genres of ancient Egyptian LITERATURE. Two categories are represented in the surviving works. *Sebayt* ('teachings'), consisting of a series of sayings or maxims for living the ideal life, include such works as the INSTRUCTION OF HORDJEDEF, INSTRUCTION OF PTAHHOTEP, INSTRUCTION FOR MERIKARA, INSTRUCTION OF AMENEMHAT I FOR HIS SON, INSTRUCTION OF AMENEMOPE, INSTRUCTION OF ANY, and the WISDOM OF ANKHSHESHONQY. More reflective works, often focusing on the theme of 'national distress', include the ADMONITIONS OF IPUWER, COMPLAINTS OF KHAKHEPERRASENEB, DISPUTE OF A MAN WITH HIS BA and the PROPHECY OF NEFERTI.

Wisdom of Ankhsheshonqy Work of WISDOM LITERATURE, written in DEMOTIC and dating from the 1st century BC. Preserved in a single copy from AKHMIM, it comprises a series of sayings which reveal a cynicism about human nature quite different from the tone of earlier wisdom literature.

women The evidence from ancient Egypt, archaeological, literary and artistic, is heavily biased in favour of the literate, male elite, hence it is difficult to be certain about the role and status of women. There is no text that can be ascribed to a female author and the position of women is under-documented. In ART, women generally feature only in subordinate roles, reflecting their relationship – as mother, wife or daughter – with a male character.

The position of women in the ROYAL FAMILY is slightly better attested than in other sections of society. Periodically, women held important and powerful positions at court; examples include MERNEITH in the 1st Dynasty, AHMOSE NEFERTARI, TIYE and NEFERTITI in the 18th Dynasty. A few royal women, notably SOBEKNEFERU at the end of the 12th Dynasty, HATSHEPSUT in the 18th and TWOSRET in the 19th, went so far as to claim the KINGSHIP. However, in order to conform to the accepted ideology, they generally presented themselves as male rulers. The institution of the HAREM existed to support kings' wives, daughters and their attendants, but also provided fertile ground for plots against the throne.

In the NEW KINGDOM, THIRD INTERMEDIATE PERIOD and LATE PERIOD, the office of GOD'S WIFE OF AMUN, usually held by a royal princess, brought with it considerable influence over the Theban region, and was often used as a political tool. Female members of the elite might serve as dancers and songstresses in the local temple; in the OLD KINGDOM, women held more administrative titles than in later periods.

Among the general population, the role of women seems to have been confined, in large part, to the running of the household. However, political power was concentrated in men's hands, and the male ideal was that women stayed at home. Hence, in art, women were usually shown with paler, yellow skin, while men, exposed to sunlight outside the house, were shown with tanned, red-brown skin. Likewise, the male concept of female subservience was reflected in the tight-fitting restrictive garments which women were often shown wearing. In practice, such dresses would have been far too impractical for daily wear. The New

Kingdom text, the INSTRUCTION OF ANY, advises its (male) audience 'do not control your wife in her house', suggesting that in domestic matters women were considered to hold the upper hand. Evidence from DEIR EL-MEDINA indicates that women often supplemented the household income by engaging in economic enterprises, especially the manufacture of textiles, an activity associated with women at all periods. Egyptian LAW enshrined the equality of men and women; for example, women could inherit property and testify against their husbands. Despite such rights, it is likely that the status of women was generally lower than that of men, at all levels of society. However, the situation was not static, and women's roles undoubtedly changed during the course of Egyptian history.

woodworking Because of its relatively poor survival in archaeological contexts, wood is not particularly well represented among artifacts from ancient Egypt. Nevertheless, woodworking was evidently carried out to a high standard from an early period. Native trees included date palm and dom palm, the trunks of which could be used as joists in buildings, or split to produce planks. Tamarisk, acacia and sycamore fig were employed in FURNITURE manufacture, while ash was used when greater flexibility was required (for example in the manufacture of bows). However, all these native timbers were of relatively poor quality; finer varieties had to be imported, especially from the LEVANT.

The development of close relations with BYBLOS in the late 2nd Dynasty gave Egypt access to regular supplies of coniferous woods, notably Lebanese cedar, favoured for ship-building and for the finest COFFINS and furniture. Ebony, used for small objects and inlays, was imported from NUBIA. Scenes of cabinet-making in private tombs and the study of surviving wooden objects provide useful sources of evidence for woodworking techniques. Ancient Egyptian carpenters made use of veneers, inlays and plywood, and a range of joints. Carpenters' tools included adzes, saws and chisels.

writing The origins of ancient Egyptian writing are unclear; the earliest examples yet discovered, dating from the late PREDYNASTIC PERIOD (c. 3150 BC), comprise fully formed signs, and belong to an already highly developed system. It is possible that the idea of writing was borrowed from MESOPOTAMIA in the late 4th millennium BC, and the Egyptian system developed

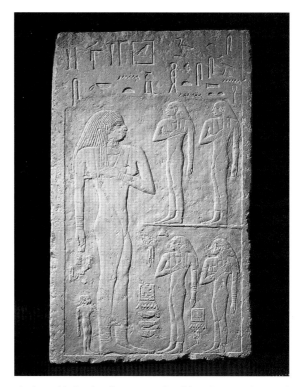

The late Old Kingdom limestone stela of the priestess Intkaes and her daughters illustrates the prominent role played by **women** *in ancient Egyptian society.*

Among the **writing** *equipment from Tutankhamun's tomb are two scribal palettes of ivory (left) and gilded wood (right), an ivory papyrus burnisher and a decorated wooden pen-case.*

fairly rapidly thereafter. However, the individual hiero-glyphic signs were drawn from the Egyptians' own world, and the writing system that was developed was ideally suited to the Egyptian LANGUAGE. The earliest use of writing was essentially economic, to record ownership of commodities. Towards the end of the Predynastic period, the Egyptians recognized the potential of writing to proclaim the ideology of KING-SHIP; HIEROGLYPHS were thus used to label the main protagonists in royal ART, on objects such as the NARMER PALETTE. Indeed, there was no formal distinction between art and writing; both were seen as elements in a unified system of representation. The earliest continuous texts that have survived date from the late 2nd and early 3rd Dynasties.

From the very beginning, writing used a combination of sound-signs (phonograms) and meaning-signs (logograms). Different scripts were developed for use in different contexts and on different media. CURSIVE SCRIPT (hieroglyphic or HIERATIC) was ideally suited for writing administrative or literary texts on PAPYRUS, whereas fully formed hieroglyphs were generally used for religious texts and other monumental inscriptions. Throughout ancient Egyptian history, the written language remained conservative, whereas the spoken language developed much more rapidly. Writing was always the preserve of a small ruling elite; the majority of the population was illiterate.

X, Y, Z

Xerxes (486–466 BC) Persian king of the 27th Dynasty, who ruled Egypt for twenty years during the first PERSIAN PERIOD.

X-Group see Nubia

Yahudiya, Tell el- see Tell el-Yahudiya

Yakubhar (throne name: Meruserra) (late 17th century BC) King of the SECOND INTERMEDIATE PERIOD (14th or 15th Dynasty), of Asiatic origin, attested on numerous SCARAB seals from the LEVANT. He probably reigned close in time to SHESHI.

Yam Foreign land to the south of Egypt. It is probably to be identified as KERMA, which is mentioned in Egyptian texts of the OLD KINGDOM, such as the auto-biographical inscription of HARKHUF. Yam is perhaps to be equated with the otherwise unidentified land of IREM, mentioned in NEW KINGDOM texts.

Young, Thomas see Egyptology

Yuya Father of TIYE. He and his wife TUYU were granted the rare privilege of a tomb in the VALLEY OF THE KINGS (KV46), indicating their influence at the court of AMENHOTEP III (c. 1390–c. 1353). Their elaborate FUNERARY GOODS included FURNITURE, JEWELRY and a CHARIOT.

Originally from AKHMIM, Yuya bore the titles 'god's father' and 'master of the horse', a combination next held by AY, who may thus have been Yuya's son. There is no firm evidence for the mooted identification of Yuya with the biblical Joseph.

Zanakht see Sanakht

Zawiyet el-Amwat (Zawiyet el-Meitin, Zawiyet Sultan) Site on the east bank of the NILE in MIDDLE EGYPT, opposite the modern city of Minya. Monuments at the site include a well-preserved step PYRAMID dating to the end of the 3rd Dynasty, as well as a series of OLD KINGDOM ROCK-CUT TOMBS, some of which are decorated.

Zawiyet el-Aryan Area of the Memphite NECROPOLIS between GIZA and ABUSIR. Besides tombs of the late PREDYNASTIC PERIOD, early 1st Dynasty, NEW KINGDOM and ROMAN PERIOD, the site contains the remains of two unfinished PYRAMIDS. The earlier one, known as the 'Layer Pyramid', is dated to the 3rd Dynasty by its architecture; it has been attributed to KHABA on the basis of stone vessels inscribed with the king's SEREKH found in a nearby MASTABA. The later monument probably dates to the 4th Dynasty, and may have been begun by an ephemeral king who reigned for a very brief period between DJEDEFRA and KHAFRA. Its main feature is a long sloping trench, at the bottom of which archaeologists discovered an unusual oval granite SARCOPHAGUS.

Zawiyet el-Meitin see Zawiyet el-Amwat

Zawiyet Sultan see Zawiyet el-Amwat

Zawiyet Umm el-Rakham Site on the Mediterranean coast, some 300 km (187.5 miles) west of ALEXANDRIA,

*Drawing of the **zodiac** ceiling in the roof chapel of the temple of Hathor at Dendera, taken from the Napoleonic* Description de l'Egypte

close to the modern city of Mersa Matruh. Excavations have revealed a fortress built by RAMESSES II to guard Egypt's western frontier against Libyan infiltration. The site also played an important role in Mediterranean trade, providing a staging-post for ships from CRETE before they continued eastwards to the DELTA and MEMPHIS.

Zer *see* Djer

Zet *see* Djet

zodiac Depictions of the classic twelve-constellation zodiac, adopted from Babylonian astrology, first appeared in Egyptian temples during the PTOLEMAIC PERIOD. The most famous, dated to 50 BC, is a relief on the ceiling of a roof-top chamber in the temple of HATHOR at DENDERA.

Zoser *see* Djoser

Site plans and maps

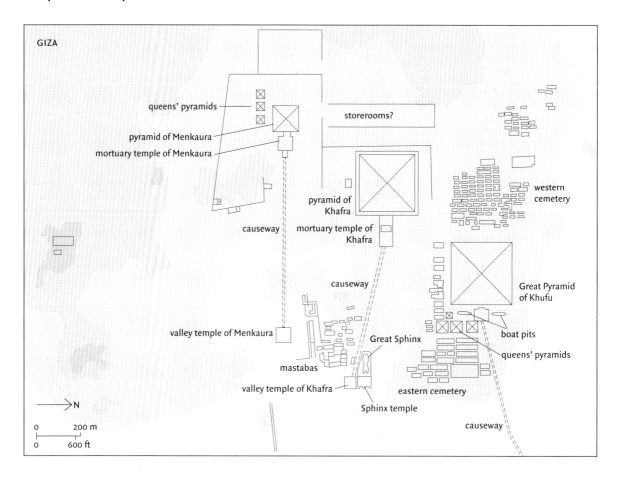

GIZA

queens' pyramids

pyramid of Menkaura

mortuary temple of Menkaura

storerooms?

western cemetery

pyramid of Khafra

causeway

mortuary temple of Khafra

causeway

Great Pyramid of Khufu

valley temple of Menkaura

Great Sphinx

boat pits

queens' pyramids

mastabas

valley temple of Khafra

eastern cemetery

Sphinx temple

causeway

N

0   200 m
0   600 ft

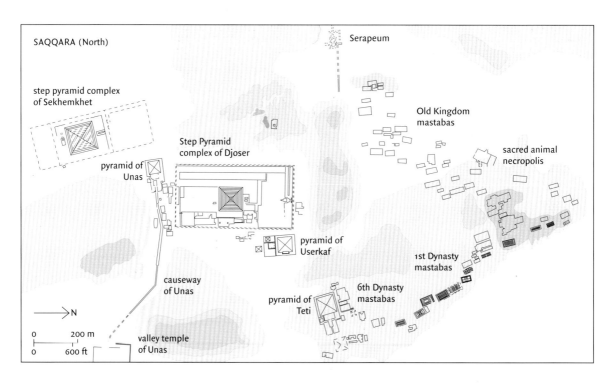

SAQQARA (North)

Serapeum

step pyramid complex of Sekhemkhet

Old Kingdom mastabas

sacred animal necropolis

Step Pyramid complex of Djoser

pyramid of Unas

pyramid of Userkaf

1st Dynasty mastabas

6th Dynasty mastabas

causeway of Unas

pyramid of Teti

N

0   200 m
0   600 ft

valley temple of Unas

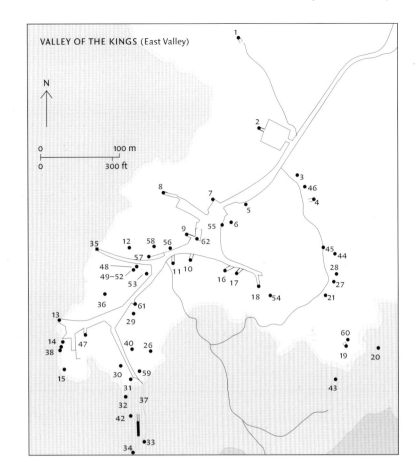

VALLEY OF THE KINGS (East Valley)

1 Ramesses VII
2 Ramesses IV
3 son of Ramesses III
4 Ramesses XI
5 sons of Ramesses II
6 Ramesses IX
7 Ramesses II
8 Merenptah
9 Ramesses V/VI
10 Amenmesse
11 Ramesses III
13 Bay
14 Tawosret/Sethnakht
15 Seti II
16 Ramesses I
17 Seti I
18 Ramesses X
19 Mentuherkhepeshef
20 Hatshepsut
34 Thutmose III
35 Amenhotep II
36 Maiherpri
38 Thutmose I
42 Thutmose II
43 Thutmose IV
45 Userhet
46 Yuya & Tuyu
47 Siptah
48 Amenemopet
54 embalming cache
55 Tiye and Akhenaten cache
57 'Gold Tomb'
57 Horemheb
62 Tutankhamun

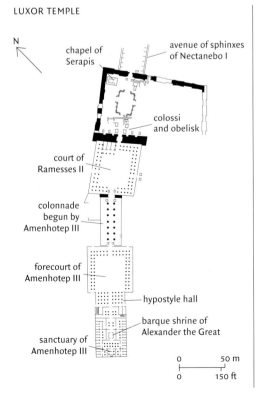

LUXOR TEMPLE

chapel of Serapis
avenue of sphinxes of Nectanebo I
colossi and obelisk
court of Ramesses II
colonnade begun by Amenhotep III
forecourt of Amenhotep III
hypostyle hall
barque shrine of Alexander the Great
sanctuary of Amenhotep III

0 50 m
0 150 ft

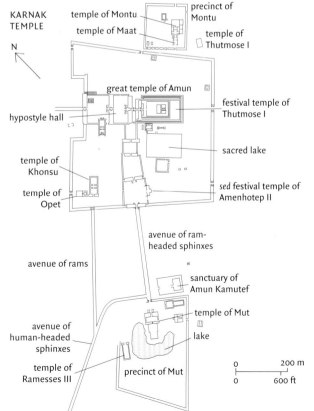

KARNAK TEMPLE

temple of Montu
temple of Maat
precinct of Montu
temple of Thutmose I
great temple of Amun
hypostyle hall
festival temple of Thutmose I
sacred lake
temple of Khonsu
temple of Opet
sed festival temple of Amenhotep II
avenue of ram-headed sphinxes
avenue of rams
sanctuary of Amun Kamutef
temple of Mut
lake
avenue of human-headed sphinxes
temple of Ramesses III
precinct of Mut

0 200 m
0 600 ft

267

Site plans and maps

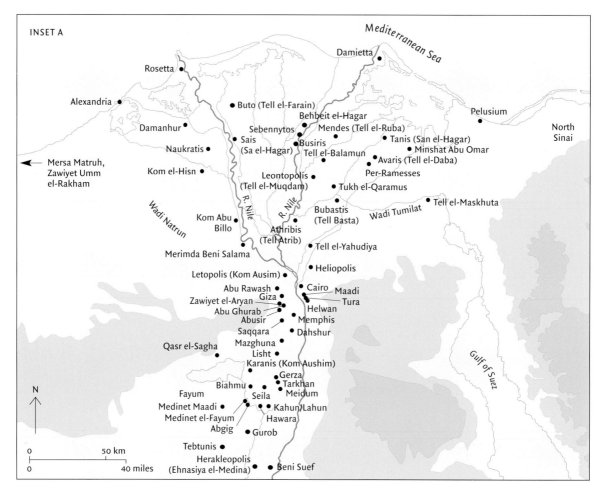

INSET A

Mediterranean Sea

Damietta

Rosetta

Alexandria

Buto (Tell el-Farain)

Behbeit el-Hagar

Pelusium

North Sinai

Damanhur

Sebennytos

Mendes (Tell el-Ruba)

Sais (Sa el-Hagar)

Busiris

Tanis (San el-Hagar)

Naukratis

Tell el-Balamun

Minshat Abu Omar

Avaris (Tell el-Daba)

Kom el-Hisn

Leontopolis (Tell el-Muqdam)

Per-Ramesses

Mersa Matruh, Zawiyet Umm el-Rakham

Tukh el-Qaramus

R. Nile

R. Nile

Tell el-Maskhuta

Wadi Natrun

Kom Abu Billo

Bubastis (Tell Basta)

Wadi Tumilat

Athribis (Tell Atrib)

Merimda Beni Salama

Tell el-Yahudiya

Heliopolis

Letopolis (Kom Ausim)

Abu Rawash

Cairo

Maadi

Zawiyet el-Aryan

Giza

Tura

Abu Ghurab

Helwan

Abusir

Memphis

Saqqara

Dahshur

Qasr el-Sagha

Mazghuna

Lisht

Karanis (Kom Aushim)

N

Biahmu

Gerza

Tarkhan

Meidum

Fayum

Seila

Medinet Maadi

Kahun/Lahun

Medinet el-Fayum

Hawara

Abgig

Gurob

Tebtunis

Gulf of Suez

Herakleopolis (Ehnasiya el-Medina)

Beni Suef

0   50 km

0   40 miles

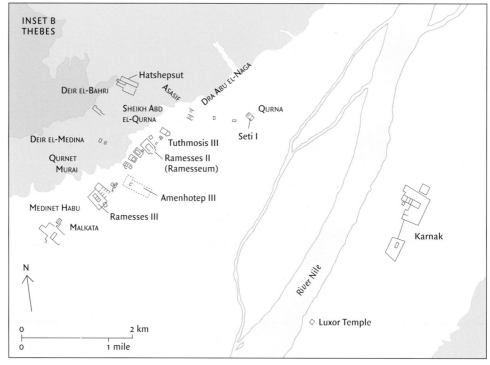

INSET B
THEBES

Hatshepsut

DEIR EL-BAHRI

ASASIF

DRA ABU EL-NAGA

SHEIKH ABD EL-QURNA

QURNA

Seti I

DEIR EL-MEDINA

Tuthmosis III

QURNET MURAI

Ramesses II (Ramesseum)

Amenhotep III

MEDINET HABU

Ramesses III

MALKATA

Karnak

N

River Nile

Luxor Temple

0   2 km

0   1 mile

268

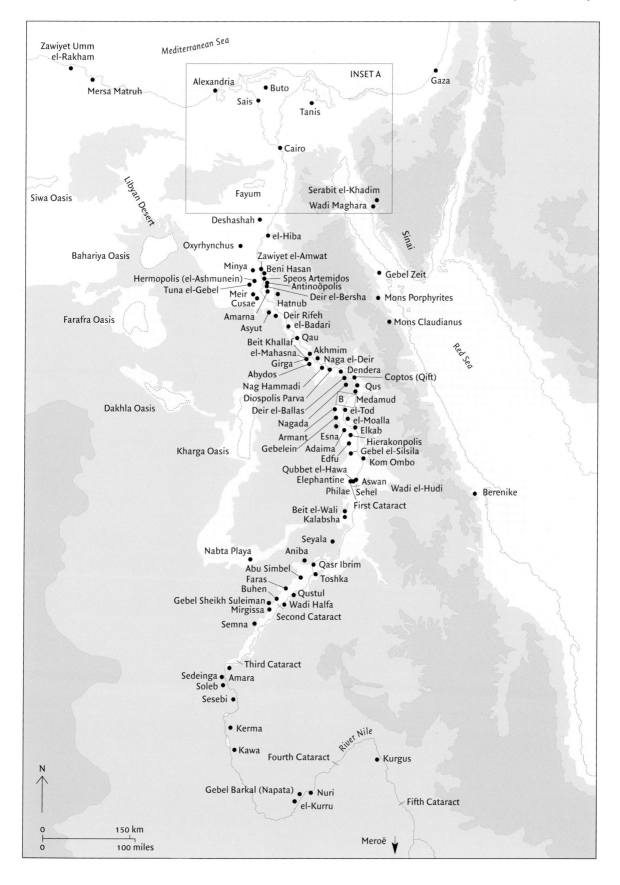

Zawiyet Umm el-Rakham

Mediterranean Sea

INSET A

Gaza

Alexandria
Buto
Sais
Tanis

Mersa Matruh

Siwa Oasis

Libyan Desert

Cairo

Fayum

Serabit el-Khadim
Wadi Maghara

Sinai

Baharyia Oasis

Deshashah

el-Hiba

Oxyrhynchus

Zawiyet el-Amwat

Gebel Zeit

Minya
Beni Hasan
Speos Artemidos
Hermopolis (el-Ashmunein)
Antinoöpolis
Tuna el-Gebel
Meir
Deir el-Bersha
Cusae
Hatnub
Amarna
Deir Rifeh
Asyut
el-Badari
Beit Khallaf
Qau
el-Mahasna
Akhmim
Girga
Naga el-Deir
Abydos
Dendera
Nag Hammadi
Diospolis Parva
Qus
Deir el-Ballas
Medamud
B
Nagada
el-Tod
Armant
el-Moalla
Gebelein
Esna
Elkab
Adaima
Hierakonpolis
Edfu
Gebel el-Silsila
Qubbet el-Hawa
Kom Ombo
Elephantine
Philae
Aswan
Sehel
Beit el-Wali
First Cataract
Kalabsha

Coptos (Qift)

Mons Porphyrites

Mons Claudianus

Red Sea

Farafra Oasis

Dakhla Oasis

Kharga Oasis

Wadi el-Hudi
Berenike

Seyala

Nabta Playa
Aniba
Abu Simbel
Qasr Ibrim
Faras
Toshka
Buhen
Qustul
Gebel Sheikh Suleiman
Wadi Halfa
Mirgissa
Second Cataract
Semna

Third Cataract
Sedeinga
Amara
Soleb
Sesebi

Kerma

Kawa
Fourth Cataract
River Nile
Kurgus

Gebel Barkal (Napata)
Nuri
el-Kurru
Fifth Cataract

N

0   150 km
0   100 miles

Meroë

Suggestions for further reading

General

Baines, J. & Malek, J., *The Cultural Atlas of Ancient Egypt* (New York, rev. ed., 2000)

Bard, K.A. (ed.), *Encyclopedia of the Archaeology of Ancient Egypt* (London & New York, 1999)

Brewer, D. & Teeter, E., *Egypt and the Egyptians* (Cambridge, 1999)

David, R., *The Experience of Ancient Egypt* (London & New York, 2000)

Davies, V. & Friedman, R., *Egypt* (London, 1998)

Kemp, B.J., *Ancient Egypt: Anatomy of a Civilization* (London, 1999)

Manley, B. (ed.), *The Seventy Great Mysteries of Ancient Egypt* (London & New York, 2003)

Redford, D.B. (ed.), *The Oxford Encyclopedia of Ancient Egypt* (3 vols) (Oxford & New York, 2001)

Reeves, N., *Ancient Egypt: The Great Discoveries* (London & New York, 2000)

Rice, M., *Who's Who in Ancient Egypt* (London & New York, 1999)

Schulz, R. & Seidel, M. (eds), *Egypt: The World of the Pharaohs* (Cologne, 1998)

Shaw, I., *Ancient Egypt: A Very Short Introduction* (Oxford, 2004)

Siliotti, A., *Egypt: Splendours of an Ancient Civilization* (London, 1996)

Vercoutter, J., *The Search for Ancient Egypt* (London & New York, 1992)

Art, Architecture and Monuments

Arnold, D. (tr. Gardiner, S.H. & Strudwick, H.), *The Encyclopaedia of Ancient Egyptian Architecture* (Princeton, 2003)

Davies, W.V. (ed.), *Colour and Painting in Ancient Egypt* (London, 2001)

Lehner, M., *The Complete Pyramids* (London & New York, 1997)

Metropolitan Museum of Art, *Egyptian Art in the Age of the Pyramids* (New York, 1999)

Reeves, N. & Wilkinson, R.H., *The Complete Valley of the Kings* (London, 1996)

Robins, G., *The Art of Ancient Egypt* (London, 1997)

Russmann, E., *Egyptian Sculpture. Cairo and Luxor* (London, 1989)

Russmann, E. (ed.), *Eternal Egypt: Masterworks of Ancient Art from the British Museum* (London, 2001)

Smith, W.S. (rev. Simpson, W.K.), *The Art and Architecture of Ancient Egypt* (New Haven, 1981)

Stafford-Deitsch, J., *The Monuments of Ancient Egypt* (London, 2001)

Strudwick, N. & Strudwick, H., *Thebes in Egypt* (London, 1999)

Strudwick, N. & Taylor, J.H. (eds), *The Theban Necropolis: Past, Present and Future* (London, 2003)

Tiradritti, F., *Ancient Egypt: Art, Architecture and History* (London, 2002)

Verner, M., *The Pyramids. Their Archaeology and History* (London, 2002)

Wilkinson, R.H., *Reading Egyptian Art* (London & New York, 1994)

Wilkinson, R.H., *Symbol and Magic in Ancient Egyptian Art* (London & New York, 1994)

Wilkinson. R.H., *The Complete Temples of Ancient Egypt* (London & New York, 2000)

History

Clayton, P., *Chronicle of the Pharaohs* (London & New York, 1994)

Dodson, A. & Hilton, D., *The Complete Royal Families of Ancient Egypt* (London & New York, 2004)

Manley, B., *The Penguin Historical Atlas of Ancient Egypt* (London, 1996)

Shaw, I. (ed.), *The Oxford History of Ancient Egypt* (Oxford & New York, 2000)

Trigger, B.G., Kemp, B.J., O'Connor, D. & Lloyd, A.B., *Ancient Egypt: A Social History* (Cambridge, 1983)

Individual rulers and periods

Aldred, C., *Akhenaten: King of Egypt* (London, 1988)

Flamarion, E., *Cleopatra: From History to Legend* (London & New York, 1997)

Fletcher, J., *Egypt's Sun King: Amenhotep III* (London, 2000)

Freed, R., Markowitz, Y. & D'Auria, S. (eds), *Pharaohs of the Sun: Akhenaten, Nefertiti, Tutankhamen* (Boston & London, 1999)

Kozloff, A.P. & Bryan, B.M., *Egypt's Dazzling Sun: Amenhotep III and his World* (Bloomington, 1992)

Malek, J. & Forman, W., *In the Shadow of the Pyramids: Egypt During the Old Kingdom* (London & Norman, 1986)

Midant-Reynes, B. (tr. Shaw, I.), *The Prehistory of Egypt: From the First Egyptians to the First Pharaohs* (Oxford, 2000)

Reeves, N., *The Complete Tutankhamun* (London & New York, 1995)

Reeves, N., *Akhenaten: Egypt's False Prophet* (London & New York, 2001)

Tyldesley, J., *Hatchepsut: The Female Pharaoh* (London, 1996)

Tyldesley, J., *Nefertiti: Egypt's Sun Queen* (London & New York, 1998)

Tyldesley, J., *Ramesses: Egypt's Greatest Pharaoh* (London, 2000)

Walker, S. & Higgs, P. (eds), *Cleopatra of Egypt: From History to Myth* (London, 2001)

Wilkinson, T., *Early Dynastic Egypt* (London, 1999)

Language, Literature & Writing

Allen, J.P., *Middle Egyptian: An Introduction to the Language and Culture of Hieroglyphs* (Cambridge, 1999)

Collier, M. & Manley, B., *How to Read Egyptian Hieroglyphs* (London, rev. ed., 2003)

Gardiner, A., *Egyptian Grammar*, 3rd ed. (Oxford, 1982)

Lichtheim, M., *Ancient Egyptian Literature* (3 vols) (Berkeley, Los Angeles & London, 1975, 1976, 1980)

Parkinson, R., *Voices from Ancient Egypt: An Anthology of Middle Kingdom Writings* (London & Norman, 1991)

Parkinson, R., *The Tale of Sinuhe and Other Ancient Egyptian Poems 1940–1640 BC* (Oxford & New York, 1997)

Parkinson, R., *Pocket Guide to Ancient Egyptian Hieroglyphs* (London, 2003)

Religion

Forman, W. & Quirke, S., *Hieroglyphs and the Afterlife in Ancient Egypt* (London, 1996)

Ikram, S. & Dodson, A., *The Mummy in Ancient Egypt* (London & New York, 1998)

Pinch, G., *Magic in Ancient Egypt* (London, 1994)

Pinch, G., *Egyptian Myth: A Very Short Introduction* (Oxford, 2004)

Pinch, G., *Egyptian Mythology* (Oxford, 2004)

Quirke, S., *Ancient Egyptian Religion* (London, 1992)

Quirke, S., *The Cult of Ra: Sun-Worship in Ancient Egypt* (London & New York, 2001)

Schafer, B. (ed.), *Religion in Ancient Egypt* (London & Ithaca, 1991)

Taylor, J.H., *Death and the Afterlife in Ancient Egypt* (London, 2001)

Taylor, J.H., *Mummy: The Inside Story* (London, 2004)

Wilkinson, R.H., *The Complete Gods and Goddesses of Ancient Egypt* (London & New York, 2003)

Sources of Illustrations

a - above, b - below, c - centre, l - left, r - right.

Cyril Aldred 18; The Art Archive/Dagli Orti (A) 42; Photo Audrain 36; Walters Art Gallery, Baltimore 20a; Staatliche Museen zu Berlin, Preussischer Kulturbesitz 85, 167b, 169b, 188b, 208b, 248l; Courtesy, Museum of Fine Arts, Boston 150, 206; Brooklyn Museum of Art 183; Egyptian Museum, Cairo titlepage, 17, 23b, 28a, 40, 49ar, 49bl, 51, 54, 57, 72, 84, 87a, 95, 120b, 154, 169l, 185a, 196a, 210a, 214a, 223, 228a, 230, 247, 251, 253, 254r; Luxor Museum, Cairo 32a; Fitzwilliam Museum, University of Cambridge 33, 74, 134, 263a; © Peter Clayton 27b, 34, 57, 194, 210b, 232; From Norman de Garis Davis, *Tomb of Nakht at Thebes* (1917) 261; Michael Duigan 20b; Aidan Dodson 151, 152bl; National Museums of Scotland, Edinburgh 125a; Egypt Exploration Society 46; Werner Forman Archive 14, 31, 61b, 80, 142b, 170, 191, 223b, 239; Photo Heidi Grassley, © Thames & Hudson Ltd, London frontispiece, 10, 11, 55, 58, 61a, 62, 63, 66, 76, 79, 97, 107a, 122, 125b, 132a, 133, 140, 164, 187, 192, 202a, 211, 234; Pelizaeus Museum, Hildesheim 101, 160; Photo Hirmer 73, 91, 105a; Michael Hughes 199a; © Andrea Jemolo 6–7, 16a, 71, 88b, 93, 148, 153, 173, 201, 205a, 221, 227, 241, 248r; G. B. Johnson 27a, 86, 171; Rijksmuseum van Oudheden, Leiden 70, 99a; © Jürgen Liepe 15, 32, 49al, 56, 59b, 98, 99b, 102b, 106, 108, 112c, 112b, 117, 119, 137, 149, 165, 174, 184, 218, 219, 238; University of Liverpool, Mo'alla Expedition 158a; British Museum, London 16b, 19, 21, 24a&b, 26, 41, 43, 45b, 47, 53, 64b, 65, 81, 92, 104b, 109, 110, 112a, 175, 188a, 198, 202b, 208a, 226a, 231, 260; Petrie Museum of Egyptian Archaeology, University College, London 13, 103b, 118r; Lotos-Film, Kaufbeuren 110; J. Paul Getty Conservation Institute, Malibu 128; The Metropolitan Museum of Art, New York: 49br (Harris Brisbane Dick Fund, 1956), 78 (Purchase, Edward S. Harkness Gift), 88a (Rogers Fund and Edward S. Harkness Gift 1920), 115 (Rogers Fund, 1913), 120a (Rogers Fund and Henry Walter Gift, 1916), 132 (Gift of Theodore M. Davis, 1907), 158–59 (Museum Excavations, 1919–1920; Rogers Fund supplemented by contribution of Edward S. Harkness), 166, 207, 213b, 218a (Gift of Henry Walter, 1915); Ashmolean Museum, Oxford 162, 182, 216, 249; Copyright Griffith Institute, Oxford 50, 87b, 113a, 180, 228b, 263b; Musée du Louvre, Paris: 215a; Photo RMN 39b, 67a, 142a, 152br, 157; © John G. Ross 28b, 38, 68a, 77, 118l, 126, 130b, 131, 141b, 167a, 176b, 197, 214b, 233; William Schenck 121, 130a, 145, 156, 200a; From G. Segato, *Atlante del Basso e Alto Egitto* (1835) 265; Abdel Ghaffar Shedid 113b; Albert Shoucair 68b, 136, 256; Edwin Smith 215; From G. Elliot Smith *The Royal Mummies* (1901) 225, 237; Steven Snape 129; © Jeremy Stafford-Deitsch 30, 52r, 102a, 111, 124, 141a, 179, 258; State Hermitage Museum, St Petersburg 52l; E. Strouhal 35a, 39a, 178a, 193, 200b, 244; Frank Teichmann 11b; Museo Egizio, Turin 89a; © Derek Welsby 89b; © Archivio Whitestar/Araldo da Luca 168; © Archivio Whitestar/Giulio Veggi 196b; Toby Wilkinson 25, 35b, 45c, 46, 69, 82, 83, 96, 103a, 104a, 105b, 116, 127, 135, 138a, 138b, 139, 147, 155, 160b, 161, 163, 176a, 178b, 185, 189, 199b, 204, 205b, 212, 213a, 217, 229, 235, 245, 254l, 255, 262; Joachim Willeitner, Munich 67b; Provost & Fellows of Eton College, Windsor 259; Philip Winton 37; Milan Zemina 167b